Clerical Celibacy in the West: c.1100–1700

Clerical Celibacy in the West: c.1100–1700

HELEN PARISH
University of Reading, UK

ASHGATE

© Helen Parish 2010

All rights reserved. No part of this publication may be reproduced, stored in a retrieval system or transmitted in any form or by any means, electronic, mechanical, photocopying, recording or otherwise without the prior permission of the publisher.

Helen Parish has asserted her moral right under the Copyright, Designs and Patents Act, 1988, to be identified as the author of this work.

Published by
Ashgate Publishing Limited
Wey Court East
Union Road
Farnham
Surrey, GU9 7PT
England

Ashgate Publishing Company
Suite 420
101 Cherry Street
Burlington
VT 05401-4405
USA

www.ashgate.com

British Library Cataloguing in Publication Data
Parish, Helen L.
 Clerical celibacy in the West, c.1100–1700. – (Catholic Christendom, 1300–1700)
 1. Celibacy – Christianity – History.
 I. Title II. Series
 253.2'524–dc22

Library of Congress Cataloging-in-Publication Data
Parish, Helen L.
 Clerical celibacy in the West, c.1100–1700 / Helen Parish.
  p. cm. – (Catholic christendom, 1300–1700)
 Includes bibliographical references and index.
 ISBN 978-0-7546-3949-7 (hardcover : alk. paper) – ISBN 978-1-4094-0263-3 (ebook) 1. Celibacy – Christianity – History. 2. Clergy – Sexual behavior. I. Title.
 BV4390.P37 2009
 253'.2524–dc22

2009043768

ISBN 9780754639497 (hbk)
ISBN 9781409402633 (ebk)

Printed and bound in Great Britain by
TJ International Ltd, Padstow, Cornwall

Contents

Series Editor's Preface		*vii*
Acknowledgements		*ix*
Abbreviations		*xi*
Introduction – 'For the sake of the kingdom of heaven'?: Shaping the Celibacy Debate		1
1	'If there is one faith, there must be one tradition': Clerical Celibacy and Marriage in the Early Church	15
2	'Preserving the Ancient Rule and Apostolic Perfection'?: Celibacy and Marriage in East and West	59
3	'A concubine or an unlawful woman': Celibacy, Marriage, and the Gregorian Reform	87
4	'In marriage they will live more piously and honestly': Debating Clerical Celibacy in the Pre-Reformation Church	123
5	'The whole world and the devil will laugh': Clerical Celibacy and Married Priests in the Age of Reformation	143
6	'Contrary to the state of their order and the laudable customs of the church': Clerical Celibacy in the Catholic Church after the Reformation	185
Conclusion – 'One of the chief ornaments of the Catholic clergy'?: Celibacy in the Modern Church		209
Bibliography		*235*
Index		*277*

Series Editor's Preface

The still-usual emphasis on medieval (or Catholic) and reformation (or Protestant) religious history has meant neglect of the middle ground, both chronological and ideological. As a result, continuities between the middle ages and early modern Europe have been overlooked in favor of emphasis on radical discontinuities. Further, especially in the later period, the identification of 'reformation' with various kinds of Protestantism means that the vitality and creativity of the established church, whether in its Roman or local manifestations, has been left out of account. In the last few years, an upsurge of interest in the history of traditional (or catholic) religion makes these inadequacies in received scholarship even more glaring and in need of systematic correction. The series will attempt this by covering all varieties of religious behavior, broadly interpreted, not just (or even especially) traditional institutional and doctrinal church history. It will to the maximum degree possible be interdisciplinary, comparative and global, as well as non-confessional. The goal is to understand religion, primarily of the 'Catholic' variety, as a broadly human phenomenon, rather than as a privileged mode of access to superhuman realms, even implicitly.

The period covered, 1300–1700, embraces the moment which saw an almost complete transformation of the place of religion in the life of Europeans, whether considered as a system of beliefs, as an institution, or as a set of social and cultural practices. In 1300, vast numbers of Europeans, from the pope down, fully expected Jesus's return and the beginning of His reign on earth. By 1700, very few Europeans, of whatever level of education, would have subscribed to such chiliastic beliefs. Pierre Bayle's notorious sarcasms about signs and portents are not idiosyncratic. Likewise, in 1300 the vast majority of Europeans probably regarded the pope as their spiritual head; the institution he headed was probably the most tightly integrated and effective bureaucracy in Europe. Most Europeans were at least nominally Christian, and the pope had at least nominal knowledge of that fact. The papacy, as an institution, played a central role in high politics, and the clergy in general formed an integral part of most governments, whether central or local. By 1700, Europe was divided into a myriad of different religious allegiances, and even those areas officially subordinate to the pope were both more nominally Catholic in belief (despite colossal efforts at imposing uniformity) and also in allegiance than they had been four hundred years earlier. The pope had become only one political factor, and not one of the first rank. The clergy, for its part, had virtually disappeared from secular governments as well as losing much of its local authority. The stage was set for the Enlightenment.

Thomas F. Mayer,
Augustana College

Acknowledgements

This project had its roots in a pleasant conversation with Thomas Mayer, rather longer ago than I would like to admit. At the time, and perhaps lulled into a false sense of security and optimism by the summer sunshine, the scale of the undertaking was perhaps less apparent than it should have been. As a result, friends, family, and colleagues have heard more about the history of the church, the discipline of celibacy, and the marriage of priests, than they might have thought necessary. Their forbearance is much appreciated. I am particularly grateful to staff in the History department at the University of Reading who have provided much encouragement and intellectual stimulation along the way, and to the numerous friends outside the university who have resisted the temptation to ask 'but why?' in response to a description of my research plans. Colleagues with interests in medieval and early modern history have tolerated with good humour my intrusions onto their turf, and provided a gentle guiding hand that has preserved me from many egregious errors. Any that remain are entirely my own work. I am particularly grateful to Frank Tallett, who read the later parts of the book in an earlier draft and provided many helpful suggestions for improvement, and to Felicity Heal, who cast an expert eye over the Reformation material.

I am indebted to the patience of staff in the Reading University Library, and to the Bodleian Library in Oxford, and the British Library for permission to use their collections. The text of this book was completed during a period of research leave funded by the Arts and Humanities Research Council; I am appreciative of their financial support, and of the accompanying sabbatical provided by the Department of History at Reading. Tom Mayer and Tom Gray at Ashgate have offered friendly encouragement from the early days of this project, and provided valuable advice.

A period as head of department in Reading allowed administrative matters to intrude into already precious research time, but perhaps also provided valuable insights into the machinations that might have underpinned the bureaucracy and conciliar discussions of the medieval and early modern church. The birth of my daughter, Ruth, in December 2007, presented an entirely different set of preoccupations, but for the very best of reasons. Already, at two years, she is capable of demonstrating in a multitude of ways that there are many things in life that are much more important than the history of clerical celibacy. Her response to the first complete typescript of this book was to enjoy the many possibilities for destruction and reconstruction that it afforded, but I dedicate the final product to her, in the hope that one day she will read and enjoy what follows.

Helen Parish, January 2010

Abbreviations

AAS	*Acta apostolicae sedis*
CCCC	Corpus Christi College, Cambridge
CIC	*Corpus Iuris Canonici in tres partes distinctum*
CJC	*Corpus Juris Civilis: Codex Justiniani*
Corp. Cath.	*Corpus Catholicorum*
Corp. Ref.	*Corpus Reformatorum*
Ep.	*Epistola(e)*
LW	*Luther's Works* (American Edition)
MGH	Monumenta Germaniae Historica
PG	*Patrologia Cursus Completus: Series Graeca*
PL	*Patrologia Cursus Completus: Series Latina*
WA	*Weimarer Ausgabe: Martin Luther Werke*
WABr	*Martin Luthers Werke. Briefweschel*

INTRODUCTION

'For the sake of the kingdom of heaven'?: Shaping the Celibacy Debate

In February 1549, the passage of a bill through the upper house of the English parliament was secured against the objections of eight bishops and four secular Lords. It would be 'better for the estimation of priests and other ministers in the church of God to live chaste, sole and separate from the company of women and the bond of marriage' the Act declared, 'that they might better attend to the ministration of the Gospel, and be less intricated and troubled with the charge of household'.[1] The English legislation was not, however, a defence of the discipline of obligatory clerical celibacy. Since, it was suggested, many of the clergy did not keep to this 'chaste and sole life', it would be to the good of the realm if those priests who could not contain were permitted to marry. Of all the acts of the Edwardian Reformation, the abrogation of the law of celibacy was perhaps the one with which cooperation was most evidently voluntary. However, this was no minor issue.[2] The legalisation of clerical marriage in England was a highly visible sign of doctrinal change, a tangible break with the discipline and laws of the Catholic church, and an act of iconoclasm which shattered both the medieval image of priesthood, and the established economy of sexuality and the sacred. Increasingly vocal demands for the abrogation of the law of celibacy spilled from the pages of printed books published in defence of the Reformation, and this polemical debate was conducted against a backdrop of the reality of clerical marriage in western Europe for the first time since the eleventh century.

Early Modern writing on clerical celibacy, both Catholic and Protestant, owed much in terms of content and structure to earlier manifestations of the same controversy. Each generation might have stamped its own considerations and concerns upon the discussion of clerical celibacy, but the fundamentals of the debate had, and have, remained remarkably consistent.

---

[1] 2 & 3 Edward VI c.21.
[2] For further discussion of the English context, see H.L. Parish, *Clerical Marriage and the English Reformation* (Aldershot, 2000); E.J., *Marriage and the English Reformation* (Oxford, 1994).

Questions of scriptural mandate, apostolic precedent, ecclesiastical tradition, sacramental function and pastoral role were repeatedly aired and analysed, and the rationale behind obligatory clerical celibacy, and the desirability or acceptability of a married priesthood, considered and contested. The nature of the debate reflects the breadth and complexity of the issue. As one recent commentator has suggested, 'theology, scripture and history do not provide unambiguous arguments for the obligatory union of priesthood and celibacy'.[3] The malleability of the evidence has created an enduring controversy, in which scripture and tradition become a palimpsest, as successive protagonists layer the experience of their age upon the texts of the past. Yet the history of clerical celibacy can be made, at one level, remarkably simple. Early Christians lived in an age in which family and fertility were prized, but in which it was also possible to lead a life that was so firmly centred on discipleship that marriage was not an option. Christ had spoken of those who 'made themselves eunuchs for the sake of the kingdom', and contemporary philosophy, both Christian and non-Christian, set great store by the prioritisation of the spiritual over the material and physical. As the faith spread, some believers found fulfilment in a life of withdrawal and isolation, while others assumed positions of leadership in the nascent Christian communities and churches. The development of a Christian ministry that was permanent and perpetual brought with it assumptions about the conduct and character of the presbyter, informed by Scripture, especially the Pauline epistles, but also by questions about the nature of ministry and the emerging sacrificial function of the priest. These assumptions provided the foundation for the insistence upon, first, clerical continence, and then clerical celibacy, in the Latin church, although it was only after the eleventh century that the discipline was universally enforced. The advent of the Reformation, and evangelical criticisms of the laws and traditions of the Catholic church, reawakened the debate over clerical marriage, and paved the way for the presence of a married ministry in the Latin church for the first time in half a millennium. The reassertion of clerical celibacy at the Council of Trent established the issue as a permanent marker of the divisions within Christendom, and defined a discipline for the Catholic church which has continued to the present day.

However, the history of clerical celibacy, both the ideal and the reality, has as times a Delphic ambiguity to it. What, exactly, does the phrase 'clerical celibacy' mean? Only by considering this question does it become apparent at what point, and with what consequences, practice became obligation. An understanding of the meaning of 'clerical celibacy' also

---

[3] J.E. Dittes, 'The Symbolic Value of Celibacy for the Catholic Faithful', in W. Bassett and P. Huizing (eds), *Celibacy in the Church* (New York, 1972), p. 84.

helps to explain the basis upon which it has been possible for successive generations of protagonists, on both sides of the debate, to lay claim to 'apostolic' precedent, and what implications this has had for the understanding of history and tradition in the church. And, looking briefly beyond the discipline and practice of the Latin church, a consideration of the nature of clerical celibacy illuminates the apparently divergent traditions of East and West, and how it is that the church in East came to adopt a model of married priesthood and celibate episcopate. As Roman Cholij, writing in the context of praxis in the East, demanded, why can a priest be married, if it is wrong for a priest to marry? [4] The term celibacy, *caelebs*, in its literal meaning, indicates the single life; a celibate clergy is, therefore, an unmarried ministry, and in the twenty-first century Catholic church, clerical celibacy is evidenced in the ordination of men who commit to remain unmarried. No individual may be presented for ordination and service in a diocese until 'in a prescribed rite he has assumed publicly and before God and the Church the obligation of celibacy'.[5] This is the form in which the term is most commonly understood in the equation of ordination to the Catholic priesthood with the renunciation of marriage.

When applied to the history of the church, however, clerical celibacy thus defined is an inadequate concept. Since it is evident that the early Christian priesthood comprised both married and unmarried men, there is, with this definition, no obvious root for the law of clerical celibacy in the practice of the primitive church. By searching in the past for the modern discipline of the church, it is easy to conclude that the origins of clerical celibacy lie in the post-apostolic period, possibly as late as the eleventh century. Yet it is clear that there were not only unmarried men in the service of the primitive church, but also married men who, after ordination, led a life of continence within marriage. The practice of prohibiting marriage to men after they received holy orders, and denying the possibility of re-marriage to married priests whose wives pre-deceased them, raises the possibility that the rejection of such unions embodied an underlying principle of clerical continence. Marriage (or re-marriage) after ordination was rejected on the basis either that it implied an inability to live in continence, or that such unions would not be valid because the discipline of clerical continence required that they be unconsummated. The assumption that continence would be demanded of all who entered higher Christian orders might then provide a backdrop to the legislation of the Latin church which excluded married men from the ministry. It is this process of definition and redefinition which has reinvigorated the debate over the apostolic origins of clerical celibacy. Defined as 'unmarried', the celibate priesthood has been argued to

---

[4] R. Cholij, *Clerical Celibacy in East and West* (Worcester, 1988), preface.
[5] CIC 132.2 and 132.3, *Code of Canon Law* 1037.

be an invention of the medieval church; defined as 'continent' the celibate priesthood has been presented as the practice of primitive Christianity.[6]

It is this seemingly semantic distinction that lies at the heart of some of the most violent printed exchanges on the history of clerical celibacy, and which has shaped the debate over clerical celibacy and marriage for centuries. The representation of clerical celibacy as innovation provided a springboard for critics of the ecclesiastical reforms of the eleventh century, while the view that clerical continence was the tradition of the church underpinned the assertions of the reformers that what they demanded was a rigorous enforcement rather than a new direction. The question of the apostolic origins of clerical celibacy was revisited by both Catholic and Protestant in the early modern period, each determined to locate evidence of departure from the traditions of the primitive church and the law of Scripture in the disciplines and dogmas of the other. Evangelical critics argued that clerical celibacy had its origins in the mind of the medieval papacy, and concluded that this was simply another example of innovation in the Catholic church, a sign of decay and disregard for the apostolic heritage, a departure from the scriptures, and evidence of the presence of Antichrist on the throne of St Peter. At the hands of Catholic propagandists, the first generation of evangelical clergy wives were depicted as no better than concubines, testimony to the lack of moral integrity that attracted individuals to the Reformation, and proof that Protestantism was little more than the reincarnation of earlier heresies already condemned by fathers, popes, and doctors of the church. Nineteenth century polemical and academic exchanges on the subject were again dominated by the question of whether or not the roots of clerical celibacy lay in the practice of the primitive church.[7] The centrality of the 'apostolic origins' question to the celibacy debate in successive generations

---

[6] The modern debate is most effectively played out in the pages of C. Cochini, *The Apostolic Origins of Priestly Celibacy* (San Francisco, 1995); Cholij, *Clerical Celibacy in East and West*; S. Heid, *Clerical Celibacy in the Early Church. The Beginnings of Obligatory Continence for Clerics in East and West* (trans. Michael J. Muller) (San Francisco, 2001); A.M. Cardinal Stickler, *The Case for Clerical Celibacy. Its Historical Development & Theological Foundations* (trans. B. Ferme) (San Francisco, 1995); R. Gryson, *Les origins du celibate ecclesiastique* (Gembloux, 1970).

[7] See especially G. Bickell, 'Der Colibat eine apostolische Anordnung', *Zeitschrift fur Katholische Theologie*, 2 (1878): 20–64; Bickell, 'Der Colibat dennoch eine apostolische Anordnung', *Zeitschrift fur Katholische Theologie*, 3 (1879): 792–9; F.X. Funk, 'Der Colibat keine apostolische Anordnung', *Tübinger theologische Quartalschrift*, 61 (1880): 202–21; Funk, 'Colibat und Priesterehe im Christlichen Alterum', in *Kirchengeschichtliche Abhandlungen und Unterschungen*, I (1897): 121–55; E.F. Vancandard, 'Les origines du Celibat Ecclesiastique', *Etudes de Critique d'histoire religieuse* 1st ser. (Paris 1905; 5th edition Paris 1913) 71–120; 'Celibat' in *Dictionnaire de theologie catholique*, 2 (Paris, 1905): 2068–88; H. Leclerq, 'La legislation conciliaire relative au celibat ecclesiastique' in the extended French edition of *Conciliengeschichte* by C.J. von Hefele, vol. 2 part 2 (Paris

positions the consideration of the practice and precedents established in scripture and the patristic era as a necessary preamble to the analysis of the history of the controversy in the medieval and early modern church. Refracted through the prism of competing polemical concerns, biblical and patristic texts were open to a multiplicity of interpretations. The intention of the councils and synods of the church were readily obfuscated by the (at times) limited availability of accurate narratives, and this same process by which a narrative of the ecclesiastical past was constructed in the service of the needs and concerns of the present.

The question of the 'origins' of clerical celibacy is not confined to chronology alone. The debate over the foundations of the principle of clerical continence or clerical celibacy in any age has revolved around the fundamental question of why it was that abstinence from sexual relations and marriage carried with it a reputation for holiness, or implied characteristics that were necessary to the priesthood. Two routes to this question are readily identifiable. The first is the argument that freedom from marriage equipped the priest with the ability to devote himself to the service of God, the service of the church, and the service of his flock. This practical value accorded to clerical celibacy was given expression in the *Decree on the Ministry and Life of Priests* at the Second Vatican Council, but also in the 1549 Act which legalised clerical marriage in England: it was preferable that priests remained unmarried so that 'they might better attend to the ministration of the Gospel, and be less intricated and troubled with the charge of household'. The second approach argues from the assumption that purity, by which is understood sexual purity, is a necessary companion to the sacred function of the priest. Drawing upon the precedent of the Levitical priesthood, and the sacrificial role of the priest at the altar, continence, or celibacy, emerged as a requirement for all who would fulfil such duties in the church.[8] The function of the priest as mediator between God and man has certainly been used to justify the demand for continence from clergy in higher orders in both East and West. J.P. Audet, for example, concluded that the decisive factor behind the law that imposed continence upon the clergy was 'the encounter, within the same pastoral consciousness, of the double perception of impure and sacred, the first being present in the shadows, under the form of sexual activity, and the second, in full light, under the form of service of the *sacramenta*'.[9] The

---

1908), appendix 6 1321–48; 'Celibat' in *Dictionnaire d'Archeologie chretienne et de liturgie*, 2 (Paris, 1908) 2802–32; discussed in Conclusion below.

[8] For a discussion of the 'cultic purity' question, see B. Verkamp, 'Cultic Purity and the Law of Celibacy', *Review for Religious*, 30 (1971): 199–217.

[9] J-P. Audet, *Mariage et celibat dans le service pastoral de l'Eglise, Histoire et Orientation* (Paris, 1967), p. 114.

defence of clerical celibacy on the basis of the 'cultic purity' demanded of those who serve at the altar dominated the literature on clerical marriage in the period of the eleventh century reforms, and continued to be debated in the early modern period. The path to Donatism was repeatedly blocked by the medieval church, in the assertion that the moral conduct of the priest made no difference to the efficacy of the sacrament. However, evangelical polemicists in the sixteenth century capitalised upon the vocabulary of Catholic devotional and disciplinary writing to argue that the concubinary priest who handled the body and blood of Christ in the consecrated elements did not only dishonour himself, and commit an act of sacrilege, but also called into question the theology and sacramental structure of the church.[10] The argument from 'cultic purity' has become rather less dominant in the modern church as the value of clerical celibacy is commonly articulated on the basis of the relationship of the priest with Christ, and in particular the function of the priest *in alter Christus*. *The Code of Canon Law* (1983), for example, describes priests as those who 'are consecrated and deputed to shepherd the people of God, each in accord with his own grade of orders, by fulfilling in the person of Christ [*in persona Christi*] the Head the functions of teaching, sanctifying, and governing'.[11] The sharing of the ordained priest in the office and priestly function of Christ requires the commitment and character that celibacy manifests, and this spiritual union and rejection of material concerns is presented as a fundamental part of the identity and nature of the priesthood.

The issue of clerical celibacy is, at its narrowest level, a debate over the ordination of married men to the priesthood, and the marriage of men once they have received higher orders. It is an issue, however, which is rarely seen or understood in this narrow definition; the history of clerical celibacy is more than a narrative of the evolution of a discipline. The capacity for the debate to spill out into areas of sacraments and sexuality, priesthood and politics, history and hermeneutics, has imbued the issue with a life which is still vigorous and active. Each generation has brought its own context to the controversy, even where the basic principles and preoccupations have remained remarkably consistent. Questions of scriptural interpretation, apostolic precedent, the nature and order of the priesthood, the value of celibacy to the faithful in practical and symbolic terms, and the desirability and attainability of a celibate priesthood feature as prominently in modern writing on the topic as they did in the literature

---

[10] See chapter 5 below.

[11] M.J. Scheeben, *Die Mysterien des Christentums* (Mainz, 1931), pp. 543–6; *Code of Canon Law (1983)*, c.1008; see also John Paul II, *Da Vobis*, 25 March 1992 c.29; Joseph Cardinal Ratzinger (Pope Benedict XVI), *Zur Gemeinschaft Gerufen, die Kirche heute verstehen* (Freiburg, 1991), pp. 98ff.

of the medieval and early modern periods. The contributions of each era to the debate rapidly became part of the corpus of material available to successive generations, as the history of clerical celibacy was remodelled and reworked in light of contemporary pressures and emergent concerns. Critics of obligatory clerical celibacy in the eleventh century, for example, provided evangelical polemicists in the sixteenth century with a vocabulary and framework for an assault upon the papal church and its laws, and the lexicon of Reformation debate was to shape the content and approach of nineteenth century controversy. But more immediate, personal, or local concerns could also intrude into the debate. The radical rhetoric of Peter Damian in defence of a specific image and form of church and clergy, the proclivities and preoccupations of princes and popes, the turmoil that faced the clerical estate in post-revolutionary France, and the personal concerns of individual authors have all done much to shape the historical controversy.

English-language writing on the history of clerical celibacy continues to be dominated by the work of the nineteenth century American author, Henry Charles Lea. Despite the opening assertion that 'it has been my intention to avoid polemics', Lea's work remained determinedly critical of the law of celibacy in particular, and indeed of the Catholic church more generally. It remains, however, the starting point for many modern investigations of the subject. His *History of Sacerdotal Celibacy* was, perhaps, the product of Lea's outlook and environment. Philadelphia in the civil war era was a city with a large Catholic immigrant population, and one in which the position of the church was already hotly disputed. The priest William Hogan had been excommunicated after falling foul of the bishop, Henry Conwell, in the 1820s, but resurfaced after two marriages and a stint on the public lecture tour, putting his criticisms of the church into print in the middle decades of the century in strident criticisms of the history of 'popery', and its pillars, auricular confession and monasticism.[12] Perhaps encouraged by the atmosphere in the city, Lea the publisher became Lea the historian, and turned his energies to the history of the Christian church and canon law.[13] It was, he believed, in the history of its laws that the nature of an institution was best understood, and this principle guided the composition of Lea's massive *History of the Inquisition of the Middle Ages,* and the later *History of the Inquisition in Spain.* The first edition of the *History*

---

[12] W. Hogan, *A Synopsis of Popery as It was and Is* (Hartford 1847) and *Auricular Confession and Popish Nunneries* (2 vols, Hartford 1847).

[13] E. Sculley Bradley, *Henry Charles Lea. A Biography* (Philadelphia, 1931); E. Peters, 'Henry Charles Lea 1825–1909', in H. Damico and J. Zavadil (eds), *Medieval Scholarship: Biographical Studies in the Formation of a Discipline. Volume One: History* (New York, 1995), pp. 89–100; J.M. O'Brien, 'Henry Charles Lea: The Historian as Reformer', *American Quarterly*, 19 (1967): 104–113; see also W. Ullmann's historical introduction to the Harper Torchbook edition of *The Inquisition of the Middle Ages* (1969).

of Sacerdotal Celibacy was printed in 1867, and, for all its flaws, was based upon extensive research in the primary sources, including the newly available volumes of Migne's *Patrologia Latina*. Indeed Lea, responding to his critics, asserted the primacy of such materials over the subjective interpretations that were presented in recent writing, and defended his decision to present the facts as he found them, rather than engaging in the polemic that had characterised the mid-century debates.[14] The *History of Sacerdotal Celibacy* was an account of the theory and practice of clerical celibacy across a broad chronological sweep from the primitive church to the Christianity of Lea's own day, drawing upon the laws of the church, the criticisms of its opponents, and a range of authoritative and more minor sources that lent substance to the narrative and colour to his criticisms. The history of clerical celibacy, through Lea's pen, was presented as a history of the expansion of an institution, a history of decay and decline, and a history of ecclesiastical immovability in the face of clerical immorality. The Catholic church, he concluded, had long been in error in its insistence that a priest must live in celibacy, and although radical change was necessary, it was not, in any likelihood, imminent.

Lea's sense that the sources should be allowed to speak for themselves has parallels in the work of the Hungarian theologian Augustin de Roskovány, although it is immediately apparent that the sources in question spoke with little unanimity on the subject of clerical celibacy. Roskovány, bishop of Neutra, had compiled a massive collection of 'monumenta' and literature devoted to the history of clerical celibacy, from which he adduced that the law of the church had its origins in the age of the apostles. For each era in the history of the church, a list was provided of works and commentaries written in favour of, or against, the law of celibacy, in a summary of scholarly and popular literature that ran into the thousands. Roskovány's compilation amounts to an extensive if not exhaustive bibliography for the history of clerical celibacy until the late nineteenth century, and despite its flaws and shortcomings, the weight of the volumes alone is testimony to the capacity of the subject to inspire debate and controversy. It is possible to chart through its pages, for example, the rising tide of criticism and complaint in the sixteenth century as the evangelical assault upon the laws and traditions of the medieval church sought to erode the edifice of half a millennium of clerical celibacy, while Catholic churchmen and propagandists mounted a spirited defence of the necessity and narrative of the discipline. In Roskovány's eyes, the sources that he presented exposed the roots of the law of celibacy in the precedent of the primitive church; for Lea those same sources provided evidence of disunity, innovation, and infidelity in Catholic history.

---

[14] O'Brien, 'Henry Charles Lea', 108–10.

These themes of tradition and innovation have continued to guide modern scholarship on the history of clerical celibacy. The battleground, and indeed the armoury, was still remarkably similar nearly a century after the publication of Lea's work. Georg Denzler, in his *Das Papsttum und der Amstzolibat* (1973) promised an annotated bibliography of papal laws and literature that would correct some of the misconceptions and misrepresentations that had marred the works of Lea and Roskovány. Again, it was argued, the intention was to allow the sources to speak for themself. But Denzler clearly regarded clerical celibacy as a post-apostolic innovation, and one that had done untold damage to the morality and reputation of the Catholic church. There was no biblical warrant, he suggested, for the assumption that celibacy was necessary to the fulfilment of the obligations of Christian ministry, even if such a ministry were taken to require some form of ritual purity. The law of celibacy, as the second part of the work was clearly intended to prove, was imposed at the instigation of the papal, not the primitive church, and the repeated efforts that were necessary to enforce the discipline were testimony to the dangers inherent in such innovation.[15] Jean Paul Audet, in his study of the *Structures of Christian Priesthood*, argued that a married priesthood was an accepted aspect of the life of the church well beyond the apostolic era, undermined only by the false equation of holiness with chastity that characterised the thought of the early Christian centuries. Clerical celibacy was the natural consequence of the assumption that abstinence presented a path to purity, but this was not, he argued, a natural assumption. To permit clerical marriage would be to restore the discipline and tradition of the church of the apostles. Roger Gryson, similarly, took issue with the 'apostolic origins' thesis, arguing that it was in a negative, and flawed, view of sexuality in which the origins of the law of celibacy were to be found. Such attitudes, he suggested, came from outside Christianity, setting the discipline of the church on a collision course with the views on marriage contained in scripture and apostolic tradition.[16]

The evolution of the law of celibacy in the primitive church and beyond has continued to command substantial attention. By far the most comprehensive contribution to the modern analysis of the legislation is Martin Boelens' *Die Klerikerehe in der Gesetzebung der Kirche unter besonder Berucksichtilgung der Strafe,* from which obligatory celibacy

---

[15] G. Denzler, *Das Papsttum und der Amstzolibat. Erster Teil: Die Zeit bis zue Reformation; Zweiter Teil: Von der Reformation bis in die Gegenwart* (Papste und Papsttum, Band 5 I, II: Stuttgart, 1973, 1976).

[16] Audet, *Mariage et celibat*; Gryson, *Les Origines*; for an assertion of the 'apostolic origins' thesis, heavily informed by Bickell's nineteenth-century work, see H. Deen, *Le Celibat des pretres dans les premiers siecles de l'Eglise* (Paris, 1969).

emerges as a harsh discipline, subject to vigorous enforcement, but based upon erroneous assumptions about the relationship between celibacy, purity, and sacramental function.[17] Samuel Laeuchli's study of the Council of Elvira did much to re-establish the place of the fourth century synod in the history of clerical celibacy, but also argued that the imposition of sexual discipline upon the clergy was not simply a reflection of ascetic trends in Christian and non-Christian thought, but a manifestation of the determination of the church in Spain to exercise and extend its authority.[18] A rather longer chronological sweep is taken in Charles Frazee's account of the 'Origins of Clerical Celibacy in the Western Church', which encompassed not only the legislation of the fourth century, but also the vigorous attempts to impose clerical celibacy in the eleventh and early twelfth centuries.[19] The importance of this latter period, long recognised in the more polemical histories of clerical celibacy, has received rather more even-handed analysis and interpretation in recent studies of the medieval reforming popes, and the church as a whole. Vacandard's study of the early history of clerical celibacy encouraged a reappraisal of the discipline of the medieval church, and exerted a profound influence over Augustin Fliche's investigation of the so-called *Reforme Gregorienne*.[20] The most lucid study of the literature on marriage and celibacy in the 'Gregorian' era remains Anne Llewellyn Barstow's *Married Priests and the Reforming Papacy*, but understanding of the priorities and scope of the reforms has been further enhanced by more recent contributions, particularly the series of essays contained in Michael Frassetto's *Medieval Purity and Piety: Essays on Medieval Clerical Celibacy and Religious Reform*.[21] The breadth and depth of debate over the issue is here immediately apparent, ranging from questions of cultic purity and monastic spirituality, to the history of

---

[17] M. Boelens, *Die Klerikerehe in der Gesetzebung der Kirche unter besonder Berucksichtilgung der Strafe: Eine rechtsgeschichtliche bis zum Jahre 1139* (Paderborn, 1968); see also Boelens, 'Die Klerikereche in der kirchlichen Gesetzgebung zwischen den Konzilien von Basel und Trent, *Archiv fur katholisches Kirchenrecht* 138 (1969): 62–81; M. Dortel-Claudot, 'Le Pretre et le Mariage: Evolution de la legislation canonique des Origines au XIIe Siecle', *L'Année Canonique*, 17 (1973): 319–44.

[18] S. Laeuchli, *Power and Sexuality: the Emergence of canon law at the synod of Elvira* (Philadelphia, 1972).

[19] C.A. Frazee, 'The Origins of Clerical Celibacy in the Western Church', *CH* 41 (1972).

[20] A. Fliche, *La reforme gregorienne* (Paris and Louvain, 1924–37).

[21] A.L. Barstow, *Married Priests and the Reforming Papacy, The Eleventh Century Debates* (Lewiston, NY, 1982); M. Frassetto, *Medieval Purity and Piety: Essays on Medieval Clerical Celibacy and Religious Reform* (New York and London, 1998). See also, J. Brundage, 'Sexuality, Marriage and the reform of Christian Society in the thought of Gregory VII', *Studia Gregoriani*, 14 (1991): 69–73; F. Liotta, *La Continenza dei chierici nel penserio canonistico classico da Graziano a Gregorio IX* (Milan, 1971).

doctrine, canon law, and the understanding of both marriage and clerical status in medieval society. The assertion that the origins of the law of celibacy lie outside the first Christian centuries has certainly sharpened appreciation of the Gregorian reforms, and positioned the debates over clerical celibacy in this period more firmly within their wider context.

Images of clerical celibacy as ideal, clerical celibacy as tradition, and clerical celibacy as obligation have continued to shape writing on the subject throughout its history. Attempts to locate the origins of the modern discipline in the constraints of Levitical law, the model of the Old Testament priesthood, the life of Christ, or the practice of the apostles have positioned the consideration of Judaeo-Christian attitudes to sex, marriage, and the body as the starting point for debate. Speculation over the apostolic origins of clerical celibacy has secured for the primitive church, patristic writings, and the councils and synods of the first Christian centuries, a position of pre-eminent authority in discussions of the relationship between ministry and marriage in the church. The following chapter presents an overview of the texts and contexts that were to prove so critical to subsequent participants in the celibacy debate. The intention is not to attempt to prove that clerical celibacy is (or is not) 'apostolic' in its origins – the abundance of literature on this topic exposes both the heat of polemical controversy and the apparently irreconcilable differences in approach and outcome – but to establish the practices and precedents that were to be so central to later writers. The seemingly divergent traditions of East and West, on occasion sharpened and polemicised, shared, in many respects, the same inheritance. In theory and in practice, the example of the Greek church has rarely been ignored in the Latin west, and recent scholarship, particularly that of Roman Cholij, has restored the analysis of clerical celibacy 'in east and west' as a necessary precursor to the understanding of either tradition. The basic assertion that the married clergy of the Greek church amount to a conclusive argument against the law of celibacy that obtains in the west is too simplistic, but still a commonplace in medieval and early modern debate, and indeed in some later scholarship. A consideration of the origins of Greek praxis, and perhaps particularly of the representation of that practice, has the potential to shed light upon the debates within the Latin church.[22]

The forceful imposition of celibacy upon the Latin clergy in the eleventh century provided a more definite assertion of the principles that were argued to underpin the unmarried priesthood, presented a history of the early church in which ascetic values were tied to the service of the altar, and embedded the image of the celibate, rather than simply continent, priest in the minds of the faithful. The Gregorian era was significant in its own

---

[22] See chapter 2 below.

right, but also within the narratives of clerical celibacy constructed in the early modern period and beyond. Viewed through the mirror of evangelical history writing, this period in the history of church emerged as a defining moment in the evolution of sacerdotalism and papal power, but also in the history of false faith and doctrine, innovation and invention, and the rise of Antichrist within the medieval Catholic church. The legislation and debates of the eleventh and twelfth centuries provided evangelical writers in the sixteenth century with a vocabulary, and a version of events that fitted their polemical and, at times, political needs.[23] Reformation dialectic on marriage, ministry, and the sacraments imbued the celibacy issue with a broader, and popular significance, but calls for change in the law had been articulated a century before the division of Christendom, in the polemical exchanges of the fifteenth century, particularly in the dialogue between Saignet and Gerson.[24] It was with the advent of Protestantism, however, that the debate over clerical celibacy was conducted once again in a context in which a married priesthood was not only argued to be legitimate, but was rapidly becoming a practical reality in parts of the Latin church. Clerical marriage was for many a highly visible sign of the rejection of Catholic discipline and practice, for some a badge of confessional affiliation, and for evangelical polemicists both a solution to the ills of the church and a manifestation of the authority of biblical precedent over medieval practice.[25] The Catholic church was strident in its response, but the simple *anathema sit* at the Council of Trent did not bring to an end the debate over clerical marriage and celibacy.[26] Criticism and crisis were not, in themselves, sufficient grounds to change Catholic tradition, and political and pastoral pressures in the centuries that followed did not force a universal modification of the law of the church.[27]

The debate over clerical celibacy and marriage had its origins in the early Christian centuries, and is still very much alive in the modern church.[28] The content and shape of controversy remain remarkably consistent, but

---

[23] See chapter 3 below.
[24] See chapter 4 below.
[25] See chapter 5 below.
[26] See chapter 6 below.
[27] See Conclusion below.
[28] Recent contributions to the debate have been both academic and more personal in tone and content. See, for example, C. Fairbank, *Hiding Behind the Collar* (Frederick, MD, 2002), and P. Jenkins, *Paedophiles and Priests* (Oxford, 2001), which use personal testimony in the consideration of what is portrayed as the moral crisis of modern Catholicism. Similarly, R. Schoenherr, *Goodbye Father: The Celibate Male Priesthood and the Future of the Catholic Church* (Oxford, 1997) examines the future of the celibate priesthood in the light of current challenges, but gives little attention to the historical origins of clerical celibacy. A fuller discussion of the modern debates may be found in Conclusion.

each age has selected and shaped the sources that underpin its narrative, and imbued an ancient issue with an immediacy and relevance. The basic question of whether, and why, continence is demanded of those who serve at the altar has been asked, and answered, in much the same terms, but the implications of that question, and of the answer given, have changed with each generation. Concluding his study of the history of sacerdotal celibacy, Henry Charles Lea expressed his hope that the Catholic church would modify the obligation to celibacy expected of its priests, but also his belief that in order for this to happen, 'the traditions of the past must first be forgotten; the hopes of the future must first be abandoned'. However, the debate over clerical celibacy and marriage demonstrates the extent to which the traditions of the past have not and, on this issue, cannot, be forgotten. Continence and celibacy, tied to the sacramental and pastoral function of the priest, imposed by the law and authority of the church, has remained a historical issue. To ground the unmarried Christian ministry in the priesthood of the Levites was to lay claim to the traditions and history of the Hebrews. To debate the origins of clerical celibacy in the primitive church was to revisit the history of the apostles and Fathers. To represent clerical celibacy as innovation was to turn to the records of the councils and synods of the church and the pages of papal history. To defend the marriage of priests as the restoration of the church to its former purity was to reconstruct and rewrite the narrative of the medieval past. Celibacy and marriage are intensely personal and private matters, but in the context of the Christian priesthood, very public, and at times polemical statements. The commitment to a life of celibacy demanded of the Catholic clergy reaches to the heart of the individual, but also to the heart of the history of the church that he serves, and clerical celibacy continues to be defined in relation to Scripture, apostolic tradition, ecclesiastical history, and papal authority. 'The Latin Church has wished, and continues to wish', Pope John Paul II reminded the priests of the church, 'referring to the example of Christ the Lord himself, to the apostolic teaching and to the whole Tradition that is proper to her, that all those who receive the sacrament of Orders should embrace this renunciation "for the sake of the kingdom of heaven".'[29]

---

[29] Holy Thursday, 1979.

CHAPTER ONE

'If there is one faith, there must be one tradition': Clerical Celibacy and Marriage in the Early Church

Central to the medieval and early modern debates surrounding the legitimacy and necessity of a celibate priesthood was the issue of whether the origins of clerical celibacy were to be found in the church of the apostles. The significance of biblical and apostolic precedent turned the example of the first centuries of the Christian era into a hunting ground for churchmen and protagonists on both sides of the debate. This focus is equally evident in modern scholarship, with recent studies of clerical celibacy returning to the theme of the inheritance of the primitive church, either as a necessary preamble to an understanding of the present and historical discipline, or as a topic in its own right.[1] As Stefan Heid has demonstrated, this approach is not without its problems; there are dangers in any attempt to read backwards from the modern discipline in an attempt to find an identical praxis in the early history of the church, not least if the apparent absence of a universal obligation to remain unmarried is read as an equal absence of any motivation or inclination towards a celibate clergy.[2] The assertion that there was no coherent and binding prohibition of marriage to the clergy of the early church becomes, in this approach, a validation of the assumption that compulsory celibacy in the modern church is the culmination of the erosion of clerical freedom by an

---

[1] See, for example, R. Cholij, *Clerical Celibacy in East and West* (Leominster, 1988); C. Cochini, *The Apostolic Origins of Priestly Celibacy* (San Francisco, 1990); Stefan Heid, *Celibacy in the Early Church. The Beginnings of a Discipline of Obligatory Continence for Clerics in East and West* (San Francisco, 2001); R. Gryson, 'Dix ans de recherches sur les origines du célibat ecclésiastique', *Revue Théologique de Louvain* 11 (1980): 164–5; Gryson, *les Origines du Celibat Ecclesiastique du Premier au Septieme Siecle* (Gembloux, 1970); L. Legrand, 'St Paul and Celibacy', in J. Coppens (ed.) *Priesthood and Celibacy* (Milan, Rome, 1972), pp. 427–50; E-F. Vacandard, *Celibat Ecclesiastique* (DTC 2, 2068–88); Vacandard, *Les Origines du Celibat Ecclesiastique* (Paris, 1905); Charles A. Frazee, 'The origins of clerical celibacy in the Western Church', *Church History*, 41 (1972): 149–67.

[2] Heid, *Celibacy*, p. 14.

increasingly institutional papal church in the centuries that followed.[3] Such an approach has been substantially undermined by the contributions of Christian Cochini and Roman Cholij to the debate. Rather than searching for complete parallels between ancient and modern, Cholij and Cochini have suggested that the presence of a continent, if not unmarried, higher clergy in the primitive church requires that we ask a rather different question of the history of clerical celibacy. The issue, they suggest, is not whether a married man might be ordained as a priest (as many undoubtedly were) but whether enduring and exclusive continence was required of all those, married and unmarried, who entered higher orders.[4] In whatever form the question is posed, however, it is clear that the precedent provided by the primitive church remains a critical component of the argument over the origins and history of clerical celibacy.

The debate over the 'apostolic origins' of clerical celibacy does not limit the chronology and polemical geography of the controversy to the immediate post-Christian era. It is, for example, evident that continence and celibacy had been prized among certain pre-Christian groups, and it was not just the primitive church, but also Jewish tradition that was used to provide fuel for subsequent debate and legitimation for later legislation. The Judaic precedent was to become particularly important as an argument for clerical celibacy developed from the principle that the Christian priesthood was a continuation of the Aaronic priesthood of the Old Testament.[5] The requirement that the priests of the Old Law abstain from their wives during their period of service in the temple (Lev. 8:33) coupled with, for example, the expectation that the same demand was made of participants in a holy war, lent weight to the assertion that there was a link between sacred function, the encounter with the divine, and moral purity. Thus, for the duration of the revelation of God on Mount Sinai, Moses instructed that the Israelites refrain from sexual intercourse (Exodus 19:15). When David led his troops against the Philistines, the fact that they had abstained from intercourse permitted them to partake of the consecrated bread (1 Sam. 21:4–6). Yahweh would abide with his troops, it was promised, if the holiness of the camp was maintained (Deut. 23:10–15).[6] The obligations imposed in the Pentateuch were underpinned

---

[3] This is the natural conclusion to be drawn from, for example, J-P Audet, *Mariage et Celibat dans le service pastorale de l'eglise* (Paris, 1967); A. Franzen, *Zölibat und Priesterehe in der Auseinandersetzung der Reformationszeit und der katholischen Reform des 16. Jahrhunderts* (Munster, 1969), and Gryson, *Les Origines*.

[4] Cochini, *Apostolic Origins*; Cholij, *Clerical Celibacy*.

[5] See, for example, Peter Lombard, *Libri Quatuor Sententiarum*, IV.d.24, 9 [PL 192].

[6] The demand for purity extended beyond conjugal activity to include skin disease, contact with a corpse, and nocturnal emissions (Deut. 23:10, Lev. 15:16–19).

by the assumption that the priest occupied a sacred sphere, and reinforced the sense of separation between priest and layman. A priest was set apart from his people by divine mandate: 'Thus shalt thou separate the Levites from among the children of Israel: and the Levites shall be mine' (Num. 8:14; Deut. 10:8). This separateness extended to laws which constrained the marriage of priests. It was forbidden for a priest to marry a woman who had been divorced, or who had been a prostitute, 'for he is holy unto his God' (Lev. 21:7). The sons of Aaron were deemed to be ceremonially unclean and not permitted to handle the sacred elements at the tabernacle until they had washed in the evening (Lev. 22:4–6), and it was unlawful for an individual to approach the sacred in a state of uncleanness. The demands placed upon the priests, and the constructs of purity upon which they were based, established the requirements of the state of holiness in which the priests dwelled, separate from the life of the people. Entry to that state was made possible by ritual purification, usually through washing, which has led Gerard Sloyan to suggest that the purity required of the priestly legislation was not contingent upon ethical virtue; rather, Sloyan suggests, the ritually fit person is not the one who has abstained but the one on whose body or clothing there remains no trace of such engagement.[7]

However, these stringent regulations did not amount to a complete deprecation of the physical, nor to a total rejection of the value of marriage. The universal nature of marriage in Jewish custom, the assertion in Genesis that it was not good for man to be alone, and the command to 'be fruitful and multiply' (Gen. 1:28) suggested that marriage and procreation were part of the divine plan. Indeed, inherent in the limitations placed upon the marriage of the Levites, for example in the obligation that a priest marry a virgin of his own people (Lev. 21:13–14), was the existence of the married priesthood itself, in which the office of the priest was hereditary. Sexuality was thus undoubtedly an important element in human life, but one that was to be controlled in proximity to the holy. Sacred and sexual activities were regarded as mutually exclusive, but the expectation was that continence and ritual purity would be practised for a specific time. The abstinence required of a priest before he served at the Temple was temporary rather than perpetual; there was, it has been argued, no sense in which marriage itself was 'morally contaminating', and no sense in which virginity was expected to be a permanent state.[8] The legacy provided to the

---

[7] Gerard Sloyan, 'Biblical and patristic motives for the Celibacy of Church Ministers', in W. Bassett and Peter Huizing (eds), *Celibacy in the Church* (New York, 1972), pp. 13–29, especially pp. 15–16.

[8] W. Phipps, *Clerical Celibacy. The Heritage* (London and New York, 2004), p. 9; there is, Phipps notes, no Hebrew word for perpetual virginity.

emergent Christian churches was in this sense ambivalent. The controls exerted over the conduct of the Levitical priesthood implied a relationship between sacred function and sexual abstinence, yet it is abundantly clear that marriage was held in high esteem and was certainly not prohibited to those who served at the temple. And as Christian Cochini has already noted, this insistence upon a liturgical 'purity' from those who served at the altar was alone among the Levitical prohibitions in its retention in the apostolic church; 'if we go back to the Old Testament's prescriptions concerning the sanctity of priests, we cannot help but be struck by the fact that only sexual interdictions survived the deep mutations that put a definitive end to the rules of purity and impurity'.[9] The means by which such purity was to be preserved, for example in the avoidance of contact with the bodies of the dead, or in the ritual cleanness attained by washing, were not detailed in the new law, yet the Levitical insistence upon sexual abstinence was to remain a critical part of the foundations of the obligation to celibacy placed upon ministers in the Christian church.

One of the more problematic precedents for the association of celibacy with holiness and access to the sacred lies in the Essene communities in the centuries immediately prior to the birth of Christ. It has been suggested that the response of many Jews to the changes in the world around them in this period encouraged the radicalisation of the sexual codes that were already apparent in Levitical law.[10] The accounts by two Jewish writers, Josephus and Philo, and by Pliny the Elder, all suggest that the Essenes led a communal life in which celibacy was both strictly observed, and indeed demanded of certain members for an indefinite period. Such a life of purity would reach fulfilment in the inheritance of the promised land. Yet the evidence is far from conclusive; the most famous documentary record, the *Dead Sea Scrolls*, makes no such link between the priestly sect and an obligation to complete continence, and the presence in the Qumran cemetery of the bodies of men and women and children suggests a separation that was less than complete. The validity of the Scrolls (and indeed the forensic excavations) as a record of Essene life has been vociferously challenged, particularly given this divergence between the textual and physical evidence.[11] Marriage appears to have been deferred rather than disavowed in the community, although it is worthy of note

---

[9] Cochini, *Apostolic Origins*, p. 429; see also J. Coppens 'Le Sacerdoce Veterotestamentaire', in Coppens (ed.) *Sacerdoce et Celibat* (Gembloux/Louvain, 1971), pp. 3–21.

[10] P. Brown, *The Body and Society. Men, Women and Sexual Renunciation in Early Christian Society* (New York, 1988), p. 34.

[11] N. Golb, *Who Wrote the Dead Sea Scrolls? The Search for the Secret of Qumran* (New York, 1985).

that even if perpetual celibacy was not required, the postponement of marriage beyond the age of puberty was unusual.[12]

There are also dangers in extrapolating from the Essene example to assume that such practices were common, or served as the building blocks of later Christian monasticism. The relationship between the Qumran community, the Scrolls, and the Essenes remains uncertain, and the account of Essene life provided by Philo may well be less than typical. It is not clear why the Essenic life of continence was expected of, or attractive to, specific sections of Jewish society.[13] However, some degree of influence of Persian and neo-Pythagorean thought on Jewish communities would not be out of place, and would certainly accommodate effectively the structures described in Philo's narrative of the Essenes. There were clearly those who perceived celibacy through the mirror of asceticism, and articulated the more radical principle that sexual intercourse debased and constrained the soul, and that its freedom could be won only through the practice of complete continence. The ascetic imperative of the Stoic and Epicurean philosophies, and even the celibacy of Indian monasticism, exerted a profound influence over the Mediterranean world.[14] Platonic assertions of the superiority of the soul over the body, and the moral peril of sexuality, established a dichotomy between idea and matter that extended into the thought of the first Christian centuries. The nascent religion was born into a world already 'fertilised with sexual asceticism',[15] both in this separation of spiritual and material, and in the separate life of religious communities.

The association of prophetic authority, continence, and repentance in the life of, for example, John the Baptist, perhaps exemplified this trend in the minds of early Christian writers and observers of the new religion. Certainly, the fact that Christ was unmarried at the start of his fourth decade occasioned little comment. However, despite the absence of a clear statement on the subject, both the personal example and the instruction of Jesus were to prove central to later debates over the merits and necessity of a celibate priesthood. While the proponents of clerical marriage posited that the Gospels provided little direct evidence that the prohibition of marriage was expected by Christ or practised with any rigour in the first Christian centuries, defenders of clerical celibacy have

---

[12] G. Vermes, *The Dead Sea Scrolls in English* (Harmondsworth, 1968), pp. 103ff.

[13] A. Marx, 'Les Racines du celibat essenien', *Revue de Qumran*, 7 (1970): 323–42; S.D. Fraade, 'Ascetical Aspects of Ancient Judaism', in A. Green (ed.) *World Spirituality vol. 13: Jewish Spirituality from the Bible to the Middle Ages* (New York, 1986), pp. 253–88.

[14] See W. Phipps, 'Did Ancient Indian Celibacy Influence Christianity?', *Studies in Religion*, 4 (1974): 49–50.

[15] Elizabeth Abbott, *A History of Celibacy* (Cambridge Mass: 2001), p. 44.

argued it to be a necessary feature of a priesthood modelled on Christ. An unmarried Christ is often assumed in writings on clerical celibacy and marriage,[16] and the Second Vatican Council echoed this long tradition in its commendation of those priests who 'have freely undertaken celibacy in imitation of Christ'.[17] There is little agreement, however, as to why (or if) Christ remained celibate. The commendation of those who remained unmarried 'for the sake of the kingdom' (Matt. 19:12) might point to a more general preference for virginity or celibacy over marriage, but, as Gerald Sloyan has indicated, precisely what conduct was expected from the early followers of Christ is still less than perspicuous from this text. Jesus' teaching on the indissoluble nature of marriage (Matt.19:10), for example, suggests a respect for the merits and bonds of matrimony, but his praise for those who had 'made themselves eunuchs' has continued to be regarded through the centuries as a biblical and apostolic warrant for the discipline of clerical celibacy.[18]

Such claims, however, remain contested, and the apparently contradictory voice of scripture on the subject has served to enliven the debate over the biblical foundations of clerical celibacy. The assertion of a scriptural mandate for either clerical marriage or clerical celibacy tends to focus around a relatively small selection of key passages from the Gospels and Epistles. Two texts might be described as eschatological in their tone: Mark 10:29 and Luke 14:26. A third, taken from Matthew's Gospel, is the widely debated reference to those who made themselves 'eunuchs for the sake of the kingdom'. All three imply some benefit from the renunciation of marriage or family life, but historically there has been little agreement as to the precise meaning, and indeed wider implications, of these texts. The vocabulary is problematic, as is the extent to which the injunctions or commendations were to be applied to the wider

---

[16] See, for example, A-M Cardinal Stickler, *The Case for Clerical Celibacy. Its Historical Development & Theological Foundations* (trans. Fr Brian Ferme) (San Francisco, 1995); K. Niederwimmer, *Askese und Mysterium. Ubere Ehe, Ehescheidung und Eheverzicht in den Anfangen des christlichen Glaubens* (Gottingen, 1975) p. 40, quoted in Heid, *Celibacy*, p. 24.

[17] *Decree on the Ministry and Life of Priests*, 16; cf John Paul II, letter to Priests, 9 April 1979, c.8. In his study of early asceticism and attitudes to virginity, Peter Brown notes that it was at least a century before the followers of Christ began to model their own celibacy upon his example: Brown, *Body and Society*, p. 41; Ignatius, *Letter to Polycarp* 5.2 [PG 5].

[18] Mark 10:2–12; Sloyan, 'Biblical and Patristic', 17; Pope John Paul II, *The Theology of Marriage and Celibacy*, (Boston, 1986) pp. 90, 102; Pope Paul VI, *Priestly Celibacy*, c.6, 20–1. The debate over the marriage (or celibacy) of Christ has continued in academic and popular literature. See, for example, Philip Schaff, *History of the Christian Church* (New York, 1914), vol. 2, p. 397 for the argument that the divinity of Christ prevented his marriage; Charles Davis' contention that that evidence points to a married Christ (the London *Observer*, 28 March 1971, p. 25); R.J. Bunnik, 'The Question of Married Priests', in *Cross Currents* XV.4 (Fall, 1965): 407–14; J. Blenkinsopp, *Celibacy, Ministry, Church* (New York, 1968).

community of followers of Christ, or a smaller group within it. The literal interpretation has some famous devotees, most famously Origen, but a multiplicity of other meanings are inferred. Thus Edward Schillebeeckx suggests that the 'eunuchs' of Matthew's Gospel were not the unmarried, but the unmarriageable, whose inability or failure to procreate was unacceptable under the Old Law.[19] The term 'eunouchos' has been taken to mean not those who, literally or figuratively, castrated themselves for the sake of the kingdom, but rather those with a military commission, which need not imply emasculation.[20] Such variation in the interpretation of what was to become a critical verse in the celibacy debate has led others to argue that the phrase comes not from Jesus at all, but from local Encratite groups whose rejection of the body was widely known.[21] Stefan Heid proposes a solution that occupies the middle ground between those who reject the authenticity of the record and those who argue for a strict interpretation, arguing that the strict understanding of the word 'eunuch' makes little sense in the context of the first followers of Christ. Instead, in Heid's exegetical framework, it is assumed that although some of the first Christians and indeed immediate circle of Christ's disciples were married, they lived in an 'unmarried' state, or separate from their wives. Eunuchs in this context were the unmarried disciples, or even Jesus himself, those who had abandoned their previous life, and adopted a form of 'spiritual castration', choosing to lead a life of continence.[22] Heid goes as far as to suggest that in this analysis it is possible to see the beginnings of the obligations placed upon the clergy to be celibate, in a gospel narrative of men, both married and unmarried, who were willing

---

[19] E. Schillebeeckx, *Clerical Celibacy Under Fire. A Critical Appraisal* (London and Sydney, 1968), p. 12; William Phipps suggests that the 'eunuchs' were not the unmarriageable, but those who had become estranged from their spouses but rejected divorce, and therefore lived in continence: Phipps, *Clerical Celibacy*, p. 24; Brown, *Body and Society*, p. 42; Jean-Paul Audet, *Mariage et Celibat dans le service pastoral de l'Eglise* (Paris, 1967), pp. 50–51 argues that the passage refers to those who were continent, and continent through their own volition; for a discussion of several interpretations, see J. Blinzer, '"Zur Ehe unfahig ..." Auslegung von Mt. 19,12' in *Gesammelte Ausfatze* 1 (1969): 30–40.

[20] Sloyan, 'Biblical and Patristic', 19; for a more detailed discussion of the passage, see Q. Quesnell, 'Make themselves Eunuchs for the Kingdom of Heaven (Mt. 19:12)', *Catholic Biblical Quarterly*, 30 (July, 1968): 335–8. The literal understanding was sufficiently widespread that the church was moved to condemn mutilation in the fourth century. Origen's actions were recorded by Eusebius, but the authenticity of the account has been questioned (see, for example, Daniel F. Caner, 'The Practice and Prohibition of Self Castration in Early Christianity', *Vigilae Christiani*, 51 (1997): 396–415). Patristic commentators tended to assume continence rather than castration was implied here. For a further discussion, see D.S. Bailey, *Sexual Relations in Christian Thought* (New York, 1959) pp. 72ff, especially note 11.

[21] See Niederwimmer, *Askese und Mysterium*, pp. 57ff, for further discussion.

[22] Heid, *Celibacy*, p. 26.

to forswear physical procreation for the sake of the kingdom. There is little or no sense of obligation here, but from elsewhere in the Gospels, including Mark 10:29 (*para* Matt. 19:29 and Luke 18:29), it is apparent that leaving home and family in order to lead a life of discipleship was to be rewarded in the life to come, notwithstanding Christ's insistence upon the indissoluble nature of the marriage bond. Luke's Gospel is cited in, for example, Pope Paul VI's commentary on clerical celibacy, to underpin the assertion that Christ held out such a promise for those who surrendered everything to follow him.[23] The suggestion that it was in a life freed from the cares of family that devotion to God might best be expressed has certainly proved persuasive across the centuries. Writing in the early third century, Tertullian described the conduct of certain clerics for whom the service of God was made possible by the renunciation of marriage, and more than a millennium later Francis Bacon commented that 'a single life does well with churchmen, for charity will hardly water the ground when it must first fill a pool'.[24] Celibacy appeared to have benefits both for the priest at his devotions and for the congregation who enjoyed the full attention of a minister unencumbered by the cares of marriage. However, this rejection of the demands of spouse and family in order to facilitate a deeper devotion to God has not always found such favour among scholars and commentators. John Calvin, for example, wrote that he had married in order that he might be better able to devote himself to God, freed from the domestic distractions of daily life.[25]

The generality of the calling to the renunciation of marriage is less than apparent in these passages alone, as is any specific association between chastity and the requirements of Christian priesthood. It is not immediately evident that sexual abstinence, rather than a more general rejection of family ties, is required, and the Gospels do not assert that the exercise of sexuality is unfitting for those who preach the word. Where detachment from worldly affairs was lauded, it certainly served to validate the single life, but no obvious connection was made here between such a life and ministry within the church. These renunciatory statements of Christ might be seen as a step away from the assumption that all adult males would marry towards the assertion that a devotion

---

[23] Paul VI, *Priestly Celibacy*, c. 22. For a fuller discussion of this text, see pp. 222–3 below.

[24] Tertullian, *De Exhort. Cast.* 13 [PL 2.920]; W.P. Le Saint, *Tertullian, Treatises on Marriage and Remarriage* (Westminster, Md., 1951), pp. 42–64; C. Tibiletti, 'Verginità e matrimonio in antichi scrittori cristiani', Annali della Facoltŕ di Lettere e Filosofia dell'Universita di Macerata 2 (1969): 9–217; Francis Bacon, *Of Marriage and Single Life*, J. Pitcher (ed.), *The Essays of Francis Bacon* (Penguin Classics, 1985) p. 81; see also Pope Pius XIII, *Holy Virginity* (1954), c. 20–1.

[25] J. Calvin, *Jean Calvin Opera* (Brunswick, 1871), vol. 10a:228.

to the kingdom of God might encourage the avoidance of married life, but it is less clear that they provides a scriptural mandate for celibacy as a precondition for entry into the priesthood or the kingdom.[26] Indeed, several commentators have noted the lack of any cogent link between sexual abstention and priesthood in the Gospels; while these passages might be marshalled in support of a calling to celibacy, they do not appear to have been directed towards a specific group in society, and nor do they impose obligatory continence upon the followers of Christ.[27] However, if the teachings of Christ did not establish a binding link between the service of the church and celibacy, they still left open the belief that a life of faith might make marriage impossible or unnecessary. Celibacy was for many a consequence of a life of total surrender to the divine will, but it was not (yet) something that was imposed upon those who felt called to the ministry and preaching of the word.

Debate over the biblical origins of clerical celibacy was not confined to the words and example of Christ alone. Among the first generation of followers of Christ, it is St Paul whose attitude to marriage has been the most closely studied and debated. Paul's letters predate the composition of the Gospel narratives, and therefore offer one of the earliest accounts of the life and faith of the primitive church. However, the experience of Paul was rather different from that of the early Christians in Palestine, and his preoccupations were shaped by specific problems and by his own position. A sense of the imminent return of Christ certainly coloured his expectations of Christian life, but his epistles are also a response to a very particular set of concerns to do with human conduct in the period prior to the parousia.[28] Most critical, but also perhaps most ambiguous, among Paul's writings on the subject, is the seventh chapter of the first Epistle to the Corinthians, written in AD54 in response to questions received from the church in Corinth relating to social order, including marriage and sexual conduct.[29] These themes dominated this epistle to a far greater

---

[26] Frazee, 'Origins', 149; Audet, *Mariage*, p. 49.

[27] Sloyan for example suggests that both Mark's and Luke's Gospels pointed to the more general surrender of family ties rather than the specific renunciation of marriage (Luke is alone in including 'wife' among the list of family members) and argues that there is no foundation here for the argument that these sayings of Christ were intended to relate to a specific class: 'Biblical and Patristic', 10. Schillebeeckx offers some clarification here, in the observation that the vocabulary might be dictated by the audience: for readers of Mark's and Matthew's Gospels, the instruction to leave one's house would imply also one's wife; for Luke's audience, it would have been necessary to make this clear: *Clerical Celibacy*, p. 14.

[28] Brown, *Body and Society*, 44ff; Sloyan, 'Biblical and Patristic', 21.

[29] L. Legrand, 'Saint Paul et le celibat', in J. Coppens (ed.), *Sacerdoce et Celibat* (Gembloux/Louvain, 1971), pp. 315–31; C.B. Cousar, *The Letters of Paul. Interpreting Biblical Texts* (Nashville, 1996); J. Murphy-O'Connor, *Paul the Letter-Writer: His World,*

extent that any of Paul's other writings, and indeed most of the epistolary section of the New Testament, but despite the critical place the letter, and especially this chapter, assumed in the history and study of clerical celibacy, it contains no explicit observations on the continence or otherwise of the apostles, or any leaders of the church. From Paul's response, it would seem that some of the community in Corinth had begun to adopt a strict form of life, abstaining from their spouses, renouncing marriage, and leading a life of perpetual continence.[30] Paul's Epistle opened with what has become an infamous statement in defence of chastity: 'it is not good for a man to touch a woman' (I. Cor. 7:1), but what follows does much to uphold the value of marriage, particularly for those who might not be able to contain. Both marriage and celibacy were described as holy, and gifts from God (I. Cor. 7:14, 34) and in the face of the potentially short time before the second coming, he advised, it would be better for the married to remain married, and the unmarried to refrain from marriage. In the absence of any clear directive from Jesus on celibacy (I. Cor. 7:10, 25), Paul counselled a moderate approach. Stopping short of suggesting that sexual relations within marriage were in any way defiling, Paul portrayed marriage, like much human activity, as a distraction from prayer (I. Cor. 7:5, 32, 34). However, it would be ill advised, he warned, for married men and women to withhold themselves from each other except on a temporary basis in order to allow time for prayer (I. Cor. 7:5), and only with the mutual consent of both parties.[31] The gift of continence had not been given to all, and therefore marriage was the appropriate remedy for those who might otherwise 'burn with passion' (I. Cor. 7:9). This apparently ambivalent attitude to marriage, in which it appeared to serve as remedy for fornication rather than a positive good, was, as Brown suggests, 'a fatal legacy' for the future, raising the spectre that a married Christian might be only 'half' a Christian.[32]

The Epistle to the Corinthians contained a series of observations that did much to fuel the debate over marriage and celibacy in context of the Christian priesthood, and sexual conduct more generally. Whether

---

His Options, His Skills (Collegeville, MN: Liturgical, 1995); W. Deming, *Paul on Marriage and Celibacy: The Hellenistic Background of I Corinthians 7* (Cambridge/New York/Oakleigh, 1995), argues that in fact Paul was writing against extreme views of celibacy. I. Cor. 7 is the passage cited most frequently in, for example, Pope Pius XII's encyclical *On Holy Virginity*, and featured prominently in patristic writing on celibacy as well as in the Reformation debates over clerical marriage.

[30] N. Baumert, *Ehelosigkeit und Ehe in Herrn: Eine Neuinterpretations von I Kkor 7* (Wurzburg, 1984) pp. 20ff.

[31] Phipps, *Clerical Celibacy*, p. 61, suggests that Paul made this recommendation not with any real enthusiasm, but as a concession to the ascetically minded Corinthians.

[32] Brown, *Body and Society*, p. 55.

the letter is read as a commendation of sexual asceticism or as evidence of the Christological foundations of celibacy, it is immediately apparent why Paul's correspondence with the church in Corinth should assume such a prominent place in subsequent debate.[33] However, it is in Paul's other writings that his views on marriage and the ministry are more transparent. The letters to Timothy and Titus, for example, are a more obvious and indeed 'fundamental and perennial reference point for the discussion of clerical continence',[34] not least because these letters do relate rather more explicitly to the character and conduct expected of aspiring candidates for the ministry. Deacons, elders and bishops, Paul urged, were to be temperate, hospitable, beyond reproach, and significantly 'mias gynaikos aner' (I. Tim. 3:12; Tit. 1:5–9; 1 Tim. 3:8–12). They were to be experienced in the running of a household, in order that they might better understand and fulfil the demands of their congregations. In these words it might appear that Paul offers the most concrete evidence that marriage was permitted to, and even encouraged for, those who preached the word. But even here the phrasing is unclear. Paul's recommendation might be interpreted as a demand that the minister be monogamous (rather than bigamous), that he be married only once (rather than digamous), or, as some later commentators claimed, that the clergy should be drawn only from the ranks of the married. Certainly it is possible that there were perceived advantages in appointing married men as leaders of the early Christian communities, although with no understanding that marriage would be essential to ministry. Edward Schillebeeckx proposes that given the domestic nature of the early church, and the reliance upon the homes of the faithful as a meeting place for the congregations, it was natural to expect that the leaders of the church would share the attributes of the head of a family; a faithful husband who attended to the needs and the discipline of his children.[35] However, it is less clear whether the characteristics expected of ministers of the church in the Pauline letters were simply that, expected, or whether they were intended to be rather more prescriptive. Given that the intended recipients of the letters were

---

[33] For the suggestions that it was celibacy rather than asceticism that was at stake here, see Heid, pp. 38–9, in debate with Niederwimmer, *Askese und Mysterium*, p. 113.

[34] Heid, *Celibacy*, p. 41; see also his 'Grundlagen des Zolibats in der fruhen Kirche', in K.M. Becker and J. Eberle (eds), *Der Zolibat des priesters* (St. Ottilien, 1995), pp. 51–68.

[35] Schillebeeckx, *Clerical Celibacy*, p. 9; H-J. Klauck, *Hausgemeinde und Hauskirche im fruhen Christentum*, (Stuttgart, 1981) pp. 66ff; cf. Phipps, *Clerical Celibacy*, p. 73, who argues that fidelity in a marriage was more critical than whether it was a second marriage. A candidate for church offices was required to show that he could exercise leadership in the household and in the family of the church, hence the terminology of the priest as 'father'. See also Sloyan's interpretation of the phrase as 'a one-woman man', implying a reputation for fidelity: 'Biblical and Patristic', 22.

not ministers in the church but rather the wider congregation involved in their selection, Heid suggests that Paul's recommendation concerning the conduct of church leaders was certainly intended to shape the choice of candidates after proper examination. The letters to Titus and Timothy set out impediments to orders, in the hope that those who were appointed would be 'above reproach'; candidates did not need to demonstrate that they were married, but they needed to prove that they had been married only once.[36] The prohibition of orders to digamists was certainly the practice of the early church, but the more extreme interpretation of the passage as a suggestion that the clergy might be forced to marry did become a staple for Catholic writers seeking to discredit the evangelical legalisation of clerical marriage on the basis of the Pauline epistles.[37] Importantly for the defenders of the apostolic origins of clerical celibacy, this concern that bishops, priests and deacons should be married only once would imply that the ministry was not the exclusive preserve of married men in the first decades after Christ, and that the prohibition of second marriages for the clergy was rather part of a wider discipline of continence imposed upon the first generation of church leaders.

St Paul died around 60AD, although letters attributed to him continued to be written after this date.[38] But the legacy and reputation of Paul remained significant, albeit as contested as the interpretation of his letters. Within the context of the debate over the origins of clerical celibacy, Paul's own actions, as well as those of the other early followers of Christ, were to assume a position of importance. However, despite the forceful statement that he wished that 'all men live as I do', Paul gave little clue as to his own marital status, and the sources are frustratingly ambiguous.[39] Later commentators, particularly in the polemical vein, have been rather more definite, although their combined arguments are

---

[36] Heid, *Celibacy*, pp. 42–5, and his summary of H. Schlier, 'Die Ordnung der Kirche nach den Pastoralbriefen', in K. Kertelge (ed.), *Das Kirchliche Amt in Neuen Testament* (Darmstadt, 1977), and A. Harnack, *Enstehung und Entwicklung der Kirchenverfassung und des Kirchenrechts in den zwei ersten Jahrhunderten* (Darmstadt, 1980); see also G. Bickell, 'Colibat eine apostoliche Anordnung', *Zeitschrift für katholische Theologie* 2 (1878): 26–64, especially at 28.

[37] See, for example, Cholij, *Clerical Celibacy*, pp. 12–13, 75–8, with a focus on the Council of Trullo; H. Deen, *Le Celibat des Pretres dans les premiers siecles de l'eglise* (Paris, 1969) pp. 33–4; Stickler, *Clerical Celibacy*, p. 91; on Catholic suggestions that Protestantism would usher in compulsory marriage for priests, see H.L. Parish, *Clerical Marriage and the English Reformation* (Aldershot, 2000) pp. 60–62.

[38] D. Guthrie, *New Testament Introduction* (Nottingham, 1990), which defends Pauline authorship, and Raymond E. Brown, *An Introduction to the New Testament* (New Haven, 1997) provide an introduction to ongoing debates over the authorship of the epistles.

[39] For a discussion of the controversial 'letter of Ignatius to the Phladelphians', see Parish, *Clerical Marriage*, pp. 64–6.

ultimately no more conclusive. St Jerome, for example, in his *Letter to Eustochium* rejected any suggestion that Paul had married 'because when he writes about continence and advises perpetual chastity, he argues from his own case'. In contrast, Ambrose and Clement of Alexandria were both convinced that Paul had been married, although disagreed over the equally vexed question of whether his wife had still been alive at the time of his conversion.[40] The debate continued in later periods of controversy over celibacy and marriage. In the sixteenth century, Martin Luther believed it to be more likely that Paul had married, given Jewish custom of the time, but that at the time of writing to the Corinthians, he counted himself among the unmarried. By contrast, Catholic writers objected to any assertion that the apostle was the 'patrone of maried priests'.[41] The assumption that men would marry under Judaic law might well suggest the likelihood that Paul had been married, but need not lead to the assumption that he was still married at the time of conversion or at the time of writing to the Corinthians. Thus, Gerard Sloyan argues that although the law expected marriage, Paul might well have had a preference for the unmarried life, albeit not linked explicitly to his apostolic work.[42] Both Jean-Paul Audet and Edward Schillebeeckx conclude that Paul's celibacy was that of a man who had either left his wife, or been left by her, by the time of his conversion or by the time the letter to the Corinthians was composed.[43]

It was this latter question of the continuation, and particularly the continued use, of marriage by Paul and the first apostles that was rather more critical, particularly to later commentators confronted by priests who wished to marry after ordination. While it was clear that married men had made up some of the first followers of Christ, and that the leaders of the early church might well have been drawn from the ranks of the married, this precedent did not necessarily support a contract of marriage after ordination, or the continued use of marriage after entry into higher orders. It was these questions that were to form the basis of the earliest ecclesiastical legislation on the subject of clerical marriage in the western church. Again, the ongoing debate over the marriage of the first followers of Christ, and their relationship with their wives

---

[40] Ep. 22.20; CSEL 54.170–1; Clement of Alexandria, Stromata III.6 [PG 8], although Clement suggests that after their calling the apostles treated their wives as sisters; Ambrose, *De Virginitate* [PL 16.315a].

[41] Luther, LW 54:353–4; Thomas Martin, *A traictise declaryng and plainly prouyng, that the pretensed marriage of priestes, and professed persones, is no mariage, but altogether vnlawful* (London, 1554), sig.Hh1r.

[42] Sloyan 'Biblical and Patristic', 19–20.

[43] Schillebeeckx, *Marriage: Human Reality and Saving Mystery* (New York, 1965), p. 128; Audet, *Mariage*, p. 69.

after their calling, exposes the biblical evidence as less than conclusive; it is certainly a controversy that has continued to be invigorated by the reappearance of clerical celibacy on the polemical agenda in the medieval, modern and early modern church. There are clear references to women who accompanied the early apostles on their travels, most evident in Paul's assertion 'do we not have the right to be accompanied by a sister as wife, as the other apostles and the brothers of the Lord and Cephas'.[44] However, the vocabulary used to describe such women (or wives) in the epistles or the gospels is disputed, and for the defenders of the apostolic origins of clerical celibacy, not consonant with the claims of, for example, Peter to have 'left everything and followed you'.[45] The term 'gune', while used to describe a woman, might more commonly be understood as 'wife'; Luke the evangelist used the word to refer to particular women who were the spouses of his subject, but also more generally to describe married and unmarried women.[46] In some cases, the evidence is more explicit. The gospel narrative of the healing of Peter's mother in law is in itself testimony to his marriage (Mark 1:29–31), but the role of his wife in his mission, or indeed the survival of his marriage after his calling, are less transparent.[47] Among later patristic commentators, Clement of Alexandria suggested that the women who accompanied the apostles were a vital part of their mission, allowing the gospel to be preached more effectively to other women. Arguing that all apostles were married men, Basil upheld their wives as examples of Christian life to those for whom asceticism has no appeal.[48] However, others were less enthusiastic about the possibility that the wives of the married apostles had any role to play in the life of the church. Tertullian concluded that the women described in the Gospels were simply in the service of the apostles, rather than their wives, and that their role was correspondingly limited. Although he accepted that Peter had been married, Tertullian argued that all the other

---

[44] I. Cor. 9:4–5; this text was of course a subject of consideration for the medieval church in its insistence upon continence for the clergy: see, for example, Gratian, *Decretum*, in *Corpus iuris canonici in tres partes distinctum*, A. Naldi (ed) (3 vols, Lyons, 1671), P. 1.Dist 31.c.11.

[45] Matt. 19:27; Heid, *Celibacy*, p. 31.

[46] See, for example, Luke 8:1–3.

[47] For further discussion, see Gryson, *Les Origines*, pp. 9–10; later apocryphal writings, including the Acts of Peter, asserted that St Petronilla was Peter's daughter. Audet argues for a clear distinction between the 'genuine' narratives of the lives and deeds of the apostles that make no such claims, and the later writing, primarily from the second and third centuries, in which the continence of the first followers of Christ is more frequently considered: Audet, *Mariage*, p. 64.

[48] Basil, *De Renuntatione Saeculi* 1.

apostles had practised continence or remained virgins.[49] Likewise, Jerome, writing against Vigilantius and his defence of marriage for the clergy, conceded that Peter had been married, but denied that this provided any precedent for the legitimacy of the unions of priests, because either he had ceased to exercise his marriage after being called to preach, or his wife had died.[50] Jerome also asserted that John, 'the disciple that Jesus loved', was held in such esteem because he had remained a virgin, and made the argument from silence that where no explicit mention was made of a wife in scripture, the apostles should be assumed to have been unmarried.[51] Such silence was not, however, entirely conclusive. Were it not for the record of Christ healing Peter's mother-in-law, there would be no formal mention of his marriage in Scripture, yet it is clear that he had a wife. Other patristic commentators present a mixed picture of the marital status of the apostles. The virginity of John appeared to be assumed through tradition, while Epiphanius, for example, listed Andrew and James the son of Alpheus among the married, although the latter with no direct scriptural support.[52] Indeed the Gospels remained tantalisingly silent on the subject of the marriage of James the brother of John, Andrew, Matthew, Thomas, Bartholomew, Simon and Jude. Confusion resulting from the potential conflation of the biographies of Philip in the Gospels (John 1:45) and Philip the deacon (Acts 6:5) introduces a further complication, although Cochini concludes that the weight of evidence points to both as married men.[53] In light of such varied interpretations, Jean-Paul Audet is sensibly cautious about assuming that any of the apostles went further than Christ had done towards continence in the service of the Gospel.[54] Given that the precise views of Christ on marriage and virginity have been as hotly disputed as the actions of his followers, it is perhaps no surprise that these apparent ambiguities have fuelled centuries of polemical controversy.

---

[49] Miscellanies 3.53; Tertullian, *De Monogamia* 8; cf. Jerome, *Adv. Jov.* I.26; for a more detailed discussion, see Cochini, *Apostolic Origins*, p. 80. Audet dismissed Tertullian's assumptions as lacking in any evidential basis and the consequence of the fact that Tertullian 'had montanism on the brain'.

[50] Jerome, *Adv. Jov.* 1.26 [PL 23.246b] cf Epist. 118.4, where the suggestion is that he left his wife when called. See Cochini, *Apostolic Origins*, p. 66.

[51] Jerome, *Adv. Jov.* 1.26 (PL 23.246a–c); see also Epiphanius, *Adv. Haer.* 58 [PG 41.1061a].

[52] *Adv. Haer.* 78 [PG 42.720a, 714c]; Cochini, *Apostolic Origins*, pp. 68–9.

[53] Cochini, *Apostolic Origins*, p. 69.

[54] Audet, pp. 64–5; compare with Vern Bullough's suggestion that there was no systematic treatment of sexuality in the Christian scripture: V.L. Bullough, 'Introduction: The Christian Inheritance', in V.L. Bullough and J. Brundage (eds), *Sexual Practices and the Medieval Church* (Buffalo: Prometheus, 1982) p. 4.

Whatever the precedent set by the example of the unmarried and married apostles, by the second century there was a sense in the works of Christian and non-Christian writers that at least some of the adherents of the new religion practised a form of continence. Galen, in the second half of the century described a 'restraint from intercourse' as a characteristic of Christian believers, while Justin Martyr in his *Apology* identified the strict sexual code of its members as a defining feature of the faith.[55] Peter Brown writes of a parting of the ways between Jewish and Christian leaders on the subject of marriage and continence in the mid-second century; the martyrdom of Peter and Paul marked the shift from a Jewish to a Gentile leadership in the church, and a pagan 'ascetic syncretism' gradually exerted a more powerful influence over the growing church.[56] Despite the paucity of evidence for the nature of religious life in the second century after Christ, it is possible to glean some insight into attitudes to marriage and continence, and the discipline of the clergy, from the pastoral letters and apologetic writings of the time. Christian ministry and belief may have lacked a rigid institutional structure and organisation, but it is in this period that it is possible to see a greater unification of religious life, and a gradual shift towards uniformity in faith and discipline.[57] Such developments within the church were accompanied by challenges and influences outwith its embryonic structures, which were, in relation to clerical discipline, most evident in ascetic movements, including Encratism.[58] The hostility to marriage that characterised such groups was roundly condemned by orthodox authorities, but views of sexuality, continence and ministry in the second century and beyond continued to be shaped by a mix of biblical, orthodox and more controversial views of humanity, the body, and the service of the word. Clerical discipline in the west, including its ascetic constructs, was defined not only in relation to the needs and priorities of the church, but also as a result of the imperative to reclaim certain practices from the more radical groups whose particular form of asceticism was rejected as erroneous. Although central to the history of the church in its own right, this period was also critical to the evolution of later debates over clerical celibacy and continence; controversialists in

---

[55] Quoted in Brown, *Body and Society*. Brown contrasts such statements with the attitude of first-century writers such as Ignatius of Antioch who were unwilling to allow celibacy and continence to become a divisive issue in the church (Letter to Polycarp 1.2).

[56] Brown, *Body and Society*, p. 61; Phipps, *Clerical Celibacy*, chapter 5.

[57] For further discussion of these themes, see H. Chadwick, *The Early Church* (Penguin 1968), chs 3 and 4; Heid, *Celibacy*, pp. 58ff.

[58] The link between clerical continence and the views of Encratite groups hostile to marriage has been made by, for example, K. Muller, *Aus der Akademischen Arbeit: Vortage und Aufsatze* (Tubingen, 1930) p. 79; Abbott, *History of Celibacy*, pp. 49–54, suggests that Christianity was born into a world in which there was already a strong ascetic current.

subsequent centuries continued to regard the testimony of the Fathers as authoritative, even if not normative, in the dispute over the origins and necessity of the continence discipline.

Among the epistolary evidence of the second and third centuries in the west, the name of Tertullian looms large. It is with his writings, it has been suggested, that we see the 'first consequential statement ... of the belief that abstinence from sex was the most effective technique with which to achieve clarity of the soul'.[59] An orator in the North African city of Carthage, Tertullian converted to Christianity around 195, and (in Jerome's account at least) was ordained a priest prior to his drift into heresy. If he remained a layman, he was a layman with strong theological interests. The interpretation of his writings is coloured by two difficulties; a master rhetorician, Tertullian displayed a marked tendency towards exaggeration in form and content, and as an enthusiast for the Montanism in the early third century, his writings cannot always be taken as an accurate record of the prevailing Christian orthodoxy of the time. His counsels on continence and celibacy come from this later period, but can still shed a useful light upon the general mores of the age.[60] From his *De Exhortatione Castitatis*, written to dissuade a widow from a second marriage, it would seem that continence had already become, in the eyes of some, a key part of ministry: 'Quanti igitus et quanta in ecclesiasticis ordibinus de continentia censentur, qui deo nubere maluerunt, qui carnis suae honorem restituerunt'.[61] His formulation that there are those among this group who 'prefer to marry God' has been argued by Bickell, and more recently Heid, to be indicative of the self-nature of clerical continence, for both married and celibate clergy, in the second century; the bishops of the church were chosen from those men who had been married only once, or those who were virgins.[62] For Tertullian, the argument in favour of a continent clergy was both practical and moral, and tied in with the purity expected of those who served at the altar of God. Tertullian suggested that the apostles had been sent to preach the 'sanctity of the

---

[59] The writers of the East are considered in more detail in chapter 2; see also Brown, *Body and Society*, p. 78, quoting De Ieiunio 5.1.

[60] For a fuller discussion of the 'orthodoxy' of Tertullian, see Douglas Powell, 'Tertullianists and Cataphrygians', *Vigiliae Christianae*, 29 (1975): 33–54 and David Rankin, *Tertullian and the Church* (Cambridge, 1995), p. 27. After his conversion to Montanism, Tertullian wrote to his wife of the high value of celibacy over marriage: Tertullian, *To His Wife* 1.2–3.

[61] 13.4 (CCL 2.1035); see also Gryson, *Origines*, p. 30; for the opposing view, see Cochini, *Apostolic Origins*, pp. 143–6.

[62] *De Exhortatione Cast.* 11.12, but with the qualifier 'aut etiam' which implied that the latter was more unusual. Bickell, 'Der Colibat', 38–9; Heid, *Celibacy*, p. 74; see also L. Crouzet, 'Le celibat et la continence dans l'Eglise primitive: leurs motivations', in Coppens, *Sacerdoce et Celibat*, pp. 333–71.

flesh' and therefore abided in a manner (i.e. without their wives) that was a living example of this model. Re-married men were not to be admitted to the priesthood (or re-married women to widowhood) in order that the altar might remain pure.[63] The extrapolation of clerical continence from these phrases has certainly been questioned by those who argue against the early origins of the discipline. Cochini advocates a more moderate interpretation, suggesting that Tertullian instructed his friend that by refusing a second marriage he could be ordained; some men were deemed appropriate candidates for holy orders because they were continent, although not lifetime celibates.[64] There were evidently married bishops in the second century, openly referred to by Polycarp and Irenaeus, but also those for whom celibacy was clearly a badge of honour, or an epithet to be acquired.[65] Contemporaries of Tertullian certainly voiced objections to the esteem in which celibacy was held in the first and second centuries. Perhaps the most famous is the letter of Ignatius, cited above, in which he condemned the boasting of a man who lived in continence. There is, however, little to suggest here that Ignatius' criticism was levelled against the continent; more likely it was any hint of boastfulness that was unwelcome.[66] In a more detailed analysis of the Greek text, Cochini identified two possible interpretations, the first implying that it would be detrimental to the individual if the news of his conduct were to go any further than the bishop's ears, the second warning of the consequences if an individual believed himself to be superior to the bishop. Since there was nothing to suggest that the church was unsupportive of the virginal state, there seems no reason why a celibate priest should have to keep his life-style a secret. The more plausible interpretation, and that advanced by Cochini, is that Ignatius was critical of those who regarded themselves as superior on account of their virginity, a view that came to be associated

---

[63] *De Monogamia* 8.4–7; *De Exhort. Cast.* 7.1; Sloyan warns that this final assertion is based upon a biblical citation that Tertullian appears to have invented (*sacerdotes mei non plus ubent*) which does not feature in Leviticus.

[64] Cochini, *Apostolic Origins*, p. 145.

[65] Polycarp, *Letter to the Philippians* 11.4 [printed in The Ante-Nicene Fathers, vol. 1, A. Roberts, J. Donaldson, and A. Cleveland Coxe (eds) (Buffalo, NY: Christian Literature Publishing Co., 1885)]; Irenaeus, *Against Heresies* I.13.5 [PG7]; See also Sloyan, 'Biblical and Patristic', 23; H. Leclerq, 'Celibat' in *Dictionnaire d'Archeologie Chretienne et Liturgie* (Paris, 1896), 2.2808.

[66] For various interpretations of this passage, and a modern commentary on the text, see *St Irenaeus of Lyons against the heresies*, D.J. Unger and J.J. Dillon (eds) (Newman Press, 1992), and Gryson, *Les Origines*, p. 22. Ignatius instructed Polycarp to advise the Christian community that 'if somebody is capable of passing all his days in chastity, in honour of the Lord's body, let him do so without boasting; for if he boasts of it he is lost, and if the news gets beyond the bishop's ears it is all over with his chastity' (M. Staniforth (ed.), *Early Christian Writings: The Apostolic Fathers* (Middlesex, 1968), p. 129).

with heresy in later centuries.[67] The key issue, at least insofar as later arguments over the apostolic origins of clerical celibacy are concerned, was less whether the clergy were married or not, but whether they continued to use their conjugal rights, but it is less than obvious whether this was a distinction that was in practical force as early as the second century.[68]

By the fourth century, the debate over the use of marriage by ordained priests was becoming rather more nuanced. The notion of conjugal chastity was to feature in the writings of Ambrose, bishop of Milan (c.333–397), in a context that suggests that it was an issue over which there was a diversity of opinion. In his *Letter to the church of Vercelli*, Ambrose returned to the contested passages in the Pauline epistles in order to address the intention behind the suggestion that the bishop should be the husband of one wife. He debated the necessary qualities of those called to high office in the church, and argued that Paul's recommendation had in no way been intended to exclude unmarried men from ordination, but rather to encourage the appointment of those who, through 'conjugal chastity', remained in grace of their baptism. Thus, although it was perfectly acceptable to ordain married men, and even married men who had fathered children, Ambrose did not countenance marriage after an individual had been elevated to a bishopric, and assumed that those appointed would refrain from intercourse even within marriage. This requirement was spelled out more clearly in the *De Officiis Ministrorum*, in which Ambrose advised that those who were called to the priesthood must know that 'the ministry must be immune from possible conjugal relations', on the basis that this purity that was required of the clergy was necessary to the exercise of this sacred function. The law of the New Testament, he argued, demanded perpetual service of the priest, and therefore perpetual chastity. Peter Brown suggests a divergence between ideal and reality here; although there was clearly a current of thought that favoured a celibate clergy, Ambrose was well aware that the best that he could hope for at a local level was that the clergy might have 'had sons, and not continue to have sons'. The ministry of married priests was a necessity outside the large diocesan centres if local churches were to be served, although the ideal of a celibate priesthood appeared to be gathering some momentum. The suggestion that it was the perpetual character of priestly function that required celibacy was echoed in the works attributed to Ambrosiaster, and often published with those of Ambrose; as the 'representatives of

---

[67] Cochini cites the condemnation at the council of Gangres (340) of those who refused to accept the sacrament from married clergy: Cochini, *Apostolic Origins*, pp. 140–41.

[68] J. Colson, *Les Fonctions ecclesiales aux deux premiers siecles* (Paris, Desclee de Brouwer, 1954), p. 228 n.2; cited in Cochini, *Apostolic Origins*, p. 141.

God' the priest was obliged to lead a life of purity that was not demanded of the laity, and to do so in perpetuity.[69]

The full implications of this intellectual current were to become apparent in the next two generations of Christian thought and apologetic. Ambrose's understanding of the relationship between church and society was to resonate in the thought of Augustine, and his interpretation of the Pauline epistle was to be echoed in the writings of Jerome, and in the eventual papal intervention in the debate by Siricius. Evidence of a more negative general attitude to sexuality and marriage is identifiable in the records of the early church and in patristic writing, but also in the doctrine and practice of emergent ascetic groups including the Encratites, and followers of Marcion and Tatian. The more extreme amongst them were ultimately condemned by the church, but their influence in practical and polemical terms was still potent. To many in such groups, contact with women was defiling, sex the invention of the devil, and the sacraments reserved for those who renounced both marriage and the use of marriage. To undermine what Peter Brown refers to as the 'unidirectional' process of procreation to which humans contributed was to bring to an end human society in anticipation of the return of Christ, and to make a powerful symbolic gesture via an 'attitude of noncollaboration with all the Creator's purposes'. Human sexuality was not a remedy for death in the propagation of the species, but a cause of death as the means by which mankind first lost its freedom.[70] The full potential of this theology was most obviously realised in the Manichaean dualism, but the dividing line between orthodoxy and heterodoxy was less than clear, and the influence of Manichaean thought on the developing church is apparent both in the condemnation of dualist heresies, and in the thought of

---

[69] Ep. 63.62–3 [PL 16.1257]; *De Officiis Ministrorum*, 1.50 [PL 16:104a–5b]. In his condemnation of the heresies of Jovinian, Ambrose argued that Christ had honoured virginity by choosing a virgin as his mother [PL16:1124], and in his treatise *On Educating Virgins* argues that Mary called all to virginity [5.36]. Marriage itself was a 'galling burden' and those who entered into it entered into a form of bondage: *De Vidius* XIIII.31; XV.88; XI.69; *De Virginitate* I.6; Brown, *Body and Society*, p. 357–8; on Ambrosiaster, see Cochini, *Apostolic Origins*, pp. 222–4 ; PL 17.497a–d; CSEL 50.414–5.

[70] A. Voobus, *Celibacy. A Requirement for Admission to Baptism in the Early Syriac Church* (Stockholm, 1951), pp. 19ff; L.W. Barnard 'The Origins and Emergence of the Church in Edessa during the First Two Centuries AD', *Vigiliae Christianae*, 22. 3 (Sept. 1968): 161–75; Tertullian, *Adversus Marcionem*, (E. Evans trans and ed.) (Oxford, 1972), 4:24–34; Clement, *Stromata* III.c.12, c.17, in *Ante-Nicene Fathers. Vol. 2: The Fathers of the Second Century*, A. Roberts and J. Donaldson (eds) (Edinburgh, 1865); Justin Martyr, *Apology* 1 c.29 [PG.6]; Tatian, *On Perfection According to the Saviour*, in *Ante-Nicene Fathers*, vol. 2, p. 84; Brown, *Body and Society*, pp. 83–7.

authoritative figures within the orthodox church.[71] Marriage and sex were spoken of with disdain by both orthodox and heterodox. Arnobius the Elder denounced 'obscenitas coeundi', an Egyptian monk suggested that a priest lost his dignity if he was unchaste, and Augustine presented sexual desire as a permanent reminder of the sin and shame of mankind descended from Adam.[72] This sense that sex was inherently sinful, and more particularly that intercourse might render an individual impure, was to underpin some of the most determined demands for a celibate priesthood.[73] With the disparagement of marriage, virginity was to become the 'pinnacle of Christian achievement', although not necessarily one that was accessible to all. The ascetic heights climbed by a minority were a symbol of perfection, rather than a practical possibility for the majority, and attempts to enforce celibacy on the priesthood became a 'manifestation of prestigious separation from other Christians'.[74] Such separation could be that of distance between a priestly caste and Christian laymen, or the physical separation from the world that characterised the life of renunciation and poverty adopted by the desert fathers. But one of the most visible signs of withdrawal from the temptations and distractions of the world was the rejection of marriage, and the adoption of a strict sexual abstinence, whether in the practice of primitive monasticism, the cultivation of the ascetic impulse within the church, or the rejection of the prevailing orthodoxy in a search for a deeper spiritual experience.

Interaction between orthodox and heterodox ideas concerning marriage and sexuality are equally apparent in the fourth century in the writings of St Jerome. His works dominate many modern studies of celibacy in the patristic period, not least that of H.C. Lea, who suggested that Jerome did more than anyone to establish celibacy as the only acceptable form of life

---

[71] The most obvious example of this intellectual cross-current is Augustine, who converted from Manichaeism in 387. Despite his subsequent denunciations of the heresy, some scholars still argue that his earlier experience continued to exert a profound influence over his later work. See, for example, A. Adam, 'Das Fortwirken des Manichäismus bei Augustin', *Zeitschrift fur Kirchengeschichte*, 69 (1958): 1–25; F. Beatrice, 'Continenza e matrimonio nel Christianesimo primitivo', in R. Cantalamassa (ed.), *Etica sessuale e Matrimonio nel Cristainesimo delle Origimi* (Milan, 1976), pp. 43–7.

[72] Arnobius, *Contra Nationes* 3.9; Gryson, *Les Origines*, p. 51; Augustine, *City of God* 14:17–18. Modern writers have emphasised this negative view of marriage that was common in this period: Muriel Porter, *Sex, Marriage and the Church. Patterns of Change* (Victoria, Aus., 1996), pp. 17–22; Brown, *Body and Society*, pp. 242–54.

[73] B. Lohkamp, 'Cultic Purity and the Law of Celibacy', *Review for Religious*, 30 (1971): 119–217; J.E. Lynch, 'Marriage and Celibacy of the Clergy: The Discipline of the Western Church: An Historico-Canonical Synopsis', *The Jurist*, 32.1 and 2 (1972): 14–38 and 189–212; Frazee, 'Origins', 149–67; M. Douglas, *Purity and Danger. An Analysis of Concept of Pollution and Taboo* (Routledge, 2002).

[74] Brown, *Body and Society*, p. 254.

for those who entered into the ministry.[75] Jerome's polemic against Jovinian, Vigilantius, and Helvidius on a variety of subjects including marriage and clerical celibacy rearticulated, albeit in a more vigorous form, his more pastoral epistolary encouragements to virginity and chastity addressed to his female correspondents. His views on clerical celibacy were closely associated with the high esteem in which he held virginity and chastity for all Christians; those who lived as virgins on earth, he proposed, would gain the promise of a 'head start' in paradise.[76] From his work it is possible to glean not only a picture of Christian asceticism and cult of the virginity of the age, but also a (rather more fragmentary) picture of the attitudes of those who sought to establish virginity and marriage on an equal footing. Insights into the views of those who took up the defence of marriage in the face of such outpourings come almost entirely from the vigorous denunciations that Jerome wrote of such views. In 393 he composed a powerful and vitriolic response to a pamphlet written by a monk, Jovinian, who had argued for the equality of virginity and marriage as Christian callings. Jovinian had criticised strongly those clergy who boasted of the dignity that celibacy gave them, as well as the proponents of celibacy who, he alleged, had twisted Scripture in order to root their erroneous views in authoritative text. Married clergy were equally deserving of respect as their celibate colleagues, he argued, and all who remained faithful to their baptismal vows would find equal reward in heaven. Scripture was, after all, replete with examples of holy men and women who had fulfilled their calling in wedlock, including Abraham, Sarah, and Simeon, several disciples were married, and Christ had honoured marriage at the feast in Cana.[77] Jerome's reply has been described as 'one of the most blistering denunciations in all of patristic literature'.[78] Rebutting Jovinian, Jerome argued for a scriptural mandate for celibacy, found in the example of Old Testament figures such as Elijah, and the apostles and disciples of the New Testament who, he claimed, were themselves celibate. It would be better for the faithful Christian to refrain from intercourse as an occasion of sin that threatened salvation, Jerome believed, but for those who were married, the primary function of their union was the birth of those who

---

[75] H.C. Lea, *History of Sacerdotal Celibacy in the Christian Church* (third edition, 2 vols, London, 1907), vol. I, p. 13: 'No Doctor of the Church did more than St Jerome to impose the rule of celibacy on its members, yet even he admits that at the beginning there was no absolute injunction to that effect'.

[76] Jerome, *Adversus Jovinianum* 1.36 in PL 23.

[77] Jerome, *Adv. Jov.* 1.3.

[78] James A. Brundage, *Law, Sex and Christian Society in Medieval Europe* (Chicago and London, 1987), p. 85. The pamphlet was not well received; Jerome's friend Pammachius withdrew it from circulation. Jerome, *Epist.* 48 (CSEL 54.347); Brown, *Body and Society*, p. 377.

might lead a virginal life. Not even the suffering of martyrdom could cleanse the soul of a Christian woman from the stain of marriage.[79] The parable of the soil that yielded three different yields, one hundred fold, sixty fold and thirty fold, was interpreted by Jerome as a figure of the reward awaiting three groups of Christians, consecrated virgins, chaste widows, and finally pious spouses.[80]

This conviction that virginity was a higher way of life was to shape Jerome's attitudes to clerical marriage. In his *Commentary on the Epistle to Titus* he used the example of the purity that was demanded of the priests of the Old Law to argue that such obligations were all the more incumbent upon the priests of the New Law, whose daily intercession bound them to a life of abstinence. Laymen might benefit from temporary continence, but those who served at the altar were expected to make a perpetual commitment, in order that they might be protected from distractions of the eye and temptations of the mind, and lead the life of purity that was demanded of those who administered the sacraments.[81] Marriage was a diversion, particularly for a priest who was obliged to lead a life of prayer. A married man, Jerome suggested, might be ordained a priest if he professed continence, but any priest who fathered children after ordination was guilty of adultery. 'Either', he challenged Jovinian, 'you allow priests to exercise their nuptial activity so that there is no difference between virgins and married people, or if priests are not allowed to touch their wives, they are holy precisely because they imitate virginal purity.' The exalted position of virginity over marriage was confirmed by, but also required, married clergy living in continence.[82] The fact that there were married men serving as priests in the church in the first place was not evidence of any divine mandate, but simply a result of the exigencies of an age in which there was a shortage of men called to serve; the holiness of the priest was

---

[79] Despite the weight lent to scriptural precedent, Jerome also made use of idea more commonly linked with Stoicism. See, for example, *Adv. Jov.* 1.49; *Adv. Jov.* 1.3, 1.13, 1.16, 1.26, 1.28 [PL 23.229–30, 246, 247, 249]; Jerome, Epist. 22.19 [PL 22.406]; 'I praise marriage and wedlock but I do so because they produce virgins for me, I gather roses from thorns, gold from earth, and pearl from the shell': Ep. 22 to Eustochium in St. Jerome: *Letters and Select Works*, W.H. Fremantle (trans.), *Select Library of Nicene and Post-Nicene Fathers*, ser. 2, vol. VI (Edinburgh, 1892); P. Delehaye, 'Le Dossier Antimatrimonial de l'Adversus Jovinianum et son influence sur quelques ecrits latins du XII siecle', *Medieval Studies* 13 (1951): 65–86.

[80] Jerome, Ep. 48.2; 123.9.

[81] Jerome, *Comm. In Tit.* [PL 26:603b–4a]; *Adv. Jov.* 1.14, perhaps influenced by Pope Siricius' exposition of the rationale behind clerical continence. For further discussion, see D.G. Hunter, 'Rereading the Jovinianist Controversy: Asceticism and Clerical Authority in Late Ancient Christianity', in *Journal of Medieval and Early Modern Studies* 33.3 (2003): 453–70, especially 465.

[82] Jerome, *Adv. Jov.* 1.34.

predicated upon his lifelong virginity.[83] Jerome was similarly strident in his denunciation of the views of Vigilantius, and his rejection of Vigilantius' views on faith and practice in the Gallic church has been likened to an 'unpleasant fly-sheet' in its tone and content.[84] Jerome mocked Vigilantius for his apparent assertion that no men should be ordained unless they were married and had children, derided his refusal to credit clerics with chastity, and suggested that he revealed the manner of his own living 'by engaging in wicked speculation about others'. Vigilantius, he claimed, and those bishops who supported him, would refuse to ordain a man unless he brought with him a pregnant wife or wailing infants.[85] The apparent enthusiasm of Vigilantius for clerical marriage no doubt contributed to his acquisition of the dubious epithet 'Protestant of his age', and Jerome and Vigilantius both certainly had a presence in the early modern debate over clerical celibacy.[86] But the polemical controversy between the two was very much rooted in the ideas and tensions of their age; the evident presence of married clergy (and indeed married clergy who did not abstain from conjugal relations) in the fourth century church, and the growing tensions in the Gallic church between the critics and proponents of asceticism which were increasingly difficult to resolve.[87]

One of the most striking attempts to reconcile the lofty demands of Christian asceticism, religious calling, and human experience, is apparent in the personal struggle of Augustine of Hippo and his writings on human sexuality, marriage, and religious faith. Of all the writers of the age who tackled the issue of continence, Augustine provided his reader with perhaps the most detailed insight into his own life. As bishop of Hippo, he participated in the Council of Carthage at which the discipline of celibacy was imposed upon the clergy, on the basis of apostolic precedent, but Augustine was a man who had been promised in marriage himself, who had maintained a concubine, and fathered a son, in a series of relationships which underlay his famous plea 'da mihi castitatem et continentiam, sed noli modo'.[88] An adherent of Manichaeism in his youth, Augustine was

---

[83] Jerome, *Adv. Jov.* 1.34.

[84] J.N.D. Kelly, *Jerome, His Life, Writings and Controversies* (New York: Harper and Row, 1975), p. 289; the full text of the *Contra Vigilantium* is in PL 23:353–68.

[85] Contra Vig. 2 [PL 23:355, 356, 368].

[86] E. Gibbon, *The History of the Decline and Fall of the Roman Empire*, J.B. Bury (ed.) (8 vols, London, Methuen 1909), vol. 3 p. 489. The use of the controversy between Jerome and Vigilantius during the Reformation is discussion on p. 168 below.

[87] C. Stancliffe, *St Martin and his Hagiogapher: History and Miracle in Sulpitius Severus* (Oxford, 1983), chapter 21.

[88] Augustine, *Confessions* 8.7.17 [Library of Christian Classics volume 7, A.C. Outler (ed.)]. Modern biographies of Augustine include P. Brown, *Augustine of Hippo* (Berkeley, 1967); J. O'Donnell, *Augustine: A new biography* (New York, 2005); G. Matthews, *Augustine*

reconciled with orthodoxy while studying in Milan, under the influence of his mother, Monica, and St Ambrose, and following a damascene moment in the summer of 386. He committed his life to the church, its service as a priest, and to a celibate life, and wrote extensively on marriage and virginity.[89] His admiration for both virginity and continence is apparent; writing on the 'good' of marriage against the heretic Jovinian, Augustine rejected the proposal that marriage and virginity were of equal merit, arguing for the superiority of the latter. Marriage had admittedly been ordained by God and its value reinforced by Christ, and the total rejection of marriage by some heretical groups was to be condemned, but Augustine argued that even if marriage were indeed 'good', virginity was better still.[90] It was in virginity, or in the renunciation of physical passions, that victory over sin might be attained, although it was nigh impossible to remove the impulse and therefore the danger or occasion of sin. Sexual desire, he postulated, was the result of original sin, the consequence of the expulsion of Adam and Eve from Eden which continued to be passed from generation to generation by the procreative act.[91] From this perspective, Augustine's advocacy of clerical celibacy or continence appears all the more considered. The tendency to see all sexual activity as accompanied by ritual pollution placed a clear obligation upon all Christians, but particularly the clergy, to avoid such physical causes of contamination.[92]

(Oxford, 2005); for a modern edition of the Life of St Augustine, see H.T. Weiskotten, *The Life of Saint Augustine: A Translation of the Sancti Augustini Vita by Possidius, Bishop of Calama* (Merchantville, NJ, 2008); D.S. Bailey, *Sexual Relations in Christian Thought* (New York, 1959) discusses the impact of Augustine.

[89] See particularly *De Continentia, De Bono Coniugali, De Sancta Virginitate, De Bono Viduitatis, De Coniugiis Adulterinis, De Nuptiis et Concupiscientia*.

[90] Since the union of man and woman was the result of lust, it had its origins in sin even within marriage: Augustine, *De Nuptiis at Concupiscientia* 1.4. Porter emphasises the central role of procreation in marriage, which was offered to those who could not contain, and proposes a clear link between Augustine's views and those expressed in the modern day Roman Catholic church, particularly in *Humanae Vitae* (1968). William Phipps complains that Augustine, even more than Jerome, was responsible for 'molding the prevailing sin-sex syndrome' that has affected billions of churchgoers: Phipps, *Clerical celibacy*, p. 107; M. Muller, *Die Lehre des hl. Augustinus von der Paradiesesehe und ihre Auswirkung in der Sexualethik des 12. und 13. Jahrhunderts bis Thomas von Aquin* (Regensburg, 1954). Augustine did, however, defend the merits of marriage against those who were more forceful in their condemnations, including Manichaeans and Priscillianists: Augustine, *De Haeresibus* 87; D. Callam, 'Clerical Continence in the Fourth Century: Three Papal Decretals', *Theological Studies*, 41 (1980): 3–50.

[91] Augustine, *De Civitate Dei* 14.9; *De Nuptiis et Concupiscentia* 1.23.15; for the suggestion that infants are subject to original sin by the 'contagion' of procreation rather than their own mind, see *Opus imperfectum contra Iulianum* 4.98, *De Peccatorium Meritis* c.57; *City of God* 14.17.19.

[92] Brundage, *Law, Sex and Christian Society*, p. 82.

That said, Augustine was all too aware of the very practical problems confronted by the church in North Africa. The higher orders were not closed to married men, but rather it was to be expected that should a married man be ordained as a priest, he would be the recipient of the necessary divine grace that would enable him to live in continence.[93]

The writings of Ambrose, Jerome, Augustine and their contemporaries were to exert a profound influence on subsequent debates over clerical celibacy and marriage. Patristic testimony, argued to provide clear insights into the faith and the tradition of the early church, has proved particularly valuable to those theologians and controversialists seeking to establish the origins of the obligation to clerical celibacy in the primitive church. Thus, Cardinal Stickler argues that the evidence from patristic writings points not to clerical celibacy as an innovation, but rather as an unbroken tradition, handed down orally long before it was fixed in the written laws of the church.[94] Others have argued that the writings of the Fathers are evidence of the fourth century 'onslaught' of the ideal of asceticism, undermining the married ministry established in the New Testament, in which men proved their ability to govern the church by the manner in which they ran their household. The view of Jerome, Ambrose and Augustine in particular have drowned out other voices to the extent that celibacy appears to be at the core of Christianity. Indeed, their opponents argue, the only evidence of opposition to the cult of virginity that they established comes from their own condemnations of the heresies of Vigilantius, Helvidius and Jovinian, with the result that celibacy carried the day.[95] Similarly divergent interpretations of the patristic testimony are to be found in the debates over clerical celibacy at other critical periods in the history of the church, particularly in the eleventh and twelfth centuries and in the controversies of the Reformation.[96] The importance that subsequent generations attached to the writings of the Fathers is recognised in Christian Cochini's discussions of the 'catalogues' of patristic texts that were produced to facilitate the composition of more accurate histories of clerical celibacy. As early as the Council of Trent, he demonstrates, theologians were commissioned to compile collections of patristic material in order to examine and rebut Protestant objections to the enforcement of clerical celibacy. The first systematic catalogue of such materials was published in 1631, and these early collections and commentaries on the patristic period were greatly

---

[93] Augustine, *De Conjugiis Adulterinis* 2.20.22.

[94] See, for example, Stickler, *Case for Clerical Celibacy*, p. 37–40.

[95] See, for example, Porter, *Sex, Marriage and the Church*, p. 26; Phipps, *Celibacy*, pp. 88 and 109, where he is particularly critical of Abbott, *History of Celibacy*, p. 17; Bullough 'Introduction', in Bullough and Brundage (eds) *Sexual Practices*, p. 8.

[96] See chapter 3 and chapter 5 below.

enriched and expanded in the eighteenth and nineteenth centuries.[97] The foundations upon which the historical debate over the celibacy of the clergy was constructed are tantalisingly narrow, but from these origins a vast literature has been spawned.

The words of the Fathers, while regarded by many subsequent commentators as intrinsically valuable in the evolution of the obligation to priestly continence, did not of themselves establish the law of the church. Their writings must therefore be considered alongside the early conciliar legislative framework, and the decrees of the popes, which sought to impose sexual discipline upon the clergy. A handful of conciliar decrees and papal instructions have provided the focus for those investigating the origins and evolution of compulsory clerical celibacy across the centuries; like the writings of the Fathers, these texts have assumed a significance even in the minds of those who would not otherwise have accorded authority to such sources, precisely because they have become part of the lexicon of debate.[98] Controversy over the immediate (and indeed longterm) effectiveness of these attempts to regulate the conduct of the clergy has a narrative as lengthy as the history of the discipline itself, but whether or not the enforcement of sacerdotal celibacy was practicable, it is evident that calls for such a discipline were becoming more insistent by the end of the fourth century. The asceticism counselled by figures such as Ambrose and Augustine, coupled with the changing demography of church leaders – it was the appointment of a wealthy landowner as bishop of Vercelli in 396 that occasioned Ambrose's laudatory comments on the value of virginity – pushed the issue to the foreground.[99] It is also possible to see in this period the increased use of what might be termed a 'sacrificial' language in relation to the eucharist, and a sacerdotal terminology in relation to the clergy, which itself contributed to a growing insistence that

---

[97] Cochini, *Apostolic Origins*, p. 137; referring to Georg Calixtus, *De Conjugio Clericorum* (1631); F.A. Zaccaria, *Storia Polemica del celibato sacro da contraporsi ad alcune detestabili opera uscite a questi tempi* (Rome, 1774); A. Roskovany, *Coelibatus et Breviarum: duo gravissima clericorum official e monumentis omnium seculorum demonstrate* (vols 1–4 Pestini, 1861; vols 5–8 Nitrae 1877; vols 9–10 Nitrae 1881); *Supplementa ad collections monumentorum et literaturae* (vols 3–4 Nitrae, 1888); Johann Anton Theiner and Augustine Theiner, *Die Einfuhrung der erzwungenen Ehelosigkeit bei den christlichen Geistlichen und ihre Folgen. Ein Beitrag zur Kirchengeschichte* (3 vols Altenburg, 1828); Bickel, 'Der Zolibat'.

[98] Despite the evangelical insistence upon the principle of sola scriptura for example, the defenders of clerical marriage in the era of the Reformation peppered their works with reference to the Fathers, Councils, and decrees of the popes. For a fuller discussion of this, see chapter 5 below; Parish, *Clerical Marriage*, chapter 3; S. Greenslade, 'The authority of the Tradition of the Early Church in Early Anglican Thought', *Oecumenica* (1971–2): 9–33.

[99] D. Callam, 'Clerical Continence in the Fourth Century: Three Papal Decretals', *Theological Studies*, 41 (1980): 3–50.

the purity expected of the priests of the Old Testament be demanded of the priests that served at the altars of the Christian church.[100]

Events at the Council of Elvira (c.305) generally provide the starting point for studies of the institutional origins of clerical celibacy. Debate over the apostolic origins of priestly continence and celibacy continues, but at Elvira it is possible to see the first concerted, and indeed controversial, attempt by a council of the church to impose sexual discipline on its clergy.[101] The relative paucity of prior evidence obfuscates the issue of innovation at the Council, and while it is clear the bishops who met at Elvira reached a decision on the question of married clergy, it is less obvious whether this was a break with tradition, or a simple consolidation of existing practice. The fact that some attempt was made to regulate clerical marriage certainly suggests that there was still a substantial number of married priests in the church, but whether these men made up the minority or majority of clergy in higher orders is less certain.[102] The significance of the council for the development of clerical celibacy is also contested, despite its prominent position in the history of the discipline. Funk's proposal that Elvira marked a watershed in the history of clerical celibacy has been downplayed more recently by John Lynch, who argues that the critical canon was an 'isolated event' rather than the true starting point for subsequent legislation, and by Samuel Laeuchli, who sees the decrees of the council as the outworking of a 'patristic crisis of sexuality' which had its origins in the decades and centuries prior to the council.[103]

The gathering of bishops at Elvira, in southern Spain, was the first formal ecclesiastical council held in Spain, and the earliest surviving to hand down disciplinary canons. There were nineteen bishops in attendance, twenty four priests, and a number of deacons and laypersons. The council promulgated 81 decrees, which covered a vast array of topics relating to liturgy, sacrament, and clerical discipline. It met at the instigation of bishop Ossius of Cordoba, but was presided over by the most senior bishop in attendance, Felix of Accitum, and the content of its decrees no doubt reflected the context in which the council was convened,

---

[100] Lynch, 'Marriage and Celibacy', 18–19; R. Aubert (ed.), *Sacralisation and Secularisation* (Concilium 47, New York 1969).

[101] For a summary of recent contributions to the 'apostolic origins' debate, see above, n. 1.

[102] Gryson, for example, suggests that the married men were in the majority: Gryson, *Les Origines*, p. 42.

[103] Funk, 'Colibat und Priesterehe im Christlichen Altertum', *Kirchen Geschichtliche Abhandlungen und Untersuchungen*, 1 (1897): 121–2; Cochini, *Apostolic Origins*, p. 160; Lynch, 'Marriage and Celibacy', 23; S. Laeuchli, *Power and Sexuality. The Emergence of Canon Law at the Synod of Elvira* (Philadelphia, 1972), p. 106, with reference to E.R. Dodds, *Pagan and Christian in an Age of Anxiety* (Cambridge, 1965).

and the problems confronted by the Iberian church in the early fourth century.[104] For historians of clerical celibacy, the most significant canon is the thirty-third, although it is worth nothing that several others relate to the conduct of the clergy, and particularly their sexual conduct, and nearly half the canons deal with sexual relations more generally. The canons are not ordered by subject, and the lack of clear structure to the topical sequence of the decrees may imply that rather than proceeding according to a pre-prepared agenda, each member of the assembly was able to initiate a discussion.[105] Canon 33 instructed that the clergy were not to have intercourse with their wives: 'Placuit in totum prohibere episcopis, presbyteris et diaconibus vel omnibus clericis positis in ministerio abstinere se a coniugibus suis et non generare filios. Quicumque vero fecerit, ad honore clericatus exterminetur'.[106] The canon should, Cochini argues convincingly, be read as an attempt to regulate the conduct only of those in orders down to the subdiaconate, and be understood as referring not to single men, but to those married men who had been ordained. The canon makes no attempt to ground its demands in other legislation, but Cochini rejects any notion that the bishops imagined that they were innovating in their decision. Given the potential magnitude of the decree, he suggests, the bishops surely believed that they were acting in accordance with current praxis rather than making new demands.

The interpretation of the canon is complicated by the double negative contained in its formulation, which Cochini ascribes to an error in transcription, and Heid suggests causes little real difficulty once

---

[104] A.W. Dale, *The Synod of Elvira and Christian Life in the Fourth Century* (London, 1882); L. Duchesne, 'Le concile d'Elvira et les flamines chrétiennes, *Mélanges Renier* (Paris, 1887), pp. 159–74; Cochini, *Apostolic Origins*, p. 158; Laeuchli, *Elvira*, p. 3; C.J. Hefele and H. Leclerq (eds), *Histoire des Conciles d'apres les documents originaux* (vol. 1, Paris, 1907). The precise date of the council is not known: Hefele-Leclerq suggest 305, Laeuchli suggests 309, and Duchesne proposed a date between 300 and 303. See also E. Griffe, 'Le Concile d'Elvire et les origins de celibate ecclesiastique', *Bulletin de Litterature Ecclesiastique*, 77 (1976) 123–7. Several canons were added later to the records of the council, and there are suggestions that canon 33, which dealt with clerical celibacy, might be one of these: M. Migne, 'Concile ou collection d'Elvire', *Revue d'Histoire Ecclesiastique*, 70 (1975): 361–87. For a full discussion of the issue, see Heid, *Celibacy*, pp. 109–10.

[105] Canon 27, for example, enjoins that no cleric is to live with a woman who is not of his kin. Laeuchli suggests that forty-five per cent of the canons address sexual issues, but that this reflected a spontaneous drift in discussions from the major issues of apostasy to more specific matters to do with discipline. Married clergy were the subject of canons 30, 33, 65 and 81.

[106] 'it has seemed absolutely good to forbid the bishops, the priests and the deacons i.e. all clerics in the service of the ministry to have intercourse with their wives and procreate children; should anyone do so, let him be excluded from the honour of the clergy'. Translation from Cochini, *Apostolic Origins*, p. 159; see also his discussion of the original text and of the commentary provided by E. Griffe, 'A propos du canon 33 du concile d'Elvire', *Bulletin de Litterature Ecclesiastique*, 74 (1973): 142–5.

contextualised.[107] However, Heid also argues forcefully, on the basis of the formulation of the canon, that the council intended that the continence of married clergy be permanent, rather than required simply for the time of service at the altar; 'ministerium' referred to the office and not to the daily sacred ministry. The term 'ministerium' might also be taken to refer to the particular functions of priests and those in higher orders, which were not fulfilled by, for example, lectors. This would certainly tie the continence of the clergy to their sacramental function, and the belief that those who performed such a significant role in the church should maintain a kind of ritual purity by abstaining from their wives.[108] It seems clear that the Fathers at Elvira did not demand celibacy of Spanish clerics, but the precise meaning of the canon is still debated. However, the council was secure enough in its intent to impose a severe penalty for disobedience which was articulated more precisely than the punishment to be meted out to, for example, an unmarried priest who cohabited with a woman who was not of his kin (c.27).[109] Certainly, the canon does not correspond exactly with clerical celibacy as it is understood in the modern church, but neither is this first written law the earliest sign that celibacy, or continence, was expected of those in higher orders.[110] The imperative was not so much the imposition of celibacy, but the prohibition of the sexual act to those in orders; the canon demanded continence from the married clergy of Spain, and established that ordination required that the marital relationship be conducted without sexual intercourse. As the earliest apparent reference to a requirement for perfect continence from those clergy who were already married, however, the 33rd canon of the Council of Elvira was to acquire a central position in debates over the origins of clerical celibacy in the centuries that followed, as testimony to the existence of a married clergy in western Europe at the start of the fourth century, and to the probable earlier origins of attempts to regulate clerical marriages that made the decisions at Elvira appear as consolidation rather than innovation.

Despite its reputation in subsequent histories, the Council of Elvira was a local synod, and its decrees did not command the obedience of churches outside its area of jurisdiction. The broader influence of the 33rd canon lies in part in the efforts of bishop Ossius, whose likely participation at the council of Arles and at the first ecumenical council

---

[107] Cochini, *Apostolic Origins*, p. 160; Heid, *Celibacy*, p. 111; for a fuller discussion see Griffe, 'Concile d'Elvire, 124–6.

[108] Heid, *Celibacy*, p. 112; Audet, *Mariage*, p. 20; Gryson, *Les Origines*, p. 40; and particularly B. Verkamp, 'Cultic Purity and the Law of Celibacy', *Review for Religious*, 30 (1971): 199.

[109] Laeuchli, *Elvira*, p. 95.

[110] Cochini, *Apostolic Origins*, p. 160.

at Nicaea in 325 might explain some of the similarities in the discussions and resultant canons.[111] However, it is also possible to identify similar preoccupations in the decrees of other local and regional councils. The first Council of Arles, convened in 314, had as its primary function a solution to the Donatist controversy, but its 29th canon sought to regulate the conduct of married priests, and with some accounts claiming that there were 600 bishops in attendance, the council was more than simply a local assembly.[112] The canon made similar demands of the clergy to those required at Elvira: 'moreover [concerned with] what is worthy, pure, and honest, we exhort our brothers [in the episcopate] to make sure that priests and deacons have no relations with their wives, since they are serving the ministry every day. Whosoever will act against this decision will be deposed from the honour of the clergy'. However, the records of the council have been transmitted in several different sources and formats, and the accuracy of each account, and indeed the list of the canons of the council, is disputed. The 'Letter to Sylvester' details only nine canons, the 'Canons to Sylvester' some twenty-two.[113] Cochini, in seeking to resolve some of these ambiguities, notes that although the 29th canon reads as an exhortation, it carried with it a punitive weight. Its compass echoed that of the decree at Elvira, but its motives were more clearly articulated, in explaining that for those priests whose function is fulfilled on a daily basis, abstaining from intercourse is both worthy and pure. The general tenor is such, however, that it seems plausible again that the bishops believed that they were defending a principle rather than creating a new law. The similarity with the Council of Elvira, and the references to the Donatists in the other 'disputed' canons all point to an early fourth century context and preoccupations.[114]

A similarly complex narrative exists for the Council of Ancyra, a gathering of bishops from Asia Minor and Syria in the same year. The

---

[111] V. de Clerq, *Ossius of Cordova* (Washington, 1954), pp. 277–8; Hefele-Leclerq, *Conciles*, I.1.621, write of the resemblances between the legislation at Elvira and Nicaea 'cette coincidence porterait a faire croire que c'est un des Peres d'Elvire, Osius, qui proposa au concile de Nicee le loi sur le celibat'.

[112] Translation from Cochini, *Apostolic Origins*, p. 161; the council is discussed by Eusebius, *Church History*, 10.5.21–24, C. Munier, *Concilia Galliae a.314–a.506* (Turnhout: Brepols, 1963), pp. 14–22; P. Coustant, *Epistolae Romanorum pontificum, et quae ad eos scriptae sunt, a S. Clemente I. usque ad Innocentium III. . . .*, vol. 1 (Brunsbergae, 1721), De Clercq, *Ossius of Cordova*; J.M. O'Donnell, *The Canons of the First Council of Arles, 314 AD* (Washington, 1961).

[113] C. Munier, *Concilia Galliae*, pp. 4–6, pp. 9–13. Lea argues that the celibacy canon is to be found in only one of the manuscript sources, repeating Mansi's suggestion that it belongs to a later synod. Mansi 2.474; cf. Hefele-Leclerq, *Conciles*, I.i.295.

[114] Cochini, *Apostolic Origins*, p. 162.

canons were transmitted in at least six versions to a Greek and Latin audience, but there is less dispute over their content, and the variant sources are in agreement that the tenth addressed the issue of clerical continence and marriage.[115] However, its content diverges substantially from the early conciliar decisions on the subject in the West. The bishops agreed that those deacons who announced at the time of their ordination that they were unable to live a celibate life and who later married would be permitted to remain in orders, but those who did not make such a declaration would be deprived of their ecclesiastical function if they later married. The interpretation of the canon in subsequent generations was less than straightforward. By the sixth century, one edition of the canons appeared to suggest that the bishop had no such right to dispense, and later Byzantine councils make no reference to the possibility that a deacon might petition for a later marriage at the time of his ordination.[116] It seems unlikely that the Council of Ancyra marked a decisive and considered deviation from the discipline of Latin Christendom, but its tenth canon was to provide valuable ammunition for those in later generations who sought to establish a precedent for the legality of marriage after ordination when the issue became critical in the life of the church.[117]

The first ecumenical council of the church, held at Nicaea in 325, was, despite its association with the condemnation of Arius, dominated by disciplinary decrees intended to regulate the conduct of the clergy. Accorded ecumenical status, the decrees of the council were as influential in the West as in the East, and featured prominently in canonical collections.[118] The majority of the twenty decrees impacted upon clerical life and discipline, and the third decree specifically tackled the question of 'women who live with clerics'. The Fathers agreed that 'the great Council has stringently forbidden any bishop, priest, deacon, or any of the clergy, to have a

---

[115] R.B. Rackam, 'The Texts of the Canons of Ancyra', in *Studia Biblica et Ecclesiastica* (Oxford, 1891); Cochini, *Apostolic Origins*, pp. 168ff.

[116] Cochini, *Apostolic Origins*, pp. 171–2 notes that when the canons of Ancyra were confirmed by the Fathers at Trullo, they did not repeat this clause allowing subsequent marriage. Likewise, Roman Cholij suggests that if the concession were indeed authentic, it fell into disuse shortly after the council: Cholij, *Clerical Celibacy*, pp. 12–13.

[117] See for example the eleventh century *Tractatus pro clericorum conniubio* and the protests of a group of Normandy clergy against the imposition of clerical celibacy, and in the sixteenth century Peter Martyr's use of the council in his *Defensio Doctrinae Veteris et Apostolicae de Sacrosanto Eucharistiae Sacramento* (Zurich, 1559), sig.u2r, G5v. The proceedings and records of the council are discussed in more detail in chapter 2, pp. 92–4.

[118] Cochini, *Apostolic Origins*, pp. 186ff gives numerous examples of later councils and papal letters that echoed the words of the decree at Nicaea, including councils at Hippo 393, Toledo 400, Arles 442–506, the *Directa* of Pope Siricius to Himerius, and Pope Leo's Letter to Rusticus of Narbonne: L.D. Davis, *The First Seven Ecumenical Councils (325–787)*, (Liturgical Press, 1983); N.P. Tanner, *The Councils of the Church: A Short History* (New York, 2001).

woman living with him, except a mother, sister, aunt, or some such person who is beyond all suspicion', although the decree is tantalisingly imprecise about who these women might be.[119] If the decree referred to the wives of the clergy, it appeared to assume that priests continued to live with their wives, but made no reference to whether they lived in continence, or indeed whether such marriages had been entered into before or after ordination.[120] The decree was certainly cited in support of compulsory clerical celibacy in subsequent generations. Some five hundred years after the council, Ratramnus used the Nicene decree to defend clerical celibacy in the western church, arguing that the reference to '*virgins subintroductae*' in its third canon was a prohibition of marriage to the clergy.[121] In 1022, at the Synod of Pavia, the pope's opening address referred to the 'law of Nicaea' to justify the exclusion of all women from the homes of priests and the removal of married clergy from their benefices.[122] In contrast, Bishop Otto of Constance was to find in 1075 that his attempt to enforce the celibacy legislation promulgated at the Lenten Synod left him open to the accusation that the pope had departed from the sentiments expressed at Nicaea, which was in this instance being cited in defence of those priests who were married.[123] The precise mind of the bishops at Nicaea is all the more difficult to fathom as a consequence of the development of the legend of Paphnutius, a bishop alleged to have attended the council, who intervened at the eleventh hour to prevent the passage of legislation that would have denounced clerical marriage on the basis that it were better for those who could not live in chastity to marry.[124] Paphnutius, although in all likelihood a fictional character, was to feature prominently in later debates over clerical celibacy, and although he became famous for his defence of marriage, the story served to lend weight to the suggestion that the council had adopted a negative stance with regard to the wives of the clergy.

It was not the ecumenical council of Nicaea, but the smaller assembly of bishops in Carthage in 390 that was to provide the *locus classicus* for later writers seeking to locate obligatory clerical celibacy in the decrees of

---

[119] Hefele-Leclerq, *Conciles*, I.1.503–28; J. Alberigo, J. Dossetti, P. Joannou, C. Leonardi (eds) *Conciliorum Oecumenicorum Decreta* (Freiburg im Breisgau: Herder, 1962), p. 6 (the Latin text does not mention deacons).

[120] Cochini, *Apostolic Origins*, p. 186.

[121] Ratramnus, *Contra Graecorum Opposita* c.6 [PL 121.324–32].

[122] L. Weiland (ed.), *MGH Legum Section IV, Constitutiones et acta publica imperatorum et regum* (Hanover, 1893), vol. 1 no. 34, pp. 70–88.

[123] H.E.J. Cowdrey (ed.), *The Epistolae Vagantes of Pope Gregory VII* (Oxford, 1972), No. 9.

[124] For a full discussion of the story and its development, see chapter 2, pp. 69–70.

the early church. Some 390 bishops were in attendance, but the overall purposes of the council have been described as 'modest'.[125] However, its decisions were incorporated into the *Codex Canonum Ecclesiae Africanae* of 419, and thereafter much more widely disseminated through the work of Denys the Minor.[126] The Carthage canon paid lip-service to early conciliar attempts to impose the rule of continence and chastity, but recommended that the application of the rule to bishops, priests and deacons be emphasised, and that these higher clergy be exhorted to obedience. The clergy of the Christian church were compared to the Levitical priesthood, and expected to observe perfect continence because of their sacramental function. All were obliged to abstain from conjugal intercourse with their wives, in keeping with 'what the apostles taught and what antiquity observed'.[127] Clerical continence was predicated upon the liturgical and sacramental function of the priest, and was presented as a long-standing obligation. The decision at Carthage was to provide the basis for arguments in favour of clerical celibacy (not only clerical continence) in the era of the Gregorian reform, and in the aftermath of Protestant advocacy of clerical marriage in the sixteenth century.[128] For those seeking evidence of the apostolic origins of clerical celibacy, a fourth century council which affirmed that its deliberations had been guided by teachings of the first followers of Christ was a compelling source. For those who defended clerical marriage, the decree at Carthage, like those of other fourth century assemblies of the church, testified to the continued presence of married men in Christian ministry.

Neither the Council of Nicaea nor the Council of Carthage had imposed celibacy upon the clergy as a whole. The most significant step towards the formalisation of the discipline of clerical continence in the fourth century was taken not in conciliar assembly, but at the instigation

---

[125] Cochini, *Apostolic Origins*, p. 3; Munier, *Concilia Africae*, p. 149; Hefele-Leclerq, *Conciles*, II.1.76–8.

[126] Cochini, *Apostolic Origins*, p. 4.

[127] Mansi, *Sacrum Conciliorum*, vol. 3, 692D–693A; F.L. Cross, 'History and Fiction in the African Canons', *Journal of Theological Studies*, 12 (1961): 227–47. A subsequent council in Carthage in 401 added the sanction that those who did not cease having relations with their wives were to be deprived of their ecclesiastical functions [canon 3; Mansi, *Sacrum Conciliorum*, vol. 3, 969A).

[128] Cochini, *Apostolic Origins*, p. 4, referring to MGH *Libelli de Lite Imperatorum et Pontificum Saeculius XI et XII*, II (Hanover, 1892) pp. 7ff, *Concilium Tridentium Diariorum, Actorum, Epistolarum, Tractatuum Nova Collectio*, Societas Goerresiana (ed.) (Freiburg im Breisgau 1965), vol. IX pt. 6, pp. 380–82 and 425–70, and 'Responsum a Pio IV datum consiliariis electorum et principum imperii, qui sacerdotum conjugia petebant', in L. Leplat, *Monumentorum ad Historiam Concilii Tridentini Amplissima Collectio* VI (Louvain, 1876) p. 336.

of Pope Siricius.[129] His views were articulated in a letter addressed to bishop Himerius of Tarragona, in response to a series of questions that the bishop had earlier sent to pope Damasus in the context of the Priscillianist controversy.[130] Clearly, the issue of married clergy was still of concern, although the only limitation placed on ordination was the refusal to admit re-married men to major orders; the pope stopped short of prohibiting the ordination of those who had entered into monogamous marriage. However, Siricius was strident in expressing his concern about the number of priests and deacons who appeared to have fathered children after their ordination, and in his condemnation of monks and nuns who were guilty of 'sacrilegious passion'. Rejecting the appeals of such men to the precedent provided by the temporary abstinence expected of the priests of the Old Testament, Siricius instructed that 'all priests and deacons are bound by the indissoluble law of these provisions, in such a way that from the day of our ordination we subject both our hearts and our bodies to sobriety and purity'. God had demanded of the priests of the Old Law 'be ye holy for I am Yahweh your God', and such an obligation was all the more incumbent upon the priests of the new law. The pope instructed that for any priest or deacon who failed to live in continence there was to be no mercy, and that all pardon should be refused 'for one must cut out with a knife wounds that resist all remedies'.[131] The pope made no reference to the decrees of earlier councils on the subject, but his letter was clearly occasioned by the anxiety of bishop Himerius over the apparent violation of agreed codes of conduct for the clergy. Siricius did, however, anchor his exhortations in biblical and apostolic precedent, suggesting that he did not regard his instruction as a new departure for the Roman or Spanish church.

The demands of the pope were repeated a year later. Following a council held in Rome in 386, letters were sent out to the bishops who were unable to attend, and to those of other provinces, detailing its determinations. The opening phrases made clear that the decisions of the council were not innovations, but an attempt to ensure that the church remained faithful to the practice of the apostolic church, 'the question is not one of ordering new precept, but ... to have people observe those

---

[129] Lynch, 'Marriage and Celibacy', 24.

[130] PL 13.1131b–1147a; P. Coustant, *Epistolae Romanorum Pontificum* (Paris, 1721), pp. 623–38.

[131] Siricius, *Ad Himerium* c.7 n. 11 [PL 13.1138a–39a, 1140–1]; The letter has been referred to as a 'milestone in the history of celibacy', Heid, *Celibacy*, p. 218. Translation from Lynch 'Marriage and Celibacy', 26, who notes that the fact that clergy were appealing on the ground of ignorance suggests that the legislation passed at Elvira had been forgotten. See also Cochini, *Apostolic Origins*, pp. 8ff.

that ... have been neglected'.[132] The ninth canon of the Roman council called upon the bishops to act in order to put an end to the 'scandal' that afflicted the church and which had occasioned a good deal of criticism from outside its members. The source of the scandal was the conduct of the clergy, and the decree set forth the argument, based upon biblical and patristic sources, that the priests of the church, who were bound to serve God every day, were therefore required to lead a life of perpetual sexual abstinence in order to devote themselves to prayer. The pope demanded continence from all in higher orders 'as it is worthy, chaste and honest to do so' on the basis of Levitical law, and particularly the Pauline injunction contained in I. Cor 7:5. He rejected the argument that the 'husband of one wife' phrase in the Letter to Timothy was simply a bar to the ordination of digamists, arguing that Paul did not commend a man 'persisting in his desire to beget' but counselled a commitment to matters spiritual rather than unspiritual (Rom. 8:8–9).[133] Continence was an obligation, and a permanent obligation for those who were required to make themselves available for the service of the altar on a daily basis.[134]

The same demands were made in a second Roman synod, the decisions of which have been attributed variously to Siricius, his predecessor Damasus, and the later Pope Innocent I (401–17).[135] A papal decretal was composed as a response to a series of questions from bishops, this time from Gaul, and clerical continence was again high on the agenda. Concern was expressed that the higher clergy failed to heed the obligation to continence, and therefore violated not only the decrees of the church but also the divine ordinance in scripture.[136] In his decretal *Dominus Inter*, addressed to the Gallic bishops, the pope protested that 'many bishops in various churches have challenged the tradition of the fathers, out of human

---

[132] The decretal *Cum in Unum* is preserved only in the records of a fifth century African council which discussed it; Gryson, *Les Origines*, p. 139, Hefele-Leclerq *Conciles* II.68ff [PL 13.1156a] 'non quae nova praecepta aliqua imperent, sed quibus ea qaue per ignasiam desidiamque aliquorum neglecta sunt, observari cupiamus, quae tamen apostolic et partum constitutione sunt constituta sicut scriptum est *State et temete traditions nostra sive per verbum, sive per epistolam*' (2 Thess.2:14).

[133] PL 13.1160a–1161a.

[134] Siricius was not alone in this interpretation of the Pauline epistle; Cochini cited a similar exegesis in the writings of Epiphanius of Salamis: 'the man who goes on living with his wife and begetting children is not admitted [by the church] as deacon, priest, and subdeacon, even if he is married only once, but [only the one 'who being monogamous, observes continence or is a widower', *Panarion (Adversus Haereses* 79.4).

[135] PL 13.1181a–94c; Cochini, *Apostolic Origins*, p. 13 citing Coustant, *Epistolae*, pp. 685–700 and E.C. Babut, *La Plus Ancienne Decretale* (Paris 1904), pp. 69–87. See also Gryson, *Les Origines*, pp. 127ff, and Lynch 'Marriage and Celibacy'.

[136] Coustant, *Epistolae*, pp. 689–91; PL 13.1184a–85b, especially 1184b 'quos non solum non sed et scriptura divine compellit esse castissimos'.

presumption and to the detriment of their reputation', particularly in relation to the conduct of the clergy, and the requirement to continence.[137] Communicating the decisions taken at the Roman Synod of the same year, the pope wrote that the church considered two groups of candidates for ordination: those who had remained virgins after baptism as infants, and those baptised as adults who had married only once, and had remained chaste. The latter, as a condition of ordination, were to promise to live in continence, in order to tend to the pastoral needs of widows and virgins, to avoid the temptations of the flesh that might distract them from the service of God, and to preserve the purity that was necessary for the successors of the priests of the Old Law, who offered sacrifice daily. The dignity of the clergy required that they provide an example to the faithful, and, the pope asserted, 'not only we, but the sacred scriptures compel them to be perfectly chaste, and the Fathers commanded that they observe bodily continence'. This requirement to purity in the handling of the sacraments and the administration of baptism must be permanent, 'for they must be ready at all times'.[138] The tone and content of the letter certainly suggested a hardening of papal attitudes to clerical marriages and conduct, perhaps in light of the Jovinianist controvsery, and a more explicit enunciation of views that had previously been implied rather than stridently stated.[139] The attempts of Siricius to enforce continence upon the married clergy were echoed in the labours of his successors, and in subsequent councils, which suggests that if not novel, the requirement was at least unpopular or unheeded in some quarters.[140] *Dominus Inter* concluded with the demand

---

[137] The document is most commonly attributed to Pope Siricius, although some sources suggest that it was composed by Pope Damasus. For further discussion, see P. Pampaloni, 'Continenza e celibate del clero: Leggi e motive nelle fonti canonistiche dei sec IV et V', *Studia Patavina* 17 (1970): 18–19; Gryson, *Les Origines*, pp. 127–31; PL 13.1182–1188, quoting 1182a 'scimus fraters charissimi, multos episcopos per diversas ecclesias ad famam pessimam nominis sui humana praesumptione partum traditionem mutare properasse, atque per hanc causam in haeresis tenebras cecidisse ...'; see also D.G. Hunter, 'Reading the Jovinianist Controversy: Asceticism and Clerical Authority in Late Ancient Christianity', *Journal of Medieval and Early Modern Studies* 33.3 (2003): 453–70; Hunter, 'Clerical Celibacy and Veiling of Virgins: new Boundaries in Late Ancient Christianity', in W.E. Klingshirn and M. Vessey (eds), *The Limits of Ancient Christianity: Essays on Late Antique Thought and Culture in Honour of R.A. Markus* (Ann Arbor, 1999), pp. 139–52.

[138] Siricius, *Ad Gallos Episcopos*, Ep. 10.3 [PL 13.1184b–5a, 1187].

[139] Hunter, 'Jovinian', 453.

[140] Innocent I Ep. 2 (to Vitricius of Rouen) [PL 20.475–7]. Ep. 6 [PL 20.496] which recalled the injunctions of Siricius; Leo Ep. 14 [PL 54.672]; Ep. 167 [PL54.1204a]; Gregory I Ep. 1, 20 in MGH *Epist* 1–1, 76, 31–2; 9, 110; Ep. 2 1; 116, 21–4]. The council of Toledo (400) made reference to clerics who still claimed ignorance of the obligation to continence [canon 1; Vives 20]; see also Co. Agde (506) c.16 in D.C. Clercq (ed.) *Concilia Galliae*, in CCSL 148 (Turnhout, 1963), p. 125; co.Epaone (517) c.37 in *Concilia Galliae*, pp. 34, 233.

that there must be one, unified faith in the church, and 'if there is one faith there must be one tradition as well. If there is one tradition, one discipline must be observed in all churches'.[141] Establishing clerical continence or celibacy as a discipline that was observed in all churches was to present a substantial challenge to the successors of Siricius.

The debate surrounding attitudes to clerical continence in the first four centuries, and the legislation enacted to enforce it, are evidence of the concern to regulate the conduct of the clergy, but also of the continued presence of married priests and bishops in the patristic era. At the close of the second century, bishop Polycrates of Ephesus addressed a letter to the pope and church of Rome in which he commended the 'tradition of my relatives', as the eighth in an Episcopal line.[142] Gregory of Nyssa had married, probably before his appointment as bishop, and Hillary of Poitiers was both married and a father.[143] Anastasius, pope between 399 and 402, may have been father to his successor, the fifth century pope Felix III was the great-great-grandfather of Gregory the Great, and, as late as the sixth century, it was possible for the son of a priest to occupy the throne of St Peter.[144] Legislation in sixth century Gaul intended to regulate the conduct of the wives of the bishops suggests that married men continued to hold high ecclesiastical office, and regulatory interventions were common in meetings of the regional and universal churches.[145] Early in his pontificate, Pope Innocent I addressed a letter to Vitricius of Rouen (February 404) in which he echoed Siricius' concerns about the conduct of the clergy. In order that the church might maintain what was 'pure, worthy and honest', he wrote, it was imperative the priests

---

The councils held in Gaul in the fifth and sixth centuries do continue to make reference to the wives of the clergy as 'episcopa', 'presbyteria' and 'diaconissa', and the requirement that they give their consent at the time of their husband's ordination: see, for example, canon 16 of the Council of Agde 'san esi soniugati iuuenes consenserint ordinary, etiam exorum uluntas ita requirenda est, ut sequestrate mansionis cubiculo, religion praemissa, posteaquam partier conuersi fuerint, ordinentur' [*Corpus Christianorum* 148.281].

[141] 'si ergo una fides est, manere debet et una traditio. Si una traditio est, una debet disciplina per omnes ecclesias custodiri' [PL 13.1188a].

[142] Eusebius, *Historica Ecclesiastica* V.24.6–7, [English Translation in A. Roberts and J. Donaldson (eds) *Nicene and Post-Nicene Fathers*, series 2 (Edinburgh, 1885) vols 1 and 2.

[143] Gregory Nazianzen, Ep. 197 [PG 37.321a–24b; Venantius Fortunatus, *Vita Sanci Hilarii* III.VI.XIII; quoted in Cochini, *Apostolic Origins*, pp. 93–5.

[144] Jerome, Ep. 130.16 [PL 22.1120a], Gregory, *Homiliae XI in Evangelio*, II.38.15 [PL 76.1291b]. Pope Agapetus (535–6).

[145] B. Brennan, 'Episcopae: Bishops' Wives Viewed in Sixth Century Gaul', *Church History* 54.3 (1985): 313–23; a year's continence was necessary before a married man could be appointed deacon, and the consent of the wife was required prior to ordination. Husband and wife were instructed not to share a bedroom, and those clergy who did return to conjugal relations were viewed as guilty of incest.

and deacons abstain from relations with their wives. Such a requirement was incumbent upon the clergy in accordance with the law of the Old Testament, but also under the demands of the new law, which required that priests be ready to serve on a daily basis. St Paul, Innocent claimed, had countenanced temporary abstinence for the laity as a precondition for prayer, but for the clergy who led a life of prayer, this abstinence was to be perpetual. The 'ceaseless sacrifice' of the priests imbued this obligation with an even greater significance, because 'if anyone has been soiled by carnal concupiscence, how would he dare to offer the sacrifice? Or with what conscience does he believe [his prayers] would be granted?' A priest might be the 'husband of one wife', but the apostle did not countenance a continuation of sexual desire within marriage, but rather commended continence 'because those who are unspiritual cannot please God'.[146] The following year a similar letter was sent to Exuperius of Toulouse, referring again to the instructions of Siricius, and repeating the references to the purity expected of the priests of the Old Law, and the Pauline injunction to abstain for the purposes of prayer. The pope conceded that there might still be some who were ignorant of the law in this respect, but demanded that those who were simply disobedient be expelled from their offices.[147]

Despite their insistence that the law of continence was both longstanding and widely promulgated, the popes continued to receive questions from local bishops on the subject. Leo the Great replied to a letter from Rusticus of Narbonne in 458/9 which had again raised the question of whether it was permitted for married priests to continue in conjugal relations. The pope responded with a reminder that continence was required of all higher clergy, who, if married, must live with their wives 'as if they did not have them', changing the nature of their union from 'carnal to spiritual'.[148] The issue was again debated at councils of the church in the fifth and sixth centuries. At Toledo in 400, the first canon of the council reinforced the expectation that deacons must lead continent lives, and the continence requirement was detailed in several Gallican councils of the fifth century.[149] The seventeenth council of Carthage, held in 419, produced a collection of some 133 canons, renewing the decisions reached by earlier African councils. The *Codex Canonum Ecclesiae Africanae* contained five canons that imposed clerical continence, ascribed to earlier councils held

---

[146] *Ep. Ad Victriciun Episcopum Rothomoagensem* IX.12 [PL 20.475c–477a], see especially at 476b 'qui si contaminates fuerit carnali concupiscentia, qho pudore sacrificare usurpabit? Aut qua conscientia quove merito exaudiri se credit'.

[147] *Ep. Ad Exuperium Episcopum Tolosoanum* [PL 20.496b–98a]; cf *Ep Ad Maximum et Severum Episcopos per Brittios* [PL 20.650b–c].

[148] PL 54.1204a.

[149] Cochini, *Apostolic Origins*, pp. 270ff.

in Carthage and Hippo. Continence was demanded of all priests in the service of the sacraments, and subdeacons, deacons, priests, and bishops were to abstain from their wives under threat of deprivation.[150]

Still the issue at stake was less the celibacy of the clergy, the expectation that the priests of the church would be unmarried, and more the continence of married clergy after their ordination. J-P Audet warns students of ecclesiastical history against the alluring assumption that the church was from the outset inexorably moving in the direction of a law of perfect celibacy for its priests, and that the married clergy of the early church were simply the 'residue' of practical considerations that would soon be overcome.[151] It is certainly apparent that the first generation of Christian ministers were not trained and organised professionals, most were married, their household providing a meeting place for the faithful, and many had children.[152] However, there were certainly some for whom religious obligation brought with it a reluctance to marry, or a decision to practise marital continence, both inside the nascent church and outside it. Christians of the second and third centuries faced the problem of reconciling baptism, marriage, and a life of religious service. For those who were to find themselves outside the church, including Encratites and Gnostics, the solution was a life of celibacy; for those inside the church, there was a need to balance the defence of marriage from its critics with the emerging sense that marriage was a remedy for those who could not live in the ideal state of virginity.[153] The assertion of a biblical justification for a life of celibacy in the service of the kingdom of God, and the argument that marriage and ministry were not easy bedfellows, were easily modified to suggest that holiness and sexuality were mutually exclusive. The influence of monasticism in reshaping the model of Christian perfection further served to associate religious devotion with the renunciation of the flesh, and at a practical level provided a group of chaste men who could be called upon to fill ecclesiastical office. At the same time, the physical location of the church gradually shifted from the home to the dedicated building, in which pastoral married domesticity came to be less important than the sacred function of the priest. As those proximate to the holy, priests were expected to lead a life that met the requirements of this access to the sacred, a life modelled upon the precedent of the priestly

---

[150] Cochini, *Apostolic Origins*, pp. 267–9.

[151] Audet, *Mariage*, p. 4 criticises those who would see the history of clerical celibacy as a long and eventually hard-won battle to eliminate this 'residue' of married priests.

[152] H. Von Camenhausen, *Ecclesiastical Authority and Spiritual Power in the Church of the First Three Centuries*, (Peabody, Mass., 1997); Audet, *Mariage*, p. 4; Frazee, 'Origins', 151ff.

[153] Schillebeeckx, *Clerical Celibacy*, pp. 19–21.

caste of the Levites. Thus, in the third and fourth centuries the liturgical lexicon, and the vocabulary used to describe the priest, acquired a more sacral and sacrificial tone, a tone reflected in the writings of the Fathers and the popes, the decrees of the councils described above, and even in the observations of the laity on the priests who served them. The function of the bishop, in particular, was defined increasingly by his liturgical role rather than his didactic obligations, and as a deeper sense of the sacred came to be attached to the celebration of the eucharist, the position and perfection of the priest were pushed to the fore. Purity and perfection were closely associated with sexual abstinence, with the result that the 'decisive factor' in requiring continence from the clergy was, as Audet suggests, 'the encounter, within the same pastoral consciousness, of the double perception of impure and sacred, the first being present in the shadows under the form of sexual activity, and the second, in full light, under the form of service of the *sacramenta*.[154]

The debate over the 'apostolic' origins of clerical continence and celibacy is a vibrant one, and has been for the last millennium. Just as Siricius, Jerome, Leo and the early councils of the church argued for a scriptural mandate for the boundaries that they placed upon the conduct of the higher clergy, so the reformers and opponents of reform of different types in the period between 1100 and 1700 continued to argue that their beliefs were rooted in the practice of the primitive church. The nineteenth century debate between Bickell and Funk reinvigorated these attempts to recover, reconstruct, and repossess the precedent of the apostles, and twentieth-century scholarship has continued in this vein.[155] Among those who argue for the novelty of the discipline, there is a sense of the history of celibacy as a shift from freedom of choice to obligation in the law of the church after the apostolic period. Roger Gryson sought to demonstrate that the primitive church was staffed with more married priests than unmarried priests, and rooted the obligation to celibacy in non-Christian texts rather than the New Testament and the example of the apostolic church. There was, he believed, a fundamental discontinuity between the discipline of the church and the mandate of scripture, and a later preoccupation with ritual purity that was used to impose obligatory celibacy upon a historically married clergy.[156] Audet depicts a married

---

[154] Pope Innocent, Ep. 38 [PL 20.605b]. For a more detailed discussion of these themes than space here allows, see E. Durkheim, *The Elementary Forms of the Religious Life* (trans. J.W. Swain) (London, 1915); Audet, *Mariage*, chapter one, quotation at p. 114; Abbott, *Celibacy*, pp. 111–12, 207ff; Brown, *Body and Society*, Epilogue; Frazee, 'Origins', 151ff; Porter, *Sex, Marriage and the Church*, pp. 28ff.

[155] The nineteenth-century debates are discussed in chapter 7.

[156] Gryson, *Les Origines*, passim.

priesthood as the 'dominant reality' of the third century church, but one which was to be unbalanced by the elevation of virginity and the sacralisation of ecclesiastical function in the decades that followed.[157] Charles Frazee likewise sees a difference between the ascetic value of celibacy which might be used to argue in defence of the discipline, and the legislation and preoccupations that established the discipline in law in two critical periods in the life of the church, the fourth and eleventh centuries.[158] If the 'origins' of clerical celibacy are argued to be found in the laws of the church, particularly for example the law established at Elvira, the moral conduct of the clergy becomes a matter of an institutional obligation that saw the position of married clergy eroded by the apparently superior character of their unmarried colleagues.[159] In contrast, as we have seen, Roman Cholij, Christian Cochini, and Stefan Heid have argued convincingly that the modern law of celibacy has firm roots in the continence discipline of the early church. The dedication of the priest to God was evidenced in his commitment to live in marital continence after ordination, and in this respect it mattered little whether the priest was married prior to ordination or not; the prohibition of the use of marriage, and of subsequent marriages, created in effect a priesthood in which purity won by abstinence was prized. Rather than searching for an unmarried priesthood in the first Christian centuries, it is possible to locate in the insistence of the early church upon clerical continence the origins of the modern law. The insistence upon clerical continence after ordination presented an implicit objection to marriage after ordination, by effectively prohibiting the consummation of such unions. This apparent cause and effect relationship between the law of continence and the prohibition of marriage to those in holy orders makes it possible to identify the principle of the law of celibacy in the continence discipline of the primitive church. The 'apostolic origins' debate revolves around the interpretation of scripture, conciliar decrees, and papal pronouncements, but also, and more particularly, the understanding of the multiple meanings and implications of continence for the clergy. Indeed, concluding his summary of the modern debate, Stefan Heid concedes that the 'advances in scholarship' made in his work lie not in its overall conclusions, but in its elaboration or correction of the interpretation of particular source texts.[160] This process of reinterpretation and reworking of a limited body of evidence has been the hallmark of the controversy over clerical

---

[157] Audet, *Mariage*, pp. 13–22.

[158] Frazee, 'Origins', 149–50.

[159] See also Franzen 'Zolibat'; G. Denzler, *Papsttum: Geschichte und Gegenwart* (1997); B. Kottin, *Der Zolibat in der Alten Kirche* (Munster, 1970).

[160] Heid, *Clerical Celibacy*, p. 23, n. 19.

celibacy throughout its history; on each occasion that the issue has proved controversial, the similarities in the foundation of the arguments in each generation are striking. Pope Siricius' attempt to suppress diversity of opinion so that there might be one faith, one tradition, and one discipline, was, rather than the final word on the subject, just one line in the dialogue of debate.

CHAPTER TWO

'Preserving the Ancient Rule and Apostolic Perfection'?: Celibacy and Marriage in East and West

The history of clerical marriage in the Eastern churches is not only a compelling narrative in its own right, but has assumed a position of importance in the debates over the origins and necessity of clerical celibacy in the Latin church. While the modern Latin church demands a complete and permanent commitment to celibacy from its priests, the Orthodox church requires such a commitment only from its bishops, and in the expectation that those entering the priesthood will be either married men or members of monastic communities. Notwithstanding the apparent divergence in practice, the ecclesiastical legislation underpinning each tradition claimed a foundation in the precedent provided by the early church and councils; both the law of celibacy in the West and the married priesthood of the East were argued to be rooted in the canons and praxis of the first centuries of Christianity. Possession of the apostolic heritage was a significant component in the defence of clerical celibacy and continence in the West, but also a priority for those who legislated for a married priesthood in the East. Thus, the incontrovertible presence of a married priesthood in the East provided ammunition for those who would contest the validity and origins of the law of celibacy in the West, while the enforced celibacy of the Latin clergy was roundly condemned as a corrupting innovation by protagonists in the East. The married clergy of the Greek church were vigorously denounced by the leaders of the ecclesiastical reforms of the eleventh century, held up as exempla by the defenders of clerical marriage during the Reformation, and have been used as evidence both for and against the apostolic origins of clerical celibacy in more recent debates. The discussion of the example of the Greek church raises questions about the ecumenicity of particular church councils, the accuracy of the historical narrative of key events, the authenticity of vital documents and collections, the relationship of clerical celibacy and marriage to the established tradition of continence in the early church in East and West, and the extent to which the principle of the celibate priesthood is embedded in both traditions. The narrative of the origins of clerical marriage in the East is thus significant not only within that particular tradition, but also to the history of clerical celibacy and marriage in the wider church.

The articulation of the ascetic impulse in the writing of the Latin fathers in the third and fourth centuries charted in chapter one has clear echoes in the letters and treatises of their contemporaries in the East; indeed for peregrinatory figures such as Jerome, the distinction between east and west is perhaps an artificial construct. From the writings of the Greek Fathers, it is clear that questions were being asked as early as the second century about the relative merits of virginity and marriage, and the necessity that those who approached the altar should be of a pure character.[1] Later in the century, pressure from heretical groups including the Valentinians, prompted further discussion of the position of marriage in the church and particularly among the clergy. Clement of Alexandria, commenting upon the 'husband of one wife' passage in Paul's Letter to Timothy, encouraged the 'respectable' use of marriage by priests, deacons, and laymen, who would be 'saved by begetting children'. Cochini presents this section of the *Stromata* as a defence of the sanctity of monogamy in the face of the criticisms of the ascetics, although earlier commentators tended to focus upon the question of differentiation between priest and layman in the use of marriage.[2] Cochini's interpretation is convincing; Clement would certainly have been aware that his audience was susceptible to the views of Gnostic teachers in the School of Alexandria, and he was highly critical of their teaching on marriage and creation. The use of marriage was, he argued, permitted in the service of God, and marriage was therefore no obstacle to the attainment of Christian perfection for either the faithful or their leaders.[3] Evidence of the more radical ascetic impulse in the Alexandrian schools is most apparent in the life and writings of Origen, who had reportedly accepted castration in his early twenties, although subsequently preached against such a literal interpretation of Christ's praise for those who 'made themselves eunuchs for the sake of the kingdom'.[4] However, virginity was still lauded in Origen's writings as a state which provided a bridge between

---

[1] See for example Ignatius, 'Letter to Polycarp' c.5, discussed in chapter one above.

[2] C. Cochini, *The Apostolic Origins of Priestly Celibacy* (San Francisco, 199) pp. 147, 150–51, citing G. Bickell, 'Der Colibat eine apostolische Anordnung', *Zeitschrift fur Katholische Theologie*, 2 (1878): 20–64 and 'Der Colibat dennoch eine apostolische Anordnung', *Zeitschrift fur Katholische Theologie*, 3 (1879): 792–99; F.X. Funk, 'Der Colibat keine apostolische Anordnung', *Tübinger theologische Quartalschrift*, 61 (1880): 202–21 and 'Colibat und Priesterehe im Christlichen Alterum', in *Kirchengeschichtliche Abhandlungen und Unterschungen*, I (1897): 121–55; E.F. Vacandard, *Les Origines du Celibat Ecclesiastique* (Paris, 1905).

[3] Clement, *Stromata* [PG 9] 3.6.52.4; 7.11.64.2; P. Brown, *Body and Society Men, Women and Sexual Renunciation in Early Christian Society* (Columbia, 1988), chapter 6.

[4] Origen, *Commentary on the Gospel of Matthew* [PG 13]: 15:1–3.

earth and heaven. Just as God had come into the world through the body of a virgin, he wrote, so those who committed themselves to perpetual continence acquired a special position as representatives of the divine.[5] In his sermons on Numbers and Leviticus, Origen presented freedom from sin as a necessary precondition for those in the service of the Lord. Perpetual prayer and sacrifice required a perpetual chastity, which was not possible for those who were married, even if they were to follow the instructions of the apostle and abstain from one another, on a temporary basis, in order to make time for prayer. Complete chastity was, therefore, required of those who served as priests under the new law.[6] Even if continence was not demanded explicitly of the clergy by law, it is apparent that by the third century the connection between ministry and chastity was being articulated strongly in the schools of the East.[7]

Such views continued to be expressed in the writings of the Fathers in the East in the centuries that followed. Eusebius, Bishop of Caesarea, devoted one section of his *Demonstratio Evangelica* (c.315) to the nature and dignity of the Christian priesthood. While the priests of the Old Law were permitted, even expected, to be married men with families, Eusebius argued that for those devoted to Christian ministry it would be fitting to abstain from the use of their marriage. There was much in Scripture in praise of Christian marriage, but, he suggested, the specific calling of the priest required a total commitment to service which was not possible for those still encumbered by the demands of matrimony.[8] Eusebius' *Church History* certainly provided evidence of the continued presence of married men among the leaders of the church, evidence which was to be cited by the defenders of clerical marriage in later generations, but his own writings testify to a preference, if not a requirement, for clerical continence.[9] Such preferences, however, continued to be balanced against the asceticism of heretical groups, and even writers who argued for the positive contribution of a continent priesthood were often also forceful in their defence of the benefits of marriage. Epiphanius of Constantia, writing in the late fourth century, was strident in his criticisms of those such as the Montanists

---

[5] Brown, *Body and Society*, pp. 161–76.

[6] Origen *Homilies on Numbers* [PG 12] 23.3; *Homilies on Leviticus* [PG 12] 6.6.

[7] The practical situation was most likely rather more complex. As Audet notes, the ideals expressed by Origen were not necessarily grounded in the reality of the times in which he lived: J-P Audet, *Mariage et Celibat dans le service pastorale de l'eglise* (Paris, 1967), pp. 10–11.

[8] Eusebius, *Demonstratio Evangelica* [PG 22.81]; Cochini, *Apostolic Origins*, pp. 180–81; E. Schillebeeckx, *Clerical Celibacy Under Fire. A Critical Appraisal* (London and Sydney, 1968), p. 25.

[9] For the identification of married bishops, see Eusebius, *Historica Ecclesiastica* [PG 20] V.24.26-7; Audet, *Mariage*, pp. 20–22.

who disparaged Christian marriage, but also clear in his articulation of the merits of virginity and chastity. In the *Expositio Fidei*, Epiphanius presented virginity as the foundation of the church, and extolled the value of continence and widowhood. Chastity was identified as a central part of Christian priesthood, and those who served in the church were to be chosen ideally from the ranks of the virgins, or monastics, or, failing that, the widowed or continently married. Those ordained to the priesthood who went on to father children, he claimed, did so out of human weakness rather than custom.[10] The intention here was not to disparage marriage, and Epiphanius argued in his writings against heresy that both marriage and virginity were states commended by God. However, continence, including continence within marriage, was presented as a precondition for admission to the clerical estate, except in cases of pastoral need.[11]

The continence that was demanded within marriage from priests who had taken wives prior to their ordination was, in the eyes of many, as strict a discipline as celibacy. Commenting upon Paul's Letter to Timothy and the recommendation that the bishop be 'the husband of one wife', for example, St John Chrysostom argued that there was in reality no difference between an unmarried and married bishop in the manner of their living. A married bishop, if he were to devote himself fully to the service of God, was expected to live as if he had no wife. Marriage was not a bar to salvation, and where necessary conditions prevailed, it was permissible for a married man to serve as a bishop in the church 'though it is difficult for a rich man to enter the Kingdom of heaven, there have frequently been rich people who did so; the same is true for marriage'.[12] As Cochini reminds us, such sentiments present an indirect witness to the practice of the fourth century church rather than a canonical statement on the subject of clerical marriage and continence.[13] However, the weight of evidence from the patristic writings suggests that clerical continence was at least widely assumed, and this apparent expectation that the married clergy would practice continence was commented upon by Jerome in his response to the complaints of Vigilantius. The custom in the East, Jerome argued, was, by this time, clerical celibacy, as demonstrated in the churches of Antioch and Alexandria. Despite this optimism, however, even in the fifth century there was still a variety of local custom. Socrates' *Historia*

---

[10] Epiphanius, *Expositio Fidei* [PG 42] 823ff.

[11] Epiphanius, *Expositio Fidei* c.21; *Adversus Haeres* [PG 41], cc.48 and 59.

[12] *Commentary on the First Epistle to Timothy* c.3 [PG 62.549a]; a rather less positive view of marriage was presented in Chrysostom's writings on virginity, in which he suggested that the virgin life was as superior to marriage as heaven was to earth: Lib.de Virg. C.x. For a fuller discussion, see Brown, *Body and Society*, chapter 15.

[13] Cochini, *Apostolic Origins*, p. 292.

Ecclesiastica described the separation of priests from their wives as a novelty, and presented a picture of priests and bishops who continued to live with their wives 'as sister and brother' in the church of Thessalony, Greece, and Macedonia.[14]

More concrete evidence concerning the canonical status of married clergy in the East is to be found in the records of provincial and ecumenical councils that defined the discipline of the church over a period of five centuries until the decision reached at the Council in Trullo (692), which established a distinctive praxis, if not sentiment, in the eastern churches. The first council at which clerical celibacy and continence were discussed in detail was the Council of Ancyra held in 314. The deliberations of the council were to be far-reaching in both chronological and geographical terms. Although attendance was small, with only around a dozen bishops present, the lists of subscriptions suggest a broad representation of churches in Asia Minor and Syria. The decrees of the council were transmitted in a number of manuscript versions, and their content varies, particularly on the subject of the marriage of clergy. The oldest Greek text dates from the tenth century, but three Latin manuscript versions from the period between the mid-fifth and early sixth centuries are extant, of which the version of Denys the Minor is the most commonly used.[15] In this text, the tenth canon permitted, with Episcopal concession, the marriage of deacons. The council determined that deacons, prior to their ordination, were permitted to declare an intention to marry, but that those who did not make such a declaration were to be prohibited from entering into a subsequent marriage on pain of deprivation.[16] The permission to marry was based upon notice of intention and individual capacity; such marriages were admitted where the ordinand did not believe that he had the ability to maintain a life of chastity outside marriage: 'Quicumque Diaconi constituti in ipsa constitutione testificati sunt et dixerunt oportere se uxores ducere, com non possint sic manere, ii si uxorem postea duxerint sint in ministerio eo quod hoc sit illis ab episcopo concessum'. Such a concession was clearly out of line with the emerging canonical tradition in the West, which did not

---

[14] Jerome, *Adversus* Vigiantium [PL 23] l. c.2; Socrates, *Historia Ecclesiastica* [PG 67] 5.22.

[15] P. Joannou, *Discipline générale antique. t.I, ptie. 1. Les canons des conciles oecuméniques (IIe–IXe s.)–t.1, ptie. 2. Les canons des synodes particuliers (IVe–IXe s.)–t.II. Les canons des pères grecs* (Grottaferrata, 1962–4), II.2. p. 64; Hefele-Leclerq offer a summary: *Histoire des Conciles d'Apres les Documents Originaux*, C.H. Hefele and J. Leclerq, (eds) (19 vols, Paris, 1907–52). I.i.299 n. 1; see also R.B. Rackam, 'The texts of the canons of Ancyra', in *Studia Biblica et Ecclesiastica*, 3 (1891): 139–216, and Cochini, *Apostolic Origins*, pp. 169ff.

[16] Hefele-Leclerq, *Conciles*, I.1.213–3 c.10.

provide for subsequent marriages after ordination.[17] However, Christian Cochini's closer study of the surviving versions of the Ancyran decrees raises the possibility that the Fathers at the council did not intend that the tenth canon should permit such unions. In a sixth-century Latin translation of the canons undertaken by Archbishop Martin of Duma, and perhaps manipulated in order to ensure concordance with the law of the West, the tenth canon demanded that chastity be promised by deacons at ordination, and that without this promise, the candidate should not be ordained. Such an understanding is not without its problems.[18] It is possible, for example, that the Archbishop was working from a different version of the decrees, not least because, as Cochini notes, the tenth canon in the form that Denys presented it was not confirmed by subsequent councils of the Byzantine church, or indeed in imperial law.[19] In the absence of any references to the post-ordination marriage of deacons at later councils, Cochini's contention that the intention of the fathers at Ancyra was to separate those subdeacons who wished to marry and continue to exercise the functions of the subdiaconate from those who were prepared to commit to celibacy and therefore be ordained deacons seems convincing.

Shortly after the Council of Ancyra, another assembly of bishops took place in Neocaesarea. The council promulgated fifteen canons, later given ecumenical authority at the Council of Chalcedon in 451, the first of which prohibited the marriage of priests after ordination. Those who transgressed, like those found guilty of fornication, were to be subject to deprivation.[20] The canon made no mention of clergy in other orders, particularly the deacons who had been the focus of the discussions at Ancyra, and, interestingly, given the law of clerical continence that was taking shape in the West, the Fathers made no mention of the use of marriage after ordination. On this basis, H.C. Lea argued that there was nothing in the canons of Ancyra or Neocaesarea that threatened to disturb the conjugal relations of clergy and their wives, lending weight to his assertion that any such law would clearly be regarded as an innovation.[21] However, it

---

[17] See for example Council of Elvira discussed at pp. 41–3 above.

[18] C.W. Barlow, *Martini Episcopi Bracarensis Opera Omnia* (New Haven, Conn., 1950), p. 85; Cochini, *Apostolic Origins*, pp. 171ff.

[19] R. Gryson, *les Origines du Celibat Ecclesiastique du Premier au Septieme Siecle* (Gembloux, 1970), p. 125, conceded that the concession, if it were ever made, soon fell into abeyance.

[20] *Sacrorum Conciliorum Nova et Amplissa Collectio*, J.D. Mansi (ed.), continued and reprinted by L. Petit and J.P. Martin (53 vols in 60, Paris/Leipzig: Weller, 1901–1927). pp. 539–51; Joannou, *Discipline*, I.2.75; D. Constantelos, 'Marriage and Celibacy of Clergy in the Orthodox Church', in W. Bassett and Peter Huizing (eds), *Celibacy in the Church* (New York, 1972), pp. 30–38, especially p. 33.

[21] H.C. Lea, *History of Sacerdotal Celibacy* (2 vols, London 1907) vol. 1, p. 47.

would be valid to assume that the absence of such a prohibition, in a conciliar decree directed against marriage after orders, need not imply an acceptance of the continued use of marriage by those priests who had taken wives prior to entering the church. After all, the connection between the requirement to continence after ordination and the prohibition of subsequent marriages presumably lies in the use of marriage; subsequent marriages could be considered invalid on the basis of non-consummation if permanent abstinence was demanded from those clergy who were married at the time that they had received orders.

Part of the reasoning that underpinned Lea's interpretation of the canons of Ancyra and Neocaesarea was the determination to demonstrate that the participants at the Council of Nicaea (325) could not have intended its decrees to be read as an attack on clerical marriage, since such an innovation would have required a more explicit articulation than the Nicene canons offer. It is easy to see why the deliberations of the council were so critical to protagonists on both sides of the debate over clerical celibacy. With ecumenical authority, its canons rapidly acquired a prominent position in the canonical collections, and were repeatedly referenced by subsequent councils and popes. To lay claim to the inheritance of the first great ecumenical council was to lend substantial weight to any argument over the origins of the law of celibacy. The decisions taken at Nicaea, but also the legend that developed surrounding the apparent intervention of one 'Paphnutius' in the discussion of clerical discipline, exerted a profound influence over both subsequent legislation, and the shape of later debates over the validity and historicity of the celibacy rule. However, the debate over the view of the Nicene fathers on clerical marriage revolved around not only the figure of Paphnutius and his involvement in the discussions, but also the vocabulary and meaning of the third canon agreed at the council. In Lea's interpretation, the reference in the third canon to 'subintrodoctam mulierem' was deliberately constructed to exclude the wives of priests; these women, along with the mothers, sisters, and aunts of priests were 'above suspicion'. The Fathers at Nicaea, he concluded, had no intention of preventing the cohabitation of married clergy with their wives, and the canon offered no support to those who would seek to root clerical celibacy in the discipline of the fourth century church. It was only when later writers attempted to apply the words of the canon to clerical wives that the apparent dichotomy between the third canon and the narrative of Paphnutius' intervention became problematic.[22]

In contrast, Christian Cochini concludes that there was a common consensus in subsequent synods and councils that the intention of the third canon was indeed to preserve the chastity of the higher members of the

---

[22] Lea, *Sacerdotal Celibacy*, pp. 48–9.

clergy, who were obliged to live in perfect continence, by isolating them from the temptations of women. It was only permitted for a priest to live with his wife after his ordination if she also promised continence, and the consequence of such a promise was that she would no longer be regarded as 'suspicious'.[23] This is certainly a persuasive explanation for the omission of clerical wives from the third canon, especially if the text is taken to refer only to those clergy who were not permitted to exercise their marriage rights. Higher clergy, whether married-continents or celibates, would be subject to the canon, but those who were married and in lower orders would not, because the use of marriage remained open to them. The third canon was based upon, and consolidated, already-established expectations about the relationship between married priests and their wives, and particularly the assumption that those who received higher orders would commit to perpetual continence. If the Fathers at Nicaea did not believe themselves to have innovated in relation to the position of the married clergy, it seems plausible that their conclusions were informed by a recognised law and practice, and that no further clarification was required. The likely presence at the Council of Nicaea of Bishop Ossius of Cordoba has led both Gryson and Hefele-Leclerq to conclude that it was the Council of Elvira that provided the impetus behind the discussion of clerical celibacy in 325, and in the western canonical tradition the third canon is commonly bound up with the discipline of clerical celibacy that dates to Elvira. When more forceful action was taken in the Latin church of the eleventh and twelfth centuries to eradicate clerical immorality and incontinence, the wives of the clergy ceased to be regarded as above suspicion, and this shift in perception was reflected in later summaries of the Nicene canon.[24] However the trajectory in the East was rather different. The practice which had been affirmed at Ancyra and Neocaesarea would enable the third canon at Nicaea to be accepted as the custom of the church, and subsequent references to the third canon in the East, including fifth century Theodosian Code, tended to make explicit reference to clerical wives in the list of women with whom clergy

---

[23] Cochini, *Apostolic Origins*, p. 194; see also R. Cholij, *Clerical Celibacy in East and West* (Leominster, 1988), pp. 81–2.

[24] The similarity in the tone of the legislation at the two councils led Hefele-Leclerq to conclude (I.1.621) that 'cette coincidence porterait a faire croire que c'est un des Peres d'Elvire, Osius, qui proposa au concile de Nicée la loi sur le celibat'; cf Gryson, *Origines*, pp. 87ff; Cholij, *Clerical Celibacy*, pp. 79ff. See, for example, the third canon of the Lateran Council of 1123: 'We absolutely forbid priests, deacons, and subdeacons to associate with concubines and women, or to live with women other than such as the Nicene Council for reasons of necessity permitted, namely, the mother, sister, or aunt, or any such person concerning whom no suspicion could arise': H.J. Schroeder, *Disciplinary Decrees of the General Councils: Text, Translation and Commentary* (St. Louis, 1937), pp. 177–94.

could be permitted to reside.[25] However, at the Council in Trullo of 692, it was suggested that the Nicene canon was intended to apply to celibate clergy alone; the failure to mention clerical wives implied that the canon was of more limited scope. At the second Council of Nicaea in 787, and in the views of later canonists, it was assumed that the third canon of 325 referred only to unmarried bishops, celibates and monastics, and was not intended in any way to limit the activity of married clergy and their wives.[26]

At a superficial level, there is some common ground to be found in the assumption that the third canon did not apply to the wives of the clergy, but this common ground is narrow, and masks a fundamental disagreement. For Lea, clerical wives were not mentioned because the council made no attempt to regulate clerical marriage and its use, but for Cochini and Cholij the absence of any explicit reference to married clerics simply reflected the assumption that such women were already above suspicion by virtue of their promised continence. When confronted by the story of a debate during the council, in which Paphnutius intervened to prevent the prohibition of clerical marriage, the implications of this disagreement are apparent. In Lea's eyes, the Paphnutius legend was unsettling only for those later writers struggling to find evidence of a celibate priesthood in the early church. If it is accepted that the third canon made no attempt to regulate clerical marriage, the account of Paphnutius' intervention can be readily accommodated. However, if it is argued that the council attempted to legislate for clerical celibacy, the persuasive powers of Paphnutius in convincing the bishops to do otherwise are more problematic. Such tensions in the evidence might explain why the apparent contribution of an obscure figure to discussions at one council was to exert such a powerful influence over the writing of the history of clerical celibacy and marriage in the centuries to come. From rather uncertain beginnings, the legend of Paphnutius' defence of clerical marriage was to become a staple of the debate over the law of celibacy in the twelfth century, during the Reformation, and indeed in more recent scholarship. The legend was

---

[25] J. Lynch, 'Marriage and Celibacy of the Clergy. The Discipline of the Western Church: An Historico-Canonical Synopsis', *The Jurist*, 32 (1972): 14–38, especially 24.

[26] For a fuller discussion, see Cholij, *Clerical Celibacy*, p. 83; canon 18. 'Be irreproachable even for those outside, says the divine apostle. Now for women to live in the houses of bishops or in monasteries is a cause for every sort of scandal. Therefore if anybody is discovered to be keeping a woman, whether a slave or free, in the bishop's house or in a monastery in order to undertake some service, let him be censured, and if he persists let him be deposed. Should it happen that women are living in the suburban residence and the bishop or monastic superior wishes to journey there, no woman should be allowed to undertake any sort of work during the time that the bishop or monastic superior is present; she should stay on her own in some other area until the bishop has retired, in order to avoid all possible criticism', in *Decrees of the Ecumenical Councils*, Norman P. Tanner (ed.) (London, 1990).

certainly not part of the canonical record of the council, but its polemical potential ensured it a prominent position in the hermeneutic of the third Nicene canon.

The story was widely disseminated through the Greek historian Sozomen's assertion that Paphnutius had intervened at the Council of Nicaea in order to stall an attempt to impose absolute continence upon married clerics. Paphnutius' intervention was critical to the understanding of the third canon, because if such an attempt was made, it would imply that the contested canon was not intended to refer to married priests and their wives. The origins of the story lay not in Sozomen's work, but in the rather more detailed narrative presented in Socrates' *Ecclesiastical History*. The legend ran thus:

> Paphnutius then was bishop of one of the cities in Upper Thebes: he was a man so favoured divinely that extraordinary miracles were done by him. In the time of the persecution he had been deprived of one of his eyes. The emperor honoured this man exceedingly, and often sent for him to the palace, and kissed the part where the eye had been torn out. So great devoutness characterized the emperor Constantine. Let this single fact respecting Paphnutius suffice: I shall now explain another thing which came to pass in consequence of his advice, both for the good of the Church and the honor of the clergy. It seemed fit to the bishops to introduce a new law into the Church, that those who were in holy orders, I speak of bishops, presbyters, and deacons, should have no conjugal intercourse with the wives whom they had married while still laymen. Now when discussion on this matter was impending, Paphnutius having arisen in the midst of the assembly of bishops, earnestly entreated them not to impose so heavy a yoke on the ministers of religion: asserting that 'marriage itself is honorable, and the bed undefiled'; urging before God that they ought not to injure the Church by too stringent restrictions. 'For all men,' said he, 'cannot bear the practice of rigid continence; neither perhaps would the chastity of the wife of each be preserved': and he termed the intercourse of a man with his lawful wife chastity. It would be sufficient, he thought, that such as had previously entered on their sacred calling should abjure matrimony, according to the ancient tradition of the Church: but that none should be separated from her to whom, while yet unordained, he had been united. And these sentiments he expressed, although himself without experience of marriage, and, to speak plainly, without ever having known a woman: for from a boy he had been brought up in a monastery, and was specially renowned above all men for his chastity. The whole assembly of the clergy assented to the reasoning of Paphnutius: wherefore they silenced all further debate on this point, leaving it to the discretion of those who were husbands to exercise abstinence if they so wished in reference to their wives. Thus much concerning Paphnutius.[27]

---

[27] Socrates, *Hist. Ecc.* [PG 67] 1.11; see Sozomen's similar account, Lib.1 c.22 [*Die Griechischen christlichen Schriftsteller der Ersten drei Jahrhundert*, 50.44].

The Fathers at Nicaea, in this account, had determined to introduce a *new* law, which would require total continence from clergy who had married prior to their ordination. While such continence was, it appeared, possible for Paphnutius, whose credentials were here presented, he articulated a concern that the inability of all men to live in continence might bring scandal and immorality into the church. If such a debate did take place, it was evidence of both the novelty of clerical continence and celibacy, and of a deep-seated concern that attempts to regulate the lives of married clergy ran counter to biblical authority and might present an occasion for sin. In this respect, it is easy to see why Paphnutius became such a popular figure in arguments against clerical celibacy. Despite its condemnation by Pope Gregory VII, the story of Paphnutius found its way into canonical collections in the West, including Gratian's *Decretum*.[28] It was a prominent part of the condemnation of the eleventh century reform of clerical marriage in the *Rescript of Ulric,* and was cited by William Tyndale, Martin Luther, and Philip Melanchthon in their defences of clerical marriage in the sixteenth century.[29] The story has continued to be debated in more recent scholarship. Paphnutius had a key role to play in nineteenth century exchanges on the history of clerical celibacy, and the story of his intervention at Nicaea was detailed in both von Hefele's *Conciliengeschichte* (1855), and in Funk's continuation. Von Hefele argued that the law which Paphnutius sought to block was that which had been accepted and promulgated at Elvira, and that Paphnutius' views were in keeping with the praxis of the East established at Ancyra and outlined in the Apostolic Constitutions. His intervention was a defence of tradition, and an attempt to prevent the implementation of the novel laws of the West which imposed continence upon the married clergy. Elphège Vacandard cited the legend in his study of clerical celibacy for the *Dictionnaire de théologie catholique* (1905), and Roger Gryson argued that the stance taken by Paphnutius was readily accommodated into the practice of the Eastern church.[30]

However, the veracity of the legend of Paphnutius has been vigorously challenged. As the story became popular in the eleventh and twelfth centuries, and was reproduced in pamphlets directed against the imposition of clerical celibacy, Gregory VII intervened to condemn the narrative as a fiction. Bernold of Constance, in his exchange with Alboin in the 1070s, argued that the story must be false, since it was incompatible with the

---

[28] Pars I Dist 31 c.12, based upon the narrative in Cassiodorus' compilation, the *Historia Tripartita*.

[29] For a discussion of the *Rescript*, see pp. 171–2 below; On reformation uses see pp. 171–2 below, and H.L. Parish, *Clerical Marriage and the English Reformation* (Aldershot, 2000) pp. 90, 94.

[30] Gryson, *Les Origines*, p. 92.

third canon of the council, and concluded that Sozomen had presented inaccurate information.[31] Baronius' *Annales*, printed between 1588 and 1607, dismissed the story altogether. The third canon at Nicaea had made no mention of the wives of the clergy, he argued, and it was clear that a law of celibacy had been agreed, making it impossible to argue that Paphnutius had prevented its passage. Baronius' assertions were vigorously criticised in a strident response from the Lutheran Georg Calixtus, but the authority of Sozomen's narrative continued to be questioned. The seventeenth century editor of Sozomen's history, Valesius, dismissed the story as an invention, lacking any foundation in the records of the council, while the Augustinian Christian Lupus argued that Paphnutius' comments referred to the subdiaconate alone, and were not intended to countenance clerical marriage for those in higher orders.[32] Robert Bellarmine simply rejected the story as an invention on the part of Socrates, who on this occasion, he argued, had betrayed his sympathies for the Novatian heresy. In the eighteenth century, Zaccaria's *Storia polemica del celibato sacro* cited the legend, but accorded it no authority. The most fundamental criticisms are of the insubstantial nature of the evidence. The figure of Paphnutius is not mentioned in other authoritative sources, particularly Eusebius' *Ecclesiastical History*, and although Socrates claimed to have received information about the council from a personal source, the passing of time makes this assertion dubious. There is a reference to Paphnutius and to the deliberations at Nicaea in the history of the council composed by Gelasius of Kyzikos (d. c.475), who suggested that in light of the warnings of Paphnutius about the dangers inherent in imposing celibacy upon a clerical estate that was unable and unwilling, the council opted to demand only optional celibacy for the benefit of the church.[33] However, the paucity of evidence to support Socrates' narrative has led many to condemn the story as a fabrication, and a fabrication that was apparently recognised as such in the centuries that followed.[34] In 1968, the Paphnutius story was dismissed in a detailed examination of its origins and foundations by Friedhelm Winkelmann as a 'progressive hagiographical confabulation'. The legend, he claimed, had evolved and become corrupted over time, rendering the identification of the real Paphnutius increasingly complex. Greek sources certainly record figures of that name in the early fourth century, but none held an Episcopal title. Indeed this status, Winkelmann

---

[31] For a fuller discussion of Bernold see p. 116 below.

[32] C. Lupus, *Synodorum generalium et provincialium statuta et canones cum notis et historicis dissertationibus* (Louvain, 1665–73).

[33] Gelasius of Kyzikos, *Historia Concilii Nicaeni* XXXII [PG 85:1336–7].

[34] A.M. Cardinal Stickler, *The Case for Clerical Celibacy. Its Historical Development & Theological Foundations* (tr. Brian Ferme, San Francisco, 1995), pp. 62–3.

argued, was accorded first by Rufinus, and later cemented by Socrates and Sozomen, who positioned Paphnutius in Thebes. The most accurate lists of participants at the council do not include the name of Paphnutius, and even in the variants in which his presence is recorded there is a marked lack of consistency.[35]

Given the importance attached to the Council of Nicaea throughout the history of the church, it would be expected that the story of Paphnutius would acquire a similar authority as part of the history of the council. However, in neither East nor West was there an attempt to ground any subsequent legislation on Paphnutius' intervention. Christian Cochini effectively undermines the arguments of Gryson that the practice recommended by Paphnutius was to become the discipline of the Greek church, on the basis that there is no evidence that early canonical tradition in the East permitted the use of marriage after ordination. When the Trullan Fathers legislated for temporary continence for the married lower clergy, this was done without any reference to the Paphnutius legend, despite the support that it might have offered for their stance. Either the story was unknown in the East, or it was known, but recognised as a fabrication and therefore excluded from both subsequent conciliar deliberations, and from commentaries on canon law, including the *Canonum Adauctum* of the twelfth century.[36] The failure of the Trullan Council to make use of the Paphnutius story might also be attributed to the interpretation of the 'discretion' that Socrates asserted was accorded to married priests with regard to abstinence. If this discretion is seen, as Roman Cholij does, as being exercised in relation to strict and perpetual continence, rather than temporary continence, Paphnutius' suggestion is more evidently in keeping with contemporary practice, as Socrates described it.[37] However, even this position is not concordant with the law of the eastern church as laid down in Trullo, which explains the silence of the council on the subject, and further undermines Hefele's assertion that Paphnutius' demands were in harmony with the practice of the Greek church. Even in the polemical exchange between Nicetas and Humbert in the eleventh century, no mention was made of Paphnutius in defence of the tradition of the Greek church.[38]

The position of married priests in the Eastern church was defended at the Council of Gangres, which met in 340. Some twenty canons were

---

[35] F. Winkelmann, 'Paphnutios, der Bekenner und Bischof', *Probleme der Koptischen Literatur*, 1 (1968): 145–53; E. Honigmann, 'The Original Lists of the Members of the Councils of Nicaea, the Robber-Synod, and the Council of Chalcedon', *Byzantion*, 16 (1942/3): 20–28.

[36] Cochini, *Apostolic Origins*, pp. 199–200; Stickler, *Clerical Celibacy*, p. 64.

[37] Hist. Ecc. V.22 [PG 67. 637a] quoted in Cholij, *Clerical Celibacy*, p. 85.

[38] Cholij, *Clerical Celibacy*, p. 88.

promulgated by this assembly of thirteen bishops, and both the synodal letter and the content of the canons suggest that the main focus of the council was the threat posed by the Eustathian heresy.[39] The fourth canon stated 'if anyone affirms that one should not receive communion during the holy sacrifice celebrated by a married priest, let him be anathema'.[40] It is clear that there were married clergy who continued to officiate at the altar, presumably those who had married prior to ordination, but also that there was some debate surrounding the legitimacy of their service. Such debate was liable to have been spawned by the Eustathian antipathy toward marriage, and in particular the proposition that communion was not to be received from the hands of married priests; there is certainly nothing in the canon to suggest that the council intended to legislate in favour of clerical marriage after ordination. Neither is there any obvious sense that the canon was intended to permit the continued use of marriage by those priests who had taken orders after marriage. As Cochini suggests, the most likely target were either widows or continent married clergy, whose position had perhaps been undermined by the criticisms of radical heretics who saw marriage in a negative light.[41] The canon was not used to support the Trullan decision on married priests, but it did, however, cause problems for later writers seeking to demonstrate the antiquity of the law of clerical celibacy, and argue against the celebration of the sacraments by married clerics. Manegold of Lautenbach's *Liber ad Geberhardum*, composed in 1086 to counter Wenric of Trier's polemic against Pope Gregory VII, argued that the pope had been too lenient in his treatment of the married clergy. With the weight of patristic testimony on his side, Manegold argued, Gregory should have mounted a more determined campaign against clerical marriage. In particular, the pope was quite justified in his instruction that the faithful were to refuse the sacraments of married clergy, the decree of Gangres notwithstanding.[42] Such views on the sacraments of married priests were echoed in the work of Bernold of Constance, thus necessitating his rather dismissive attitude towards the

---

[39] For further information, and detail on the date of the council, see Joannou, *Discipline*, 1.2.92; the council featured in the collections of Dionysius and Isidore, and through the latter its decrees found their way into Gratian's *Decretum*, Dist XXVIII c.15.

[40] Cholij, *Clerical Celibacy*, p. 91; Hefele-Leclerq, *Conciles*, I.1.1034 c.4.

[41] Mansi, *Sacrum Conciliorum*, v.2.1095ff; Cochini, *Apostolic Origins*, pp. 201–2; citing C. Knetes, 'Ordination and Matrimony in the Eastern Orthodox Church', *Journal of Theological Studies*, 11 (1910): 481–513 for a discussion of criticisms of marriage and married clergy; see also Schillebeeckx, *Clerical Celibacy*, p. 24.

[42] *Libelli de lite imperatorum et pontificum saeculis XI. et XII. Conscripti I*, Ernst Dümmler, Friedrich Thaner, Lotkar von Heinemann (eds) (Hanover: Monumenta Germaniae Historica, 1891), pp. 308–430 especially c.2.

canon of Gangres that seemed to stand in opposition.[43] The Council of Gangres was widely cited in defence of clerical marriage, or at least in defence of the validity of the celebration of the sacraments by married clergy during the era of the Gregorian reform. The Italian author of the *Tractatus pro clericorum connubio* certainly saw the fourth canon as evidence that the eleventh century injunctions against the sacraments of married clergy were erroneous and ran contrary to the traditions and canons of the church.[44] The canons had already acquired a new polemical weight during the ninth century, when the patriarch of Constantinople, Photius, condemned the 'errors' of the Latin church and its clergy in Bulgaria, and particularly the perpetual and compulsory celibacy demanded of priests. Pope Nicholas' reply to the questions of the recently converted Boris I suggested that the married clergy were reprehensible, although their position in the church was not to be denied. The issue appeared to be one of continence rather than marriage; it was the continued use of marriage to which the pope objected, and even then he stopped short of suggesting that the sacraments of incontinent clergy (in either geographical context) were invalidated by their actions.[45] It was this assertion of the efficacy of the ministrations of married clergy that was to make the fourth canon so significant, and its use by Greek commentators in their criticisms of the law and practice of the Latin clergy was focused primarily around this issue, rather than the question of whether the use of marriage was permitted to the priesthood.[46] However, even if the impact of the council upon the praxis of the Greek church was minimal, its concrete denunciation of those who refused the ministrations of married clergy was to ensure that its fourth canon occupied a significant place in later debates over clerical celibacy in the West.

A century later, at the fourth ecumenical Council of Chalcedon (451), the focus of the discussion was the issue of the marriage of lectors and cantors. More than five hundred bishops, the majority drawn from the

---

[43] Bernold of Constance, *Apologeticus*, 17–19 in LdL II, esp. 83.

[44] *Tractatus pro Clericorum Connubio*, LdL III.591–2; see also Burchard, *Decretum* 3.75 [PL 140:689].

[45] *Responsa Nicolai ad Consulta Bulgarorum*, [PL 119.978–1016, especially 1006d]. Anne Barstow, in her study of married clergy in the era of the Gregorian reform, has highlighted a neglected chapter in the history of the debate. The monk Ratramnus responded to the arguments advanced by the pope, and in his defence of papal primacy also set out a defence of clerical celibacy in his *Contra Graecorum Opposita* [PL 121.324–32] chapter 6. Despite the evident esteem in which marriage was held by Christ and the disciples, he argued, it was not possible for a priest to serve both God and his wife. The decree at Nicaea then, Ratramnus argued, became a prohibition of clerical marriage, because the wives of the clergy were not mentioned in the list of those women who were above suspicion. A.L. Barstow, *Married Priests and the Reforming Papacy, The Eleventh Century Debates* (Lewiston, NY: 1982), pp. 36–7.

[46] Cholij, *Clerical Celibacy*, pp. 94–5.

East, attended debates over issues of doctrine and practice that ranged from the humanity and divinity of Christ to a variety of disciplinary questions.[47] The fourteenth canon attempted to impose limitations upon the women that cantors and lectors might take as their wives,

> Since in certain provinces readers and cantors have been allowed to marry, the sacred synod decrees that none of them is permitted to marry a wife of heterodox views. If those thus married have already had children, and if they have already had the children baptised among heretics, they are to bring them into the communion of the catholic church. If they have not been baptised, they may no longer have them baptised among heretics; nor indeed marry them to a heretic or a Jew or a Greek, unless of course the person who is to be married to the orthodox party promises to convert to the orthodox faith. If anyone transgresses this decree of the sacred synod, let him be subject to canonical penalty.[48]

However, the council made no clear statement on clerical continence after ordination, either for the higher clergy or for those in lower orders to whom the fourteenth canon applied. There was no obvious attempt made to prohibit marriage to cantors and lectors, but the decree does not make clear whether such marriage were part of a longstanding ecclesiastical tradition, or simply tolerated under local practice and custom in some parts of the church. Again, perhaps, the significance of the canon to the debate was to lie in its exploitation by later writers and canonists. The author of the *Tractatus pro clericorum connubio*, arguing that marriage was permitted to those in holy orders who had not made a promise of continence, cited the Council of Ancyra and the ratification of its decrees at Chalcedon in support of the legality of clerical marriages.[49] The freedom to marry in lower orders, which appeared to be implicitly accepted at Chalcedon, was certainly accepted as part of the apostolic tradition by the Fathers in Trullo in 691.

It was at the Council in Trullo that the most significant, and also the most controversial, statement on clerical marriage in any of the councils of the Eastern church was to be made. The council in Trullo (literally, 'in the hall') was convoked late in 691, with the purpose of promulgating decrees that would enforce the decisions taken at the fifth and sixth ecumenical councils of 553 and 680–1. Some two and a half centuries had elapsed since the enactment at Chalcedon of the previous disciplinary decrees intended to regulate the conduct of the clergy, and the determination of the Trullan council to attempt to breathe new life into the traditional laws of the

---

[47] Tanner, *Ecumenical Councils*, pp. 75–6.
[48] Tanner, *Ecumenical Councils*, p. 76.
[49] MGH LdL, vol. 3, p. 592.

church is therefore understandable. The church was also confronted by the deepening divisions opened up by the Monothelitic controversy, political uncertainty, and the advance of Islam which had left Constantinople as the sole surviving patriarchate. The decrees were focused primarily on matters of discipline, and took what Cholij has described as a hostile stance towards other churches, including those of Rome and Armenia.[50] The opening decree of the council revealed an expectation that it would be treated as an ecumenical council, but the failure of several of its decisions, particularly those relating to the celibacy of the clergy, to find favour in Rome left its decrees without papal ratification. Both Pope Sergius II and Pope John XII refused to confirm the canons, and when papal approval was finally obtained from Adrian I, it was limited to those canons which were deemed to be in accordance with the already established laws and traditions of the church.[51] The reception of the canons in the western tradition was generally hostile; Bede referred to the council as a 'reprobate' synod, and Paul Casinensis as 'erratic'. Writing in the eleventh century, Humbert was equally dismissive, although some of the canons were presented in Gratian's *Decretum*.[52] The text of the canons was published in the West in the sixteenth century, and their position as part of the canonical tradition of the eastern, although not universal church, accepted by Pope Sixtus V. However, the refusal of the popes to give their full assent to the Trullan decrees did not limit their impact and force in the East; the canons were deemed to be of ecumenical standing at the second Council of Nicaea in 787 (although at least partially in the mistaken assumption that they had the authority of the pope). The discipline that they established for the married clergy has endured until the present day, and the synod in Trullo is often regarded as the final statement on ecclesiastical discipline in the East.[53]

---

[50] Cholij, *Clerical Celibacy*, pp. 5ff.

[51] Cholii, *Clerical Celibacy*, p. 6; Cochini, *Apostolic Origins*, p. 1933; Mansi, *Conciliorum*, XII 3c and 164, 982; H.J. Hefele, *Conciliengeschichte* (Freiburg im Breisgau, 1973) 3.345–8.

[52] 'Council in Trullo', in C.G. Hebermann (ed.), *Catholic Encyclopedia volume* 4: *Clandestinity – Diocesan Chancery* (15 vols, New York: Appleton, 1907–12); Paul Casinensis, *Historia gentis Langobardorum*, in *Scriptores rerum Langobardicarumet Italicarum saec. VI–IX*, Georg Waitz (ed.) (Hanover: Monumenta Germaniae Historica, 1878), pp. 45–187; PL 145:402; Cholij, *Clerical Celibacy*, p. 8.

[53] For discussion of the 'ecumenical' nature of the council, see Hefle-Leclerq, *Conciles*, III.i.560ff; Barstow, *Married Priests*, pp. 28–9; Cochini, *Apostolic Origins*, pp. 396ff, Cholij, *Clerical Celibacy*, pp. 62ff; A. Vasiliev, *History of the Byzantine Empire* (Madison Wisconsin, 1952), pp. 225ff; E.F. Vacandard, *Les Origines du Celibact Ecclesiastique* (Etudes de Critique et d'histoire religieuse, 1re ser., Paris, 1905), p. 101.

The council affirmed obligatory celibacy for bishops, and prohibited marriage to those in holy orders, but its import lay in the sanction that it offered to the continued use of marriage by priests and deacons.[54] The third canon was directed against those clergy who had entered into second marriages, and those who had married women who were deemed inappropriate spouses for priests. Reform was deemed necessary in order that priests might be 'pure and blameless', and those who did not repent of their sins were to be removed from office:

> that he who has been joined in two marriages after his baptism, or has had a concubine, cannot be bishop, or presbyter, or deacon, or at all on the sacerdotal list; in like manner, that he who has taken a widow, or a divorced person, or a harlot, or a servant, or an actress, cannot be bishop, or presbyter, or deacon, or at all on the sacerdotal list.[55]

There was nothing particularly novel in this condemnation of twice-married clerics; the issue of digamy had been addressed in previous councils and in patristic literature in both East and West.[56] As Cholij has argued, the issue here seems to have been one of continence rather than the illicit nature of such unions. To enter into a second marriage was to concede to the demands of the flesh over those of the spirit, and there was already an expectation that those who had taken holy orders would not re-marry after the death of their spouse.[57] If continence was demanded of those in orders, including those clergy who had married prior to entering the church, such a commitment surely extended also to the prohibition of marriage, and indeed second marriage, after ordination.

This suggestion that the third canon, in its attempts to regulate the marriages of priests, was inspired by the assumption that continence was to be expected of all in higher orders makes sense in the context of the sixth Trullan canon. Cholij suggests that there was little that was innovative or indeed controversial about the sixth canon, which simply articulated the natural consequences of the decision expressed at Elvira nearly four centuries previously to demand continence from all who entered into higher

---

[54] The council and its decrees have been well studied by scholars in both East and West. The fullest and most recent survey is that of Roman Cholij, but see also V. Laurent, 'L'Oeuvre Canonique du Concile in Trullo 691–2', *Revue des Etudes Byzantine*, 23 (1965): 7–41; Vacandard *Les origines*, p. 101; Joannou, *Discipline*, I.1.98.

[55] *The Seven Ecumenical Councils of the Undivided Church*, (tr. H.R. Percival), in *Nicene and Post-Nicene Fathers, 2nd Series*, P. Schaff and H. Wace (eds) (repr. Grand Rapids MI: Wm. B. Eerdmans, 1955), pp. 362–3.

[56] As, for example, at the Council of Ancyra 314.

[57] Cholij, *Clerical Celibacy*, pp. 15ff; the decree of the Council of Neocaesarea 'if a presbyter marry, let him be deposed' [Joannou, *Discipline*, 1.2.75].

orders. The marriage of priests in higher orders had been prohibited at the council of Neocaesarea, and even in the contested canons of the Council of Ancyra it was established that clergy were not permitted to marry once they had been ordained priest. The Fathers at the council were at pains to establish the apostolic foundations of the tradition that they defined, arguing that it had been determined in the Apostolic Canons that of 'those who are advanced to the clergy unmarried, only lectors and cantors are able to marry'. On this basis, the council instructed that 'it is in nowise lawful for any subdeacon, deacon or presbyter after his ordination to contract matrimony but if he shall have dared to do so, let him be deposed. And if any of those who enter the clergy, wishes to be joined to a wife in lawful marriage before he is ordained subdeacon, deacon, or presbyter, let it be done'. The Fathers at Trullo also considered the obligatory nature of the celibacy discipline for bishops, and the position of Episcopal wives. The twelfth canon expressed the concern that those bishops who continued to live with their wives were a cause of scandal in the church, and suggested that would be better if the Episcopal state were beyond reproach. Canon 48 required that the wife of a bishop, upon his elevation and consecration, be removed to a monastery where she would enjoy the provision of the bishop, and might in some instances prove herself worthy to be appointed as a deaconess.[58] The separation of bishops from their wives was already common practice in, for example, the church of Gaul, but the most likely basis for the legislation at Trullo was the law of Justinian a century before which had condemned cohabitation in an attempt to ensure that the property of the church was not dispersed to the family of the bishop.[59] The canon did not close the ranks of the episcopate to married men, and there was nothing in the text of the canon to suggest that only celibates were eligible for Episcopal appointment. However, the fear that a married bishop might be tempted to alienate the lands of the church to the benefit of his family fuelled a developing tendency to assume that celibates, rather than continent priests, were preferable. The fact that the Trullan canon required that married bishops separate from their wives implied an acceptance of the principle that married men might be appointed to high office, but in later centuries it was to become the established norm that monastic communities would supply candidates for the episcopate. Ample precedent was to be found in the example of the monastic leaders of the early church, and

---

[58] Joannou, *Discipline*, I.i.138–9; I.i.186.

[59] Cholij, *Clerical Celibacy*, p. 108; *Corpus Juris Civilis: Codex Justiniani Repetitae Praelectionis a 534; Digesta a.533; Institutiones Junstiniani a.533*, P. Kreuger, T. Mommsen, R. Schoell, G. Kroll (eds) (3 vols, Berlin: Berolini: Weidman, 1877), III. 615–16. This situation was not unique to the Greek church; Cholij makes the useful comparison here between the concerns expressed by the emperor and those articulated by Pope Pelagius [PL 79.414].

Cholij suggests that even a century before the council in Trullo there was a preference for the appointment of monastic bishops. By the fourteenth century, it was rare for secular clergy to secure such appointments, not least because the expectation that secular clergy would marry before receiving orders encouraged celibates to take the monastic habit.[60]

However, it was the thirteenth canon which was to give the council in Trullo its defining position in the history of the church, and the history of clerical celibacy and marriage in particular. The canon is significant not only for its impact upon subsequent debate and practice in the eastern church, but also because of its representation of the 'apostolic' origins of the married priesthood, and a married priesthood that was not required to live in perfect continence. Given its importance, the text is worth reading in full:

> Since we know it to be handed down as a rule of the Roman Church that those who are deemed worthy to be advanced to the diaconate or presbyterate should promise no longer to cohabit with their wives, we, preserving the ancient rule and apostolic perfection and order, will that the lawful marriages of men who are in holy orders be from this time forward firm, by no means dissolving their union with their wives nor depriving them of their mutual intercourse at a convenient time. Wherefore, if anyone shall have been found worthy to be ordained subdeacon, or deacon, or presbyter, he is by no means to be prohibited from admittance to such a rank, even if he shall live with a lawful wife. Nor shall it be demanded of him at the time of his ordination that he promise to abstain from lawful intercourse with his wife: lest we should affect injuriously marriage constituted by God and blessed by his presence, as the Gospel saith: "What God hath joined together let no man put asunder;" and the Apostle saith, "Marriage is honourable and the bed undefiled;" and again, "Art thou bound to a wife? seek not to be loosed." But we know, as they who assembled at Carthage (with a care for the honest life of the clergy) said, that subdeacons, who handle the Holy Mysteries, and deacons, and presbyters should abstain from their consorts according to their own course [of ministration]. So that what has been handed down through the Apostles and preserved by ancient custom, we too likewise maintain, knowing that there is a time for all things and especially for fasting and prayer. For it is meet that they who assist at the divine altar should be absolutely continent when they are handling holy things, in order that they may be able to obtain from God what they ask in sincerity.
>
> If therefore anyone shall have dared, contrary to the Apostolic Canons, to deprive any of those who are in holy orders, presbyter, or deacon, or subdeacon of cohabitation and intercourse with his lawful wife, let him be deposed. In like manner also if any presbyter or deacon on pretence of piety has dismissed his

---

[60] Cholij, *Clerical Celibacy*, pp. 111–12; J. Dauvillier, C. de Clerq, *Le Mariage en Droit Canonique Oriental* (Paris, 1936).

wife, let him be excluded from communion; and if he persevere in this let him be deposed.[61]

Thus the Fathers at Trullo provided a defence of, and justification for, the continued use of marriage after ordination. The thirteenth canon was not a simple articulation of the principle that married men might be ordained, but moved significantly beyond this in asserting that the higher clergy had no obligation to perpetual and complete celibacy. The 'legitimate marriages' of men in holy orders were not to be undermined by the law of the church. There was a strident rejection of the obligatory and perpetual continence that was demanded of the Latin clergy; while it was 'meet that they who assist at the divine altar should be absolutely continent when they are handling holy things', such continence was temporary. The apostolic tradition had taught that those who carried the responsibility for intercession, and who touched the sacred objects, should be pure, but had also counselled a specific time for prayer and fasting, rather than a perpetual commitment. This principle of temporary continence, Cholij argues, was the 'hinge on which all the rest of the Greek discipline hangs'.[62]

It was, however, a rather creaky hinge, not least because the thirteenth canon required a more explicit and indeed creative articulation of its 'apostolic' origins if it was to be viewed as concordant with the traditional practice of the church. In order to locate a canonical precedent, the Trullan Fathers turned once more to the Apostolic Canon, but also to a more awkward manipulation of the canons of earlier councils, in order to establish a continuity of law and practice. It was argued to be contrary to the Apostolic Canon, for example, to deprive a priest in holy orders of the right to cohabit and enjoy conjugal relations with his wife, and those clergy who put away their wives 'on pretence of piety' were to be excluded from their offices. However, as recent commentators have noted, there was a degree of inconsistency in the postulations of the Fathers, not least in the fact the sixth Trullan canon demanded that bishops should dismiss their wives and place them in convents.[63] Equally, there was nothing in the Apostolic Canons that sanctioned the anathematisation of those who prevented married clergy from exercising their marital rights. If the canon was conceived a riposte to Latin practice, it was based upon a rather shaky understanding of the practice of the Western church in the seventh century if it was assumed that married clergy were forced to live apart from

---

[61] *The Seven Ecumenical Councils*, pp. 356–408.

[62] Joannou, *Discipline*, I.i.140–3; Cochini, *Apostolic Origins*, p. 405; Cholij, *Clerical Celibacy*, p. 115.

[63] Hefele-Leclerq, *Conciles*. III.i.565 note 1; Cholij, *Clerical Celibacy*, p. 100; Cochini, *Apostolic Origins*, p. 406.

their wives.[64] The primary purpose behind the embedding of the Trullan legislation in the precedent of the Apostolic canon was most likely to have been the attempt to assert an apostolic authority that was not immediately apparent for the thirteenth canon.

A similar process can be seen at work in the references made to other early councils of the church in order to justify the use of marriage after ordination. It was at Trullo, for example, that it was first argued that the third canon of Nicaea (325) applied only to those clergy who had already made a commitment to celibacy, although there was no mention of the alleged intervention of Paphnutius at the council in defence of clerical marriage. From the context, it is apparent that the confirmation of the Nicene canons in the fifth canon of the Trullo synod implied the inclusion of the wives of clerics among the groups of women who were not regarded as 'suspicious' by the Fathers at Nicaea, although it is worth noting that the Trullan synod was unique in its assertion that perfect continence was not required in this situation.[65] More significantly, the Council of Carthage (419) was presented as the basis of the thirteenth canon, alongside the texts of councils held at Carthage in 390 and 401, which were manipulated in order that they might be counted as consonant with the Trullan canon. The evidence of the Carthaginian canons presented in the Trullan text is, at least superficially, a conflagration of two canons from two councils; the second canon of the Carthage Council of 390, and the fourth canon of the council that was convened a decade later in 401. The consequence of this misconception or misrepresentation is evident in the assertion that the Carthaginian Council of 390 permitted the continued use of marriage after holy orders; it was this same council which was so significant in the development of an argument in favour of perpetual continence in the west.[66] The pivotal role accorded to the Carthage canons in East and West is not surprising if it is considered that the discipline in both churches was predicated upon the assumption that there was some kind of intrinsic association between the continence of the priest (whether married or not) and the fulfilment of his liturgical role, but the practice established at Trullo marked a significant divergence in the understanding of how this was to be achieved, in advocating a temporary rather than perpetual continence in preparation for the exercise of priestly function.

The justification for this, and indeed for much of the celibacy legislation enacted at Trullo, was the 'Apostolic Canons', a collection of 85 canons which formed part of the 'Apostolic Constitutions' of the fourth and fifth centuries. Although widely used, particularly in the East, the provenance,

---

[64] Cholij, *Clerical Celibacy*, p. 100.
[65] Cochini, *Apostolic Origins*, p. 193.
[66] Cholij, *Clerical Celibacy*, p. 122; Cochini, *Apostolic Origins*, pp. 3ff.

and particularly the authenticity of the canons has been disputed, and their reliability as a statement of the practice of the apostolic church called into question. The descriptor 'apostolic' is attached to a number of collections of statements on doctrine and practice dating from the fourth and fifth centuries, on some occasions rather optimistically. The *Canons of the Apostles*, composed in Egypt or Syria around the turn of the fourth century, for example, have been dismissed as 'pseudoapostolic' by at least one modern commentator. Although clearly limited as a source for the study of the apostolic church, the canons do offer insights into the practice and preoccupations of the fourth century, and still hold some significance for modern scholars given the weight that was attached to them in the east.[67] In the passages of the canons that address the issue of married clergy, the assumption is that it was the unmarried who were deemed most appropriate to take on the office of bishop, and that those who were married would be committed to a life of continence. However, it was not this collection, but rather the *Apostolic Constitutions* of the late fourth century that were to become so important in the context of the Trullan canons. The *Constitutions* themselves were drawn from a variety of earlier documents, including the third century *Didascalia*, and were commonly associated with the name of Clement of Rome. They were widely used in the East, but the first Latin edition of the text was not published until 1578.[68] One chapter was devoted to the question of clerical marriage and continence, and included a detailed consideration of the Pauline recommendation that the bishop should be the husband of one wife. Digamists were excluded from holy orders on this basis, and those who had been ordained were not permitted to enter into a subsequent marriage. The way in which a cleric governed his household and family was deemed to be a measure of his fitness for office, and any priests in orders who attempted to put away their wives were threatened with excommunication.[69] The question of whether married men ordained as priests were permitted to continue in the use of their marriages was not addressed, although Cochini argues forcefully that the prohibition of marriage after ordination certainly resonates with the law of continence that had been established in the West and advanced by Pope

---

[67] Cochini, *Apostolic Origins*, p. 203; see also F.X. Funk, *Didascalia et Constitutiones Apostolorum* (2 vols, Paderborn 1905); J.W. Bickell, 'Apostolischen Kirchenordnung', in *Geschichte des Kirchenrechts* (Giessen, 1843), pp. 107–32.

[68] F. Turrianus, *Apostolicarum Constitutionum et Catholicae Doctrinae Clementis Romani Libri VIII* (Antwerp, 1578). For a further consideration of Turrianus and his work, see p. 202 below.

[69] PG 1 956a; PG 1 957; Vacandard, *Les Origines*, p. 2077; Funk, *Didascalia* 2.2.33–4. This same theme was taken up in the fourteenth century by Theodore Metochites, *Miscellanea Philosophia et Historica*, C. Muller and T. Kiessling (eds) (Leipzig, 1821), pp. 370–77.

Siricius.[70] The *Constitutions* themselves were not viewed as problematic in the West, but the *Apostolic Canons* contained in the eighth book of the *Constitutions* were more controversial. The canons were claimed to have their origins in councils held in Antioch and Laodicaea, although their authentic canonicity and therefore authority was undermined after their rejection by Pope Gelasius I in the late fifth century. The first fifty canons were translated into Latin by Denys the Minor in the sixth century, and this subset of the *Apostolic Canon* did circulate more widely and enjoyed rather better repute. However, all 85 canons were accepted as authentic in the East, even sustaining a pre-eminent position above the Nicene canons in the conclusions of the synod in Trullo, at which they were used to assert the apostolic origins of several decrees.[71] In defence of the third canon, against the ordination of digamists, the Trullan decree cited canons 17 and 18 of the Apostolic Canons, which had excluded from orders those who, once baptised, had entered into second marriages or who had maintained a concubine, and laid down the qualities demanded of the wife of a bishop. In denying higher clergy the liberty to marry after ordination (Trullo can. 6), canon 26 of the Apostolic Canon was used to justify the limiting of marriage to those in lower orders.

The sixth of the Apostolic Canons was to prove more complex in its interpretation, and acquired a significance not only in the Greek church, but also in the debates over clerical marriage between East and West in the eleventh century. The canon addressed the issue of cohabitation of married clergy and their spouses, and instructed 'let no bishop, priest, or deacon send his spouse away under pretext of piety; if he does so let him be excommunicated, and if he persists, let him be deposed'.[72] Although the canon clearly required that the married clergy continue to live with their wives, there was no explicit instruction as to the use of marriage, and Cholij is quick to assert that the context of the Apostolic Canons leaves the matter in no doubt. The practice of the churches of Rome, Africa and Gaul at this time was of marital continence after ordination, and such an interpretation would be entirely in keeping with the sentiments expressed by Pope Leo in his letter to Rusticus, which criticised those clergy who dismissed their wives, and recommended that they should continue to live with them,

---

[70] Cochini, *Apostolic Origins*, pp. 309–10. Cochini notes that there are variations in the Latin rendering of the text in the early modern period, with at least one translation suggesting that it was indeed legitimate for married clergy to continue in the use of their marriage. This edition, published in 1672, however, he regards as inferior in its understanding and interpretation of the Greek.

[71] Cholij, *Clerical Celibacy*, p. 11; Cochini, *Apostolic Origins*, pp. 203ff; Joannou, *Discipline*, 1.2.121.

[72] Joannou, *Discipline*, 1.2.10.

but 'have them as if they had them not'.[73] However, a rather different interpretation was placed upon the sixth canon by the Fathers in Trullo, who argued that it not only threatened with excommunication any priest who dismissed his wife, but also anathematised anyone who attempted to deprive priests, bishops or deacons of 'cohabitation and conjugal relations with his lawful wife'. Such an assertion was, unsurprisingly, condemned in the mid-eleventh century by Cardinal Humbert in his exchange with Nicetas. Humbert attempted to break apart the association between the Apostolic Canons and the thirteenth canon of the council in Trullo, arguing that while the sixth Apostolic Canon was clear in its intention that married clergy should not put away their wives, their obligation was to provide food and other necessary items, but to abstain from carnal relations.[74] The attempt of the Trullan council to bestow an apostolic authority upon the decision to allow married clergy to use their marriages was roundly dismissed, and the fidelity of the West to the traditions of the apostles strongly articulated.

The assumption extrapolated from the Apostolic Canon by the Fathers at Trullo that the Latin church was guilty of separating married clergy from their wives was to become a critical part of the debate between pope and patriarch in the eleventh century. Nicetas, in his *Libellus Contra Latinos*, demanded of the church of Rome 'who is it that taught you to prohibit and dissolve the marriage of priests? Which of the Doctors of the Church taught you such depravity?' and fell back upon the authority of the Apostolic Canons to defend the tradition of the East. The Latin church, he alleged, dishonoured marriage by its insistence upon clerical celibacy, and imposed upon an unwilling or unable clergy an impossible discipline that simply opened the door to immorality.[75] The thirteenth canon of Trullo continued to be the primary authority cited in defence of Greek praxis, although it was, of course, not a canon which was accepted as authoritative in the West. The reply to Nicetas from Humbert alleged that the Greek church forced its clergy into marriage, and that celibacy was the solution to, not the cause of, clerical misconduct. The *Adversus Nicetam* portrayed the Greek church as a brothel, and for the first time articulated the link between clerical marriage and heresy, in accusing Nicetas and his church of Nicolaitism. There was no hint of any respect for the Trullan decrees and their claims to apostolicity.[76] However, the example of the Greek church continued to be marshalled in the defence of clerical marriage in the West. The married Archbishop of Spalato refused

---

[73] See p. 53 above and also Cholij, *Clerical Celibacy*, p. 99.
[74] PL 143.997d.
[75] PL 143.981ff.
[76] PL 143.996–1000.

to give up his wife, arguing, not entirely accurately, that such marriages were permitted in the Greek church, and Peter Damian was compelled to denounce the use of the canons of Trullo in defence of marriage in the Latin church on the basis that the decrees of the council had not been approved by the pope.[77] The practice of the East was raised at the Fourth Lateran Council, and again at the Council of Florence in 1439, but without any judgement being passed, and without debate. The example of the married clergy of the Greek church was to become critical again in the context of Reformation debates over clerical marriage and in the dialogues between the Tübingen Lutherans and the patriarch in the second half of the sixteenth century.[78] However, the foundations of the Greek discipline were also re-examined, and found wanting by more hostile writers. Caesar Baronius, in his history of the church, examined the thirteenth canon and the text from Carthage upon which it purported to be based, and argued that the Fathers in Trullo had been guilty of falsifying the evidence of the apostolic church to support their ill-conceived opinions.[79] The same period also witnessed a revival of papal interest in the practice of the East, with what Roman Cholij identifies as the first intervention by Rome in the discipline of Catholic priests in the Oriental churches, although the sixteenth century popes, and their successors clearly did not wish to be seen to innovate in their interventions in local rites when the question of clerical marriages arose.[80]

Commentators and canonists in both East and West were well aware of the geographical variations in the practice that prevailed. The canons at Trullo were at least in some respects a thinly veiled criticism of the celibacy legislation of the Latin church, and although the Trullan decrees were accorded neither approval nor authority in the West, the example of the Greek church continued to punctuate debates within Latin Christianity, and shape exchanges between the two churches in the centuries that followed. It is certainly worth noting that there was a good deal of common ground despite the controversial nature of the thirteenth canon of Trullo. Practice in East and West was to exclude from ordination any man who had been married more than once, and to demand that the wives of the clergy be women of suitable moral standing.[81] Neither church permitted marriage after ordination, and both demanded continence of bishops. The

---

[77] Barstow, *Married Priests*, p. 55, although noting the lack of concrete evidence on the Spalato story, which comes from Lea.

[78] See p. 174 below.

[79] Baronius, *Annales Ecclesiastici*, G.D. Mansi (ed.) (30 vols, Lucca, 1738–59), vol. I:499.

[80] Cholij, *Clerical Celibacy*, p. 168; for a fuller discussion, see pp. 224–5 below.

[81] The ruling that excludes digamists from higher orders was challenged in more modern times, and spawned a lively debate in *Gregorios o Palamas*, vols 2 and 3; *Ekklesiastikos Kyrex*

thirteenth Trullan canon did not in itself create a married priesthood in the East; there were clearly married clergy in both the Latin and Greek tradition, although it is evident that these married priests were expected to live in perpetual continence after ordination, in the West. As Cholij has demonstrated, the established practice in the Latin church by the seventh century was effectively summarised in the third, sixth and twelfth canons of the Council in Trullo. In these circumstances, in which continence was demanded after ordination and chastity was to be preserved, there was no question of the use of marriage or of entering into marriage after orders, because such unions would remain invalid on the simple basis of non-consummation. 'The principle of a celibate priesthood', Cholij asserts, is evident in the Trullan decrees, and throughout the Byzantine church in the prohibition of marriage after ordination, and also in the demand for temporary continence even from those married clergy who were able to continue in the use of their marriages after ordination in the aftermath of 692.[82] The point of fracture between East and West lay in the question of whether it was the law of perpetual continence that provided the true impediment to marriage after ordination. Where the Latin church saw the two as inextricably linked, and came to regard clerical celibacy as the best guarantor of clerical continence, in the East it was assumed that marriage provided the only such assurance, and therefore only married men were deemed suitable for entry into holy orders. Continence was demanded in both East and West, but was preserved by different means.

From this significant difference came the assumption that marriage was a necessary part of Christian priesthood in the East. There was nothing in the Trullan decrees that prevented the ordination of celibates, although the thirteenth canon appeared to anticipate that priests would be married. Such was the importance attached to marriage that Nicetas suggested that it would be appropriate for priests who were widowed to resign from their cure, and despite the apparent misconceptions upon which the argument was based, many clergy did retire to monasteries after the death of their wife.[83] From the twelfth century, married clergy, although permitted the use of their marriages, were required to practise temporary continence before service at the altar. It was assumed, however, that candidates for ordination would have taken wives, and even suggested that those who

---

vol. 8; *Ekklesiastikos Pharos*, Vol.1; *Ekklesiastike Aletheia*, vol. 33. For a fuller discussion of these debates, see Constantelos, 'Marriage and Celibacy', 37.

[82] Cholij, *Clerical Celibacy*, p. 2.

[83] PL 143.981; Cholij, *Clerical Celibacy*, pp. 138ff. The question of the remarriage of widowers has been debated more recently. For a survey of the twentieth-century arguments, see Constantelos, 'Marriage and Celibacy', 37.

were unmarried were 'not worthy to be a priest'.[84] Those with a preference for celibacy either took the monastic habit, or pursued a career as a monk in all but name in the Episcopal tribunal. Particularly in rural areas, clerical dynasties created by the ordination and appointment of the sons of priests (a practice condemned in the West) were almost expected, and by the early twentieth century the law prohibited the nomination of a celibate priest to a parochial curacy. The basis of the perpetual continence demanded of the Latin clergy was the daily nature of the service and prayer that they offered, particularly as the daily celebration of the eucharist became common practice. Such frequent liturgical celebration, combined with the obligation only to temporary abstinence in the East, was perhaps sustainable in urban parishes, but rather more problematic in areas served by a small number of priests, where either daily celebration was not possible, or the continence demanded of the priest was, to all intents and purposes, perpetual. Such practical problems are perhaps a manifestation of the same concerns that preoccupied the Latin church in the medieval period. The legacy of the apostolic church when it came to the celibacy of the clergy was sufficiently contested (and prized) that the disciplines of both East and West were claimed to be anchored in the traditions of the first centuries, but in the centuries that followed, the outworking of these claims took on a different form. The guiding principle, though, was not as divisive as its outward manifestation in the married ministry of the East and the celibate priesthood of the West might suggest. As Cholij concludes, even after Trullo, the discipline of the East held that where temporary continence was not practised, the exercise of the ministry was prohibited.[85] In the Latin West, the sacred function of the priest carried with it an obligation to celibacy; the perpetual nature of that sacred function demanded a perpetual continence if the sacraments of the church were to be celebrated. The married ministry of the Eastern church might appear to stand in stark contrast to perpetual continence of Latin priests, but the law which committed them to temporary continence was constructed on the same foundations as the celibacy obligation which bound the clergy of the Roman church.

---

[84] *Statutes of Gergios of Kiev*, quoted in Cholij, *Clerical Celibacy*, p. 134.
[85] Cholij, *Clerical Celibacy*, p. 202.

CHAPTER THREE

'A concubine or an unlawful woman': Celibacy, Marriage, and the Gregorian Reform

The practice of the apostolic church acquired an authoritative, if not normative, position in debates over clerical celibacy within the medieval church. Its legacy, however, was a complex one. In the centuries that followed, married men continued to service as priests, but against a backdrop of increasing efforts to regulate their conduct, and a more confident insistence on the part of popes, bishops and councils that the precedent of the Old Law and the demands of the New placed an obligation to purity, equated with continence, upon those who served at the altar. The records of the early church provided ammunition for what was at times an eristic dialogue between protagonists on both sides of the celibacy debate, but despite the centrality of 'apostolic precedent' in the literature, the picture that it provides is incomplete. The continence issue continued to confront the institutional and local church as it embraced its mission in the world; the development of the requirement to compulsory clerical celibacy remains 'one of the central problems of church history and a question of great controversy'.[1] Both those writers seeking to establish the continence demanded by the early church as the foundation for modern-day clerical celibacy, and those who argue for the entirely post-apostolic origins of the discipline, are compelled to look beyond the testimony of the patristic era to a period in the history of the church that each side recognises as a potential turning point in the development of the unmarried priesthood. Concerns over clerical continence did not disappear in the centuries that followed the attempts to regulate the conduct of priests at the council of Elvira and beyond, but the debate reached a new climax during the eleventh- and twelfth-centuries ecclesiastical reforms, and particularly in the pontificate of Hildebrand, Gregory VII.

From the perspective of subsequent writers on the history of clerical celibacy, the person of Gregory was to bestride the issue like a Colossus, but the roots of the debate were spread more widely and deeply. The purity

---

[1] M. Frassetto 'Introduction', in Frassetto (ed.), *Medieval Purity and Piety. Essays on Medieval Clerical Celibacy and Religious Reform* (New York and London, 1998), p. x.

of the clergy had certainly been an issue in the Carolingian church, and one recent commentator has identified clerical celibacy as a prominent feature of ninth-century religious thought.[2] Bishop Theodulf of Orleans, for example, argued that the perpetual ministry of the Christian priest demanded a permanent commitment to celibacy, for those who handle the 'immaculatam corpus et sanguine domini'.[3] Gone was the hereditary priesthood of the Levites, replaced by men from 'all peoples' who were called to baptism, and created not by procreation, but by imitation of the priesthood of Christ. The anointing of the hands of the priest was part of the liturgy of ordination, a symbol of sacrificial function, but also of the purity of those who would consecrate kings. Priestly celibacy was not simply a matter of ecclesiastical discipline, but of political import and social function.[4] Agnellus' ninth century *Pontifical Book of the Church of Ravenna*, composed in the context of Carolingian antipathy towards clerical marriage, examined examples of earlier married churchmen which appeared to stand in accordance with the 'husband of one wife' provision in I. Tim. 3:2. Although his *Vita* of the eighth-century married bishop Sergius had the potential to enhance the reputation of married priests in subsequent generations, at least one of the miracles recorded paid lip-service to the idea that the clerical wife occupied too much space in the church.[5] Beyond the Carolingian precedent, the origins of the 'Gregorian reform' have been located in the Cluniac monastic renewal that preceded it, and, conversely, in the challenges to conventional modes of morality raised by heterodox voices in the eleventh and twelfth centuries.[6]

The positioning of clerical celibacy at the centre of the reform movement owes much to the work of Vacandard and Fliche, who presented the first

---

[2] M. De Jong, 'Imitatio Morum. The Cloister and Clerical Purity in the Carolingian World', in Frassetto (ed.), *Purity and Piety*, pp. 49–80.

[3] Theodoulf, *Capitulare* II.8.4. in *Capitularia regum Francorum*, Alfred Boretius (ed.) (Hanover: Monumenta Germaniae Historica, 1883), Ep. I.170.

[4] J.L. Nelson, 'Kingship, Law and Liturgy in the Political Thought of Hincmar of Rheims', *English Historical Review*, 92 (1977): 241–79; P. Beaudette, 'In the World but not of it: Clerical Celibacy as a Symbol of the Medieval Church', in Frassetto (ed.) *Purity and Piety*, chapter 2; De Jong, 'Imitatio Morum'; A. Dresdner, *Kultur-und Sittengeschichte der Italienischen Geistlichkeit im 10 un 11 Jahrhundert* (Breslau, 1890).

[5] D. Elliott, 'The Priest's Wife. Female Erasure and the Gregorian Reform', in C.H. Berman (ed.), *Medieval Religion. New Approaches* (London and New York, 2005), pp. 123–56, especially 127ff.

[6] H.E.J. Cowdrey, *The Cluniacs and the Gregorian Reform* (Oxford, 1970); A. Fliche, *La Reforme Gregorienne* (3 vols, Paris, 1927–37); M. Lambert, *Medieval Heresy: Popular Movements from the Gregorian reform to the reformation* (Oxford, 1992); R.I. Moore, *The Origins of European Dissent* (Oxford, 1985); A. Dondaine, 'L'origine de le'heresie medievale', *Rivista di Storia della Chiesa in Italia* 6 (1952): 47–78; A. Borst, *Die Katharer* (Stuttgart, 1953).

detailed surveys of the attempts made to regulate the conduct of the clergy in the century between 1050 and 1150.[7] H.C. Lea's *History of Sacerdotal Celibacy* was typically untimid in its assertion that the law of celibacy was the most ambitious and damaging innovation on the part of the reforming popes. A 'blunder' driven through in the 'stormy pontificate' of Gregory VII, he argued, the destruction of the married priesthood was accomplished within half a century, as 'the sacrament of marriage [became] powerless in comparison with vows of religion'.[8] Such a focus upon the morality and conduct of the clergy as the driving force behind the papal programme is not without its critics. Gerd Tellenbach, for example, has suggested that celibacy was a secondary concern, while Norman Cantor's study of the English church dismissed the notion that the imposition of clerical celibacy might serve as a barometer for the impact of papal reform in the country.[9] And if the eleventh century did not mark the beginning of the controversy, neither did it mark the end. Debates over the celibacy of the clergy certainly did not come to a conclusion with the legislation enacted by Gregory; Filippo Liotta has charted a controversy that continued into the thirteenth century, while Anne Barstow, in the most substantial modern study of the Gregorian legislation and particularly its impact, focuses in much-needed detail upon the views of those who came to the defence of clerical marriage in the face of the reform.[10] However, the era of the 'Gregorian reform' has continued to occupy a central place in the history and historical narrative of clerical celibacy, whether through the character of the popes, the enactment of decrees regulating the conduct of the clergy, or the burgeoning polemical debate over marriage and celibacy. The figure of Gregory VII and his contemporaries loomed large in the controversies

---

[7] E.F. Vacandard, 'Les Origines du Celibat Ecclesiastique', *Etudes de Critique et d'Histoire Religieuse* (Paris, 1906); Fliche, *La reforme gregorienne*, pp. 1924–37; G. Tellenbach, *Libertas. Kirche und Weltordnung im Zeitalter des Investiturstreites* (Stuttgart, 1936); B. Verkamp, 'Cultic Purity and the Law of Celibacy', *Review for Religious*, 30 (1971): 199–217.

[8] H.C. Lea, *History of Sacerdotal Celibacy* (2 vols, London, 1907) vol. 1, pp. 242, 264–5.

[9] N.F. Cantor, *Church, Kingship and Lay Investiture in England 1089–1135* (Princeton, 1958); C.N.L. Brooke 'Gregorian Reform in Action: Clerical Marriage in England 1050–1200' and 'Married Men among the English Higher Clergy 1066–1100', both in *Cambridge Historical Journal*, 12.1 1–21 and 12.2 187–8 (1956), quoted in A.L. Barstow, *Married Priests and the Reforming Papacy, The Eleventh Century Debates* (Lewiston, NY: 1982), p. 10; J. Lynch, 'Marriage and Celibacy of the Clergy: The Discipline of the Western Church. An Historico-canonical synopsis', *The Jurist*, 32.1 and 32.2 (1972): 14–38 and 189–212.

[10] Filippo Liotta, *La Continenza dei chierici nel penserio canonistico classico da Graziano a Gregorio IX* (Milan, 1971); for a study of the families of the married clergy, see Bernard Schimmelpfennig, 'Zolibat und Lage der 'Priestersohne' vom 11 bis 14 Jahrhundert', *Historische Zeitschrift*, 27 (1978): 2–44; Barstow, *Married Priests*.

of the Reformation, and the rhetoric of eleventh-century literature and legislation entered into the vocabulary of subsequent generations.[11]

In his study of the foundations of the law of celibacy in the church, Edward Schillebeeckx conceded that 'the Latin church until the twelfth century allowed its clerics to be married but required them to practice complete continence. Because of this psychologically abnormal situation, the law of continence remained ... a dead letter'.[12] The requirement to continence laid down at successive councils and synods from the fourth century had reflected the weight attached to the symbolic value of celibacy, but the practical and ascetic concerns of the twelfth century turned this symbol into reality. Certainly, there was no overtly articulated obstacle to a priesthood of married men in the intervening centuries, and Schillebeeckx's comment that the law was a 'dead letter' carries some weight. The evidence is less than precise, but it still seems likely that many of clergy in the western church between the sixth and tenth centuries were married men, often in rural parishes and appointed by laymen who owned the land on which the church was built, and leading a life almost indistinguishable at first glance from that of their parishioners.[13] However, as the land of the church fell into private hands, concerns over the alienation of ecclesiastical property were articulated increasingly strongly, and married clergy were identified by many as the root of the problem. As early as the sixth century, Pope Pelagius had instructed that any married man appointed as bishop should promise that his children would not inherit the property of the church, but by the tenth century this law appeared to be honoured largely in the breach. Ratherius of Verona dedicated two lengthy treatises to the problems caused by married clergy, detailing his attempts to impose financial penalties upon those who refused to live apart from their wives, and bemoaning the apparently common practice of the marriage of priests to the daughters of other clergymen in order to maintain family control over church

---

[11] For the treatment of this period at the hands of early modern polemicists, see pp. 176–8.

[12] E. Schillebeeckx, *Clerical Celibacy Under Fire. A Critical Appraisal* (London and Sydney, 1968), p. 42; Charles Frazee suggests that the authorities were happy to ignore the actual state of affairs and conduct of married clergy: 'The origins of clerical celibacy in the western church', *Church History*, 57 (1988): 158.

[13] R.J. Bunnik, 'The Question of Married Priests', *Cross Currents*, XV.4 (Fall, 1965): 418; S. Bailey, *Sexual Relations in Christian Thought* (New York, 1959), p. 148; Barstow, *Married Priests*, p. 37; Frazee, 'Origins', 159; F. Kempf, *The Church in the Age of Feudalism*, suggests that it was all the more necessary for a priest to have a family in order to farm the land; Albert Dresdner makes the same point, but in relation to exploitative landowners who left the clergy impoverished without marriage and the additional income that it might bring: Dresdner, *Kultur-und Sittengeschichte*, pp. 149–57; M. Dortel-Claudot, 'Le Pretre et le marriage: evolution de la legislation canonique des origins au XII siècle', *L'Année Canonique*, 17 (1973): 319–44.

offices.[14] Long-standing dynasties of clerical and Episcopal families were particularly common where the authority of the institutional church was weakest, outside the urban centres.[15] The legal position of the children of priests, however, was ambiguous. Emperor Otto I instructed that the sons of clergymen were to be excluded from certain lay offices, and were to be deemed ineligible themselves for ordination, but when the council of Tours (925) considered an appeal from two priests, father and son, for the return of detained tithes, it granted the income to them and their successors in perpetuity, suggesting a legal recognition of their legitimacy.

Legitimacy and custom, however, did not confer respect or immunity from criticism. There were complaints in tenth-century England that the married clergy 'decorate their wives with what they should the altars' and that clerical wives were the 'snares of the devil'.[16] The eradication of the hereditary benefice was, Kemp suggests, a formidable task for those who sought to abolish the married priesthood and the 'associated evil' of ecclesiastical offices that passed from father to son.[17] Throughout the eleventh, twelfth and thirteenth centuries, for example, the church of Whalley in Lancashire was passed from generation to generation within the same family, and a similar situation prevailed in Hexham.[18] Kemp's study of the Herefordshire parish of Eye exposes a relationship between the local lordship and the hereditary benefice which seemed to persist well beyond the arrival of the continental reform movement in England;

---

[14] Frazee, 'Origins', 159; Lea, *Sacerdotal Celibacy*, p. 167; E. Martene, *Thesaurus Novus Anecdotorum* (Paris, 1717); Ratherius, *De Contemptu Canonum* [PL 136.491]; *De Nuptio Illicitu* [PL 136.567–74]. Clerical marriage was not the only issue that Ratherius addressed at such length; one reviewer of Peter Reid's modern edition of the *Complete Works of Rather of Verona* comments that Rather was 'not the only man to lose two bishoprics in the middle ages, but he was surely the most long-winded to do so' (T.F.X. Noble, *Speculum* (1994): 553).

[15] Frazee, 'Origins', 60; Schimmelpfennig, 'Ex Fornicatione Nati', 8–9; L. Wertheimer, 'Children of Disorder: Clerical Parentage, Illegitimacy, and Reform in the Middle Ages', *Journal of the History of Sexuality*, 15:3 (2006): 382–407; S.F. Wemple, *Women in Frankish Society: Marriage and the Cloister, 500 to 900* (Philadelphia, 1985), pp. 142–3. Orderic Vitalis reported that Hugh, archbishop of Rouen, left his see to his son, Robert, himself a married man with three sons [*Historia Ecclesiasticae*, A. Le Prevost (ed.) (5 vols, Paris, 1838–55), V.43]. There were more than a handful of married popes in the first millennium (some estimates range as high as 40), and of these at least two were the sons of previous occupants of the papal throne (Innocent I was the son of Anastasius I; Silverius the son of Hormisdas). W. Phipps, *Clerical Celibacy. The Heritage* (London and New York, 2004), p. 127.

[16] B. Thorpe, *Ancient Laws and Institutes of England* (2 vols, London, 1840), vol. II.329.

[17] B. Kemp, 'Hereditary benefices in the medieval English church: a Herefordshire example', *Bulletin of the Institute of Historical Research*, 43 (May 1970): 1–15 at p. 1.

[18] Kemp, 'Hereditary Benefices', 2; W.A. Hulton (ed.), *The Coucher Book of Whalley Abbey* (2 vols, Manchester: Chetham Society, 1847–9), vol. I, pp. 186–8, 277–8; J. Raine, *The Priory of Hexham* (2 vols, Surtees Society, 1864–5), vol. 1, pp. l–lxvii.

the benefice remained in the same family for more than a century, and was occupied by at least two married men who passed the living to their sons.[19] Repeated attempts were made to ensure the continence of married men who had been ordained to the ministry, but the efforts of the church in this regard were often met with indifference, with the result that the cohabitation of clergy with their wives was increasingly frowned upon. Beyond those legally married priests who continued to live with their wives, the church was also obliged to tackle the scandal caused by clergy maintaining concubines. Clerical concubinage was treated as a legal impediment to promotion, although at least one sixth-century pope felt compelled to relax such regulation in areas where insufficient candidates presented themselves for ordination.[20] St Boniface bemoaned the shame brought on the church by priests and deacons who kept multiple women yet still secured Episcopal office, and his correspondence with Pope Zachary revealed that the church continued to accept married ordinands and struggled to enforce continence upon ordained priests.[21] Clerical continence might have been presented as the tradition of the Apostolic era, and a requirement of the medieval church, but it was certainly not universally practised.

Against this backdrop, outspoken critics of the prevailing custom of clerical conduct made their voices heard, and positioned priestly continence at the forefront of their calls for reform in the church. As martyr saints gave way to confessors, spiritual and moral virtues such as chastity were increasingly prized, and imbued with a wider significance in the cosmic battle between flesh and spirit. Such ideas are associated most clearly with the revival of monasticism in the tenth century, and particularly the reinvigoration of Cluniac Benedictinism, and, unsurprisingly therefore, one of the most strident calls for reform came from Cluny's second abbot, Odo. Although written from a monastic perspective, Odo's major work, the *Collationes*, included a more general exhortation that was clearly intended to be heard beyond the walls of Cluny, and was perhaps informed by Odo's own secular background. His writings on clerical celibacy likewise reflected the monastic emphasis on the merits of chastity, but also the very practical considerations confronting the world outside the cloister. Two strands of thought coalesced in Odo's writing: the Augustinian equation of sex and

---

[19] Kemp, 'Hereditary Benefices', 4–11.

[20] J. Brundage, *Law, Sex and Christian Society in Medieval Europe* (Chicago and London, 1987), pp. 150–51; PL 72.727 (Letter of Pope Pelagius I, ascribed to Pelagius II).

[21] Boniface, Ep. 50 in *Epistolae Selecta: Die Briefe des heiligen Bonifatius und Lullus*, M. Tangl (ed.) (Hanover: Monumenta Germaniae Historia, 1916), pp. 82–5; Zachary, *Epistola* 51 in ibid., pp. 87–8.

sin, and the Cluniac devotion to the eucharist.[22] The sanctity of the altar, he argued, required a purity of mind from those who received the eucharist, and a physical purity, including sexual purity, from those priests who served. There was no question that the efficacy of the sacrament was impugned by the actions of an unchaste priest, but the sin of the priest, albeit one that might be hidden from the eyes of his congregation, would be known by God.[23] The ritual purity demanded of the priest was coupled explicitly to the holiness of the sacrament rather than implicitly to Levitical law, and those priests whose incontinence polluted the altar were warned that they would incur the wrath of God. Effective control of the sexual conduct of the clergy would come as much through the threat of divine anger as through the sanctions of the church.

The interplay between monastic chastity and clerical continence was to be felt beyond the walls of Cluny. The increasingly common practice of ordaining priests from within monastic communities tied the permanent vowed chastity of the monks more closely to the celebration of the sacraments, and exposed the contrast between married secular priests and chaste monastic clergy. As the influence of the monastic reform spread, so these contrasts and tensions became more acute, particularly where secular clerks found their position threatened by the ordained religious. The tenth-century English church provides a clear illustration of the potential for conflict. A synod held in Winchester in 964 determined that those ecclesiastical endowments that were in the possession of secular clerks should be transferred to monastics, precipitating the expulsion of secular, often married, clergy, begun in Winchester and later in Worcester. The Anglo Saxon Chronicle for 964 noted 'in this year King Edgar drove the priests in the city [Winchester] from the Old Minster and the New Minster, and from Chertsey and from Milton [Abbas] and replaced them with monks'.[24] Monks from the community in Abingdon arrived at Winchester and entered the church at the end of Mass on 21 February

---

[22] For the suggestion that Odo had been influenced by the views of Radbertus on the transformation of the Eucharistic elements, see P.G. Jestice, 'Why Celibacy? Odo of Cluny and the Development of a New Sexual Morality', in Frassetto (ed.), *Purity and Piety*, p. 104.

[23] Odo, *Collationes* [PL 133], II.11.558; 28.572. There was an ongoing debate surrounding the sacraments of priests in a state of sin; with its origins in the Donatist controversy, the most famous articulation of the view of the church came from Innocent III: 'Thus the wickedness of the priest does not nullify the effect of the sacrament, just as the sickness of a doctor does not destroy the power of his medicine. Although the "doing of the thing (opus operans)" may be unclean, nevertheless, the "thing which is done (opus operatum)" is always clean.'

[24] D. Whitelock, D.C. Douglas, S. Tucker (eds), *The Anglo Saxon Chronicle* (London, 1961).

964.[25] In the same year, Oswald reorganised the estates of his See, and in the preamble to the Oswaldslaw charter, the king, Edgar, offered clerks a stark choice between their prebends and their wives. The rhetoric was strident: the charter referred to the replacement of the 'degraded and lascivious' married clerks of Worcester by a monastic community, although whether the secular clergy were expelled or gradually replaced by religious is unclear.[26] Whatever the process, the steering issue was celibacy; it was not possible for the reformers to establish a monastic community which was made up in part of married priests, hence the requirement that those clerks who were married must choose between their office and their wife. The essence of monastic life, Deansley argues, lay in the renunciation of personal possession, even that which had come by hereditary right. There was, therefore, a clash of principle as reformed monasticism encountered a cathedral life in which it had become customary for a portion of the minster to be allocated to its fratres, many of whom then passed this to their children. Clerical prebends attracted not only accusations of abuse, but also more fundamental criticism from monastic reformers who questioned their canonical position.[27] However, it was not only prebendaries, but married priests more generally, who found themselves on the receiving end of such criticism. Aelfric's homily written for Archbishop William of York took as its theme the denunciation of clerical marriage, drawing upon biblical testimony and the example of the early church.[28] In the laws of Ethelred there was a financial as well as spiritual inducement to forswear marriage: 'he who will turn from marriage and observe celibacy shall obtain the favour of God and in addition as worldly honour shall enjoy the wergild and privileges of a thegn during his life and after his death', but such encouragement to celibacy provides eloquent testimony

---

[25] Only three of the Winchester clerks chose to leave their wives and remain in the community: for a fuller discussion, see John, E., 'St Oswald and the Tenth Century Reformation', in *Journal of Ecclesiastical History*, 9.2 (October 1958): 159–72.

[26] Eric John suggests that the clerks may have been married in accordance with the custom of the day rather than guilty of any breach of the continence law: *Orbis Britanniae and other Studies* (Leicester: Leicester University Press, 1966), p. 164. For differing views on the speed with which the clerks were removed from the cathedral, see A. Robinson, *St Oswald and the Church of Worcester* (London, 1919); M. Deansley, *The Pre-conquest Church in England* (London, 1963); D. Knowles, *Monastic Order in England: a history of its development from the times of St Dunstan to the Fourth Lateran Council, 940–1216* (Cambridge, 1949), p. 42.

[27] Deansley, *Pre-Conquest Church*, pp. 312–13.

[28] B. Thorpe (ed. and tr.), *The Homilies of the Anglo-Saxon Church. The First Part, Containing The Sermones Catholici, or Homilies of Ælfric. In the Original Anglo-Saxon, with an English Version* (2 vols, London, 1844, 1846).

to the continued presence of married clergy in parish churches.[29] Indeed, on the eve of the Gregorian reform, marriage remained the norm for a substantial proportion of parish clergy, and many married clergy of the Latin church were, to all intents and purposes, living with little heed to the law of continence that had been established in the fourth-century church.[30] Practical concerns surrounding the property of the church and the undesirability of hereditary benefices were to acquire an added impetus from a deeper understanding of the sacred nature of priestly function in the celebration of the eucharist, particularly in the thought of monastic proponents of asceticism and reform. The impact of the monastic reform movement also continued to be felt well into the eleventh century, as the monastic schools populated senior church offices with their products, and northern European monks occupied the papal throne in the middle decades of the century. Increasingly derogatory language was attached to married clergy and their wives by those who argued for a ministry that was pure and undefiled by sexual contact, but it was not until the eleventh century that the unfolding conflict between the sacraments of marriage and ministry was resolved in the creation of a celibate priesthood.

Although this period in the life of the church bears the name of Hildebrand, Gregory VII, the reform, and particularly the attack on clerical marriage, had its origins in the early years of the eleventh century. There was a clear awareness of the efforts of an earlier age to ensure that the higher clergy led a celibate life, but also a recognition of the potential for contradiction and interpretation of the law. Burchard of Worms' twenty-volume collection of canon law, for example, included a substantial section that detailed previous attempts to regulate the conduct of the clergy, including instructions that priests must cease all carnal relations, that clergy above the rank of subdeacon were not to marry, and that those who did not abide by these prohibitions were to be deprived of their offices. This was not only an age in which new legislation was directed against married clergy and their families, but one in which the full force of the decisions taken by earlier councils was to be felt.[31] The pontificate of Benedict VIII (1012–24) witnessed the increasingly harsh treatment of the children of married clergy, after the Synod of Pavia (1022) adopted a series of canons that ordered the deposition of all priests, deacons, subdeacons who continued to live with their wives or concubines, and all bishops who kept women near them. The children of the clergy were to be treated as serfs of the church. The imperial confirmation of the decisions at the Council denounced the unchastity of the clergy as the 'root of all evil'. In

---

[29] 5 Ethelred 9.1 cf. 6 Ethelred 5.2.
[30] Barstow, *Married Priests*, pp. 44–5.
[31] Burchard, *Decretum (Brocardus)* [PL 140] 1.5, 2.114, 148, 3.108–116.

an appeal to precedent, the opening address by the pope made reference to the Council of Nicaea, but the canons at Pavia went well beyond this in excluding all women from the houses of the clergy.[32] In Hamburg, bishop Libentius abruptly dispatched the wives of canons, although the impact of such draconian measures appeared to be simply to move the location of liaison between husband and wife outside the walls of the city.[33] The Council of Bourges (November 1031) enacted similar measures against clerical families. Priests, deacons and subdeacons were to refrain from taking wives and concubines, and those already married were to separate from their wives, or face the threat of degradation. The council instructed that no bishop was to ordain a candidate who did not promise to remain without a wife or concubine, children born to clergy after their ordination were to be barred from entering the ministry, and no man was to accept the daughter or wife of a priest as his wife.[34]

Although determined efforts were made to enforce the legislation on clerical continence, the direction of the assault on the married clergy was still shaped by essentially practical concerns expressed in the decisions reached at Pavia and Bourges. The focus upon the position of the children of priests, and particularly the determination to prevent the formation of clerical dynasties and the alienation of the land of the church, did not manifest the rhetoric of purity and sacerdotalism that was to characterise later attempts to regulate clerical conduct.[35] The middle decades of the eleventh century saw further attempts to impose a more stringent discipline on the clergy, often coupling the condemnation of clerical marriage with the denunciation of those churchmen guilty of simony. At the synod of Rheims (1049), for example, the pope demanded that those clergy who had purchased their office declare the offence, and warned in powerful terms of the dangers of both apostasy and incest embodied in simony and incontinence. Canons 8 and 11 have been read as evidence of a growing distaste for married clergy, and such negativity was expressly articulated

---

[32] *Constitutiones et acta publica imperatorum et regum inde ab a. DCCCCXI usque ad a. MCXCVII (911–1197)*, L. Weiland (ed.) (Hanover, 1893), no. 34 pp. 70–88; U-R. Blumenthal, 'Pope Gregory VII and the Prohibition of Nicolaitism', in Frassetto (ed.), *Purity and Piety*, p. 240.

[33] Synod of Pavia canons 1–4; Mansi, *Sacrum Conciliorum*, 19.353; Adam von Bremen, *Gesta Hammaburgensis ecclesiae pontificum* in *Scriptores Rerum Germanicarum in Usum Scholarum Separatim Editi*, B. Schmeidler (ed.) (Hanover: Monumenta Germaniae Historica, 1917), 2.61; Brundage, *Law, Sex and Christian Society*, p. 218.

[34] Mansi, *Sacrum Conciliorum*, 19.503–6 (canons 6, 8, 19, 20); Frazee 'Origins', 161; Barstow, *Married Priests*, p. 47.

[35] In this vein, Blumenthal suggests that the Pavia canons should not, for this reason, be regarded as a landmark in the history of clerical celibacy: 'Pope Gregory VII', 241.

at the Synod of Mainz and at the Easter synod of the same year.[36] In his narrative of the discussions at Mainz, Adam of Bremen noted that 'many things were decreed for the good of the church and above all simoniacal heresy and the evil of clerical marriage were forever condemned'. Both groups of offending clergy were declared anathema, in a statement that was indicative of the growing papal preoccupation with the problem. At a synod held in Rome at Easter 1049, Pope Leo IX repeated the prohibition against clerics in major orders engaging in sexual relations with their wives, but also took the more radical step of instructing the laity to abstain from the sacraments of priests and clerks who were guilty of fornication.[37] There was no assertion that the conduct of the priest impugned the efficacy of the sacrament, but such a call to lay action had the potential to be destructive. Two years later, at the Roman synod of 1051, the wives and the mistresses of the clergy were made *ancillae* of the Lateran, effectively reduced to the status of serfs. In the same year, writing to the cathedral canons at Lucca, the pope contrasted a life lived with community of property with the luxury and wastefulness of a married clergy.[38] The direction of reform was made abundantly clear.

The appointment of the reform-minded Pope Nicholas II initiated a further assault upon the married priesthood. A council of 113 bishops called to Rome in 1059 adopted a hostile stance, particularly with regard to those clergy who continued to maintain a wife or concubine, and to those guilty of simony, who were to be removed from office. However, its most radical decision was the repetition of the instructions of Leo IX that the laity should refuse the sacraments of married priests. Concubinary priests who officiated at Mass were to be subject to the penalty of excommunication, a ruling now for the first time established in the law of the universal church. Canon 3 demanded that the laity absent themselves from any Mass offered by a priest known to keep a concubine or to live improperly with a woman [*subintrodoctam mulierem*]. The encyclical letter sent out by Nicholas to disseminate the decrees of the council was a clear declaration of the constraints to be placed upon married priests:

---

[36] Frazee 'Origins', 162, quoting Anselm, *History of the Dedication of the Church of St Remigius* (PL 142.1417); Barstow, *Married Priests*, p. 53.

[37] Adam von Bremen, *Gesta Hammaburgensis*, pp. 346–7; Peter Damian, *Contra Intemperantes* [PL 145.409]; Barstow argues that the instructions to the laity appear to have remained dormant for a decade: *Married Priests*, p. 53.

[38] Ep. 55 [PL 143.671–2]; Bernold of Constance, *Chronicon* s.a.1049, in *Annales et chronica aevi Salici. Scriptores V*, Georg Waitz (ed.) (Hanover: Monumenta Germaniae Historia, 1844), p. 426.

let no one hear the mass of priest whom he knows with certainty to have a concubine or an unlawful woman. For this reason the holy synod has decreed the following under threat of excommunication, saying: whoever among priests, deacons, subdeacons, publicly married a concubine after the constitution regarding the chastity of the clergy which had been issued by the most holy pope Leo, our predecessor of blessed memory, or did not dismiss one he had married earlier, shall not sing mass, nor read the Gospels or the Epistles, as we declare and enjoin on behalf of the omnipotent God and on the authority of the blessed Apostles Peter and Paul, nor shall he remain in the choir room for the divine offices with those who were obedient to the aforementioned constitution; neither shall he obtain a benefice from the church until we have made a judicial decision regarding him, God willing.[39]

The council did not authorise the immediate deposition of all married priests; perhaps the potential disruption that would be caused by such large-scale clerical dispossession presented a weighty practical consideration.[40] Neither was the third canon vigorously enforced, and a determined effort was made to clarify that the validity of the sacrament offered by the guilty priest remained unaffected, in order to avoid the long-condemned Donatist stance on the relationship between the morality and office of the priest. Indeed, Pope Urban II was to argue that the purpose of such a prohibition was to provide an encouragement to better conduct among the clergy rather than to impugn the validity of the Mass offered by married priests. However, the apparent interchangeability of clerical wives and concubines in the terminology of the statement has been seen as the first formal papal denial of the validity of the marriages of priests, which had previously enjoyed a legal status in the eyes of the canonists.[41]

---

[39] P. Jaffe, *Regesta pontificum Romanorum ab condita ecclesia ad annum post Christum natum MCXCVIII* (2 vols, Leipzig, 1885–8) 4405/6. Blumenthal notes that the reference to the previous prohibition of clerical marriage by Leo IX is hard to pin down; no such legislation exists in the surviving records of Leo's councils, although there is a hint in Peter Damian's account of the reforms of Stephen IX that the pope recapitulated some of the determinations of Leo: 'Gregory VII', p. 243.

[40] See Blumenthal, 'Pope Gregory VII', p. 243 and Barstow, *Married Priests*, pp. 57ff.

[41] Roman Synod of 1059 c.3 in *Constitutiones et acta publica imperatorum* (MGH) vol. 1:547; Fliche, *La Reforme Gregorienne*, pp. 28–9; Cowdrey notes that the phrase 'subintroductae mulierem' had been used in the early church to refer to women who had lived with men in spiritual marriage, but that the terms of reference in 1059 were most likely to the council of Nicaea which had ordered that clerks were to live only with a mother, sister, aunt or other person who was above suspicion. Nicholas II's letter *Vigilantia Universalis Regiminis* was later reissued by Alexander II, probably after his Roman synod of 1063. See R. Schieffer, *Die Entstehung des papstlichen Investiturverbots fur den Deutschen Konig* (Stuttgart: MGH, 1981), pp. 208–25 especially cc.3–4; and discussed in H.E.J. Cowdrey, 'Pope Gregory VII and the Chastity of the Clergy', in Frassetto (ed.) *Purity and Piety*, pp. 270ff; for the attempt to counter accusations of Donatism, see for example Peter Damian

The extent to which the decisions taken at the Roman synod marked a departure from the traditions of the church has been disputed; clearly some of the deliberations of the bishops were informed by established practice, and earlier legislation. However, as Barstow indicates, there was clearly a strong contemporary reaction to the 1059 synod, which was perhaps indicative of a sense of change of speed if not direction. The decrees of the synod were controversial enough to prompt what Barstow describes as the first known literary defence of clerical marriage for 600 years, in which bishop Ulric of Imola set out the basis of opposition to the demands of the pope, and hostile reaction to attempts to enforce the reforms was evident on the Italian streets.[42]

Attempts to both define and act upon the legal status of married clergy in the church gathered pace with the accession of Gregory VII to the papal throne.[43] Prior to his election as pope by popular acclaim of the people of Rome, Gregory had been a motivating force in the reforming councils of the mid-eleventh century, and as pope was unsurprisingly quick to act against what he regarded as failings on the part of the clergy. Appointed archdeacon of the Roman church in 1058, Gregory played a critical role in the administration of the church and papal office, and he was to exercise a profound influence over the appointment and pontificate of Alexander II in the 1060s.[44] A series of Lenten Synods, attended by senior monastic

---

Opuscula 6 c.12 (PL 145.105–6). On the validity of the marriages of priests, see Brundage, *Law, Sex, and Christian Society*, p. 218. Brundage argues that the views of Nicholas II stood in stark contrast to the traditional attitudes of the church on the sacraments of married priests established at the Council of Gangra.

[42] 'Pseudo Udalrici Epistola de Continentia Clericorum', in *MGH LdL*, vol. I, pp. 254–60; Fliche, *Reforme Gregorienne* vol. 3, pp. 1–12; H.E.J. Cowdrey, 'The Papacy, the Patarenes and the Church of Milan', in *Transactions of the Royal Historical Society*, 5th series, 18 (1968): 25–48; E. Coleman, 'Representative Assemblies in Communal Italy', in P.S. Barnwell and M. Mostert (eds), *Political Assemblies in the Early Middle Ages* (Turnhout, 2003), pp. 193–210; A. Siegel, 'Italian Society and the Origins of Eleventh-Century Western Heresy', in M. Frassetto (ed.), *Heresy and the Persecuting Society in the Middle Ages: Essays on the Work of R.I. Moore* (Leiden, 2006), pp. 43–72.

[43] *Das Register Gregors VII (Gregorii VII Registrum)*, in *Epistolae Selecta* V, E. Caspar (ed.) (2 vols, Berlin: Monumenta Germaniae Historica, 1920, 1923). Although significant to the position of married clergy in the church, Gregory's concerns over clerical marriage were confined to a small portion of his pontificate between c.1073 and 1076, when his dispute with the emperor Henry IV proved time consuming and ultimately costly.

[44] For recent studies of Gregory VII, see H.E.J. Cowdrey, *Pope Gregory VII, 1073–1085* (Oxford, 1988); H.E.J. Cowdrey (ed.), *The Register of Pope Gregory VII, 1073–1085: An English Translation* (Oxford, 2002); I.S. Robinson (ed.), *The Papal Reform of the Eleventh Century: Lives of Pope Leo IX and Pope Gregory VII* (Manchester, 2004); I.S. Robinson, *The Papacy, 1073–1198: Continuity and Innovation* (Cambridge University Press, 1990); Eamon Duffy, *Saints & Sinners: A History of the Popes* (New Haven, Conn., 1997); C. Morris, *The Papal Monarchy: The Western Church from 1050 to 1250* (Oxford, 1991); U-R. Blumenthal,

as well as episcopal representatives, was charged with the more forceful implementation of ecclesiastical reform. The first such synod, in its eleventh canon, instructed that no married priest was to officiate at the eucharist, citing the Council of Nicaea as evidence that this was reform rather than innovation.[45] The two-pronged focus of the attack, on married clergy and simoniacal clergy, continued when, in the following year, legislation was enacted to depose all clergy who were guilty of simony.[46] Writing to Archbishop Siegfried of Mainz after the synod of February 1075, Gregory denounced those clergy who had acquired their office through simony, and the married priests, declaring 'those guilty of the crime of fornication should not celebrate masses or serve at the altar in lesser orders'. The pope called upon the laity to support efforts to enforce the decrees, instructing that 'the faithful should in no way receive the ministrations [of married priests], so that whosoever is not corrected for the love of God and the dignity of their office might come to his senses by the shame of the world and the reproach of the faithful'.[47] Action against married clergy was couched in terms of the enactment of the wishes of 'the holy fathers' and Gregory's predecessors in Rome, with no suggestion that the demands of the pope were in any way innovative. The ongoing reluctance to distinguish between clerical marriage and clerical fornication is apparent in both this letter and the epistle addressed to Werner of Magdeburg in the same year,

---

The Investiture Controversy: Church and Monarchy from the Ninth to the Twelfth Century (Philadelphia, 1988); K. Cushing, *Papacy and Law in the Gregorian Revolution*, Oxford Historical Monographs (New York, 1998).

[45] The only account of the 1074 synod comes from a German chronicler, Marianus Scotus, *Chronicon c.1096 (1074)* in *Annales et chronica aevi Salici. Scriptores V*, G. Pertz (ed.) (Hanover, 1844), p. 560; Mansi, *Sacrum Conciliorum*, 20.413–5; Brundage *Law, Sex, and Christian Society*, p. 219.

[46] Again, records of the synod are scarce, and the content of its deliberations is best viewed in the papal letters that followed. For a fuller discussion, see Cowdrey, 'Gregory VII', pp. 275ff.

[47] sed nec illi qui in crimine fornicationis iacent missas celebrare aut secundum inferiors ordines ministrare altare debeant. Statuimus etiam ut si ipsi contempores fuerint nostrarum immo sanctorum partum constitutionum, populus nullo modo eorum official recipiat, ut qui pro amore Dei et officii dignitate non corriguntur uerecundia saeculi et obiurgatione populi resipiscant'; Cowdrey, *Epistolae Vagantes*, Letter 6; the German bishops were to criticise the pope's attempts to use the laity to enforce laws against the married clergy, and Gregory did seem to move away from this controversial stance in later years: J. Gilchrist, 'The reception of pope Gregory VII into the Canon Law 1071–1141', *Zeitschrift der Savigny Stiftung fur Rechtsgeschichte, Kanonistische Abteilung*, 56 (1973): 35ff; Blumenthal, 'Pope Gregory VII', pp. 251ff; Lambert of Hersfeld, *Annales*, in *Annales et chronica aevi Salici. Scriptores V*, G. Pertz (ed.) (Hanover: MGH, 1844), p. 218; the attempts to discipline him are contained in the papal register of Gregory VII, *Das Register Gregors VII*, pp. 161–2 and 248–50.

which repeated the hope that the clergy would be corrected by 'verecundia saeculi et obiurgatione populi resipiscant'.[48]

However, the assertive tone of Gregory's decrees and the canons of the reforming synods did not ensure a positive response to local efforts to implement the laws against simony and nicolaitism. Resistance took various forms. Bishop Hubert of Therouanne went as far as to instruct his cathedral clergy to refuse baptism and burial to those who opposed clerical marriage, rather than obey the orders of the pope.[49] Gregory entered into an increasingly intemperate epistolary exchange with Bishop Otto of Constance, whose own attempts to promulgate the papal decrees had met with resounding failure, to the point where the bishop had simply continued to allow his diocesan clergy to take wives. Gregory regarded the bishop's attitude as one of 'unparalleled insolence', and criticised Otto for his failure to respect the wishes of the pope, the traditions of the fathers, and the commendations of Scripture. The faithful of Constance were, on the grounds of their bishop's rebellion 'against God and the Apostolic See', absolved from all duties of obedience and fealty. If laymen who were guilty of fornication were to be excluded from the altar, the pope protested, 'how can a man be a dispenser or a minister of the holy sacraments when he can on no account even be a partaker of them?'[50] In a letter addressed to the German laity and clergy in late 1075, Gregory professed to be aware of the actions of certain bishops who 'condone, or fail to take due notice of, the keeping of women by priests, deacons and subdeacons' and instructed that the laity were to withdraw obedience from these bishops on the basis that scripture threatened equal punishment of those of committed evil and those who tolerated their so doing.[51] The pope turned to the secular arm for assurance that action would be taken against the married clergy of the Empire, writing to Rudolph of Swabia and Welf of Bavaria permitting them to use necessary force to remove offending clergy from the altar.[52] As Cowdrey notes, Gregory's excommunication and deposition of the emperor brought an abrupt end to his attempts to enforce celibacy upon the imperial

---

[48] Cowdrey, *Epistolae Vagantes*, letter 7. Further attempts were made to enforce the decrees in instructions to the Archbishop of Cologne, Anno (*Das Registers Gregors VII*, pp. 223–4), and the pope's letter to Bishop Burchard of Halberstadt (ibid., pp. 221–2). Cowdrey notes that there is some uncertainty over the date of this letter and others sent to the German bishops, and whether they were written in the aftermath of the 1074 or 1075 synods. See, Fliche, *La Reforme Gregorienne*, vol. II, p. 136; Lambert of Hersfeld *Ann* c.1074, pp. 256–8; Berthold, *Ann a.1075*, p. 277.

[49] Cowdrey, *Epistolae Vagantes*, letter 41.

[50] Cowdrey, *Epistolae Vagantes*, letters 8, 9 and 10, citing the laws of Leo I and Gregory the Great, as well as I Cor. 5:11; see also *De Damnatio Scismaticorum*, in *MGH LdL*, vol. 2, p. 45.

[51] Cowdrey, *Epistolae Vagantes*, letter 11.

[52] *Das Registers Gregors VII*, pp. 182–5.

clergy by impressing its necessity upon his correspondents. Clerical continence and celibacy, however, remained on the ecclesiastical agenda. The Council of Constance (1077) repeated the condemnations of simony and nicolaitism, and urged that the laity refuse the ministrations of incontinent priests. Bishop Altmann of Passau, papal vicar and sympathetic to the reforming ambitions of Gregory, laboured strenuously, and against a good deal of local opposition, to impose chastity upon the clergy of his diocese.[53]

The rather abrupt end to Gregory's interventions in the moral conduct of the German clergy coincided with the invigoration of his admonitions to French bishops and laymen on the subject of clerical marriage. In a letter addressed to Countess Adela of Flanders and her son Robert in November 1076, Gregory responded to questions about the position of clerks suspected of fornication by insisting that such individuals should not be permitted to celebrate Mass, and repeated his assertion that it was an obligation incumbent upon the secular arm to ensure that the law was diligently enforced.[54] The following year, the pope urged the bishop of Paris to ensure that incontinent priests were excluded from the ministry of the altar, and to admonish the laity to absent themselves from the ministrations of such clergy. Again, the assumption was not that the validity of the sacrament was undermined by the actions or character of the priest, but rather that the castigations of the laity might coerce the clergy into better conduct. The married clergy were less than receptive to the reform, however, and it appeared that a proponent of clerical celibacy had been burned alive by the clergy of Cambrai who were unwilling to heed his exhortations.[55] In 1079, the pope addressed letters to the faithful of Germany and Italy, and once more reminded them to refuse the offices of 'priests, deacons and subdeacons who are guilt of the crime of fornication ... for a blessing is made a curse and their prayer a sin, as the Lord testifies'.[56] The vigour of these attempts to enforce chastity upon the clergy was a hallmark of Gregory's pontificate, but the content of the reforms enacted in the 1070s was still clearly rooted in the actions of his predecessors. Earlier popes had struggled to regulate clerical conduct, and the level of opposition and debate over the issue after 1075 suggests that the issue was not resolved, but rather increasingly polemicised, by Gregory's campaign. This is not

---

[53] Cowdrey, 'Gregory VII', pp. 278–9; Berthold, *Annales* 1077, pp. 293–4; *Vita Altmanni Episcopi Pataviensis*, in *Historiae aevi Salici.Scriptores XII*, W. Wattenback (ed.) (Hanover, 1856), pp. 226–43 details the bishop's flight from his cathedral on St Stephen's day 1075 after he preached in defence of the papal reforms; see also Anon *Vita S. Altmanni* [PL 148.878] quoted in Barstow, *Married Priests*, p. 69.

[54] *Das Registers Gregors VII*, pp. 309–11.

[55] *Das Registers Gregors VII*, pp. 328–9; Schimpelpfenning 'Ex Fornicatione', 11.

[56] Cowdrey, *Epistolae Vagantes*, pp. 84–5.

to downplay the influence of Gregory both in his own lifetime and in the debates over clerical celibacy and marriage in decades and centuries beyond. The articulation of the principles that underpinned clerical celibacy became increasingly confident in the Gregorian decrees, and the writings of those around the pope, and when subsequent generations turned to the medieval past in the search for the origins of the celibacy discipline, it was in the Hildebrandine reforms that they claimed to find them.[57] It was also in the controversy spawned by the Gregorian reforms that later writers were to find examples of opposition to clerical celibacy, evidence of the continued existence of a married ministry and, most particularly, medieval writers and chroniclers whose works lent support to the assertion that the history of the Catholic church could be used to condemn its practices and faith.[58]

Papal attempts to impose celibacy upon the clergy of the Western church continued after the pontificate of Gregory VII. The first canon of the council of Clermont in 1095 repeated the demand that any priest, deacon, or subdeacon who was married must refrain from the celebration of Mass. Recalcitrant clerics were to be deposed, and the sons of priests were to be barred from ordination, although were permitted to enter monastic orders. The decrees of the council were widely heard; those who assembled to hear the pope, Urban II, preach the First Crusade would also have heard this condemnation of married clergy.[59] Pope Calixtus II made further attempts to enforce the prohibitions on clerical marriage at the Council of Rheims in 1119, at which it was determined that all married clergy were to be expelled from their benefices, and threatened with the penalty of excommunication if they did not separate from their wives.[60] However, even these very public demands that married clergy be excluded from the altar stopped short of asserting that their marriages were in any sense invalid. It was only with the decrees of the Lateran Council of 1123 that ordination to the higher ranks of the clergy was argued to present a diriment impediment to marriage. The council denied higher clergy permission to marry, removed legal status and protection from married priests, and prohibited clerical concubinage. The threat of excommunication was

---

[57] See pp. 177–8 below for Reformation representations of the period; see also the assertion of Innocent II in 1139 that the decrees of the second Lateran Council were anchored in the 'footsteps of our predecessors Gregory VII, Urban and Paschal': Cowdrey, 'Gregory VII', p. 291.

[58] H.L. Parish, *Monks, Miracles and Magic Reformation Representations of the Medieval Church* (London, 2005).

[59] Mansi, *Sacrum Conciliorum*, 20.817; Robert Somerville, *The Councils of Urban II* (Amsterdam, 1972), p. 144 (c.1–12); the council also repeated the decrees of the Synod of Melfi (canon 12) which deposed married clergy and the bishops who tolerated them: Mansi, *Sacrum Concilium*, 20.724. Barstow, *Married Priests*, p. 82.

[60] Mansi, *Sacrum Conciliorum*, 21.236 (canon 5).

lifted, but those clergy who had 'contracted marriage' were to be separated from their wives and 'led back to penitence'.[61] The decrees were enforced at local councils and synods, although with some variation, and repeated in the Lateran Council of 1139.[62] The marriage ties of the clergy were to be broken, those who did not leave their wives were to be removed from their cures, and the laity were ordered to refuse the sacraments of married or concubinary priests.[63] The decrees of 1123 did not suggest that holy orders invalidated previously contracted marriages, but this is clearly the sense of the subsequent legislation of 1139, and possibly even of the decrees of the earlier local council held at Pisa in 1135.[64] Married clergy were now confronted by the stigma of concubinage, and their children tainted with illegitimacy. After the labours of successive popes in the eleventh century, the real turning point in the history of clerical marriage had come in this period between 1123 and 1139. Despite the assertion by Innocent II that the Lateran Council was 'following in the footsteps of our predecessors Gregory VII, Urban [II], and Paschal [II]', by its close the church had 'transformed clerical marriage from a legally tolerated institution into a canonical crime'.[65]

Despite the confident tone of the reforming popes and councils, and the disciplinary sanctions imposed upon married priests, opposition to the decrees on clerical marriage continued to be voiced throughout the eleventh century and beyond. The enforcement of the papal reforms in the dioceses and provinces met with both passive resistance and open dissent. At the council of Paris in 1074, abbot Walter of St-Martin de Pontoise attempted to argue, against the majority view of the assembly, that a duty of obedience to the pope must override their assertion that the limitations on clerical conduct proposed were unreasonable. The hostile reception to this exhortation led to the removal of the abbot to the king's palace for his own safety. The abbot was not alone; Archbishop John of Rouen

---

[61] Brundage, *Law, Sex, and Christian Society*, p. 220; 1st Lateran Council 1123 canon 7, 21; *Conciliorum Oecumenicorum Decreta*, J. Alberigo, J. Dossetti, P. Joannou, C. Leonardi (eds) (Freiburg im Breisgau, 1962), pp. 167, 170, 191, 194 [although the decrees do not appear in all MSS]; Barstow, *Married Priests*, p. 100.

[62] Brundage, *Law, Sex, and Christian Society*, p. 221; see, for example, Westminster 1125 canon 13; Clermont 1130 canon 4; Rheims 1131 canon 4; Mansi, *Sacrum Conciliorum*, 21.438, 458.

[63] 2 Lateran 1139 canons 6–7; *Conciliorum Oecumenicorum Decreta*, p, 174.

[64] M. Boelens, *Die Klerikerehe in der Gesetzgebung der Kirche unter besonderer Berücksichtigung der Strafe* (Paderborn, 1968), p. 167; Mansi, *Sacrum Concilium*, 21.527–8; R. Somerville, 'The Council of Pisa 1135: A Re-examination of the Evidence of the Canons', *Speculum*, 45 (1970): 98–114.

[65] Brundage, *Law, Sex, and Christian Society*, p. 220; *Conciliorum Oecumenicorum Decreta*, p. 198.

was stoned by his clergy when he ordered them to leave their concubines, and several northern Italian bishops simply refused to publish the papal decrees because, they claimed, they feared for their lives.[66] Lambert of Hersfeld's picture of clerical life in eleventh-century German certainly diverged from the image of the chaste priest promoted by Gregory VII. The 'whole company' (tota factio) of the clergy stood in angry opposition to the attempted reforms, he wrote, and to the determination of the pope to compel priests to live in the manner of angels. Gregory was, in the eyes of the married clergy, a heretic, demanding of his priests a manner of life that stood in opposition to the biblical concession that those who were unable to contain should be permitted to marry. Confronted by the choice between their wives and their service, Lambert asserted, clergy were more committed to their marriages, and advised the pope that if he wished his churches to be served by angelic priests, he should call angels from heaven to fill vacant cures.[67]

French resistance to the imposition of clerical celibacy was equally vocal. Hugh of Die's attempts to use his legatine authority to enforce the decrees of the pope spawned a vigorous debate in Northern France.[68] A group of Cambrai clergy addressed a letter to the church of the province, articulating the need to defend the liberties of priests, including the freedom to marry. Those clerks who had not made a promise or vow of continence, it was argued, should be free to marry, in accordance with the scriptural principle that the bishop should be the 'husband of one wife' and the eventual decision taken against obligatory celibacy at the Council of Nicaea. As a result of the deliberations at the Roman synod of 1074, they argued, the sacraments and clergy were no longer esteemed by the laity, the sons of priest were treated harshly, and tradition and custom were undermined. In response, the clergy of Noyon wrote in favour of permitting the sons of priests to be ordained, although avoided any articulation of direct arguments in favour of clerical marriage. Citing the Council of Ancyra and its concession that deacons should be permitted to marry, the clergy argued that the offspring of married clergy were legitimate, and that even the sons of priests born of concubines were still acceptable candidates for ordination on the basis that the sins of the father are not borne by the son.[69] The Noyon group, it

---

[66] Cowdrey, 'Gregory VII', p. 287; Frazee, 'Origins', 165; Synod of Paris 1074 in Mansi, *Sacrum Conciliorum*, 20.437–38, 441–2; N. Grévy-Pons, *Célibat et nature: Une controverse médiévale. A propos d'un traité du début du XVe siècle* (Paris, 1975), p. 14; Brundage, *Law, Sex, and Christian Society*, p. 221.

[67] Lambert of Hersfeld, *Annals*, p. 218.

[68] *Camaracensium et Noviomensium Clericorum Epistolae*, in *MGH LdL*, vol. 3, pp. 573–8.

[69] The letter is printed in *Libelli de Lite*, vol. 3, pp. 576–7; Ezekiel 18:20.

has been noted, were perhaps more open to debate on the issue of reform, but the correspondence is certainly testimony to a simmering controversy surrounding the demands of the pope, and the use of not just biblical but also conciliar precedent to buttress arguments against Gregory's stance.[70]

The situation of the Anglo-Norman church was equally problematic. In 1076, Gregory VII provided King William with a summary of the scandalous life and career of one of his bishops, Juhel of Dol. The pope had already consecrated a new bishop to the See, and requested the assistance of the king in removing Juhel from his post. The former bishop, he alleged, was guilty of 'trampling on the decrees of the holy canons' and had obtained and occupied the See through the 'heresy of simony'. The bishop had also breached the law of celibacy, and had not been afraid to 'enter openly into marriage and to take a harlot rather than a wife, by whom he also begot children'.[71] Four years later, William confronted his bishops with the complaint that they had failed to enforce the decrees on celibacy, and criticised those who continued to collect a 'cullagium' from married priests who wished to remain with their wives. As Gregory had done, William appealed to the laity for support in the attempt to impose discipline on the clergy; clergy accused of concubinage were to be put on trial in a mixed court.[72] But the king had done little to assist the pope in the removal of Juhel, and confronted with the powerful clerical dynasties of the Anglo-Norman church might well have concluded that good relations with the ducal family presented greater advantages than a disciplined but disgruntled episcopate. William was not alone in recognising the enormity of the task. Lanfranc, Archbishop of Canterbury, feared that the enactment of the laws against the married clergy would leave the churches bereft of clergy, and those who dared to preach against clerical marriage in Normandy found themselves confronted by irate clergy wives determined to defend their position.[73]

In England, the campaign against the married clergy gathered pace in the first decades of the twelfth century. At the Council of London in 1102, Anselm insisted that married clergy relinquish their wives, and instructed that those who refused were to be deprived of all privileges, and prohibited from saying Mass. Chastity was demanded of all who presented themselves for ordination, and the sons of priests were not to be permitted to inherit their father's church.[74] Despite the earlier reforms of Lanfranc, there were

---

[70] *MGH LdL*, vol. 3, pp. 573–8. For further discussion, see Cowdrey, 'Gregory VII', p. 289 and Barstow, *Married Priests*, pp. 124ff.

[71] Cowdrey, *Epistolae Vagantes*, pp. 44–5.

[72] PL 20:556; Brooke, 'Clerical Marriage', 57; Barstow, *Married Priests*, p. 89.

[73] PL 172:1397.

[74] D. Wilkins (ed.), *Concilia Magnae Britanniae et Hiberniae, a synodo Verolamiensi, A.D. 446 ad Londinensem, A.D. 1717* (2 vols, London, 1737), vol. I. 382; Mansi, *Sacrum*

those, including the chronicler Henry of Huntingdon, who argued that Anselm's legislation marked a departure from the traditions of the church, and the archbishop certainly encountered resistance. A further council was held in 1108, at which Anselm made a concerted effort to regulate the contact between married clergy and their wives. Those priests who had chosen to continue in service in the church were permitted contact with their wives only in public places and before two witnesses, and those who had attempted to remain married and continue in holy orders were permitted a grace period of only eight days to reform their conduct. Clerics who did not amend their ways faced excommunication, the confiscation of their property, and the seizure of their wives as chattels of the church.[75] Sensing some material advantage, Henry I capitalised upon Anselm's absence to assert his right to the lands of any married priest who refused to separate from his wife. Anselm objected, but the king was not the only beneficiary of his exile; many of the married clergy who had been forced apart from their wives were reunited with them as the reform process stalled.[76] The decision of pope Celestine II to declare invalid all marriages contracted by clerks in higher orders was repeated in the English Councils of 1125, 1127 and 1129, and despite the scandalous story constructed around the papal legate, this rigorous legislative effort had some effect.[77] However, the labours of Anselm had not undermined the roots of the married priesthood. In his study of the impact of papal and local reforms upon the higher clergy, C.N.L. Brooke notes that of the 69 papal decretals of the twelfth and thirteenth centuries that referred to the celibacy of the clergy, some 44 related to England. As late as the second half of the twelfth century, when married bishops were an increasingly rare feature of the church, Pope Alexander III still felt compelled to denounce both the married clergy and the practice of hereditary benefices in the English church. In Wales, the bishoprics of St David's and Llandaff had strong dynastic ties, and in Durham at the beginning of the twelfth century the bishop, dean and treasurer were married men. It was only in 1231/4 that one of the most celebrated clerical dynasties in England came to an end with the death of Richard Junior, canon of St Paul's, after nearly a century of influence.[78] A century later, married clergy were the exception rather

---

Conciliorum, 20.1151 canons 5 and 6.

[75] Wilkins, *Concilia*, I.387–8, 410–11.

[76] Barstow, *Married Priests*, p. 93.

[77] Wilkins, *Concilia*, vol. I.408. 410, 411.

[78] Brooke, 'Clerical Marriage', 10; *Liber Landavensis: The text of the Book of Llan Dav*, J.G. Evans (ed.) (Oxford 1893), pp. 275ff; J. Raine, *The Priory of Hexham: its chroniclers, endowments, and annals* (Surtees Society, 1864), pp. l–lxvii.

than the rule; a successful outcome for the reformers, but a change that had been the best part of two centuries in the making.[79]

The attempts to reform the conduct of the clergy in this period have been described as a 'devastating social revolution' creating 'broken homes and personal tragedies' worthy of Hollywood.[80] At a practical level, reaction and opposition came in the form of passive resistance and outright refusal to conform, but the creation of a celibate priesthood was also a topic of vigorous and lengthy literary controversy. Papal and conciliar decisions were described, debated and disputed in letters, chronicles and open treatises, but also had their origins in contemporary writing on chastity, marriage, and the nature of the priesthood. The decrees and canons discussed above were to become the foundations for later debates over the origins of clerical celibacy, but the written debate that surrounded them was to provide subsequent generations with argument both for and against the reforms. The exchanges of the eleventh and twelfth centuries introduced a new vocabulary to the debate, and injected the issue with a new form of invective. The debate provides testimony to the existence of supporters and opponents of the reform programme, and an instructive illustration of the extent to which the question of clerical continence and celibacy was redefined in this period. Perhaps the most significant development in terms of the perception and definition of married clergy was the reference to clerical marriage as a form of heresy, 'nicolaitism'. Named after Nicholas the deacon of Antioch, who was, erroneously, identified as the founder of the heretical group mentioned in Revelation 2, nicolaitism became synonymous with fornication, and the label was applied to the married clergy for the first time in the eleventh century. Its general use is attributable primarily to the views of two men, Humbert, Cardinal Silva, and Peter Damian, in whose works the term was first and repeatedly used in this manner. Humbert had first used the vocabulary of heresy in his denunciation of the views of the monk Nicetas in 1053. The cardinal criticised the Eastern church for allowing marriage to higher clergy, and argued for a long-standing tradition of perpetual continence for those called to higher orders in the Latin church, on the basis that it was unseemly for a priest to allow his hands to touch first his wife and then the body of Christ.[81] In his examination of the compendium of heresies

---

[79] Brooke, 'Clerical Marriage', 5–7.

[80] Brooke, 'Clerical Marriage', 1; for a discussion of the date and the seeming disappearance of the wives of the clergy, see J. McNamara, 'The *herrenfrage*: The Restructuring of the Gender System, 1050–1150', in C. Lees (ed.), *Medieval Masculinities Regarding Men in the Middle Ages* (Minneapolis, 1994), pp. 3–29.

[81] See, for example, Humbert, *Adversus Nicetam* [PL 143.996–1000]; Humbert, *Responsio sive contradiction adversus Nicetae Pectorati libellum* [PL 143:983–1000], c.25–6

compiled by Epiphanius of Constantia, Humbert made the erroneous association with the deacon Nicholas that was to characterise writing, both official and unofficial, against married priests. His views on the nature of the ministry were to shape the third canon of the synod of 1059, with its insistence upon the necessity for priestly purity, and the conformity of the decrees on clerical celibacy with the traditions of the church. Most controversially, Humbert went as far as to suggest that the validity of the sacraments of an unchaste priest was impeded by his character, a charge rejected by most other reformers.[82]

Certainly Peter Damian, whose depiction of married clergy was determinedly derogatory, was careful to distance the defenders of clerical celibacy from the Donatist heresy. However, both clerical marriage, and the toleration of concubinage, were, in Damian's eyes, sinful. The consequences of the sin would be paid by the married priest, but the stain of sin fell upon the whole community. If, for example, a bishop were to lay hands on his flock that had been tainted by contact with a concubine, he defiled not only his own spirit but that of all whom he touched.[83] Consolation was to be found, however, in the fact that God continued to show his mercy and miracles through the hands of the unchaste.[84] Like Humbert, Damian adopted the term 'nicolaitan' to describe the violaters of ecclesiastical chastity. In a letter to Hildebrand in 1059, he wrote such clerks 'are called Nicolaites when they have intercourse with women ... obviously they become fornicators when they couple together in this foul commerce; they are rightly called Nicolaites when they defend their death-bringing plague as though by authority. A vice is turned into a heresy when it is confirmed by the defence of misguided teaching'. However, Peter Damian's most significant contribution to the debate was less the association of the defence of clerical marriage with heresy, and more the presentation of clerical celibacy as a necessary requirement for a priesthood whose purity must be beyond reproach.[85] Christ was born of

---

and 34; Cowdrey, 'Gregory VII', p. 270. For documents relating to the controversy between East and West in the 1050s, see Nicetas, *Libellus Contra Latinos* c.15–16 and the bull of excommunication in C. Will, *Acta et Scripta quae de controversiis ecclesiae Grecae at Latinae saeculo composite extant* (Paris, 1861), pp. 133–5; 153–4, and Leo IX's use of Humbert's reply in his own letter to Nicetas [PL 143:781–2].

[82] Elliott, 'Priest's Wife', p. 143; J. de Chasteigner, 'Le célibat sacerdotale dans les écrits de Saint Pierre Damien, *Doctor Communis*, 24 (1971): 169–83 and 261–77, especially 175–7.

[83] Ep. 61 in *Die Briefe des Petrus Damiani* in *Epistolae: Die Briefe der deutschen Kaiserzeit*, K. Reindel (ed.) (4 vols, Munich: MGH, 1983–9), vol. 2, pp. 214–16.

[84] Ep. 40 in *Briefe*, vol. 1, pp. 411–12.

[85] J. Gaudemet, 'Le célibat ecclésiastique. Le droit et la practique du XIe au XIIIe siècles', *Zeitschrift der Savigny Stiftung für Rechtsgeschichte, Kanonistisches Abteilung*, 68 (1982): 1–31.

a virgin, he argued, and therefore must not be made present on the altar by hands that were sullied by contact with a woman.[86] Married priests, Damian suggested, should be ashamed to approach the altar with unclean hands, because at that moment 'the sky is opened, the highest and lowest things rush together in one, and what sordid individual does not dread to hurl himself audaciously [into holy things]? Angelic powers assist with trembling, the divine power descends between the hands of those offering [the Mass], the gift of the holy spirit flows, and that pontiff, whom the angels adore, does not recede from the sacrifice of his body and blood [the host] and yet he [the married priest] whom the fire of hellish lust enflames, does not tremble to be present'.[87]

Damian's *Contra Intemperantes Clericos* presented the married clergy as a burden on the church. He dismissed the suggestion that St Paul's dictum 'let each man have his own wife' permitted the marriage of priests, complaining that if this text were to be universally applied it would be to the detriment of those who vowed a life of consecrated chastity. The daily liturgical functions of a priest required perpetual chastity, and Damian concluded that it would be better for those priests who could not live in continence to abandon their altars rather than cause offence by their actions.[88] Clerical wives laid themselves open to accusations of incest with their 'spiritual father' (also their husband) the priest.[89] The wives of the clergy, he argued, had no place in the work of the priest, clerical marriage was not an acceptable solution to the problems of running a household, and the women involved should not enjoy a legitimate position in society.[90] Clergy wives were 'screech owls, paramours and followers of Diana', 'the sword of souls and ... occasion of death ...', guilty of tearing apart their husbands from their ministry and turning them from Christ. Their actions not only brought their own souls into damnation, but also threatened the salvation of the faithful, because these women were unafraid to touch hands that had been anointed with oil, and opened the door by which the devil might possess the elect.[91] Such rhetoric appears mild in comparison with the vituperative language used in the *Liber Gomorrhianus*, which detailed the apparently all-encompassing sexual vices of the clergy.[92] Damian's

---

[86] PL 145.385 (*De Coelibatu Sacerdotum*), written for Nicholas II.
[87] Ep. 162, 'To the Archpriest Peter', in *Briefe*, vol. 4, p. 156; Elliott, 'Priest's Wife', p. 144.
[88] PL 145.393, 886–7.
[89] Ep. 31 in *Briefe*, vol. I, p. 299.
[90] Ep. 114 in *Briefe*, vol. 3, p. 299; Ep. 162 in *Briefe*, vol. 4, p. 154.
[91] Ep. 112 in *Briefe*, vol. 3, pp. 278–9; Barstow, *Married Priests*, pp. 60–61; Peter Damian, *Contra Intemperantes Clericos*, c.4, c.7 [PL 145:393–4, 410]; Ep. 5.13 [PL 144.359–72].
[92] Ep. 61 and 65 in *Briefe*, vol. 2, pp. 228–47; *Liber Gomorrhianus* [PL 145.159–90].

views were to resonate not only with the reforming popes, but also with more radically minded laymen. In Milan, the conflict over clerical marriage came to a head through the attitudes of the Patarene faction, whose first leader, Ariald of Carimate, had spoken openly against the immorality of the clergy in the 1050s, and acquired a new ally in the city in the form of a notary, Landulf. In their preaching, they denounced the married clergy and their wives, and in May 1057 entered the cathedral with a popular mob to expel the unworthy priests. Ariald demanded that married priests sign, on pain of death, a *phytacium de castitate servanda*. The sacraments of impure clergy were deemed to be without spiritual benefit, and the laity were instructed to refuse to attend their churches. Despite the efforts of the archbishop to have him condemned, Ariald appeared to find favour in Rome, and his return to Milan with papal support prompted further conflict with the married clergy. The atmosphere remained heated, and riots erupted when Damian and Anselm arrived in the city.[93]

The reform of clerical sexual conduct was in Damian's eyes, by necessity, a priority for the reform of the church, and at the most basic level, a question of the purity demanded of those who celebrated Mass. The language deployed by Damian and Humbert was to be repeated in a handful of papal letters and decrees, most obviously in Gregory VII's denunciation of clerical marriage as fornication. Reference to the married clergy as 'nicolaitans', and to clerical marriage as fornication, also crept into the writing of Gregory VII. His letter to the archbishop of Salzburg in November 1073 was the only expressly stated illustration of this association between clerical marriage and heresy in his pontificate, but the pope's wider vocabulary would appear to bear the influence of Damian and Humbert. In 1075 he urged the archbishop of Cologne to remove the married clergy from their cures, 'so that the service of an unspotted and pure family might be offered to the bride of Christ who knows no spot or wrinkle', and clerical marriage was referred to as fornication in a letter to the bishop of Paris.[94] It has been argued, however, that the impetus

---

[93] Arnulf of Milan, *Liber Gestorum Recentium*, in *Scriptores Germanicarum in usum scholarum separatim 67*, C. Zey (ed.) (4 vols, Hanover, 1994), especially 3.9 p. 177 and 3.10 pp. 1787–9; Bonizo of Sutri, *Liber ad Amicam* VI, in *LdL*, vol. I, p. 594; Cowdrey, 'The Papacy, the Patarenes and the Church of Milan', in *Transactions of the Royal Historical Society*, 5th series, 18 (1968): 25–48; C. Thouzellier, *Heresie et heretiques: Vaudois, Cathares, Patarines, Albigeois* (Rome, 1969).

[94] Damian, Ep. 5.13, *Opuscula*, XVII and XVIII [PL 144.358ff; 145.379–424]; Ep. 5. 4. 14–15 [PL 144.344ff]; letter 112 to AB Cunibert of Turin (Briefe, vol. 3, p. 286]; *Das register Gregors VII*, vol. I.30 p. 50; Damian, *De Caelibatu Sacerdotum* [PL 145.385–6]; *Contra Intemperantes Clericos* [PL 145.414]; Cowdrey, *Epistolae Vagantes*, no. 16, p. 44, discussed in Barstow, *Married Priests*, p. 69. See also Nicholas II's reference to the bishops of Gaul as nicolaitan heretics [Mansi, *Sacrum Conciliorum*, vol. 19.873]; Gaudemet, 'Le célibat

behind Gregory's actions against the married clergy did not come from concerns surrounding the purity of those who celebrated the sacraments alone. Gregory's rhetoric was laden with references to obedience and obligation, and the eradication of clerical incontinence, like the eradication of simony, was part of a more general attack on a base manner of life that undermined the reputation of the church. Disobedience to papal demands was a sin in itself, as the German bishops were repeatedly reminded, and as the laity were informed when they were instructed to take the reform of the clergy into their own hands. Celibacy was required of the priesthood by both church and its nature, and its enforcement was a duty of all who made up the body of Christ.[95] Despite Damian's ardent attempts to associate clerical marriage with heresy, the requirement to continence remained a matter of church discipline rather than doctrine. As such, it became an issue not only for controversialists, but also canonists, seeking to establish the ancient antecedents for the demands of the eleventh-century popes. Thus, Gratian's Decretum presented a range of materials that related to the enforcement of clerical celibacy, including the decrees of the Second Lateran Council, Gregory VII's condemnation of bishops who failed to enforce the rule, and the demands that the laity should boycott the services of married priests. Men who had been married, or indeed taken a concubine, prior to ordination, were still permitted to enter the priesthood, but only if the woman concerned had died or accepted a separation.[96] Gratian's method was to collect texts, *canones*, and expound their meaning and sense via summaries and *dicta*. Often the *canones* were contradictory, and Gratian accepted at face value the authenticity, or at least relevance, of some dubious sources, including for example the narrative of the intervention of Paphnutius at Nicaea.[97] As Roman Cholij has demonstrated, it was Gratian who provided the controversial 13th canon of the Council in Trullo with an apparent apostolic origin.[98] At the Council of Ancyra, in Gratian's interpretation, there was no obligation to continence imposed upon priests, and the early Latin tradition had, he suggested, permitted the use of marriage after ordination.[99] Celibacy was, however, an appropriate state of life for the priest, and one that created

---

ecclésiastique', pp. 1–31; Fliche, *La Reforme Gregorienne*, vol. I, p. 206–13; de Chasteigner, 'Le Celibat sacerdotal, 169–83; P. Palazzini, 'S. Pier Damiani e la polemica anticelibataria', *Divinitas*, 14 (1970): 127–33; J. Leclerq, 'S. Pierre Damian et les femmes', *Studia Monastica*, 15 (1973): 43–55.

[95] Cowdrey, 'Gregory VII', pp. 282ff.
[96] Gratian, *Decretum,* D.33 d.p.c.6 and 33.c–6–7; more generally D.26–34, 84.
[97] D.31 c.12.
[98] Cholij, *Clerical Celibacy*, pp. 63ff.
[99] D.31 ante c.1.

the necessary time and space for prayer.[100] Following Gratian, Rufinus asserted the acceptance of clerical marriage in the primitive church. In such an analysis, the impediment to marriage after ordination came not from the discipline of continence, but from the constructed notion of the 'votum' or 'votum adnexum', an obligation to chastity imposed by the discipline of the church at ordination. No vow of chastity was explicitly articulated by the ordinand, but, as Aquinas summarised, 'by the very fact of his receiving the order according to the rite of the western church, it is understood that he has taken it'.[101]

It was not the place of the decretists to debate the value of clerical celibacy, but rather to ensure that the law of the church was defined and enforced, although even in this respect there were some areas of obscurity. It was argued by some, including Aquinas, that there was an implicit vow at ordination, and that therefore observance of the continence discipline was required from admission to higher orders. For other commentators, the requirement to celibacy was simply a discipline of the church rather than an intrinsic feature of holy orders, especially given the practice of the Eastern church. There was a general consensus that men who had been married twice should be excluded from ordination, and that the sons of priests, as illegitimates, were not legally entitled to inherit the property of their parents. The position of concubinary priests was less clearly defined, and in some texts was believed to relate to the existence, or not, of 'marital affection' between the individuals concerned.[102] For some commentators, the celibacy issue was an issue of obedience. Echoing the views of Gregory VII, for example, Thomas of Chobham outlined the nature of opposition to the imposition of celibacy but concluded that even if continence were not intrinsic to holy orders, the fact that it was demanded by the discipline of the church carried with it a duty of obedience.[103] The association of Pope Lucius III with the case of a bigamous archbishop of Palermo offered an illustration of the problems that might be involved in imposing the ideal

---

[100] D.31 c.1.

[101] Aquinas, *Summa Theol*. Suppl. 53.3.

[102] I am here indebted to the excellent summary given in Brundage, *Law, Sex, and Christian Society*, pp. 316ff, citing Rolandus, and Huguccio. See also Stephen of Tournay, *Summa Stephani Tarnacensis*, V. Schulte (ed.) (Giessen, 1891). Caus xxviii q.1 (p. 233); H. Kalb, *Studien zur Summa Stephans von Tournai. Ein Beitrag zur kanonistischen Wissenschaftsgeschichte des späten 12. Jahrhunderts* (Innsbruck, 1983); for the later canonists, the best recent study is Liotta, *la Continenza*.

[103] Thomas of Chobham, *Summa* 7.2.16.1, quoted in Brundage, *Law, Sex and Christian Society*, pp. 401–2; for Chobham and other opponents of the celibacy law, see J.W. Baldwin, 'A campaign to reduce clerical celibacy at the turn of the twelfth and thirteenth centuries', in *Etudes d'histoire du droit canonique dediees a Gabriel Le Bras* (2 vols, Paris, 1965), vol. 2, pp. 1041–53.

of law upon the reality of clerical practice. In this instance, the issue was that of the dispensing power of the pope, and particularly Lucius' apparent dispensation that sanctioned appointment in a case of irregularity. The story is most likely apocryphal, but the Palermo 'case' was popular with the canonists, and serves as a demonstration of the difficulties in establishing with precision a narrative of the tradition and law of the church on marriage and ordination.[104] The 'precarious harmony between principle and practice'[105] in the work of the decretists was indicative of enduring disquiet and outright disobedience to the celibacy rule. The ongoing efforts of the local and universal church to implement the reforms, and to remove the scandal of clerical concubinage, reinforce this image, and the vibrant debate over the legality and practicality of clerical celibacy suggests that this was not an issue for the canonists alone.

References in the reforming councils of the eleventh and twelfth centuries to the decrees of past councils and the actions of previous popes had attempted to locate the foundations of clerical celibacy in the practices of the early church, and to construct a history of the discipline that presented the action against 'nicolaitan' clergy as an attempt to enforce a long-standing law of the church. The apostolic and patristic period became a battleground for controversialists on both sides of the debate, and one of the most enduring legends in the literature on the history of clerical celibacy was born as a result. One of the most outspoken denunciations of the Gregorian reform came in the form of the *Rescript or Epistle Concerning the Celibacy of the Clergy*, an influential treatise that was eventually condemned by Gregory VII in the Lenten Synod of 1079.[106] Circulating widely between 1074 and 1079, and frequently attributed to Bishop Ulric of Augsburg, it purported to present arguments in favour of clerical marriage addressed to Pope Nicholas.[107] The fictional nature of the attribution is here exposed; Ulric was indeed bishop of Augsburg, but in the tenth century, and there was no pope Nicholas whose pontificate overlapped with his episcopal career. It is more likely that the author was bishop Ulric of Imola. Both Barstow and Fliche concur in this identification, although the name of Ulric of Augsburg continued to be associated with the letter well into the early modern period.[108] The author of the *Rescript*

---

[104] S. Kuttner, 'Pope Lucius III and the Bigamous Archbishop of Palermo', in J.A. Watt, J.B. Morrall, F.X. Martin (eds), *Medieval Studies Presented to Aubrey Gwynn SJ* (Dublin, 1961) pp. 409–45.

[105] Brundage, *Law, Sex and Christian Society*, p. 404.

[106] Bernold, *Chronicon* a.1079, p. 436.

[107] *Pseudo-Udalrici Epistola de Continentia Clericorum*, in MGH LdL, vol. I:244–60.

[108] Barstow, *Married Priests*, p. 57, notes that the failure to mention the prohibition placed on married priests saying Mass might undermine this attribution; Fliche, *Reforme*

argued that while it was the duty of the pope to commend continence, he could not demand it of the clergy, since both scripture and tradition allowed the priest freedom to marry. The exhortation to chastity in Matthew's Gospel was intended only for a minority, and the lack of clear command elsewhere in the New Testament meant that there was no solid support for the prohibition of marriage to the clergy. Indeed, Paphnutius at the Council of Nicaea had reminded the church of the necessity of retaining this freedom to marry, and warned that to impose continence upon the clergy was to open the door to scandal and even greater sin.[109] The priests of the Old Testament had been married, he argued, and the authority of Scripture, including the Pauline recommendation that the bishop be the husband of one wife, was more powerful than the words of the Fathers in praise of virgnity.[110] Two sections of the *Rescript* argued from more contested evidence. Ulric suggested that the Apostolic Canons insisted that married priests and bishops must not separate from their wives, and also argued that Gregory the Great, far from being a supporter of clerical celibacy, had been persuaded of the necessity of clerical marriage by the discovery of the heads of some 6000 infants, presumably the children of priests, in the papal waters.[111]

The *Rescript* was clearly read and used widely, and Ulric appears to have been responsible for the introduction of the Paphnutius legend into the debates of the eleventh and twelfth centuries. In the mid-1060s, the story of Paphnutius' intervention at Nicaea and many of the other arguments contained in the *Rescript* were repeated in the anonymous *Tractatus Pro Clericorum Connubio*, although here supported by a more detailed discussion of the Council of Nicaea and its ruling on 'mulieres subintroductae', and a wider base in the conciliar sources, particularly those from the East.[112] A second version of the *Tractatus* was circulating in the mid-1070s, perhaps inspired by Gregory VII's Lenten Synods. Again, it was argued that the eleventh-century popes had been in error in attempting to impose obligatory celibacy, on the basis that chastity was a gift from God and not something that could be legislated or demanded by man. To do so was to lay the church open to the dangers of sin, as men who were unable to live in chastity were forced into illicit sexual encounters. The demand for celibacy was a demand for obedience to the discipline of the

---

Gregorienne, vol. 3, pp. 1–12; for the reformation uses of the letter see pp. 171–2 below.

[109] *Pseudo-Udalrici*, p. 256; for the origins of the Paphnutius legend, see chapter 2, pp. 67–70.

[110] *Pseudo-Udalrici*, pp. 255–6. For a discussion of the disputed biblical texts, see chapter 1 above.

[111] *Pseudo-Udalrici*, p. 257; Cholij, *Clerical Celibacy*; Cochini, *Apostolic Origins*.

[112] Fliche, *Reforme Gregorienne*, vol. 3, pp. 13–14; *MGH LdL*, vol. 3, pp. 591–5.

church, and it was argued that, in the absence of any scriptural mandate, the reformers could fall back only upon their own authority. The fact that clerical marriage was viewed in a positive light in the Greek church was, it was suggested, evidence enough that there was no prohibition of such unions in scripture.[113]

The defence of clerical marriage from history and scripture in Ulric's *Rescript* and its later continuations brought a vigorous response from Bernold of St Blasien, himself the son of a priest, and later canon of Constance.[114] Bernold was a staunch advocate of reform, and particularly the imposition of more rigorous clerical discipline, perhaps informed by his years in the reformed monastic community at St Blasien. His tract, *De Prohibenda Sacerdotum Incontinentia* (c.1075) took the form of a correspondence on the subject of clerical marriage with a priest named Alboin.[115] It has been described as the 'first historical retrospective on the origins of priestly celibacy', and in a series of six letters exemplified the principles of the debate over the biblical and apostolic foundations of the reforms of the eleventh century.[116] Soon after, in his *Apologeticus*, Bernold wrote in defence of the Gregorian decrees against simoniacs and incontinent clergy, and set out to demonstrate in some detail their biblical foundation.[117] Of particular importance throughout was the interpretation of the third canon of the council of Nicaea, which had ruled on the position of 'mulieres subintrodoctae'. Bernold argued that the legend of Paphnutius was incompatible with the third canon, and therefore unreliable. Alboin, in reply, sought to establish the historicity of the Paphnutius narrative by citing not only the Latin account of his intervention, presented by Cassiodorus, but also the description of the events offered by the Greek historian Sozomen. It was clear, he argued, that the church had permitted married men to enter the ministry in the past, and that the action taken against married clergy in the 1070s was not only an innovation, but one that ran contrary to the established laws of the church. Bernold's response was to argue that it was impossible that Cassiodorus, a Father of the church, had presented false information, and therefore the only conclusion could be that Sozomen's account, particularly in its apparent endorsement of clerical marriage, was flawed. Perhaps informed by this stance, the 1079

---

[113] Barstow, *Married Priests*, p. 119; E. Dummler 'Eine Streitschrift fur Priesterehe', *Sitzungberichte der koniglich-preussichen Akademie der Wissenschaften*, 21 (1902): 418–41.

[114] *Libelli Bernoldi Presbyteri Monachi*, in MGH LdL, 2.1–168; Cochini, *Apostolic Origins*; Cowdrey, 'Gregory VII', pp. 289–90.

[115] MGH LdL, 1:7–26.

[116] Cochini, *Apostolic Origins*, p. 18; Barstow, *Married Priests*, pp. 124–31.

[117] *Apologeticus super decreta contra simoniacos et incontinentes altaris ministros*, in MGH LdL, vol. 3.59–88.

Roman Synod did indeed condemn Sozomen's work, although Bernold had by this stage attempted to bring the debate over the Paphnutius legend to a close by suggesting that regardless of historical precedent, the clergy had a simple duty of obedience to the demands of the pope.

The association of clerical celibacy with the obligation to obedience to papal authority of course tied the celibacy debate to the broader conflict over papal power in the second half of the eleventh century. As Anne Barstow has argued, the response to the attack on clerical marriage and the legitimacy of the children of such unions was forceful, particularly where the issue was subsumed into a wider conflict between papal and imperial sympathisers. The monks of Lorsch, for example, intervened in defence of clerical marriage as part of a series of tracts disseminated in 1111 to commemorate the return of Henry V to Germany. They accused the papal party of demanding that which was not universally possible, and encouraging the laity to use violence against the married clergy.[118] As tensions between papacy and empire heightened, so the debate over clerical celibacy became more polarised and acrimonious. Wenric of Trier, commissioned to compile a list of the grievous errors of Gregory VII in the aftermath of the Synod of Brixen and the election of the anti-pope Clement III, alleged that the pope's actions had undermined the peace of the church. Gregory's condemnation of the emperor had threatened the stability of the church in Germany, and his ill-conceived attempt to enforce clerical celibacy was to the detriment of the authority of the prince. Innocent clergy and their families had been made scapegoats, Wenric claimed, and the implication, if not outright declaration, that the sacraments of the married clergy were invalid had brought division and distrust into the life of the church.[119] The demand that the laity refuse the sacraments of married priests was, as we have seen, not intended to call into question their validity, but this was a fine line to tread, and one that was perilously close to being crossed in the accounts of miracles disseminated by the papal party in the 1070s. Unchaste priests who celebrated Mass, for example, were reportedly stunned as the chalice was overturned by a sudden wind in the church, or as the consecrated bread vanished from their hands. Divine vengeance, Gregory's hagiographer suggested, struck down the wives of the clergy. In contrast, when Gregory had celebrated Mass in Nonantola,

---

[118] Barstow, *Married Priests*, pp. 132ff; see also the complaints of Sigebert of Gembloux in his *Apologia* that laity were seen to baptise their own children rather than employ the services of a married priest, and reportedly trampled underfoot the bread consecrated by married clergy.

[119] *Wenrici scolastici Treverensis Epistola sub Theoderici episcope Virdunensis Nomine Composita* in *LdL*, vol. 1, pp. 280–89; see also the accusations made against the pope at the Synod of Worms.

'a bright light from heaven lit up the consecrated liquid like fire and he was glorified like the ancient Fathers by this sign of divine acceptance'. [120] The miracles of the saintly pope stood in stark contrast to the dubious efficacy of the prayers of married priests.

A more historically grounded defence of the rights of married clergy was presented by the 'Norman Anonymous'.[121] The works attributed to him include a study of theocratic kingship, but also three that relate to clerical marriage, comprising a defence of such marriages, and two presentations of an examination of the rights of the sons of priests which included an unusual and rather opaque venture into the theology of predestination.[122] Although the content of the treatise on clerical marriage would not be out of place in the 1070s, the focus on the legitimacy of clerical children suggests, Barstow argues, that any serious assertion of the legality of clerical marriage had evaporated. The primary argument in the defence of clerical marriage was that the element of compulsion in the discipline of the church was not supported by scripture. The Anonymous argued that obligatory celibacy was the law of man and not of God, and that in these circumstances it was still better for those priests who could not live celibate to marry, 'melius est enim nubere quam uri' as counselled in Paul's Letter to the Corinthians. To prohibit marriage was an error, and ran contrary to the tenor of the decrees of the early church councils. In this respect the Anonymous was simply repeating the arguments of earlier writers, although without the focus on the ruling at Nicaea that had characterised much of the debate of the 1060s and 1070s. The influence of his writings is hard to assess; Brooke makes a compelling case for regarding the Anonymous as rather insignificant, given his quasi-heretical views on several issues that were unlikely to have gone unnoticed had he occupied an important office in the church. The charismatic nature of his writings, expressed in the first person, would support the hypothesis that his interests in clerical marriage were more than academic. He was, perhaps, a married priest, or the son of a priest himself. His apparent

---

[120] Paul of Benried, *Life of Gregory VII* c.117, c.116, c.7, in I. Robinson (ed.), *The Papal Reform of the Eleventh Century*.

[121] The writings of the Norman Anonymous are in *MGH LdL*, vol. 3, pp. 645ff. However it is worth noting, as Barstow does, that the Anonymous' assertion that anyone, layman or priest, might administer the sacraments, was a particularly radical statement. See Barstow, *Married Priests*, pp. 165ff, for a fuller discussion of the theology of the Anonymous.

[122] The works of the Anonymous have been well studied, although some doubt still exists over their date and provenance. See Barstow, *Married Priests*, pp. 157ff, Brooke, 'Clerical Marriage', 14ff; K. Pellens (ed.), *Die Texte des Normannischen Anonymus*, (Wiesbaden, 1966); N. Cantor, *Church, Kingship and Lay Investiture in England* (Princeton, 1958), pp. 174–97; G.H. Williams, *The Norman Anonymous of 1100 AD* (Cambridge Mass., 1951), pp. 88–127.

familiarity with English affairs suggests some experience on the other side of the Channel. However, as Brooke notes, despite the obvious continued existence of married clergy in England well beyond the eleventh-century reforms, there is little evidence of a burgeoning polemical debate on the topic, and there is nothing to imply that the Anonymous was writing as part of a controversy within the English church.

The most detailed commentary on the attempts to impose celibacy upon the English clergy comes from the *Historia Anglorum* of Henry of Huntingdon, compiled in the second decade of the twelfth century.[123] Henry had succeeded his father in the archdeaconry of Huntingdon, and perhaps for this reason was less than sympathetic to the increasingly determined efforts to undermine clerical marriage. For Henry, clerical celibacy was a novelty, and a disputed one, although his assertion that it was not until the twelfth century that clerical marriage was forbidden in England was either naive, or a reflection of the continued divergence between ideal and reality on this matter. In her study of the *Historia Anglorum* and the issue of clerical celibacy, Nancy Partner argues that the attempts to reform the English church in the tenth century were 'almost entirely inefficacious', with the result that Henry's implied ignorance of the law on clerical marriage may not have been entirely a fabrication. His deliberate references to the wives of clergy as 'uxor' rather than 'meretrice' might stem from this ignorance, or more likely a determination to represent clerical marriages as legal, given his own ancestry, and the fact that he had fathered at least one son.[124] Describing the events at the council of London in 1102, Henry described how the demand for a celibate priesthood 'seemed quite proper to some, but dangerous to others', who feared that it would force the clergy who could not contain into fornication. The implementation of the decrees of the Council was patchy at best, and Anselm was compelled to seek a dispensation from Paschal II to allow the sons of priests to be ordained 'on account of the conditions of the time'.[125] Clerical celibacy was discussed again at the council of London in 1125, which was attended by the papal legate John of Crema. Henry of Huntingdon's account of the council, and particularly the actions of the legate, were to become a staple of later works that argued for a tradition of clerical marriage in the English church, and attempted to associate clerical celibacy with debauchery and sin.[126] In the account contained in the *Historia Anglorum*, the legate was severe in his treatment of the married clergy, dismissive of their wives, and

---

[123] Henry of Huntingdon, *Historia Anglorum*, T. Arnold (ed.) (London, 1879).

[124] N. Partner, 'Henry of Huntingdon: Clerical Celibacy and the Writing of History', *Church History*, 42 (1973): 467–75, especially 468–9, 474.

[125] Wilkins, *Concilia*, vol. 1, p. 387.

[126] See chapter 5 below.

apparently motivated by the argument that it was sacrilege for a priest to make present the body of Christ with hands that had touched a woman. The polemical value of the council came from Henry's revelation that John of Crema had been apprehended after Vespers in the company of a prostitute.[127] This particular part of the history of celibacy in England was not mentioned in the chronicles, although there was clearly some suspicion surrounding the conduct of the legate.[128] If Henry did not invent the story, he at least capitalised upon it in order to tarnish the reputation of the council that enforced celibacy upon the English clergy.

John of Crema was a celebrated example, but the image of the priest who rushed from the altar to the bed of his concubine or wife continued to enjoy a literary popularity well beyond the early twelfth century. The *Apocalypse of Goliae*, attributed to Walter Map, included a reference to the payment of the 'cullagium' by priests who wished to maintain women.[129] In the early fourteenth century poem 'Handlyng Synne', Robert of Brunne described an 'amorous priest' who, once married, had steadfastly refused to leave his wife. His four sons became priests, but one was persuaded of the necessity of clerical celibacy when he witnessed the soul of his mother being carried away by demons, and took to preaching around the country against the evils of clerical wives.[130] Similar pictures of the eternal punishment of the concubines of clergy were painted in Ceasarius of Heisterbach's *Dialogus magnus visionum ac miraculorum*, again with accounts of the women pursued by demons.[131] Later in the century, the cast of Chaucer's *Canterbury Tales* included a married parson and his daughter, who had been married to the miller with a substantial dowry, and was expected to benefit substantially from the goods of the church.[132]

---

[127] *Historia Anglorum*, pp. 245–6.

[128] Partner, 'Henry of Huntingdon', 474; Brooke, 'Clerical Marriage', 19 n. 62. The story also features in Matthew Paris' (Ann 1125). In the 16th century, Baronius attempted to disprove the legend, which was still being used to criticise the implementation of clerical celibacy.

[129] Walter Map, *Apocalypse of Goliae*, in T. Wright (ed.), *The Latin Poems Commonly Attributed to Walter Mapes* (London, 1841), ll.170ff.

[130] Robert of Brunne, *Handlyng Synne*, J. Furnivall (ed.), *Early English Texts Society*, Old Series, 119 and 123 (1901 and 1903), II.7981ff; K. Greenspan, 'Lessons for the Priest, Lessons for the People: Robert Mannyng of Brunne's Audiences for Handlyng Synne', *Essays in Medieval Studies*, 21 (2004): 109–21.

[131] Caesarius of Heisterbach, *The Dialogue on Miracles*, translated by H. von E. Scott and C.C. Swinton Bland, with an introduction by G.G. Coulton (London, 1929), Dist 12.c.20.

[132] Geoffrey Chaucer, *The Canterbury Tales*, in G. Benson, C. Cannon (eds) *The Riverside Chaucer* (3rd edition, Oxford, 1988), 3942–86: 'the person of the toun, for she was faire, in purpose was to maken hire his haire, both of his catel and of his mesuage, and stranger he made it of hire marriage. His purpose was for to bestow hire hie Into som worthy blood of ancestrie.

Concubinary priests also featured in the Parson's Tale, and in *The Vision of Piers Plowman*.[133] Exploration of the theme of clerical concubinage was not confined to the written word. Medieval preachers included in their sermons *exempla* which detailed the fate of clerical wives and concubines pursued by hellish hounds at their death.[134] Such caricatures would only be resonant with their intended audience if either the reality or the fear of clerical marriage and concubinage were sufficiently firmly established in the clerical and lay mindset. By the mid-twelfth century, clerical marriages had been denounced in the strongest terms, but it is clear that even these strident declarations had not produced universal obedience. The extent to which the medieval church was forced to accommodate clerical concubinage has been the subject of much debate. Previously seen as a prime cause of lay antipathy towards the church, incontinent clergy have since been relegated to the sidelines of debate over the origins of the Reformation in England and Europe.[135] James Brundage concluded that the relationships between priests and their concubines were relatively stable and permanent, a form of quasi-mariage that was 'frequently and openly practiced' throughout the medieval period. Certainly, the repeated references to 'focaria' and 'fireside companions' in the ecclesiastical legislation of the later medieval period would suggest that these women had not been eradicated from the life of the church, even if the optimistic use of the term 'uxor' by Henry of Huntingdon was no longer used. [136] In the early thirteenth century, Pope Innocent III complained to the bishop of Norwich that there were priests in his diocese who still claimed an entitlement to their benefices despite marriage, and Pope Gregory IX addressed a strongly worded letter to the Archbishop of Drontheim demanding that he put an end to the public marriages of priests. In the mid-thirteenth century, the priests of Cordoba attempted to justify their position from ignorance of the law, claiming that they were unaware of any prohibition on concubinary priests performing sacramental functions.[137] In 1536, the Welsh clergy petitioned Thomas

---

For holy chirches good mote ben despended On holy chirches blood that is descended Therefore he wolde his holy-blood honoure, though that he holy chirche should devour'.

[133] Chaucer, *Parson's Tale*, ll. 897–9, *Vision*, ll.145ff.

[134] J.Y. Gregg (ed.), *Devils, Women and Jews. Reflections of the Other in Medieval Sermon Stories* (New York, 1997), W.14.

[135] See chapter four below.

[136] Brundage, *Law, Sex and Christian* Society, pp. 4–5; Phipps, *Celibacy*, p. 142; see for example Wilkins, *Concilia*, vol. I. 573, 590, 653, 672–3, 692, 705, vol. 2 36, 142, 169; Gaudemet, 'Le célibat ecclésiastique', 4–5.

[137] Innocent III, *Die Register Innocenz III. 6: 6. Pontifikatsjahr, 1203/1204, Texte und Indices*, O. Hageneder, J.C. Moore, and A. Sommerlechner (eds) with Christoph Egger and H. Weigl, (Graz, 1964–); E. Berger, *Les Registres d'Innocent IV* (4 vols, Paris 1884–1920) no. 1759; for the position of clergy wives and concubines in Spain, see M.A. Kelleher,'Like

Cromwell requesting that they be allowed to maintain their 'hearth companions' in accordance with tradition, and H.C. Lea concluded that clerical marriage had scarcely become obsolete in Wales before it was legalised once more in 1549.[138]

Even if the impact of the reforms of the eleventh and twelfth centuries was neither universally nor uniformly felt, the decrees of the popes and councils, and the debate that they spawned, exerted a profound influence over the understanding of the nature of the priesthood, the origins of clerical celibacy, and the history of clerical marriage in subsequent generations. If the 'sacralisation' of the priesthood has been seen to have its origins in the fourth century and tangible expression in the continence imposed upon the married clergy, it was an image that was to gain even greater force with the liturgical changes and disciplinary demands of the eleventh century. As the devotional life of the church came to focus more and more upon the eucharist, and particularly the presence of Christ in the consecrated elements, so the assertion that only those priests who were without stain should be permitted to approach the sacred acquired an added force. The image of an unchaste priest who handled the body of Christ was potent and disturbing. To assert the necessity of 'cultic purity' was to exalt both the image and the office of the priest; sacramental function set the priest apart from the laity, and his celibacy was both evidence and agent of that separation.[139] The language of liturgy and sacral function, and the lexicon of polemical debate, established the boundaries of controversy over clerical celibacy and marriage in the centuries that followed. Gregory VII loomed large on the horizon of early modern writing on the nature of the priesthood and the position of married priests, which imbued the period of 'Gregorian reform' with a significance not only in the history of clerical celibacy, but in the history and eschatology of the Christian church. The vigorous debate over clerical marriage in the era of the Reformation was to draw heavily upon the testimony provided by eleventh- and twelfth-century popes, churchmen, and critics, as the association between clerical celibacy, priestly authority, and eucharistic theology was examined, unravelled, and presented anew.

---

man and wife': Clerics Concubines in the Diocese of Barcelona', *Journal of Medieval History*, 28 (2002): 349–60; J.D. Thibodeaux, 'Man of the church or man of the village? Gender and Parish Clergy in Medieval Normandy', *Gender and History*, 18.2 (2006): 380–99.

[138] Lea, *Sacerdotal Celibacy*, vol. 1, p. 358; G. Williams, *The Welsh Church from Conquest to Reformation* (Fayetteville, 1993), pp. 341–5; C. James, 'Ban Wedy I Dynny: Medieval Welsh Law and Early Protestant Propaganda', *Cambrian Medieval Celtic Studies*, 27 (1994): 61–81, discussed in Parish, *Clerical Marriage*, p. 113.

[139] Bernard Verkamp suggests that the 'cultic purity' argument was the primary motive behind clerical celibacy until the mid-twentieth century: 'Cultic Purity and the Law of Celibacy'.

CHAPTER FOUR

'In marriage they will live more piously and honestly': Debating Clerical Celibacy in the Pre-Reformation Church

The pre-Reformation clergy, it has been suggested, 'often felt that although celibacy might require them not to marry, it did not oblige them to renounce sex'.[1] William Phipps' observation might, particularly in light of the apparent rehabilitation of the English clergy in the revisionist historiography of the Reformation, appear tongue in cheek, but the pre-Reformation clergy were not, in their totality, observing the spirit of the Gregorian reforms some four centuries on.[2] The precise role played by

---

[1] W. Phipps, *Clerical Celibacy, The Heritage* (London and New York, 2004), p. 142.

[2] For some of the more significant contributions to the debate, see W.W. MacDonald, 'Anticlericalism, Protestantism and the English Reformation', *Journal of Church & State*, 15 (1973): 21–32; H.J. Cohn, 'Anticlericalism in the German Peasants' War 1525', *Past and Present*, 83 (1979): 3–31; C. Haigh, 'Anticlericalism and the English Reformation', *History*, 68 (1983): 391–407; A.G. Dickens, 'The Shape of Anticlericalism and the English Reformation', in E. Kouri and T. Scott (eds) *Politics and Society in Reformation Europe* (1987); A.G. Dickens, The *English Reformation* (2nd edn, London, 1989); R.N. Swanson, 'Problems of the Priesthood in Pre-Reformation England', *English Historical Review*, 105 (1990): 845–69; P. Dykema and H. Oberman (eds) *Anticlericalism in Late Medieval and Early Modern Europe* (Leiden and New York, 1993); G. Dipple, *Antifraternalism and Anticlericalism in the German Reformation: Johann Eberlin von Gunzburg and the Campaign Against the Friars* (Aldershot, 1996); D.M. Loades, 'Anticlericalism in the Church of England before 1558: an "eating canker"?' in N. Aston and M. Cragoe (eds) *Anticlericalism in Britain c.1500–1914* (Stroud, 2000), pp. 1–17; E. Shagan, *Popular Politics and the English Reformation* (Cambridge, 2003); P. Marshall, 'Anticlericalism Revested? Expressions of Discontent in Early Tudor England', in C. Burgess and E. Duffy (eds), *The Parish in Late Medieval England: Proceedings of the 2002 Harlaxton Symposium* (Donington, 2006). Some debate over the 'masculinity' or 'third gender' of the late medieval clergy has been prompted by recent articles by R. Swanson, 'Angels Incarnate: Clergy and Masculinity from Gregorian Reform to Reformation', in D. Hadley (ed.), *Masculinity in Medieval Europe*, (London, 1999), pp. 160–77 and J. Thibodeaux, 'Man of the Church, or Man of the Village? Gender and the Parish Clergy in Medieval Normandy', *Gender and History*, 18.2 (2006): 380–99. See also P. Cullum, 'Clergy, Masculinity and Transgression in Late Medieval England', in Hadley (ed.), *Masculinity in Medieval Europe*, pp. 178–96, and M.C. Miller, 'Masculinity, Reform, and

clerical sexual conduct and the theoretically concomitant anticlericalism as 'causes of the Reformation' continues to be debated in books and term-papers, but it is clear that, whatever the precise conduct of the parish clergy in late medieval Europe, the issue of clerical celibacy was still contested and argued in writing and in action. The burgeoning weight of controversial literature devoted to the subject in the sixteenth century was at least in part a reflection of shifting theological sands, and of the wider doctrinal and pastoral debates which impacted upon the image of the celibate priest as well as its practical realisation. But the concerns of the reformers, both Catholic and Protestant, had their antecedents in the centuries before Luther and his contemporaries spilt their first ink. A closer study of the pre-Reformation church can provide a valuable context and texture to these Reformation debates, and evidence of the perceived position of the celibate priesthood in the life of the late medieval church.

The medieval Catholic church had, since the eleventh-century reforms, continued to uphold the value and necessity of clerical celibacy, and significant efforts were made by popes, councils, and bishops to ensure that the law of celibacy was obeyed, in order to maintain the unique status that the ordained priest enjoyed, to preserve the reputation of the church and her clergy, and to provide suitable ministers at the altar. However, individual cases of clerical misconduct, and in some cases more general failures to abide by the spirit and the letter of the law, are not difficult to find. The Council of Toledo (1302) in its second canon instructed that concubinary priests were to be deprived of the fruits of their benefices and suspended from office, and the Winchester Synod of 1308 was also motivated to act against clerical concubinage. Further attempts were made to regulate the conduct of the clergy at councils in Ravenna (1314) Toledo (1324), Florence (1346), Prague (1355) and Magdeburg (1370).[3] Part of the hagiographical reputation of Niccolo Bonafede, later papal administrator and bishop of Chiusi, rested upon his attempts to reform the conduct of the local clergy who openly maintained concubines and raised their children in the public eye.[4] Early in the sixteenth century, diocesan synods held in Leon and Seville (1512) lamented the lack of discipline in the church, and contained within their attempts to inculcate lay piety and improve clerical conduct was a condemnation of priests who either allowed their sons to

---

Clerical Culture: Narratives of Episcopal Holiness in the Gregorian Era', *Church History*, 72 (2003), pp. 25–52.

[3] A. Roskovány, *Coelibatus, et Breviarium: duo gravissima clericorum officia, e monumentis omnium seculorum demonstrate* (5 vols, Pest, 1861), vol. 2.1.6.

[4] Conte Monaldo Leopardi, *Vita di Niccolò Bonafede vescovo di Chiusi* (Pesaro, 1832), p. 18; H.C. Lea, *History of Sacerdotal Celibacy* (2 vols, London, 1907), vol. 2, p. 15. It is worth noting, however, that the despair felt by the saintly bishop when confronted by the failings of his flock was not an uncommon hagiographical topos.

assist at Mass, or officiated at the marriages of their own children.[5] Such children were most likely the fruit of unions which defied definition. The impact of the Gregorian reforms, it has been argued, was to replace the clerical wife with the clerical concubine, but such relationships were often tolerated by the local church and the women involved were accorded a recognised status.[6] Glanmor Williams' study of the Welsh church presents clerical concubinage or 'marriages' as a practice generally accepted by the faithful 'without demur', and at least three Welsh Tudor bishops were themselves the sons of priests.[7] Fifteenth century Irish friars encountered widely accepted clerical concubinage in the Gaelic church, and argued vociferously against the cultural and legal practices that lent it support.[8] The diocesan visitations undertaken by the thirteenth-century Archbishop of Rouen, Odo Rigaldus, exposed a number of cases of clerical concubinage, including some long-standing arrangements which were often regarded by the lay community as quasi-marriages. The situation appeared particularly acute in Normandy, where Jennifer Thibodeaux has shown that even after prosecution, many local clergy 'relapsed' and returned to their women. Indeed, any distinction between clerical marriage and clerical concubinage had vanished, not only in reality but also in ecclesiastical law, as the church emphasised the illicit nature of such unions and described such women not as wives but as concubines, focaria, solute, or pedisseca.[9] Whether such distinctions were significant or incidental in the eyes of parishioners is less clear. As Peter Marshall suggests, attempts to quantify the extent and the manner in which the pre-reformation clergy fell short of the celibate ideal can only be provisional, given the extent to which the visitation process depended upon the lay reporting of clerical misdemeanours.[10]

---

[5] S. Haliczer, *Sexuality in the Confessional. A Sacrament Profaned* (Oxford, 1995), p. 10; Lea, *Sacerdotal Celibacy*, vol. 2, p. 17; J.S. de Aguirre, *Collectio Maxima Conciliorum Omnium Hispaniae, et Novi Orbis* (6 vols, Rome, 1753–5), vol. 5 pp. 371–2 (1512 Can. 26 and 27).

[6] O. Chadwick, *The Early Reformation on the Continent*, in Henry and Owen Chadwick (eds), *The Oxford History of the Christian Church* (Oxford, 2001) p. 138; C. Haigh, *Reformation and Resistance in Tudor Lancashire* (Cambridge, 1975), p. 50.

[7] G. Williams, *The Welsh Church from Conquest to Reformation* (Lafayette, 1962) p. 342; F. Heal, *The Reformation in Britain and Ireland* (Oxford, 2003), p. 77.

[8] Heal, *Reformation*, p. 77.

[9] Thibodeaux, 'Man of the Church', 388; see also J. Gaudemet, 'Le Celibat Ecclesiastique. Le Droit et la Practique du XIe au XIIe siecle', *Zeitschrift der Savigny-Stiftung fur Rechtsgeschichte, Kanonistische Abteilung*, 68 (1982): 1–31 esp. 4–5; B. Schimmelpfennig, 'Ex Fornicatione Nati: Studies on the Position of Priests' Sons from the Twelfth to the Fourteenth Century', *Studies in Medieval and Renaissance History*, 2 (1980): 3–50, especially 32ff.

[10] P. Marshall, *The Catholic Priesthood and the English Reformation* (Oxford, 1994), p. 144.

Certainly, the small number of proceedings against incontinent clergy detailed in the visitation records of the English church would suggest that the majority were not guilty of the kind of conduct that was to characterise the presentation of the medieval clergy in the polemical literature of the Reformation. However, the reality of the problem cannot be entirely dismissed.[11] Of all the accusations levelled against the pre-Reformation clergy, it was sexual misconduct that most exercised the laity, and therefore featured most prominently in complaints.[12] The church continued to insist that the sons of priests were debarred from ordination, but the *Calendar of Papal Letters Relating to Great Britain and Ireland* shows that over five hundred dispensations were granted between 1447 and 1492, to remove the stigma of illegitimacy from clerical sons who wished to enter holy orders. Of these, however, only eight related to English cases; the problem in Scotland and Ireland was evidently more widespread.[13] Although there were complaints in the English Parliament in 1372 about similar practices on the part of church leaders, instances of institutional toleration of clerical concubinage for pecuniary gain were primarily a feature of the continental church. Of these, the most infamous was the enhancement of episcopal revenues by Bishop Hugo of Constance, who collected substantial fines from the priests of his diocese who maintained concubines and fathered children.[14] Erasmus was to argue that it would be better to allow the clergy to marry than to be confronted by the scandal of clerical concubinage, and to 'openly acknowledge the partners now held in infamy', if only the bishops were not so attracted by the rewards of the income from concubinage fees.[15] Even without the 'cullagium' controversy, the image of the concubinary priest was certainly familiar on both sides of the Channel. The Dominican preacher John Bromyard denounced the scandalous conduct of unchaste clergy, and John Gower presented a

---

[11] See, for example, C. Harper-Bill, 'A Late medieval visitation: The diocese of Norwich in 1499', in *Proceedings of the Suffolk Institute of Archaeology and History*, 34 (1977), p. 45; R.A. Houlbrooke, *Church Courts and the People During the English Reformation* (Oxford, 1979), pp. 178-9; M. Bowker, *Secular Clergy in the Diocese of Lincoln, 1485-1520* (Cambridge, 1968).

[12] Heal, *Reformation*, p. 76.

[13] P. Heath, *The English Parish Clergy on the Eve of the Reformation* (London, 1969), p. 107.

[14] H.G. Richardson, 'The Parish Clergy of the Thirteenth and Fourteenth Centuries', *TRHS*, 3rd series, 6 (1912): 89-128, especially 122; O. Vasella, *Reform und Reformation in der Schweiz* (Munster, 1965) 28-32; Phipps, *Clerical Celibacy*, p. 144.

[15] Erasmus, *A Right Fruitfull Epistle.... In Laud and Praise of Matrimony* (tr. Richard Taverner) (London, 1532/6), sig. C2; R. Bainton, *Erasmus of Rotterdam* (New York, 1969), pp. 49-50; E.J. Deveruex, *Renaissance English Translations of Erasmus: A Bibliography to 1700* (Toronto, 1983), p. 8.

caricature of the lecherous priest who circled his parish as a wolf circled the sheepfold, looking for women who might be seduced.[16] Complaints about clerical fornication and adultery were a staple of German lyric verse in the fourteenth and fifteenth centuries.[17] Such was the danger inherent in clerical liaisons with women, that Bernard of Pavia counselled a policy of distance and separation between priests and their female parishioners except where pastoral duty required otherwise, in order that that the reputation of the clergy be preserved.[18]

The imposition of clerical celibacy, and the disciplining of those parish priests who failed to abide by the law of the church, continued to preoccupy councils and reformers in the fifteenth century. In 1429, it was protested in the 23rd canon of the Council of Paris that "on account of the crime of concubinage, with which the multitudes of the clergy and monks are inflicted, the Church of God and the whole clergy are held in derision, abomination and dishonour among all nations; and that abominable crime has so prevailed in the House of God that Christians do not now consider mere fornication a mortal sin'. The behaviour of concubinary priests reflected poorly upon the clerical estate, and upon the church, but, it appeared, also presented a poor example to the faithful who might model their conduct upon that of their pastors. The 42nd and 43rd sessions of the Council of Constance (1414–35) engaged with the more general issue of ecclesiastical reform, and there was a purposeful denunciation of concubinage at the Council of Basle in 1435, which held over the guilty clergy the threat of deprivation and loss of title. Bishops who failed to

---

[16] J.A. Brundage, *Law, Sex and Christian Society in Medieval Europe* (Chicago and London, 1987), p. 536, quoting J. Gower, *Vox Clamantis*, in *The Complete Works of John Gower: Vol. 4, The Latin Works*, G.C. Macauley (ed.) (Oxford, 1902), lines 1624–5; see also lines 1515–24, 1597–1600, 1681–86; Bromyard, *Summa Praedicantium* s.v. *Luxuria*; G. Owst, *Literature and Pulpit. a neglected chapter in the history of English letters & of the English people* (Oxford, 1961), p. 260. See also Richardson, 'Parish Clergy', Appendix, quoting Gower's *Vox Clamantis* 'o si curates nati succedere possent Ecclesie titulo ferreque iura partum, Tunc sibi Romipetas, mortis quibus est aliene Spes, nihil aut modicum posse valere puto', and *Poem on the evil times of Edward II* 'and this ersedeknes that ben set to visite holie churche, Everich fondeth hu he may shrewedlichest worchse; he wole take mede of that on and that other, and late the parsoun have a wyf, and the prest another, at wille; coveytise shall stoppen here mouth and maken hem al stille'.

[17] See, for example, the works of Oswald von Wolkenstein (1377–1445) and Michel Beheim (mid fifteenth century) discussed in Albrecht Classen, 'Anticlericalism in Late Medieval German Verse', in P. Dykema and H. Oberman (eds), *Anticlericalism in Late Medieval and Early Modern Europe* (Brill: Leiden, London, and New York, 1993), pp. 91–114, especially pp. 97–107; for a study of the sexual misdemeanours and representations of the late medieval German clergy, see also H. Puff, 'Localising Sodomy: The "Priest and Sodomite" in pre-Reformation Germany and Switzerland', *Journal of the History of Sexuality*, 8 (1997): 165–95.

[18] Brundage, *Law, Sex and Christian Society*, p. 401.

act against clerical incontinence in their dioceses were deemed to share in the guilt of the offending priest, and the 'cullagium' paid by concubinary priests with the intention of avoiding prosecution was condemned. The decrees of the council were enacted in local synods and councils across Europe, leaving the clergy in no doubt as to the stance of the church and the course of action countenanced by the council.[19] However, the efficacy and impact of such disciplinary action is almost impossible to assess. The fact that the Basle decree was reiterated in the first of the reforming decrees of the 1549 Scottish Council testifies both to its authoritative nature, but also perhaps to the limited progress that had been made in the intervening century.[20] The York Convocation of 1518 cited a statute of Greenfield which instructed that women who lived as wives or *focaria* of priests were to be punished with excommunication, and that persistent offenders were to be handed over to the secular arm and denied burial in consecrated ground. As Peter Heath notes, even such an insistent re-statement of intent, some two centuries after the promulgation of the original statute, carried no guarantee of impact.[21]

Piecing together these pieces of evidence does not, in reality, present a clear picture of the scale of clerical incontinence on the eve of the Reformation. For every misdemeanour recorded by the courts, it is possible that there were either several others unreported, or as many clergy living a life grounded in the celibate ideal. Evidence of concern surrounding the moral conduct of the clergy provides a clearer window into the mindset of the commentator than it does into the private life of the priest. However, as Peter Marshall has argued, the fact that widespread concern about clerical conduct was without a solid empirical base did not diminish the intensity of the view that was held, either by the believer or by the critic.[22] If the labours of the Gregorian reformers had failed to eradicate entirely 'suspect women' from the houses of the clergy, their rhetoric had certainly established celibacy as a defining characteristic of the priesthood, which distinguished the priest from his congregation, and testified to his particular status as intercessor and minister at the altar. The moral integrity of the priest was a matter of both practical and soteriological importance, but as

---

[19] Brundage, *Law, Sex and Christian Society*, p. 537; Council of Basle session 20 (January 1435) in *Conciliorum Oecumenicorum Decreta*, J. Alberigo, J. Dossetti, P. Joannou, C. Leonardi (eds) (Freiburg im Breisgau: 1962), pp. 461–3; M. Boelens, 'Die Klerikerehe in der kirchlichen Gesetzgebung zwischen den Konizilien von Basel und Trient', *Archiv fur katholisches Kirchenrecht*, 138 (1969): 62ff.

[20] T. Winning, 'Church Councils in Sixteenth-Century Scotland', in D. McRoberts (ed.), *Essays on the Scottish Reformation* (Glasgow, 1962), p. 338.

[21] Heath, *Parish Clergy*, p. 107.

[22] Marshall, *Catholic Priesthood*, p. 145.

the ideal of the celibate priest was expounded in print and from the pulpit, the assertion of such extraordinary qualities had the potential to throw into relief the more ordinary nature of the clergy as a whole. The dependence of the faithful, in this world and the next, upon the intercessory and sacrificial actions of the priest, gave clerical celibacy a greater practical significance in parish life. The eucharistic sacrifice was offered not only to the people, but for the people, and anything that brought into doubt the efficacy of the propitiatory rite was liable to give rise to apprehension and antagonism.[23] Any attempt to separate the person from the office of the priest would require a degree of semantic precision that was not always communicated effectively, or within the grasp of the faithful. Even if anticlericalism on the eve of the Reformation was directed against individuals rather than the priestly caste, criticism of one priest might well become a challenge to the priesthood and its function. As Swanson suggests, 'the road to Donatism lay temptingly open, and was followed'.[24]

Despite the ongoing insistence by the church that there was no link between the moral character of the priest and the perfection of the sacrament, there was a correlation between the two which was clear in the minds of many laymen, and which was articulated in testamentary provisions for masses which specified that the celebrant should be an 'honest' priest. A precise definition of the characteristics, both personal and pastoral, required of a chantry priest, for example, was laid down in 1400 by John de Plumptre. Those engaged in service were not to frequent taverns and games, in order that they might present a better example to the faithful, and those who were unfit were to be removed from post.[25] Fuelled by the increasing devotional emphasis upon the moment of consecration, such concerns were difficult to dispel, and were at least in part encouraged by the denunciation in sermons and in writing of immoral priests who continued to handle the sacred elements. John Colet, in his statutes for the cathedral of St Paul's, insisted that it was 'fitting that those who approach so near to the altar of God, and are present at such great mysteries, should be wholly chaste and undefiled'.[26] The author of the *Doctrinal of Sapience* warned that the 'preste that lyueth in deadly synne, specialy in sinne of lecherie'

---

[23] H.L. Parish, *Clerical Marriage and the English Reformation* (Aldershot, 2000), p. 160; Swanson, 'Problems of the Priesthood', 849, talks of the 'idealisation of the priesthood in personal terms' in, for example the foundation charters of chantries.

[24] Swanson, 'Problems of the Priesthood', 859.

[25] Marshall, *Catholic Priesthood*, pp. 51–3, 161–2; Swanson 'Problems of the Priesthood', 849.

[26] J.H. Lupton, *Life of John Colet* (2nd edition, London, 1909), p. 135.

administered the sacraments under shadow of damnation.[27] The failure of the clergy to fulfil the promise of celibacy made at ordination was presented not as a danger to the faithful, but as an affront to God and as a periculous act for the priest and the salvation of his soul. To approach the body and blood of Christ with hands or mind rendered unclean by contact with women was to commit sacrilege and adultery. The sacraments, particularly the eucharist, it was argued, were so 'precyouse' that they should not be 'defyled' by those who lived in 'bestly concupiscence'.[28] The early sixteenth-century author of *Dives and Pauper* presented a dialogue on this subject, in which Pauper asserted that incontinent priests should be prevented from exercising their priestly function. Dives responded that just as a priest of good character could not improve upon the holiness of the sacraments, so a priest of poor moral standing would not diminish their efficacy.[29] Such a riposte was clearly in accordance with the doctrinal assumptions of the medieval church, although those instances, however rare, on which the faithful were encouraged to absent themselves from any Mass celebrated by unchaste clerics could only serve to deepen the suspicion that incontinence posed at least some impediment to sacramental efficacy.[30]

The value attached to clerical celibacy by the Catholic faithful had parallels in the defence of the continence discipline in sermons and treatises in the centuries before the Reformation. However, many of these advocates of clerical celibacy were contributing to a wider debate which had continued beyond the tone of presumed finality in the Gregorian pronouncements. The lively dialogue of the fourteenth and fifteenth centuries reflected changing political, cultural, and ecclesiastical circumstances, but the conceptual building blocks of the literature from both sides were hewn from earlier writing, and engaged with perennial questions about the origins and legitimacy of the celibacy discipline. As the relationship between Philip the Fair of France and Pope Boniface VIII brought a tempestuous tone to the controversy over concepts of papal authority and temporal sovereignty, both clerical celibacy and the conduct of priests and popes became part of the vocabulary of debate.[31] Strident

---

[27] *Doctrinal of Sapience*, J. Gallagher (ed.), *Middle English Texts* 26 (Heidelberg, 1993) p. 173.

[28] Dionysius the Carthusian, *The Lyfe of Prestes* (1533), sigs, C4v, C8r–v, D1r; H. Parker, *Dives and Pauper* (1536), p. 226r.

[29] Parker, *Dives and Pauper*, p. 224v.

[30] J. Thomson, *Early Tudor Church and Society 1485–1529* (London, 1993), p. 169.

[31] C.T. Wood, *Philip the Fair and Boniface VIII: State vs Papacy* (Huntingdon, NY, 1976); B. Tierney, *Crisis of Church and State* (New Jersey, 1964); M.C. Gaposchkin, 'Boniface VIII, Philip the Fair, and the sanctity of Louis IX, *Journal of Medieval History*, 29.1 (2003): 1–26.

criticisms of clerical celibacy came from the pens of the 'publicists' including Pierre Dubois, who took the side of Philip IV in his quarrel with the pope. Dubois was a layman, probably from Normandy, and an advocate for the King's position at the Council of Paris in 1302. He argued that the king of France enjoyed full sovereignty in all matters, and dismissed the claims of the pope to any temporal jurisdiction. Papal authority was limited to the cure of souls, the discipline of the clergy, and the maintenance of peace in Christendom. The root of contemporary problems, he argued, lay in the avarice of the church, including the pope, but also the parish clergy. A full reform of the church was necessary, not only to stem the tide of greed, but also to impose higher moral standards upon the clergy, most of whom failed to live in accordance with the discipline of celibacy. Dubois believed that at least part of the blame for clerical conduct was to be laid at the door of the popes. Clerical marriage had been the practice of the apostolic church, and was, he argued, still permitted in the Greek church, and the law of the Latin West was not only novel, but encouraged clerical incontinence.[32] A defence of papal authority against the publicists, which included a justification of clerical celibacy based upon its apostolic origins, came in the form Augustinus of Ancona's *De Potestate Ecclesiastica*. The author rehearsed familiar evidence of the biblical mandate for chastity, its basis in the practice of the primitive church, and the legitimacy of the discipline as established in the medieval church.[33] Such arguments did not always find favour even among the orthodox however. The Dominican writer Galvanus della Flamma presented an analysis of the evidence for and against the apostolic origins of clerical celibacy in his *Manipulo Florum Seu Chronico Mediolanensi* (1336) and concluded that the early apostles and priests of the church were married men.

The period of the Avignon papacy generated its own particular set of criticisms of clerical and papal morality, many of which betrayed a rather sceptical attitude towards the merits and necessity of clerical celibacy. At the fore was the issue of incontinence and avarice. Pope Clement VI was strident in his criticism of his clerical colleagues, demanding of them 'What can you preach to the people?... If on poverty, you are so covetous that all the benefices of the world are not enough for you. If on chastity – but we will be silent on this, for God knows what each man does and

---

[32] For Dubois' tract, see R. Scholz, *Die Publizistik zur Zeit Philipps des Schonen und Bonifaz VIII* (Stuttgart, 1903), p. 385 ff.

[33] Augustus de Ancona, *Summa de potestate ecclesiastica* (Venice: Scoti, 1487) Q.92 art. 3; For further information on the author, see M. Wilks, *The Problem of Sovereignty in the Later Middle Ages. The Papal Monarchy with Augustinus Triumphus and the Publicists* (Cambridge, 1963); some of his works are summarised in Scholz, *Die Publizistik*, pp. 172–89.

how many of you satisfy your lusts'.[34] Dante was equally expressive in his condemnations of clerical morality and the example set by the church and its leaders. Pope Boniface VIII was condemned in the *Divine Comedy* to spend eternity in suffering, and the riches of the clergy and the practice of simony condemned, but Dante also had a powerful case to make for the value of love, both for divine and humankind, in directing the universe towards God.[35] The Italian writer Petrarch referred to Avignon as the 'Babylon of the West', complaining 'instead of holy solitude we find a criminal host and crowds of the most infamous satellites; instead of soberness, licentious banquets; instead of pious pilgrimages, preternatural and foul sloth; instead of the bare feet of the apostles, the snowy coursers of brigands fly past us'.[36] Such colourful rhetoric, highlighting the contrasts between clerical ideal and the apparent reality of priestly life, was to become a staple of polemical writing against the obligatory nature of clerical celibacy in the fourteenth and fifteenth centuries. Alongside the debate over the origins and evolution of the celibacy discipline stood the argument that the conduct of the priests of the church was, in its own right, a compelling reason for reconsideration and reform.

Criticisms of clerical incontinence, coupled with a defence of the validity and desirability of clerical marriage, were a common feature of Wycliffite sermons and writings in late medieval England, and of the complaints that were made against the Catholic church by Lollards during the heresy trials. John Wycliffe's stance was clearly expressed in his *Trialogus*, which not only praised the institution of marriage, but also denounced those who would prohibit marriage against the law of the Gospel. The 23rd chapter described the twofold character of marriage, as the marriage of God and church, and the marriage of man and wife 'after God's law'. Such unions were ordained in paradise, Wycliffe wrote, and approved by Christ while on earth, and by his apostles. To forbid marriage, he argued, was to preach the 'doctrine of devils', which St Paul had identified as a heresy that would mark the coming of Antichrist. The obligation to celibacy placed upon the Catholic clergy was thus presented as grounded in error and fraught with danger, as the conduct of the contemporary priesthood revealed. Marriage had been instituted for all as a remedy of fornication, and this remedy was

---

[34] P. Bernstein, *The Power of Gold. The History of an Obsession* (New York, 2000), p. 100.

[35] Dante, *The Divine Comedy*, G.L. Bickersteff (ed.) (Oxford, 1972), *Infern*, 19.49–63; *Inf.* 19.82, *Inf.* 19.70–2; P. Acquaviva and J. Petric (eds), *Dante and the Church: Literary and Historical Essays* (Dublin,. 2007); J.T. Slattery, *Dante's attitude toward the church and the clergy of his times* (Philadelphia, 1921).

[36] Petrarch, 'Letter to a Friend', in J.H. Robinson, *Readings in European History* (Boston, 1904), p. 502.

available to all, including priests. 'Since fornication is so perilous, and men and women are so frail', Wycliffe wrote, 'God ordained priests in the old law to have wives, and never forbid it in the new, neither by Christ nor by his apostles, but rather approved it.' Marriage had been permitted to the Levitical priests, and, Wycliffe argued, there was no scriptural prohibition of marriage to those who would serve in the Christian church. Alas, however, there were priests who 'now by the hypocrisy of the fiend and of false men.... bind themselves to priesthood and chastity, and forsake wives', even although they were unable to live in chastity. There was no suggestion in Scripture that virginity was held in low repute; indeed St Paul had counselled a life of chastity for those who were able to abstain, 'thus priests who keep clean chastity, in body and soul, do best'. But chastity was not within the capacity of all. For Wycliffe, the consequence of imposing the burden of continence upon all who entered the priesthood was that many of the clergy, straining under these 'new bonds', could not fulfil their obligation, and thus 'slander themselves foully before God and his saints'.[37] Marriage, and clerical marriage in particular, was for Wycliffe desirable although in no sense obligatory. As Anne Hudson has argued, Wycliffe rejected the requirement to sacerdotal celibacy, but did not commit himself positively to the principle of a married clergy, despite the assumptions of his critics. Thomas Walden, for example, conceded that there was plenty in Wycliffe's writings to suggest that he took a positive view of clerical celibacy, but still managed to locate a passage in Wycliffe's *De officio Pastorali* which was more overtly hostile to the discipline of the church.[38]

Wycliffe's followers were more strident in their condemnations of the Catholic clergy. The third of the petitions for the reform of the church presented to parliament in 1394 denounced the scandal that was caused in the church by the prohibition of clerical marriage, and argued that it was essential that the obligation to sacerdotal celibacy be lifted. The law of celibacy, it was argued, as reason and experience demonstrated, 'brings sodomy into all the holy church'.[39] In 1389, William Ramsbury echoed Wycliffe's sentiments, arguing that clerical marriage was preferable to a

---

[37] In *Tracts and Treatises of John de Wycliffe, D.D. with Selections and Translations from his Manuscripts, and Latin Works*, Robert Vaughan (ed.) (London: Blackburn and Pardon, 1845), volume 3, c.23.

[38] A. Hudson, *The Premature Reformation. Wycliffite Texts and Lollard History* (Oxford, 1988), p. 357; *De officio Pastorali* 2.11 'nam coniugium secundum Christum eis licitum odiunt et venenum et secular dominium eis a Christo prohibitum avide amplexanture'.

[39] *Fasciculi Zizaniorum*, W.W. Shirley (ed.) (London: Rolls Series, 1858), pp. 360–69; H.S. Cronin, 'The Twelve Conclusion of the Lollards', *English Historical Review*, 22 (1907): 292–304; A.R. Myers, *English Historical Documents 1327–1485* (London, 1995), p. 502.

clergy that was nominally celibate, but in practice guilty of incontinence, and opposition to the prohibition of clerical marriage was also evident in the Norwich heresy trials of the early fifteenth century.[40] Several other Wycliffite sermons survive, in which criticisms of clerical celibacy and the incontinence of the clergy were articulated, and arguments set forth in favour of clerical marriage.[41] More controversial still was the assertion that the sacraments celebrated by unworthy priests were invalid, and in 1382 Wycliffe stood accused of advancing the erroneous opinion that a bishop or priest, living in mortal sin, did not consecrate, baptise, or ordain.[42] In 1426, the Franciscan Thomas Richmond was compelled to recant the view that 'sacerdos in peccato mortali lapsus, non est sacerdos'.[43] Such assertions were less apparent in the academic debates surrounding Wycliffe's first protests but, as Malcolm Lambert has argued, were more readily articulated in later decades as Lollard preachers took a more simplistic view.[44]

Complaints about the apparent relationship between obligatory clerical celibacy and the conduct of incontinent priests were not unique to the English context. The *Reformatio Sigismundi* (c.1438) combined an acute apocalyptic sense with a vehemently hostile appraisal of the contemporary church and society. The author of the tract depicted an Empire in turmoil and chaos, bereft of divine grace and in urgent need of reform in root and branch. Criticisms of social structures and temporal authority were accompanied by a swingeing denunciation of the ills of the church, the avarice of the popes, and the failings of the clergy.[45] It was indeed a 'good thing for a man to keep himself pure' the anonymous author argued, but with the caveat 'observe the wickedness now going on in the church.

---

[40] H. Hargreaves, 'Sir John Oldcastle and Wycliffite Views on Clerical Marriage', *Medium Aevum*, 42 (1973): 141–5; N.P. Tanner, *Heresy Trials in the Diocese of Norwich 1428–1431*, Camden Society 4th series, 20 (1977) p. 73.

[41] See, for example, *Hou Sathanas & his prestos and his feyned religious casten by pre cursed heresies to distroie all good lyuynge and meytenen alle manere of synne*, in W.W. Shirley, *A Catalogue of the Original Works of John Wyclif* (Oxford: Clarendon Press, 1855), p. 44.

[42] M. Aston, *Lollards and Reformers. Images and Literacy in Late Medieval Religion* (London, 1984), p. 67; I.C. Levy, 'Was John Wyclif's Theology of the Eucharist Donatistic?', *Scottish Journal of Theology*, 53 (2000): 137–53.

[43] D. Wilkins, *Concilia Magnae Britanniae et Hiberniae* (London, 1737), vol. 3, p. 488.

[44] M. Lambert, *Medieval Heresy. Popular Movements from the Gregorian Reform to the Reformation* (Oxford, 2002), p. 280.

[45] 'Reformatio Sigismundi', in *Monumenta Germaniae Historica, Staatsschriften des späteren Mittelalters 6: Reformation Kaiser Siegmunds* (Stuttgart 1964); English modern translation in G. Strauss, *Manifestations of Discontent in Germany on the Eve of the Reformation* (Bloomington, 1971); P.H. Freedman, *Images of the Medieval Peasant* (Stanford UP, 1999), p. 285.

Many priests have lost their livings because of women. Or they are secret sodomites. All the hatred existing between priests and laymen is due to this. In sum: secular priests ought to be allowed to marry. In marriage they will live more piously and honestly, and the friction between them and the laity will disappear'.[46] Permitting marriage to the clergy was a remedy both for those priests who could not live in continence, and for those who did so beneath a show of hypocrisy. Capitalising on the recently invented printing press, it was possible for such tracts to circulate widely in the second half of the fifteenth century, and the *Reformatio* itself ran to seven editions before Luther's protest in 1517. The purpose of the reform demanded was not simply to put matters to right, but to bring church and empire back into divinely appointed order.[47] In this context, clerical celibacy and its apparent fruits were not simply a matter of ecclesiastical law and preference, but a symptom of a disordered church which stood in need of radical reform.

Against this backdrop, it is not surprising that this period also saw the publication of a number of significant contributions to the literature on clerical celibacy and marriage. Increasingly vocal demands for change, and the eventual resolution of the papal schism which raised the possibility of reform from within, prompted a lively debate over the precise nature that such reform should take, and clerical celibacy and concubinage were considered at both the Council of Constance and the Council of Basle. The occasion of a major church council in itself served to encourage reflection and debate. Prior to the Council of Vienne (1311), the canonist William Durandus addressed the problem of clerical incontinence in his *Tractatus de modo generalis concilii celebrandi*.[48] The principle of reform 'in capite et in membris' is often attributed to Durandus, and his discussion of the problem of clerical celibacy reflected this construct. Durandus argued that although popes and councils through the centuries had attempted to impose the discipline of continence upon the clergy, and take action against the scandal of clerical concubinage, such efforts had been, in their entirety, unsuccessful. The ineffectual nature of the penalties imposed upon offending clerics was exposed in the morality of the contemporary clergy, and in the continued presence of women in the houses of priests. It was, he argued, the married priesthood of the Eastern church rather than the celibate priesthood of the West which best embodied the practice of the

---

[46] Strauss, *Manifestations of Discontent*, pp. 14–15.

[47] G. Strauss 'Ideas of Reformatio and Renovatio from the late middle ages to the Reformation', in J.D. Tracy and H. Oberman (eds), *Handbook of European History* (Leiden, 1994), pp. 1–28, esp. p. 21.

[48] W. Durandus, *Tractatus de modo generalis concilii celebrandi* (Paris, 1671) II Tit.46, pp. 157–9.

apostolic church, and with this in mind, Durandus suggested that the Latin church adopt the practice of the Greeks.

The decrees of the Council of Constance (1414–18) reflected the determination of the church to eradicate clerical concubinage, but the summoning of the council also provoked further discussion of the broader question of clerical celibacy. In part, the issue was raised as a result of the consideration by the council of the heresies of Jan Hus. Among his criticisms of the church, Hus included the assertion that clerical marriage had been permitted for the first thousand years of church history, and that the subsequent efforts of popes and councils to impose continence upon its priests were the root of all evil in the church. The canonist Zabarella adopted a similar line to that taken by Durandus a century earlier, arguing that if the actions of popes and councils against clerical concubinage were incapable of eradicating the problem, then it would be a lesser evil for the church to permit priests to marry.[49] The failure of the council to act upon such demands prompted the French canon lawyer and ambassador for the duke of Anjou, Guillaume Saignet, to set out the case for clerical marriage in more detail in his *Lamentationem ob coelibatum sacerdotum, seu dialogum Nicenaenae Constitutionis et Naturae ea de re Conquerentis* (1417/8). Saignet proposed the abrogation of the law of continence on the basis that it was both absurd, and widely violated. He professed to be concerned for the state of the church, and by the deeds that were committed in the sanctuary of God, 'ecclesie naufragia, templorum ruine, juriumque et libertatum Ecclesie violaciones, devociones, religionis et caritatis defectus, jurgia, rixe et oprobia active et passive tuis temporibus ... propter incestus, adulteria, fastus et alia nephanda michi facta opprobria, causata et eventa'. Nature was worthy of praise, he argued, as the creation of God, but also as the will of Christ, who commended it as a representation of His union with the church. In its law of celibacy, he claimed, the Catholic church created a schism within the sacraments, setting marriage and holy orders in opposition. Saignet pointed to the example of the married priesthood of the apostolic church, and to the tradition of clerical marriage in the East, in order to dismiss sacerdotal celibacy as an innovation, and one that by the fifteenth century simply served as a mandate to hypocrisy.[50]

The tract elicited a response from Jean Gerson, whose advocacy of reform in the church did not extend as far as a relaxation of the celibacy

---

[49] F. Zabarella, *Capita Agendorum in Concilio Const. De Reformatione, Magnum Oecumenicum Constantiense Concilium*, H. van der Hardt (ed.) (Frankfurt, 1700), col. 525.

[50] The most accessible version of Saignet's text is in N. Grévy-Pons, *Célibat et nature, une controverse médiévale: A propos d'un traité de début de XVe siècle* (Paris, 1975), pp. 135–61.

discipline. Gerson did not deny the problem of clerical incontinence, but argued vehemently for the desirability, indeed necessity, of clerical celibacy. There were clearly priests who failed to live in chastity and maintained concubines, he argued, but such a scandal might be tolerated if it prevented worse problems. The extreme logic of this conclusion was that it would be better to have incontinent priests than no priests at all. Gerson's four act *Dialogue* (1423) presented a debate between Natura, or Reason, and Sophia, or Theology. Natura set out the proposition that the prohibition of marriage to the clergy had its foundation in the law of man and not divine law, and suggested that the requirement to celibacy was not a necessary part of ministry. In reply, Sophia argued that unlike the priests of the Old Law, who became priests through hereditary succession, the Christian priesthood was elected. It was better that those called to the priesthood were unmarried, in order that their life might be focused entirely upon the service of God, without the distractions of family and children, and the temptation to provide for them. The abuses committed by individual priests did not constitute a compelling argument against clerical celibacy. Sophia conceded that the failure to observe continence had indeed resulted in evil and scandal in the church, but argued that the path to reform lay in the discipline of clerical celibacy and not in the legalisation of clerical marriage. There were, it was argued, different forms of chastity, either within marriage or in the 'heroic' perpetual chastity demanded of priests. The discipline of celibacy had its roots in the Gospel mandate for those who 'made themselves chaste for the sake of the kingdom', and was as natural a state as marriage.[51] The debate between Gerson and Saignet was a clash over the issue of clerical celibacy, but was also much more wide ranging, as a reflection of two different strands in late medieval thought. 'Ils sont eux-memes les successours de deux courants de pensee', Nicole Grevy-Pons suggests, 'l'un que l'on peut qualifier de mystique ou de religieux, l'autre de naturaliste'.[52]

The summoning of the Council of Basle prompted further calls for the reconsideration of the celibacy law. At the council, the Bishop of Lubeck argued in favour of the abolition of clerical celibacy, citing the judgement of the Polish humanist Jan de Luzisko, who claimed that since, in reality, clerical continence had long since been abandoned, it was time for the church to step back from the ideal.[53] Debate over clerical celibacy and marriage continued throughout the middle decades of the fifteenth century.

[51] Gerson, *Dialogus de Celibatu Ecclesiasticorum* 1423, printed in Grévy-Pons, *Célibat et nature*, pp. 162–95.
[52] Grévy-Pons, *Célibat et nature*, p. 4.
[53] Brundage, *Law Sex and Christian Society*, p. 538, quoting *Capitula Agendorum in Concilio Generali Constanciensi* 13, in H. Finke (ed.), *Acta Concilii Constanciensis*

Nicholas Tudeschi (Panormitanus, 1386–1445), who had been a participant at the Council of Basle, presented a detailed defence of clerical marriage, *Lecturam Super Can. Cum. Olim 6 de clericis coniugatis*.[54] Commending voluntary celibacy for those who were able to contain, Tudeschi argued that obligatory continence had been the occasion of much scandal and evil in the church. Clerical celibacy was not, he suggested, a law of God, but as others had argued, a law of the church, and a law that it was well within the power of the church to abrogate for the wider benefit of the clergy and the faithful. Tudeschi asserted that there was no inextricable link between priesthood and celibacy, and that it would be better for the Latin church to accommodate itself to the practice of the Greek church, where marriage was permitted.[55] The argument that the discipline of clerical continence was a law of the church rather than a custom of divine origin was debated in Aeneas Sylvius' *Dialogis Contra Bohemos*. The author's subsequent elevation to the papal see as Pius II ensured that this work enjoyed a popular readership among evangelical polemicists seeking evidence of any uncertainty over the origins of clerical celibacy, and the assertion in the *Dialogue* that the clergy of the early church had been married men was grist to the mill. Platina, in his biography of Pius II, referred to his contention that although there had been an honest motive in the past for the church to insist upon the celibacy of its priests, there were, in the fifteenth century, compelling reasons for priests to be allowed to marry. Clerical marriage would, for example, release from suffering and damnation those clergy who were unable to live in chastity.[56] Early in the sixteenth century,

---

(4 vols, Munster: Regensburg, 1896–1928), vol. IV. 569–70; Grévy-Pons, *Celibat et Nature*, pp. 52–3.

[54] *Abbatis Panormitani Commentaria in Tertium Decretalium Librum* (7 vols, Venice, 1588), vol. 3, Tit. III c.6 (Tomus VI p. 25); J. Lynch, 'Critique of the Law of Celibacy in the Catholic Church from the Period of the Reform Councils', in W. Bassett and Peter Huizing (eds), *Celibacy in the Church* (New York, 1972), pp. 57–75, p. 58.

[55] Such arguments against clerical celibacy were perhaps not entirely unrelated to attempts to undermine traditional Augustinian views of human nature and sexuality; both the French theologian Martin le Maistre (1432–1481) and the Scottish author John Maior (1470–1550) were to argue that sexual intercourse within marriage did not carry with it the burden of sin and shame. Le Maistre in his *Moral Questions* considered the marital act in Aristotelian rather than Augustinian terms, and viewed 'conjugal chastity' as that which occupied the middle ground of virtue. Marriage was, he argued, the divinely appointed remedy for fornication, and therefore marital intercourse was licit. Le Maistre, *Questiones morales magistri Martini Magistri perspicacissimi theologie professoris, de fortitudine feliciter incipiunt* (2 Parts, Paris, 1510), Pt. 2, seventh conclusion; John Maior, *Quartus Sententiarum* (Paris, 1509), 4.31. For further discussion, see M. Porter, *Sex, Marriage and the Church. Patterns of Change* (Victoria, Aus., 1996), p. 39; G.S. Kochutara, *The Concept of Sexual Pleasure in the Catholic Moral Tradition* (Rome, 2007), pp. 232–5.

[56] *Vitæ Pontificum Platinæ historici liber de vita Christi ac omnium pontificum qui hactenus ducenti fuere et XX* (Venice, 1479) II.257–75.

the Ingolstadt professor Conrad Celtis rejected the argument that the discipline of celibacy had its origins in the apostolic church, and argued that obligatory continence was an innovation of Gregory VII, and one which had done untold damage to the church.[57] Johannes Antonius' hostile commentary on the history of clerical celibacy, printed in the first decades of the sixteenth century, reiterated the arguments against the apostolic origins of the discipline. The law of celibacy, he argued, was of human origin and not divine, and marriage had been instituted by God as a remedy for those who were not able to live in perpetual continence. The conduct of the clergy, he suggested, exposed the flaws in the assumption that chastity was indeed possible for all, and Antonius argued in favour of the acceptance of clerical marriage in order to return the discipline of the church to its primitive origins.[58] A subsequent sardonic condemnation of obligatory celibacy, *Epistolae Obscurorum Virorum ad Venerabilem virum Magistrum Orthuinum Gratium Daventiensem* (Venice, 1516), was condemned by the pope, but Antonius was not deterred, and penned an equally intemperate examination of clerical concubinage, *De Fide Concubinarum in Sacerdotes*, published in Worms in 1517, the year of Luther's protest.

Such demands for the relaxation of the law on clerical celibacy did not go uncriticised, and there were still writers willing to defend the obligation to continence on the eve of the Reformation. The works of Dionysius the Carthusian, printed in the early sixteenth century, set out the value of clerical celibacy for both pastor and people, and established the existence of a necessary link between priesthood and celibacy.[59] Richard Whitford's *Pype or Tonne of the Lyfe of Perfection* praised chastity as a noble virtue 'for it doth make a man familiar w[i]t[h] god as Angell'.[60] Similar esteem for chastity and its necessity for those who ministered at the altar was expressed in *De Castitate et Munditia Sacerdotum et Ceterorum Alteris Ministrorum*. Published in the late fifteenth century but often attributed to the thirteenth century Franciscan St Bonaventure, *De Castitate* was a handbook for the moral conduct of priests. Its counsels, including the observance of the obligation to celibacy, were rooted in Scripture, both Old and New Testament, in the prescriptions of canon law, and in the writings of the Fathers, including Augustine. The third section of the treatise demonstrated that the law of continence was anchored not only in

---

[57] C. Celtis, *Quatuor libri amorum secundum quatuor latera Germanie* (Nuremberg, 1502).

[58] Antonius, *Aurea at Singularis Lectura Super IV Decretalium in Ca. De Clere. Coniugatis* (Pavia, 1497).

[59] See, for example, *The Life of Priests* (London, 1533).

[60] Richard Whitford, *Pype or Tonne of the Lyfe of Perfection* (London, 1532), fols 7r, 22r, 206r.

ecclesiastical law, but also in secular law, including the Codex of Justinian. The altar of God, it was claimed, was polluted by the actions of unchaste priests who broke the law of the church, and whose eyes turned to their concubines rather than to the worship of God. The example of the Old Testament pointed to a requirement to purity on the part of those who served at the altar, a requirement that was reinforced by Christ in his commendation of chastity to the first disciples. The assertion of the spiritual advantages of temporary abstinence for the laity placed an even greater obligation upon the clergy, and St Paul's second letter to the Corinthians was used to justify a distinction between those who walked in the flesh and those who lived in the spirit.[61] The argument from scripture, tradition, and ecclesiastical authority continued. At the turn of the sixteenth century, Gaufredus Bossardus presented an endorsement of the discipline of clerical celibacy in the context of the dispensing power of the pope, drawing upon the actions of recent popes and councils, and was underpinned by an examination of obligatory continence in the church, including the fourth century letters of Siricius and Innocent.[62]

Arguments in favour of clerical marriage, and particularly the argument that present need, set alongside the practice of the apostolic church and the Greek church, undermined the discipline of obligatory continence for priests, were stridently articulated in the century before the Reformation. Whether this amounts to a coherent campaign against clerical celibacy is another matter; while the works discussed here were impressive in their scope, and often written by men of some standing in the church, their impact upon the discipline of the church was virtually non-existent, and the Latin medium would have limited their audience. This was not the first occasion upon which there had been a polemical exchange on the subject. Anne Barstow has examined in detail the writings of those who contested clerical celibacy in the era of the Gregorian reforms, and there is some evidence of a reinvigoration of the debate in the thirteenth century.[63] However, even the briefest examination of the fifteenth-century literature makes it clear that the controversies of the Reformation did not awaken a dormant subject, but rather emerged from a context of burgeoning historical and ecclesiological interest in the celibacy discipline.

---

[61] *De Castitate et Munditia Sacerdotum et Ceterorum Alteris Ministrorum* (Paris, c.1492), unpaginated.

[62] G. Bossardus, *De Continentia Sacerdotum sub hac Quaestione: utrum papae possit com sacerdote dispensare, ut nubat?* (Paris, 1505).

[63] J.W. Baldwin, *The Language of Sex. Five Voices from Northern France Around 1200* (Chicago and London, 1994), pp. 61–3; Baldwin, 'A Campaign to Reduce Clerical Celibacy at the Turn of the Twelfth and Thirteenth Centuries', *Etudes d'Histoire du Droit Canoniques dediees a Gabriel le Bas* (2 vols, Paris, 1965), vol. 2, 1041–53.

The literature of the fourteenth and fifteenth centuries, at least in some respects, served to delineate the battle ground of Reformation debate. The example of the apostolic church had much to offer protagonists on both sides, and was to be fiercely contested. The representation of clerical celibacy as a divine or man-made law was disputed with even greater vigour in the middle decades of the sixteenth century and beyond. Clerical concubinage, which had incurred the wrath of late medieval popes and councils, and had been used to argue in favour of clerical marriage, was to be exploited by evangelical writers seeking to discredit not only the failure of discipline in the church, but also the theology which underpinned it. The condemnation of Wycliffe and Hus, which included the rejection of their views on clerical marriage, established the possibility, articulated more strongly in the centuries that followed, that clerical celibacy might become both a highly personal and highly visible badge of doctrinal allegiance in a confessional age. Perhaps even more significantly, the argument in favour of clerical marriage came to be made alongside the physical reality of married priests, if not a married priesthood. In the sixteenth century, for the first time in four hundred years, the debate over clerical celibacy was conducted in a climate in which many priests encountered 'pigtails on the pillow'.[64]

---

[64] The phrase is Martin Luther's: Luther, *Table Talk,* in LW, vol. 54, p. 191 (June 1532).

CHAPTER FIVE

'The whole world and the devil will laugh': Clerical Celibacy and Married Priests in the Age of Reformation

'Suddenly, and while I was occupied with far different thoughts', Martin Luther confessed to his friend Wenzeslaus Linck, 'the Lord has plunged me into marriage.' As late as the previous Autumn, he had suggested that he had no intention of marrying, but writing to Spalatin in summer 1525 Luther rejoiced that he had 'made the angels laugh and the devils weep'. His marriage, he felt sure, would please his father, give witness to his faith, and spite the devil and the pope.[1] Luther was not the first of the evangelical reformers to take such a step, but his marriage was one of the most iconoclastic, and hotly debated, events of the early Reformation. Canon law, explicitly hostile to clerical marriage, was even more rigorous in its condemnation of marriage involving professed religious as not only adulterous, but incestuous.[2] Luther's marriage to Katharine von Bora on 13 June 1525 scandalised Catholic commentators, and shocked even his closest friends. Philip Melanchthon, in a less guarded moment, denounced the union as 'reckless'; Luther's opponents seized upon his marriage as evidence of evangelical antinomianism, the subjugation of theology to the demands of the flesh, and the association of Protestantism with licentiousness and liberty taken to the extreme.[3] Early Reformation debates over clerical celibacy and marriage crystallised in the private wedding of a monk and a nun, a wedding which exposed the wide-ranging nature of the controversy, and the broader implications of clerical marriage for the deepening doctrinal divisions of the age.

---

[1] WABr 3.394; WABr 3.533, 541.
[2] Dist. Xxvii C.ix [CIC I.100].
[3] Melanchthon's comments were made in a Greek letter to his friend Camerarius, and preserved in the text of the letter published by W. Meyer in the reports of the München Academy of Sciences, 4 November, 1876, pp. 601–4. A modified, and less critical, text is in *Corp. Ref.*, vol. 1, p. 753. For Catholic commentary on Luther's marriage, see pp. 146–9 below.

The historiography of Reformation attitudes to marriage and ministry, and the related issue of clerical marriage, is substantial. Recent research has focused upon the impact of doctrinal change, sacramental theology, and the reform of marriage law, and raised significant questions about the extent to which Lutheran views marked a substantial break with late medieval law and tradition.[4] Evangelical attitudes to clerical marriage may be seen to have a precedent in earlier criticisms of the discipline of celibacy, but in their broader ramifications the polemical writings of the reformers reached far beyond those of their predecessors.[5] The evangelical defence of clerical marriage was part of a broader effort to redefine the nature of priesthood and the clerical estate, to undermine the sacramental theology which underpinned the sacerdotal caste and demanded celibacy of those who served at the altar, to prioritise the word of God over the laws of man, faith over works, and to reclaim the history and heritage of the primitive church from the pages of monastic chronicles. The denunciation of compulsory clerical celibacy was not simply a criticism of the morality of the contemporary clergy, but a condemnation of the doctrine, traditions, and structures of the medieval church. Just as the presence of images in churches inculcated a trust in the merits of the saints, so the presence of a celibate priesthood implied a sacrificial function for the priest, and evinced a continuation of Catholic faith and practice. Luther's marriage, and the marriages of those around him, did not simply 'spite the devil', but was

---

[4] J.F. Harrington, *Reordering Marriage and Society in Reformation Germany* (Cambridge, 1995); C. Peters, 'Gender Sacrament and Ritual. The Making and Meaning of Marriage in Late Medieval and Early Modern England', *Past and Present*, 169.1 (2000): 63–96; J. Witte Jr, *From Sacrament to Contract: Marriage, Religion and Law in the Western Tradition* (Louisville, 1997); A. Stein, 'Martin Luthers Bedeutung dur die Anfange des Evangelischen Eherechts', *Osterreichisches Archiv fur Kirchenrecht*, 34.1 and 2 (1983–4): 29–95; S. Johnson, 'Luther's Reformation and (un)holy Matrimony', *Journal of Family History*, 17.3 (1992): 271–88; L. Roper 'Luther, Sex, Marriage and Motherhood', *History Today*, 33 (1983): 33–8.

[5] For recent literature on clerical marriage, see T.A. Fudge, 'Incest and Lust in Luther's Marriage: Theology and Morality in Reformation Polemics', *Sixteenth Century Journal*, 34.2 (2003): 319–45; J.K. Yost, 'The Reformation Defence of Clerical Marriage in the Reigns of Henry VIII and Edward VI', *Church History*, 50 (1981): 152–65; E. Carlson, 'Clerical Marriage and the English Reformation', *Journal of British Studies*, 31 (1992): 1–31; Carlson, *Marriage and the English Reformation* (Oxford, 1994); M. Porter, *Sex, Marriage and the Church. Patterns of Change* (Victoria, Aus, 1996); H.L. Parish, *Clerical Marriage and the English Reformation* (Aldershot, 2000); Marjorie Elisabeth Plummer, 'Clerical Marriage and Territorial Reformation in Ernestine Saxony and the Diocese of Merseburg in 1522–1524', *Archiv für Reformationsgeschichte*, 98 (2007): 45–70; Plummer, '"Partner in his Calamities": Pastors Wives, Married Nuns and the Experience of Clerical Marriage in the Early German Reformation', *Gender and History*, 20.2 (2008): 207–27.

an act of iconoclastic destruction that broke apart false saintliness in the hearts of the faithful.[6]

This act of open iconoclasm had begun in the town of Grimma, near Nimbschen, in 1519. News of Luther's preaching in the town had reached the ears of the prior of Grimma, and through him a handful of nuns in the convent at Marienthron. Several petitioned their families to secure their liberty, but when no assistance was forthcoming, arrangements were made for their release, with the encouragement of Luther himself. Twelve of the nuns were taken to Torgau, of whom nine, including Katharine von Bora, then journeyed on to Wittenberg.[7] Luther penned a defence of their actions, in which he compared the freedom of the nuns to the release of Israel from bondage, and argued that cloistered virginity prevented women from fulfilling their God-given purpose of bearing children.[8] Despite his initial reluctance to marry (Luther exclaimed 'good God, our Wittenbergers will give wives even to the monks ... but they will not thrust a wife on me'[9]), Luther entered into a private marriage, followed by a public ceremony in June 1525. The fact that his wife was one of the former nuns of Marienthron was, in the eyes of his Catholic opponents, evidence that the evangelical reformers simply intended to empty the convents in order to satisfy their own lusts.[10] The wedding of the monk and the nun was both the consequence of evangelical licence, and an encouragement to others to follow suit. As soon as Luther's wedding bells rang, it was argued 'the lecherous monks and nuns put up plenty of ladders against the monastery walls and ran off together in masses'.[11] The birth of Luther's first child, a healthy son Hans, no doubt elicited a sigh of relief from his

---

[6] H. Oberman, *Luther. Man Between God and the Devil* (tr. E. Walliser-Schwarzbart) (New Haven and London, 1989), p. 282; Parish, *Clerical Marriage*, pp. 151ff; the importance of clerical marriage to other Reformation debates is also recognised in Roper's comment that 'when the first clerical marriage took place in defiance of church law, the Reformation embarked upon a course which involved far more than mere tinkering with the moral regulation of the priesthood', L. Roper, *Oedipus and the Devil. Witchcraft, Sexuality and Religion in Early Modern Europe* (London and New York, 1994), p. 79.

[7] P. Smith, *Luther's Correspondence and Other Contemporary Letters* (2 vols, Philadelphia, 1918), vol. 2, pp. 81, 180; J.C. Smith, 'Katharina von Bora Through Five Centuries: A Historiography', *SCJ*, 30.3 (1999): 745–74; Fudge, 'Incest and Lust', pp. 331–2; Oberman, *Luther*, pp. 272ff; M. Brecht, *Martin Luther* (tr. P. Schaff) (Minneapolis, 1985–1993), pp. 195–203.

[8] Luther, *Ursach und Antwort, das jungfrauen kloster gottlich verlassen mogen* (1523); WABr 3.353; WA 11 378–400.

[9] LW 48:290.

[10] See, for example, the condemnation of Luther's marriage in Johannes Langburg's treatise of 1528, quoted in S. Ozment, *When Fathers Ruled, Family Life in Reformation Europe* (Cambridge, Mass., and London, 1983), p. 24.

[11] Oberman, *Luther*, p. 282.

friends that was grounded in more than compassion. The belief that a two-headed monster, if not the Antichrist, would be born of the union of a monk and nun had created an air of uneasy expectation, not of all which was dissipated by Erasmus' comments that if the legend were true, the world was already populated with such creatures. Luther informed his friends in June 1526 that his son was strong, healthy, and without defect. Despite the suffering that was to follow, with the death of two girls in childhood, Luther celebrated his family life.[12]

Hostile comment was swift to come. The duke of Saxony observed that Luther's marriage to Katharine, and his sins of the flesh, would exclude him from the ultimate wedding feast with Christ, and the marriage was derided by the Catholic controversialists Johann Hasenberg and Joachim von der Hayden, who argued that Luther's actions had turned Wittenberg into a contemporary Sodom and Gomorrah, and accused the reformer of apostasy, adultery, and an inability to control his lusts.[13] Luther and his new wife appeared in hostile caricature in Simon Lemnius' dramatic representation of lustful monks and nuns, *Monachopornomachia*, and in pictorial form in mass-produced *flugschriften*.[14] Satirical wedding verses, epithalamia, were penned by Johannes Cochlaeus soon after news of the wedding was made public. Cochlaeus' later *Commentarii de Actis et Scriptis Martini Lutheri Saconis* (1549) also seized upon the marriage as evidence of Luther's lack of self control, and was equally hostile in his representation of Katherine and her conduct. Jerome Dungersheim's polemic against Lutheranism included the assertion that Luther and his followers were guilty of antinomianism in their rejection of the key tenets of Christian faith that stood in the way of their 'pretended' marriages.[15] The English king Henry VIII castigated Luther for his incestuous relationship with a nun, and the marriage was mocked on stage in a play presented by the king in 1527. Henry derided Luther for his unchaste life, and drew a

---

[12] Erasmus, 'Letter to Sylvius', in *Opus epistolarum Des. Erasmi Roterodami*, P.S. Allen, H.W. Garrod (eds) (12 vols, Oxford, 1906–58), vol. 6, 283–4; Fudge, 'Incest and Lust', p. 336; Smith, 'Luther's Reformation', p. 749; Oberman, *Luther*, p. 278.

[13] WABr 4. 517–31; Smith, *Letters*, vol. 2, pp. 452–3; J. Emser, *Epithalamia Martini Lutheri Wittenbergensis et Johannes Hessi Vratislavtensis ed Id Genus Nuptiarum* (1525); Brecht, *Luther*, p. 199.

[14] See, for example, a satirical image of Protestant pigs entering a church, with Luther and Katherine as the 'biggest pigs of all', in W.A. Coupe, *German Political Satires from the Reformation to the Second World War* (3 vols, White Plains, NY, 1993), vol. I, p. 109.

[15] J. Dungersheim, *Schriften Gegen Luther Theorismata Duodecim Contra Lutherum, Articuli Sive Libelli Triginta*, Theobald Freudenberger (ed.) (Munster, 1987) Article 17; Theobald Freudenberger, *Hieronymus Dungersheim von Ochsenfurt an Main, 1465–1540, Theologieprofessor in Leipzig: Leben und Schriften* (Munster, 1988); G. Krodel, 'Luther: An Antinomian?', *Luther Jahrbuch*, 63 (1996): 69–101.

stark contrast between the pure lives of the Fathers of the church and the pride and lechery of the reformer.[16] Catholic antipathy to Luther and his marriage in the 1520s was exemplified in the scatological denunciations penned by Thomas More, who took evident delight in the polemical capital afforded by his opponent's personal life. Luther, in his marriage, had shown 'how fondly such an hyghe pure spyrituall processe acordeth with such a baas fowle fleshly lyuyng'.[17] Luther and Katherine, he alleged, lived in shameless and open incest 'under the name of wedlock', and caricatures of friars coupling with nuns featured prominently in More's work, with more than sixty references in the *Confutation of Tyndale's Answer* alone.[18] The fundamentals of evangelical theology, including solafideianism and Christian liberty, were reduced to simple justifications for Luther's debauched conduct. Luther and his colleagues, More alleged, construed Scripture falsely in order that it might be exploited to support their actions, and extolled Gospel freedom in order to undermine morality.[19] True prophets were good and holy men, he claimed, and 'no frere out of a nonnes bedde' would be sent to preach the word of God.[20] Such views endured well beyond the storm created by Luther's marriage. Writing after the first generation of clerical marriages in England, Thomas Martin asserted that 'heresy and lechery be commonly joined together and they two be the only causes of priests pretended matrimony'.[21] His contemporary, Miles Huggarde, made the same association between the conduct of the evangelicals and their false doctrines. Lutheranism, he claimed, was a plague sent by God, and the false prophets of the Reformation were

---

[16] Smith, *Letters*, vol. 2, p. 195; Henry VIII, *A copy of the Letters Wherin ... King Henry VIII ... made answer unto ... Martyn Luther* (London, 1528), sig. B8; Henry VIII, *Assertio Septem Sacramentorum*, in *Corp. Cath.* vol. 43, p. 396.

[17] T. More, *A Dialogue Concerning Heresies*, ed. T.M.C. Lawler, G. Marc'hadour, R.C. Marius (eds), in *The Yale Edition of The Complete Works of St. Thomas More*, 6 (New Haven, Conn: Yale UP, 1981), pt. 2, p. 376.

[18] More, *Dialogue*, p. 375; More, *The Confutation of Tyndale' Answer*, L.A. Schuster, R.C. Marius, J.P. Lusardi, R.J. Schoek (eds), *The Yale Edition of The Complete Works of St Thomas More*, 8 (New Haven, Conn.: Yale UP, 1973), pp. 41–2, 48, 181; R.F. Hardin, 'Caricature in More's *Confutation*', *Moreana*, 24 (1987): 41–52.

[19] R. McCutcheon, 'The Responsio ad Lutherum: Thomas More's Inchoate Dialogue with Heresy', *Sixteenth Century Journal*, 22 (1991): 77–90; Thomas More, *Responsio ad Lutherum*, J.M. Headley (ed.), in *The Yale Edition of The Complete Works of St Thomas More 5* (New Haven, Conn.: Yale UP, 1969), pp. 59–60; More, *Confutation*, pt. 2 p. 690. Luther had, for a 'defence of hys owne shamefull synne, by the false glosynge of scripture affermeth that freres to wedde nunnys were well and virtuously done'.

[20] More, *Confutation*, pt. 1, pp. 337–8.

[21] T. Martin, *A Treatise Declaryng and Plainly Provyng that the Pretensed Marriage of Prieste ... is no marriage* (London, 1554), sig. A1r; cf. M. Huggarde, *The Displaying of the Protestantes and Sondry their Practises* (London, 1556), sig. B6v.

guilty of 'prechyng maters accordynge to theyre wayward appertytes'.[22] Evangelical theology and morality were intertwined, and the base conduct of the reformers, in the eyes of their critics, exposed the flawed nature of their faith.

Luther's marriage remained a popular topic for Catholic controversialists throughout the sixteenth century and beyond. In a derisive assessment of Luther's character and theology, the French polemicist Florimund de Raemond complained bitterly that although celibacy was a superior state to wedlock, Luther accorded celibates no place in the church. By his own marriage, he argued, Luther showed himself to be a man of little discipline, and offered a poor example to his followers by preaching and living by a principle of liberty which promoted licence. The marriage of monks and nuns was a scandal in the church, and the physical pleasures of marriage promoted by Luther were no match for the purity of chastity and celibacy.[23] The Jesuit writer Louis Maimbourg was equally vigorous in his criticism of Luther's marriage and morality in his *Histoire du Lutheranisme* (1680), and in the early twentieth century Heinrich Denifle used the argument of 'Luther's lust' to criticise not only his marriage, but the theology of the Reformation as a whole.[24] This stream of hostile commentaries did elicit some response from Luther and his supporters. Jeanette Smith suggests that certainly by the seventeenth century a more concerted effort was being made to rehabilitate Katherine von Bora in the face of a century of criticism; where the early evangelical histories of the Reformation had made little reference to her presence, both Thomas Hayne's biography of Luther and Johann Mayer's study of Katherine attempted to present both the marriage, and Katherine, in a more favourable light.[25] Luther had, himself, leapt to the defence of his marriage in a tone that mirrored that of his opponents. His 1528 *Ein Neue Fabel Aesops* included a contemptuous response to Hasenberg's letter, and *New News from Leipzig* commended a typically disrespectful function for Catholic popular pamphlets which criticised his marriage.[26] Jerome Schurf's

---

[22] Huggarde, *Displaying*, Q3v; Luther conceded that there might indeed be some priests or monks who left their orders in order to marry 'glad to have found in evangelical freedom a basis and pretext for their rascality ... Can we help that?'. Luther, *Receiving Both Kinds in the Sacrament*, LW 36, p. 260.

[23] F. De Raemond, *L'Histoire de la Naissance, Progrez et Decadence de l'heresie* (Rouen, 1647), pp. 301ff, quoted in B.S. Tinsley, *History and Polemics in the French Reformation: Florimund de Raemond: Defender of the Church* (London, 1992), p. 97.

[24] H. Denifle, *Luther und Luthertum: in der ersten Entwickelung, quellenmäßig dargestellt* (2 vols, Mainz, 1905–1906); L. Maimbourg, *Histoire du Lutheranisme* (2 vols, Paris, 1681), vol. I.I, p. 115; Fudge, 'Incest and Lust', 336.

[25] Thomas Hayne, *The Life and Death of Martin Luther* (London, 1643); Johann Mayer, *De Catharina Lutheri Conjugye, Dissertatio* (Leipzig, 1698).

[26] WA 26.534–45.

observation that 'if this monk married, the whole world and the devil will laugh' proved to be quasi-prophetic; Luther and his marriage provided substantial fuel for polemical debate, but it was not always clear which side the joke was on. Luther might have laughed 'I have legitimate children, which no papal theologian has', but as Muriel Porter has suggested, the repeated denunciations of Luther's marriage in order to undermine the Reformation as whole exposed the costs in such unions. Luther and his followers presented their marriages as evidence of their commitment to their faith, but their opponents saw clerical marriage as proof that the reformers had rejected the gospel in favour of moral licence.[27]

Catholic controversialists who used clerical marriage, and particularly the marriage of key evangelical leaders, to discredit the Reformation were exploiting, by inversion, the same argument that critics of the medieval church had used to argue that clerical concubinage betrayed the false foundations of Catholic theology. Eberlin von Gunzberg, a Franciscan convert to the Reformation, penned in 1521 a comedic picture of a group of Catholic priests debating the question of clerical celibacy. Compulsory celibacy, they concluded, was a burden, and one which required a remedy, either in masturbation, or in concubinage, which the church might tolerate if a suitable fee were paid. One of the priests expressed his concern that the unchaste lives of the clergy undermined their position and discredited their preaching. How, after all, were his congregation to listen with straight faces to his denunciations of immoral conduct, when his own children were seated among them in the church?[28] Luther was to suggest that the conduct of the supposedly celibate Catholic clergy was, in part at least, responsible for the popular acceptance of the message of the Reformation.[29] Such satirical comment on the Catholic priesthood was far from unique to the German context. In England, George Joye suggested to Stephen Gardiner that among the Catholic clergy, debauchery and licentiousness were regarded as true holiness, and John Bale used his *Actes of the Englysh Votaries* to detail those deeds that he regarded as the consequences of their feigned chastity. 'He that doth synne ... is of the deuill', Bale declaimed, asserting in eye-watering detail the symbiotic relationship between priestly immorality and doctrinal error.[30] The

---

[27] WABr. 4.210; Porter, *Sex, Marriage and the Church*, p. 54.

[28] *Syben Frumm Aber Trostloss Pfaffen Klagen Ihre Not* (Basle, Th. Wolff, 1521); discussed in Ozment, *Fathers*, pp. 7ff.

[29] LW 26.458–9.

[30] G. Joye, *The Defence of the Mariage of Priestes Agenst Steuen Gardiner* (Antwerp, 1541), sig. C8v–D2r; J. Bale, *A Mysterye of Iniquyte Contayned within the Heretycally Genealogye of Ponce Pantolabus* (Antwerp, 1545), p. 10v; Parish, *Clerical Marriage*, pp. 121ff.

vigorous insistence on the part of many evangelical polemicists that the parish clergy on the eve of the Reformation were, en masse, failing in their obligation to celibacy, facilitated their resounding condemnation of the medieval church and fuelled their demands for reform, but such rhetoric had the potential to prove counter-productive. As Marjorie Plummer's study of early clerical marriage in Germany has shown, many of the first clergy wives were indeed the former concubines of priests.[31] Such marriages, coupled with polemical criticism of what appeared to be widespread clerical concubinage, clearly reinforced the equation of clergy wives and concubines in the popular imagination. Thomas More replied to those who would argue that clerical marriage was a remedy for clerical immorality by protesting 'how can there by the marriage of priests ... be fewer whores and bawds, when by the very marriage itself being as it were incestuous and abominable, all were stark harlots that married them, and all stark bawds that should help to bring them together?'[32] Richard Smith, no doubt smarting after being removed from his post and replaced by the Italian evangelical Peter Martyr, repeatedly referred to Martyr's wife as his 'harlot'.[33] Miles Huggarde, writing during the deprivations of married clergy in England in the reign of Mary, asserted that the wives of priests were either their former concubines or 'as common as the cartway'.[34] Even without the assumption, grounded in canon law, that clerical marriages were not marriages at all, the wives of the clergy themselves were argued to belie the evangelical assumption that such unions would stem the tide of clerical immorality.

These critical caricatures of clerical marriage were encouraged by some high profile and problematic unions. Perhaps the most infamous was the marriage of Johannes Apel. Appointed canon of Wurzburg cathedral by

---

[31] Plummer, 'Calamities', 211. Plummer calculated that some 66 per cent of clerical marriages in 1521–2 were the formalisation of a relationship between priest and concubine, one third in 1523–7, and half in 1528–30. See also M.A. Kelleher, 'Like Man and Wife: Clerics Concubines in the Diocese of Barcelona', *Journal of Medieval History*, 28 (2002): 349–60; A. Fluchter, *Der Zolibat Zwischen Devianz und Norm. Kirchenpolitil und Gemeidealltag in der Herzogtumern Julich und Berg im 16 und 17 Jahrhundert* (Cologne, 2006).

[32] More, *Supplication of Souls*, F. Manley, G. Marc'hadour, R. Marius, C.H. Miller (eds), in *The Yale Edition of The Complete Works of St Thomas More*, 7 (New Haven, Conn.: Yale UP, 1990), pp. 156–7.

[33] P. Martyr, *The Commonplaces of the Most Famous and Renowned Diuine Doctor Peter Martyr*, tr. A. Marten (London, 1583), sig. Qq1v. Catherine died in Oxford, and in the reign of Mary was accused of heresy; a lack of evidence meant that her bones, once exhumed, were cast into a dunghill rather than burned. The Protestant martyrologist Foxe describes her as 'an honest, grave and sober matron'. J. Foxe, *The Actes and Monuments of these latter and perillous days* (London, 1563), fol. 1558, and details the reburial of her remains with the relics of St Frideswide in the reign of Elizabeth.

[34] Huggarde, *Displaying of the Protestants*, pp. 73v–74r.

the bishop, Conrad, Apel confessed, soon after taking up his post, to have fallen in love with a nun, and entered into a clandestine affair. She left the cloister, and the two married in 1523. However, when word of the union reached the bishop, he declared the marriage null, instructed Apel to send his wife back to the convent, and enjoined penance on the pair. Apel challenged the decision, and sought to align his cause with evangelical calls for clerical marriage. To this end, a preface by Martin Luther was appended to Apel's defence of his marriage, *Defensio Johannis Apelli ad Episcopum Herbipolensem pro suo Coniugio*, published in Wittenberg in 1523. However, Apel was arrested, imprisoned by the bishop, accused of heresy, and excommunicated, despite protestations that the case fell outside Episcopal jurisdiction.[35] Apel secured for himself a position at the newly established university in Wittenberg, but the reaction to his attempted marriage revealed both the precarious status of such unions, and the contested nature of authority in such cases. Similar controversy attended the marriage in 1524 of the Strasbourg preacher and historian Caspar Hedio to the sister of Augustin Drenss. Drenss disputed the validity of the marriage, arguing that it had been contracted without his knowledge or consent. He questioned the legality of clerical marriage, and demanded that his sister be encouraged to marry instead an honest man who would be a better match for the family. Hedio responded with the assertion that it was public knowledge that clerical celibacy was not the law of God, but the invention of Gregory VII, that obligatory celibacy was recognised as the origin of clerical incontinence, and that God had not prohibited marriage to either layman or priest. Drenss persisted in the argument that clerical marriage ran counter to the law of the church and the law of the empire; clerical marriage had arrived in the city only a few months before Hedio's match, and there was clearly some dispute over the legality of such unions.[36] For such a high profile case to come before the courts would do little to dispel the doubts of lay observers that their priests had entered into valid marriages.

A year later, similar questions of law and authority were raised after the marriages of a group of clergy in the diocese of Merseburg. The marriage of Johann Stumpf of Schonbach and Franz Klotsch of Grossbuch occupied the bishop of Merseburg and the dukes of Saxony for over two years, and exposed the complex interchanges between confessional arguments,

---

[35] For a fuller discussion of the case, see Witte, *From Sacrament to Contract*, pp. 44–6; Fudge, 'Incest and Lust', 328ff.

[36] For a fuller discussion of the Hedio case, see T. Brady '"You hate us priests": Anticlericalism. Communalism, and the Control of Women at Strasbourg in the Age of the Reformation', in P. Dykema and H. Oberman (eds), *Anticlericalism in Late Medieval and Early Modern Europe* (Leiden, 1993), pp. 194ff.

political expediency, and personal preference. The bishop of Mainz had, similarly, failed to bring a speedy resolution to the cases of three former Wittenberg students who had married in 1521, Bartholomaeus Bernhardi, Jacob Seidler and Balthasar Zeiger.[37] By 1524, Plummer argues, this first generation of married clergy were beginning to adopt a cohesive platform that was part of a wider programme of defiance. The Merseburg priests presented the bishop with a defence of clerical marriage, *Handlung des Bischoffs von Mersburg mit den zwayen Pfarhern von Schonbach unnd Buch, geschehen am Dingstag nach Bartholomei Anno M.D.Xxiii*, which was published in Erfurt, Zwickau, and in Nuremberg in 1523, and pushed interest in their case beyond their own diocese. The papal legate, Campeggio, identified clerical marriage with heresy, perhaps echoing the views of the Gregorian reformers, and authorised the punishment of those who lived 'impurely'.[38] However, the German priests presented clerical marriage as the only solution to clerical immorality, argued that their position was supported by Scripture, and claimed that although they had prayed for chastity, they had been compelled by their conscience to marry because they did not have the ability to do otherwise. Plummer highlights the extent to which these arguments resonated readily with other parish clergy, including those who were unmarried, and provided a staple defence for priests who entered into such unions. As a result, the bishop found that the married priests were united in their disobedience, and articulate in the defence of their actions. When support from the secular arm, in the form of Frederick the Wise, was not forthcoming, the law of celibacy was all the more difficult to enforce.

Debate over clerical celibacy and marriage was undoubtedly fuelled by the marriage of several evangelical leaders in the 1520s. The theologian Philip Melanchthon married in 1520, although his marriage was not in violation of holy orders. Justus Jonas married in 1522, and the following years saw the marriage of Johannes Bugenhagen, Andreas Karlstadt, Martin Bucer, Wenceslas Linck, Thomas Muntzer, Wolfgang Capito, Matthias Zell, Ulrich Zwingli, Ludwig Cellarius, and Johannes Oecolampadius, among others. The early years of the decade had also witnessed a flurry of activity on the printing presses in defence of clerical marriage and denouncing mandatory celibacy and monastic vows. The first priests in

---

[37] The protracted nature of the proceedings against individual priests who married in the first years of the reformation has been amply demonstrated by Marjorie Plummer: Plummer, 'Clerical Marriage', pp. 45–70.

[38] *Ordnung und reformation zu abstellung der Missbreuch, un auffrichtung aines erberen wesens und wandels in der gaistlichait* (1524), sig. B2r, C1r–2r quoted in Plummer, 'Clerical Marriage', p. 52. Bishops were to impose strict discipline – imprisonment if necessary.

Wittenberg married in May 1521, following the publication of Luther's *Address to the Christian Nobility* which contained a strong denunciation of obligatory clerical celibacy as an attack on Christian liberty. 'We see also how the priesthood is fallen', Luther protested, 'and how many a poor priest is encumbered with a woman and children and burdened in his conscience, and no one does anything to help him, though he might very well be helped.' The justification for action, he proposed, was to be found in St Paul's Letter to Timothy, 'the minister should not be forced to live without a lawful wife, but should be allowed to have one, as St. Paul writes, saying that "a bishop then must be blameless, the husband of one wife ... having his children in subjection with all gravity"'. The precedent of the early church was that marriage was permissible to all, although some of the Fathers had chosen to remain unmarried in order that they might better devote themselves to study. Such voluntary celibacy caused no problems, Luther claimed, until 'the Roman see has interfered of its own perversity, and has made a general law by which priests are forbidden to marry. This must have been at the instigation of the devil, as was foretold by St Paul, saying that "there shall come teachers giving heed to seducing spirits, . . . forbidding to marry"'. By prohibiting marriage to the clergy, he argued, the Catholic church had aligned itself with the falsehoods of the devil, and opened up a division in Christendom that had culminated in the separation of the Greek and Latin churches. Luther's solution was the restoration of Christian liberty, and particularly the freedom to marry. Candidates who presented themselves for ordination should make no commitment to celibacy, but instead protest to the bishop against this 'devilish tyranny', while those who were already ordained but felt unable to continue in celibacy should be permitted to take a wife, because 'the salvation of your soul is of more importance than their tyrannous, arbitrary, wicked laws, which are not necessary for salvation, nor ordained by God'. For the church to permit priests to maintain housekeepers, but not to marry, Luther warned, was akin to 'putting straw and fire together and forbidding them to smoke or burn'.[39]

The actions of the married priests in Wittenberg encouraged further debate, and the first full-length defence of clerical marriage, Carlstadt's *Axiomata Super Coelibatu, Monachatu et Viduitate*, was printed in 1521. In the same year Melanchthon's *De Votis Monasticis et an Coniugum sit Concedendum Puellae Qui in Monasterio Aliquamdiu Vixerat* set out the case against monastic vows, and defended the validity of marriage for those who were unable to keep their ill-advised promises of chastity.

---

[39] Luther, *To the Christian Nobility*, LW 44, pp. 176ff. Luther was, he claimed, surprised by the actions of the first married clergy who had taken such a radical step despite the harsh penalties that they faced in so doing: LW 48, pp. 231, 235.

Luther also entered the fray, although in part to suggest that the arguments of the Wittenbergers were not compelling.[40] Completed in November 1521 and dedicated to his father, *On Monastic Vows* (1522) was Luther's first substantial treatment of the subject, and anchored the issue firmly within his developing theology of faith and works. The principle of justification by faith was used as a battering ram against the doors of the medieval monasteries. Monastic vows, Luther argued, were mere human works that could do nothing to contribute to salvation, and to suggest otherwise was to attempt to undermine the divine prerogative and diminish the grace of God. The treatise was a detailed attack on vows of poverty, chastity, and obedience, but it was forced chastity which was most forcefully criticised.[41] Monastic chastity had no scriptural foundation, Luther argued, indeed, 'there is no doubt that the monastic vow is in itself a dangerous thing, because it is without the authority and example of scripture'. Such vows ran contrary to Christian freedom; Christ had counselled that the decision to live in marriage or in celibacy was to be voluntary (Matt. 19), yet the church demanded chastity of its monastics. The voluntary continence of the early church had been turned into law by the medieval popes. St Anthony had chosen a life of chastity 'after the pattern of the Gospel', but, Luther protested, 'pursuing human wishes, his successors made this way of life into a vow, a matter of compulsion and obligation'. The contemporary image of monasticism in itself was further and compelling evidence that such vows were ill-advised and impossible to maintain.[42]

A similar denunciation of obligatory continence and forced vows was articulated in Carlstadt's treatise on the subject, *Regarding Vows*. The Latin version of the text included a defamatory attack upon contemporary monasticism, which was less ferocious in the German translation. The basic argument, however, came not from practice, but from Scripture. The law of God expressed in the Bible, Carlstadt argued, was in all cases authoritative above the laws of men. Vows were to be made to God, and God alone, and vows made to the saints, particularly those made by monks and nuns, were

---

[40] Brecht, *Luther*, p. 21.

[41] D. Bagchi, *Luther's Earliest Opponents. Catholic Controversialists 1518–1521* (Minneapolis, 1991), p. 150.

[42] LW 44, 251–400; LW 48, 328ff; M. Mullett, *Martin Luther* (London, 2004), p. 136. Brecht suggests that Luther's critique of vows was not intended as a polemical work, but as a discussion for those already subject to vows, based on the Bible (Brecht, *Luther*, p. 22). However, the impact of the argument was rather more wide ranging, and at least one modern commentator has gone as far as to suggest that the theological basis for the critique of vows was understood in the reception process: U. Rublack, 'Zur Reception von Luthers De Votis Monasticis Iudicium', in R. Postel and F. Kopitzch (eds), *Reformation und Revolution. Beiträge zum politischen Wandel und den sozialen Kräften am Beginn der Neuzeit: Festschift für Rainer Wohlfeil zum 60. Geburtstag* (Stuttgart, 1989), pp. 224–37.

of no value. It was impossible to vow chastity, since chastity was a gift of God and not within the capacity of man to promise of his own volition. For those who were unable to live in chastity, even if they had made such ill-advised vows, he suggested, it would be better to marry in accordance with the scriptural mandate than to continue in the life of fornication that consumed many religious. To marry, even in breach of a vow, was better than to lead an impure life and reject marriage on the basis of a misdirected promise.[43] This argument that a vow of chastity amounted to an unbearable burden placed upon those who were ill-equipped to keep to it was a common argument among evangelical writers, and one that was rooted, at least in the literature, in the conduct of the pre-Reformation clergy. Robert Barnes suggested that the papal demand that priests promise celibacy at ordination was tantamount to theft, a commitment extracted in the same way as a robber might demand money from a traveller before permitting them to cross a bridge.[44] George Joye argued that any vow must be a free promise of that which it was within the capacity of the individual to achieve, and for the pope to demand chastity of the clergy was to violate both of these principles.[45]

However, the theological justification for the breaking of vows came not from the assertion that priests and religious were not capable of living in chastity, but from the assertion that monastic vows were erroneous in their conception. The magisterial reformers were no doubt reluctant to countenance the abandonment of all vows on the basis that they were hard to keep, not least because such an assertion could readily be radicalised to undermine wider legal and social structures. The primary focus was therefore the question of whether vows, and monastic vows in particular, might merit salvation for those who made them. For Luther the answer was a resounding rejection of such assumptions. Vows, as human works, could not improve upon the free gift of faith. Just as the priests of Baal, Luther claimed, had asserted for themselves a special relationship with God on the basis of their piety, so monks erroneously believed that their vows drew them closer to God.[46] Similar arguments were adopted by William Tyndale in his controversy with Thomas More. Chastity, he claimed, was

---

[43] E.J. Furcha, *The Essential Carlstadt. Fifteen Tracts by Andreas Bodenstein (Carlstadt) from Karlstadt* (Scottdale Penn, Waterloo Ontario, 1995), pp. 54, 67.

[44] R. Barnes, *That By Gods Law it is Lawfull for Priestes that hath not the gift of chastite to marry wiues*, in *The Whole Workes of W.Tyndall, Iohn Frith and Doct. Barnes, three worthy martyrs and principall teachers of this churche of Englande*, J. Foxe (ed.) (London, 1573), p. 319.

[45] G. Joye, *The Letters which Joh Ashwell ... sente secretlye to the byschope of Lincolne* (Antwerp, 1531), sig. C1r; Joye, *Defence*, sig. C7v–8r.

[46] LW 7, p. 344.

no virtue but a thing indifferent, and to make a vow of perpetual chastity did not please God, since it had nothing to do with salvation.[47] To believe that a vow of any form was meritorious was not simply to commit an error of judgement, but to erect an idol in the heart, in which hope of salvation was wrongly placed.[48] To do so was to commit a worse form of idolatry than to place trust in the image of a saint, because to trust in a vow was to create an 'image that thou hast fained of God'.[49] The distinction between the monastic vow of chastity and the priestly promise to celibacy was often blurred in the more general evangelical assault upon monasticism and the celibate priesthood. John Bale, for example, declaimed that the priesthood was 'an office in ydolatrye... and the vow y^t they cal of their chastyte a seruyce of prodigious buggerye'; secular and regular clergy were tarred with the same brush.[50] Although the foundations of priestly celibacy and monastic chastity were not identical, discussions of clerical marriage and the vows of religious orders drew upon the same polemical lexicon.

Ulrich Zwingli entered the fray with a defence of clerical celibacy expressed in the *Supplicatio Quorundam Apud Helvetios*.[51] Zwingli's arguments were set against the backdrop of his own marriage to Anna Reinhard in early 1522, celebrated in a public wedding in 1524.[52] In summer 1522 he addressed an appeal to the secular authorities to permit clerical marriage and to afford legal protection to the wives and children of those priests who had already married.[53] The attack on clerical celibacy was, for Zwingli, like Luther, part of the more general assertion of the principle of Christian freedom. Obligatory continence was a burden upon the consciences of those priests who were unable to keep to the discipline, and drove them into more shameful acts that could have been prevented by the toleration of clerical marriage. The law of the church, Zwingli argued, had no foundation in Scripture, and should be overturned. No response was forthcoming from the Diet, although it appears that several other clergy followed Zwingli's lead, particularly in the aftermath of the

---

[47] W. Tyndale, *Answer to Sir Thomas More's Dialogue*, in Foxe (ed.), *Whole Works*, pp. 313–16.

[48] Luther, *The Interpretation of the Two horrible figures: The papal Ass in Rome and the Monk Calf found in Freiburg in Meissen 1523*, in WA vol. 11, pp. 369–85; LW 2, p. 214.

[49] *Exposition of John*, in Foxe (ed.), *Whole Workes*, p. 424.

[50] J. Bale, *The Apology of John Bale Agaynste a Ranke Papyst* (London, 1550), pp. 4v, 12r, 133r.

[51] U. Zwingli, *Supplicatio quorumdam apud Helvetios Evangelistarum*, in M. Schuler & J. Schulthess (eds) *Zwingli Opera* (8 vols, Zurich, 1828–42) vol. 3, p. 18.

[52] O. Farner, 'Anna Reinhart, die Gatten Ulrich Zwingli', *Zwingliana*, 8 (1916): 230–45.

[53] *Eine Freundliche Bitte und Ermahung an die Eidgenossen*, quoted in Ulrich Gabler, *Huldrych Zwingli. His Life and Work* (tr. R.Gritsch) (Edinburgh, 1986), p. 15.

Zurich debates of 1523. The Zurich council had petitioned the bishop to take action against unworthy priests as early as 1507, and further appeals were made to the bishop of Constance to act against clerical concubinage in 1512. In the absence of a concrete response to these earlier complaints, the council was perhaps more sympathetic to calls for the toleration of clerical marriage in the first years of the Reformation. Across the confederation, the fate of married priests lay largely in the hands of the secular authorities; in Zurich there was a degree of protection provided, but in Baden, a pastor with evangelical sympathies who married was handed over to the disciplinary processes of the Episcopal court.[54] Debate continued, however, and in 1522 Sebastien Meyer published a refutation of the defence of clerical celibacy mounted by Bishop Hugo of Constance, the *Commentar zu Einem Hirtenbrief des Bischofs v. Constanz*. Zwingli's view of the religious life had found an appreciative audience in the monastic houses of Berne, and in spring 1525 the council ordered the religious to remain in their cloisters, and forbade them to marry. Several Dominican nuns at Oetenbach asked to be released from their vows after hearing Leo Jud preach, and Wilhelm Reublin, in Witikon, near Zurich, became the first priest to enter into a public marriage.[55]

By 1523, several clergy in Strasbourg had married, including Matthias Zell. Episcopal retribution was swift, and the married clergy were excommunicated in March 1524. The group published a defence of clerical marriage, the *Apellatio*, in April, and Zell's wife, Katherine, addressed a letter to the bishop setting out the biblical justifications for clerical marriage in sufficiently strident terms that the city council instructed her husband to ensure that it was not printed.[56] Zell took up the fight against clerical celibacy himself in 1523, denouncing obligatory continence as a discipline that ran contrary to nature in his *Eine Collation von der Pfaffenehe*. His wife, if at all chastened by her earlier experience, was certainly not silenced, and in the following year composed a defence of clerical marriage and of evangelism, using the marriage of priests to examine the relationship between faith and works, and scripture and tradition. She complained bitterly against clerical immorality and the financial gain afforded by episcopal taxes on concubinage, suggesting that the church was motivated to the defence of clerical celibacy primarily on financial grounds. Citing passages from Genesis, Levicitus, and the Pauline letters, she argued that

---

[54] Gabler, *Zwingli*, p. 64.

[55] B. Gordon, *The Swiss Reformation* (Manchester, 2002), p. 61.

[56] W.S. Stafford, *Domesticating the Clergy. the inception of the Reformation in Strasbourg, 1522–1524* (Missoula, Mont., 1976), pp. 153ff; T. Kaufmann 'Pfarrfrau und Publizistin – Das Reformation Amt der Katharine Zell', *ARG*, 88 (1997): 169–218.

clerical marriage was sanctioned in scripture, and the only appropriate remedy for the church.[57]

This focus on clerical marriage as a divinely sanctioned solution to the undesirable consequences of clerical celibacy remained a commonplace of evangelical writing. Justus Jonas, in his humorous response to Johannes Faber's *Opus adversus nova quaedam et a Christiana religione prorsus aliena dogmata Martini Lutheri* (Rome, 1523), both debated the origins of the discipline and denounced its contemporary manifestation.[58] Francis Lambert's critique of clerical celibacy, *De Matrimonio male inhibito Clericis* (1523), was grounded in a knowledge of the scriptures and the traditions of the church, but was likewise accompanied by a strident denunciation of what the author regarded as the fruits of a false discipline that did nothing other than drive the clergy into fornication. Lambert, a French Franciscan, had renounced his vows in the same year, and taken a wife in Wittenberg. News of such marriages was in itself propaganda for the cause, and individual clerical unions were, for this first generation, worthy of note. George Spalatin recorded the weddings of leading evangelicals in his *Annales Reformationis*, but even less significant matches were commemorated in print. The first clerical marriage in Augsburg, for example, Jacob Griessbuettel's wedding, was the subject of a 1523 pamphlet, Christoph Gerung's *Der Actus und Des Geschicht* (Augsburg, 1523).

Despite the vigorous debate, and the very obvious presence of married clergy in the parishes, the legal position of married clergy in the German principalities remained uncertain, and it was evident that some consideration of the situation was necessary. In January 1530, the Emperor Charles V issued letters from Bologna to convene a Diet in Augsburg in April of the same year, and the summoning of the Diet prompted the composition of a clear statement of evangelical doctrine, formulated in Torgau by Luther, Melanchthon, Bugenhagen and Jonas at the instigation of Elector John of Saxony. The so-called Torgau Articles were re-drafted as the *Confession of Augsburg*, which was presented before the emperor on 25 June.[59] The 28 articles of the Confession comprised 21 statements of Christian doctrine, and seven statements of the abuses that required correction in the contemporary church. Article 23 addressed the marriage of priests, Article 27 monastic vows, and both offered a succinct summary

---

[57] *Apologia of Katharina Schutz for Master Matthew Zell* (Sept 1524), printed in E.A. McKee, *Katharina Schutz Zell* (2 vols, Leiden, Boston, Cologne, 1999) vol. 2, pp. 21–47; see particularly pp. 35–40.

[58] *Defensio Adversus Johannem Fabrum ... pro conjugio sacerdotali defensio* (Wittenberg, 1523).

[59] For a recent examination of the Augsburg Confession, see L. Grane, *The Augsburg Confession* (tr. J.H. Ramussen) (Augsburg, 1987).

of evangelical objections to obligatory clerical celibacy. Article 23 opened with the assertion that the unchastity of priests was a cause of common complaint, a complaint that had been recognised by no less than Pope Pius himself, who had observed that while there had been good reasons to prohibit clerical marriage, there were now far weightier reasons why marriage should once again be permitted.[60] Those priests who had married had done so for the avoidance of scandal, and in accordance with Scripture, which offered marriage as a remedy for fornication (I. Cor. 7), and patristic writing, including those of Cyprian. However, the argument in favour of clerical marriage was based upon more than simply the conduct of the contemporary clergy. It was claimed that the priests of the early church had been married men, and that until the eleventh century there had been married priests in the German church. Such was the extent of opposition to the imposition of clerical celibacy that the publication of the Gregorian reforms had provoked violence. If marriage continued to be forbidden to the clergy, it was likely that the church would find itself with too few pastors to serve the faithful. God had created man and woman for the purpose of procreation, it was argued, and without a 'singular gift' from God, it was not within the power of man to alter this work of creation. The law of man could not, even in a vow of chastity, annul the commandment of God. An apocalyptic note of caution was added; the world was ageing, and the nature of man becoming weaker, making it all the more important that the empire be protected from further vices. God had commanded that marriage be honoured, and the prohibition of marriage had been warned against by Paul, as the 'doctrine of devils'.

Article 27 presented a criticism of the practice of monasticism which would have been familiar to the readers of Luther's works. The monastic communities of the early church were, the text asserted, free associations, and it was only as community discipline had fragmented that vows had been introduced, and even greater constraints placed upon their members. Many individuals had entered monasteries in their youth, before they had reached a sufficient age to know their mind and their abilities. Vows that should have been freely made, if made at all, were instead compelled and, in the case of chastity, demanded without knowing whether such a life lay within the power of the individual. Monastic vows had been held up as meritorious and a work of salvation that would justify the individual before God, as the Catholic church taught, 'that services of man's making satisfy for sins and merit grace'. To make such assertions was, the evangelicals contested, to detract from the glory of God and from the righteousness of faith. Monastic life was extolled as a life of Christian perfection, but from this the faithful erroneously understood that their

---

[60] 'Pius II' in Platina, *Vitae Pontificum* (Venice, 1479).

own married life was without merit. God was to be served by obedience to the divine commandments, and not by the commandments devised by man; monastic vows were not works of supererogation, but were rather null and void. The apparent 'illicit transition to marriage' commended at Augsburg produced a swift condemnation from Catholic theologians at the Diet, who asserted the merits of celibacy and were scathing in their rejection of the argument from infirmity.[61]

The practical and theological objections to obligatory clerical celibacy that were laid down in the Augsburg Confession were clearly those that preoccupied the individuals who took up the defence of clerical marriage in the first decades of the Reformation. Clerical marriage was, it appeared, the obvious remedy for clerical fornication, but the first generations of evangelical polemicists who advocated a change in ecclesiastical discipline also provided such demands with a theological justification. The debate over clerical marriage was not simply a debate over the extent to which the parish clergy were failing to fulfil their obligation to celibacy, but also a debate about the authority of scripture and tradition, the heritage of the primitive church, the role of faith and works in salvation, and the nature of the priesthood. The pivotal position occupied by the celibate priest in the theology and liturgy of the Catholic church ensured an equally prominent place for the married Protestant pastor in the eyes of the faithful and on the printed page of doctrinal controversy. Such exchanges were conducted not only in the learned works printed in Latin, but in the often rather more coarse language of vernacular polemic, and in the lives and example of those clergy who chose to marry, legally or otherwise, in the aftermath of the Reformation. The married ministry was a highly visible manifestation of changing doctrinal principles that extended well beyond the manse.

The evangelical assertion of the supremacy and sufficiency of Scripture was, unsurprisingly, reflected in the polemical defences of clerical marriage in the sixteenth century. The primacy of the word of God over and above the words of men provided a justification for the sweeping denunciation of the canon law and traditions of the church, including clerical celibacy. As Andrew Pettegree has argued, the principle of *sola scriptura* was far more accessible than other key tenets of evangelical theology. 'For most laypeople justification was too difficult to fathom', he writes, '... the doctrine of Scripture alone, in contrast, was powerful not only because of its radical rhetorical simplification, but because it was reinforced in virtually every medium: through preaching, through the image of Luther ... through the pamphlets on the streets, and finally of course through

---

[61] *Corp. Ref.*, Vol. 27, 136–45; the phrase is that of J. Schofield, *Philip Melanchthon and the English Reformation* (Aldershot, 2006), p. 105.

the publication of the Bible itself'.[62] From the start, evangelical writers in Germany and beyond asserted scripture as the ultimate foundation for faith and practice, and promised to 'digge again the wells of Abraham' that had been blocked by the laws and accretions of the 'Philistines'.[63] A stark choice was presented between the word of God and the law of the pope, in which the apparently simple principle of *sola scriptura* was set up as the antagonist to the straw man of *sola ecclesia* that personified Catholic practice. Whether such a dichotomy was sustainable in practice in debateable, and there are good reasons to suppose that the 'exegetical optimism' of the reformers was misplaced, particularly given hermeneutical uncertainties and disputes over interpretative authority.[64] However, the straightforward appeal to the authority of scripture above ecclesiastical tradition proved to be a popular line of argument for those writing in defence of clerical marriage, and one which enabled evangelical writers simply to dismiss centuries of tradition as non-scriptural 'innovation'. Debate focused upon a few key passages, which were cited or interpreted in support of a married priesthood, and to cast doubt upon the origins of the celibacy discipline. The Levitical requirement that priests abstain from their wives during their time of service in the temple, for example, provided one such focal point. The English bible translator and polemicist William Tyndale argued that this requirement offered no support to arguments in favour of the perpetual continence of the Catholic clergy, but rather served to demonstrate that there was nothing in the Old Testament to suggest that marriage was denied to the clergy. Yes, the Levitical priests abstained from their wives, but this was a temporary abstinence, and not one that provided a model for the Christian ministry. The primary message to take from the text was that the priests of the old law had been married men.[65]

---

[62] A. Pettegree, *Reformation and the Culture of Persuasion* (Cambridge, 2005), p. 169.

[63] Tyndale, *The Parable of the Wicked Mammon*, in Foxe (ed.), *Whole Works*, pp. 61–2; for a fuller consideration of the debate over scripture and tradition in the sixteenth century, see G.R. Evans, *Problems of Authority in Reformation Debates* (Cambridge, 1992); G.H. Tavard, *Holy Writ or Holy Church. The Crisis of the Protestant Reformation* (London, 1959); J.M. Headley, 'The Reformation as a Crisis in the Understanding of Tradition', *ARG*, 78 (1987): 5–22; P. Marshall, 'The Debate over Unwritten Verities in Early Reformation England', in B. Gordon (ed.), *Protestant History and Identity in Sixteenth Century Europe, vol. I The Medieval Inheritance* (Aldershot, 1996), pp. 60–77; Gordon, 'The Changing Face of Protestant History and Identity in the Sixteenth Century', in his (ed.), *Protestant History and Identity in Sixteenth-Century Europe*, vol. I, pp. 1–22; Oberman, *Dawn of the Reformation. Essays in Late Medieval and Early Reformation Thought* (Edinburgh, 1992), pp. 289–96; A. McGrath, *Reformation Thought, An Introduction* (Oxford, 1988), p. 97; Y.M. Congar, *Tradition and Traditions. An Historical and a Theological Essay* (London, 1966).

[64] P. Marshall, 'Unwritten Verities', p. 67; McGrath, *Reformation Thought*, pp. 111–12.

[65] Tyndale, *Answer*, p. 317; R. Crowley, *A Confutation of xiii articles wherunto Nicholas Shaxton ... subscribed* (London, 1548), sig. G7r–8r.

Peter Martyr argued that the priests of the Old Testament had been at prayer morning and night, but were still permitted to take wives and beget children. The daily service of the Christian priesthood was therefore no bar to marriage.[66] Attempts to regulate priestly marriage in the Old Testament were limited to restrictions placed upon the groups of women from which a wife might be chosen, and were not intended to prevent priests from taking wives. Indeed, it was argued, marriage was presented in the Old Testament as a godly state, in which man and wife enjoyed divine favour.[67]

The Pauline letters provided the most fertile hunting ground for advocates of clerical marriage in the sixteenth century. The assertion that it was 'better to marry than to burn' was used by the first generation of German married priests to defend their actions, and featured prominently in the pamphlet literature, both as a justification for clerical marriage, and as a solution to the apparent ills of the Catholic church and clergy. To deny the 'remedy' of marriage to the clergy was simply to compound their sins, it was argued, by compelling those who could not live chastely to turn to fornication rather than marriage. Rather than permit marriage as a solution to this problem, Tyndale protested, the pope believed that it was better that a priest take a concubine.[68] Luther, writing on the seventh chapter of Paul's Letter to the Corinthians argued that the married state was equal in the eyes of God to virginity. Marriage was, therefore, compatible with the priesthood, and there was nothing in the New Testament that required obligatory clerical celibacy. To insist upon such a discipline was to present an occasion for sin, for the sake of a law which was human rather than divine. Luther's *Commentary* had been composed as a wedding gift for a friend, but also as a bolster to Melanchthon's brief 1522 commentary, in which he had criticised St Jerome for using the letter of Paul as a buttress for clerical celibacy and superstition. Luther's more substantial study adopted the same critical stance. The Letter to the Corinthians had served as a defence of virginity and abstinence in Catholic hermeneutic, but Luther's exposition positioned the text as a locus classicus for the attack on clerical celibacy. To live in celibacy might free an individual from the labours of marriage, he argued, but there was nothing in Paul's letter to suggest that celibacy was in any way meritorious, or required

---

[66] Martyr, *Commonplaces*, vol. 3, p. 196.

[67] J. Bale, *Yet a Course at the Romyshe Foxe* (Antwerp, 1543), sig. K2v; T. Becon, *Book of matrimony*, in *The Worckes of Thomas Becon whiche he hath hitherto made and published with diuerse other newe books added* (2 vols, London, 1564), vol. 1, fol. HHh3r; fol. Iliv; H. Bullinger *The Golden Boke of Christen Matrimonye* (tr. M. Coverdale) (London, 1543), fol. 23r–v.

[68] Tyndale, *The Obedience of a Christian Man*, in *William Tyndale: Doctrinal Treatises*, H. Walter (ed.) (Cambridge, 1848), p. 134.

of the clergy. Celibacy was indeed possible for some, perhaps one in a hundred thousand, but marriage was necessary for most men, who were subject to the postlapsarian temptations of the flesh. This was as true for the clergy as for the laity, and so, Luther argued, it would be better to permit clerical marriage on the mandate provided by I. Cor. 7:9. 'If you had not persisted in forbidding priests to marry, there would not have been so much trouble', Luther alleged against his opponents. 'For then married men would have become priests, and many would first have tried marriage, and there would have been far fewer whoremongers'.[69]

Marriage, Luther claimed, had been ordained by God as a holy state, and was as acceptable for the priest as it was for all men. The apostles, he argued, had been married men, yet the Catholic church drove away from the priesthood not only those who might want to marry, but those who already lived in this godly state. Peter Martyr used the same Pauline letter to argue that 'it is now a thing worthy to be noted, that married folks are not despised of God'. Marriage was not, he argued, a hindrance to prayer, but rather placed the minister in 'the same state that the common people be'.[70] The exhortations to chastity in the Letter to the Corinthians were not intended to apply to all, but only to those who believed that they could maintain such a life. This was not a choice that was within the power of man, but a gift from God bestowed upon only a few; for the rest, marriage had been instituted as a remedy.[71] The argument that marriage was provided as a remedy not only for the laity but also for the clergy was used by Philip Melanchthon in his *Defence ... of the Mariage of Priestes* (1541), written for the benefit of Henry VIII. Paul's letter to the Corinthians, Melanchthon argued, 'without dowte.. pertayneth not only unto the laye men but also unto priestes. For it is a uniuersal commandement/everyman oughte to haue his wife to auoyde whoredome', with the exception of those who received a gift of chastity from God.[72] The implicit assumption was that this was a gift bestowed only upon a few, and certainly not the supposedly celibate priesthood in its entirety, for whom marriage was, therefore, a valid option. Martin Bucer's *De Coelibatu Sacerdotum* (1544) detailed the damage that had caused in the church by its continued insistence upon clerical celibacy, and Matthew Parker, later archbishop of Canterbury, clearly had an interest in this section of the work, which he annotated and marked for future use. Parker had also read and highlighted a passage in the *Apologia* of Erasmus which praised clerical marriage as a remedy for

---

[69] LW 28.1–56; see also M. Porter, *Sex, Marriage and the Church*, pp. 47ff.

[70] Martyr, *Commonplaces*, vol. 3, p. 196.

[71] Martyr, *Defensio de Petri Martyris Vermilii ...* (Basle?, 1559), sigs. C8v, D8v; S5r.

[72] Melanchthon (tr. George Joye), *A very godly defense full of lerning defending the mariage of preistes* (Antwerp, 1541), sig. A6v.

the ills of the church, using the argument that it was 'better to marry than to burn'.[73]

Marriage was not merely a remedy for fornication, however, and clerical marriage was often defended on the basis that there was a fundamental good in marriage that applied to both priests and people. Paul's assertion in the letter to the Hebrews that 'marriage is honourable and the bed undefiled' provided valuable ammunition for evangelical polemicists, but the defence of marriage was more wide ranging.[74] Martin Luther's tract *On the Estate of Marriage* (1522) presented marriage as a part of the divine creation, a remedy for prostitution, but also as a cause of delight to God who took pleasure in the actions of a man who raised children. The spiritual benefits of marriage far outweighed celibacy with all its concomitant dangers, despite what its detractors would preach.[75] Andreas Carlstadt's *Letter from Wittenberg Concerning Priests and Monks* (1522) was not only a defence of clerical marriage, but also an assertion that marriage was itself pleasing to God. Philip Melanchthon's discussion of clerical marriage asserted the prelapsarian origins of marriage, referring to the creation narrative in Genesis to argue that God 'hathe ingrassed into ether kynde a mutuall desyer to be ioyned togither', and had instituted marriage in order that man would love and honour women, produce children, and raise them in the love of God.[76] The new marriage services composed for Wittenberg and Nuremberg in the 1520s criticised the way in which marriage was mocked by its detractors, extolled its merits, and asserted its divine institution.[77] Matthew Parker, following Bucer's lead, argued that not only was compulsory clerical celibacy damaging to the church, but it also denied clergy the practical benefits of marriage, particularly in their fulfilment of the obligation to hospitality.[78] Such assertions stood in stark contrast to the rather scurrilous representations of wives and marriage in the vernacular literature of the sixteenth century, in which the marriage devil (Eheteufel) and housedevil (Hausteufel) were the cause of all discord

---

[73] CCCC SP 186; N.B. Bjorklund, '"A Godly Wife is an Helper". Matthew Parker and the Defence of Clerical Marriage', *Sixteenth Century Journal*, 34.2 (2003): 347–65, especially 351.

[74] See, for example, Becon, *Matrimony*, fols GGg5r, HHh5v–6r; H. Bullinger, *Der Christliche Ehestand* (The Golden Book of Christian Matrimony), (tr. M. Coverdale) (London, 1543).

[75] LW 45, pp. 11–49.

[76] Melanchthon, *Defence*, sigs A7r, A5r.

[77] Ozment, *Fathers*, p. 8; see also V. Reinburg, 'Liturgy and Laity in Late Medieval and Reformation France', *Sixteenth Century Journal*, 23 (1992): 526–46, for a discussion of the extent to which such ideas permeated lay understanding.

[78] M. Bucer, *De Coelibatu Sacerdotum* (Basle, 1548); Parker CCCC SP 363; Bjorklund, 'Parker', p. 353.

between man and wife.[79] Perhaps suspecting that such mythologies were ingrained in the popular imagination, Luther took the opportunity to exploit the *Eheteufel* myths in order to argue that marriage must indeed be holy if the devil laboured so hard to destroy it.[80]

The suggestion that the destruction of marriage was the work of the devil had its roots in Paul's letter to Timothy, and the warning that there would come, in the future, false prophets who would prohibit marriage. The Pauline text made no specific reference to the marriage of priests, but the assertion that the prohibition of clerical marriage was 'the doctrine of devils' was frequently exploited in evangelical commentaries.[81] Luther, in his commentary on Antichrist, translated into English by John Frith, made the connection between the 'doctrine of devils' phrase in the letter to Timothy, the celibacy of the clergy, and the influence of Antichrist in the Roman church.[82] Melanchthon also identified the 'frantik forbiddinges' of the popes with the doctrine of devils in Paul's epistle. The devilish origins of the prohibition of clerical marriage, Melanchthon argued, were betrayed in its fruits, the moral conduct of the clergy. For the pope to forbid marriage was to align the Catholic church with the very heresies that it had once condemned in Marcion and the Montanists, and to sow the seeds of the tyranny of Antichrist.[83] John Ponet, in a defence of clerical marriage printed in the year that such unions were declared lawful in England, identified the prohibition of marriage to priests as the doctrine of the devil, and argued 'the Apostles taught one thing, the byshop of Rome brought in another'. The prohibition of marriage had been identified by Paul as being of the devil, and its origins were laid bare in the conduct of the supposedly celibate clergy.[84] In a similar vein, Ponet's contemporary John Hooper asserted that compulsory clerical celibacy was indeed 'the true mark to know Antichrist by'.[85] The association of clerical celibacy with the doctrine of devils combined in evangelical literature to create an image of the papal Antichrist, feigning holiness but corrupting the church

---

[79] W. Kawerau, 'Die Reformation und die Ehe', *Reformationsgeschichte*, 8 (Halle: Verein fur Reformationsgeschichte), 1–104.

[80] Johnson, 'Unholy Matrimony', p. 280; see also R. Stambaugh (ed.), *Teufelbucher in Auswahl* (4 vols, Berlin, 1970); Nicholas Schmid, *Teufeln oder Lastern, damit die bosen, unartigen Weiber Besessen Sind* (n.p. (Leipzig), 1557).

[81] I Tim 4:1–2.

[82] J. Frith, *Pistle to the Christen Reader. The Reuelacion of Antichrist* (Antwerp, 1529), p. 71v; see also Luther, *Against the Spiritual Estate of the Pope*, LW 39, p. 292.

[83] Melanchthon, *Defence*, sigs A8v, B1v, B2v.

[84] J. Ponet, *A Defence for the Mariage of Priestes* (London, 1549).

[85] J. Hooper, 'A Brief and Clear Confession of the Christian Faith', in C. Nevinson (ed.), *The Later Writings of Bishop Hooper* (Cambridge, 1852), p. 56.

from within through doctrinal innovation and ecclesiastical laws which ran contrary to scripture.[86]

Scripture contained not only prophetic warnings, but also practical information about the life of the church in the immediate aftermath of the life and resurrection of Christ. Unsurprisingly, given the contested nature of the evidence adduced to support assertions of apostolic origins for the discipline of clerical celibacy, the New Testament was plundered ruthlessly by the defenders of clerical marriage for evidence that the first followers of Christ had been married men. The example of the apostolic church could be cited freely in debate without any detriment to the principle of *sola scriptura* in the polemic of the Reformation, but to possess the example of the primitive church, particularly that of the apostles and even the church Fathers, allowed evangelical writers to argue that their practice was 'more ancient than thou' in debate with their Catholic opponents.[87] The testimony of the apostolic church was critical, not only because this was the period in time that was in closest chronological proximity to the life of Christ, but because the historical record contained in the Acts of the Apostles and other New Testament texts was part of the canonical scriptures. The English evangelical Thomas Becon was insistent that there was a continuity of faith and practice between the church of the apostles and the reformed churches of the sixteenth century that could not be claimed by his Catholic opponents. Not only, he argued, were the apostles married men, but their wives had travelled with them in their itinerant ministry.[88] Philip Melanchthon's defence of clerical marriage drew upon the testimony of scripture and the early historians of the early church, including Eusebius, to argue that clerical marriage was the tradition of the apostolic era.[89] In his *Commentary on Corinthians*, Luther claimed that the apostles were married, and that their example would prove that the early church had permitted married men to become priests and bishops. St Paul, who Luther thought had remained unmarried, had still instructed in his letters to Timothy and Titus that 'one should choose for a bishop a man with only one wife and well-behaved, obedient children'.[90] The example of Paul was, in the era of the Reformation, as at other times in

---

[86] See Parish, *Clerical Marriage*, 123ff.

[87] D. Steinmetz, 'The Council of Trent', in D. Bagchi and D.C. Steinmetz (eds), *The Cambridge Companion to Reformation Theology* (Cambridge, 2004), pp. 233–47, 237–8; McGrath, *Reformation Thought*, p. 143.

[88] Becon, *Matrimony*, sigs GGg4v.

[89] Melanchthon, *Defence*, sig. B3v.

[90] LW 28: 22–3; on the marriage of the apostle, see also J. Calvin, *Institutes of the Christian Religion*, J.T. McNeill (ed.), (2 vols, London, 1961) vol. 2, p. 1251.

the history of clerical celibacy, hotly contested.[91] Indeed, the importance attached to the Pauline writings in evangelical polemic made his statement 'I wish that all men were as I am' increasingly problematic. Luther was willing to concede that Paul was not married, but others were less convinced, including Peter Martyr.[92] A heated debate took place in the late sixteenth century between the Catholic controversialist Thomas Harding and the Elizabethan bishop John Jewel, both of whom came to different conclusions on the basis of variant copies of the letter of Ignatius to the Philadelphians.[93] The controversy over Paul's marriage, and over clerical marriage more generally, revealed the ease with which the debate over priestly celibacy could become part of broader controversies surrounding interpretative authority and scriptural sufficiency as the implications of specific texts and exempla became clear.

Attempts to root clerical marriage in the practice of the apostolic church extended beyond the evidence of scripture and into a broader consideration of the practice of the 'primitive' church. Catholic claims to historical and doctrinal continuity across the Christian centuries were countered in evangelical polemic by the assertion that the institutional church had departed from the practice of the apostles, and entered into a period of decay and corruption that extended into the sixteenth century. The history of the church was accorded no normative value in the defence and articulation of doctrine, but it was recognised as a crucial part of the fashioning of a historical identity for the reformed churches, and of the identification of the apparent decline of the medieval church into false religion and idolatry which made reform so necessary.[94] Thus, the Reformation debate over the origins of clerical celibacy opened anew the records of the councils of the early church, the writings of the Fathers, and the papal reforms of the eleventh century. There was polemical capital to be made from the condemnation of Catholicism in the words of the Fathers and councils that the medieval church claimed as its own. Luther claimed in his preface to Steffan Klingebeil's *Von Priester Ehe* that scripture, the Fathers, and traditions of the church and the precedent

---

[91] See pp. 23–5 above.

[92] Martyr, *Defensio* S1r; W. Turner, *The Rescuyng of the Romishe Fox other vvyse called the Examination of the Hunter* (Bonn, 1545), sig. M1v.

[93] Parish, *Clerical Marriage*, p. 64; J. Booty, *John Jewel as Apologist of the Church of England* (London, 1963), pp. 106–8. The existence of different versions of the letter is discussed in M. Parker (ed.), *A Defence of Priestes Mariages* (London, 1567), sig. S2r; T. James, *A Manvduction or Introdvction unto Divinitie* (Oxford, 1625), p. 23.

[94] For a fuller discussion of these issues, see H. Parish, *Monks, Miracles and Magic. Reformation Representations of the Medieval Church* (London and New York, 2005); Gordon, *Protestant History and Identity*; E. Cameron, 'Medieval Heretics as Protestant Martyrs', in D. Wood (ed.) *Studies in Church History*, 30 (Oxford, 1993): 185–207; L.P. Fairfield, *John Bale. Mythmaker for the English Reformation* (West Lafayette, Indiana, 1976).

of the early popes all pointed to a married clergy in the first Christian centuries, until the medieval church had disrupted that tradition by imposing obligatory celibacy.[95] The Catholic image of a historical and institutional continuity that stretched back to the primitive church was subjected to the iconoclastic hammers of evangelical polemicists, and traditional narratives were reconstructed to demonstrate the novelty of specific doctrine and practice. The key texts and figures that had made up the traditional history of clerical celibacy provided the building blocks for the assertion of a radically different narrative penned in defence of clerical marriage in the sixteenth century. The Reformation debate over clerical celibacy, for example, was presented as a re-enactment of the fourth-century controversy between Jerome and Vigilantius and Jovinian. The English Catholic apologist Richard Smith cast himself in the role of a new Jerome, battling against critics of clerical celibacy who were driven by their own lack of self-control. Luther, he claimed, was simply repeating the errors of Vigilantius.[96] Cesar Baronius, in his *Annales*, accused the 'recent heretics' of 'digging up again the sewer of Jovinian's filth', and argued that the heresies of the Reformation had already been marked as such in the early church.[97] Just as criticisms of virginity had been responsible for the moral decay of the fourth century, Baronius alleged, so the evangelical arguments against clerical celibacy spread the seeds of sin in the sixteenth century. Martin Luther was well aware of the allusions to the heresies of the early church that permeated the writings of his opponents, including the attempts to associate those who argued in favour of clerical marriage with Vigilantius and Jovinian.[98] From the evangelical standpoint, those who leapt to the defence of clerical celibacy in the sixteenth century were as mistaken in their reading of Scripture as Jerome had been. Jerome, it was argued, had failed to appreciate that chastity was a gift of God, and had ignored St Paul's instruction that the bishop was to be the husband of one wife, and Catholic controversialists in the sixteenth century simply repeated Jerome's mistakes.[99]

---

[95] S. Klingebeil, *Von Priester Ehe* (Wittenberg, 1528).

[96] R. Smith, *Defensio Sacri Episcoporu[m] & sacerdotum coelibatus contra impias & indoctas Petri Martyris* (Paris, 1550), sigs B1, C3v– 4r.

[97] C. Baronius, *Annales Ecclesiastici Ann.390* c.47 (Venice, S. Monti: 1740), vol. 6, p. 84; cf T. Martin, *A Treatise Declarying and Plainly Provyng that the Pretensed marriage of Priestes is no Mariage* (London, 1554), sigs A1v–3v.

[98] *Judgement on Monastic Vows* (1522) LW 44, pp. 305–6; see also LW 54 pp. 9–11, 18–20; Calvin, *Institutes*, p. 1251.

[99] M. Bucer, *The Gratulation of the Most Famous Martin Bucer* (tr. T. Hoby), (London, 1549), sig. B8v–C1r; Turner, *Huntynge and Fyndynge Out of the Romyshe Foxe which more than seuen years hath bene hyd among the bisshopes of England* (Basle 1543), sig. E5v; Melanchthon, *De Ecclesia et de Auctoritate Verbi Dei*, in C.L. Hill (ed.), *Melanchthon, Selected Writings* (Minneapolis, 1963), p. 161; see also Calvin, *Institutes*, pp. 1250, 1253.

Like the writings of the Fathers, the decrees of popes and councils were accorded no objective authority in the definition of doctrine, but the determination of both sides to possess the heritage of the primitive church ensured for them a prominent position in the debates of the Reformation. Several Protestant histories of clerical celibacy took as their starting point the letters of Pope Siricius to the church of Gaul.[100] The letters had significance, it was argued, not because they carried the authority of the bishop of Rome, but because they served as evidence that the clergy of the fourth century were married, and as an indication of widespread resistance to the demands of the pope. Siricius' efforts to regulate the sexual conduct of the clergy were regarded as an unwarranted intrusion and innovation.[101] Papal attempts to introduce clerical celibacy in the fourth century, Melanchthon argued, amply demonstrated that 'we ar not the autors of any newe exa[m]ple in the chirche / but that we call agene the olde and godly usage'.[102] Celibacy, not marriage, was the innovation. Such 'old and godly usage' was to be found not only in the canons of the councils, but also in the occasional lone voice raised in objection to innovation. The figure of Paphnutius, whose legendary intervention at the Council of Nicaea had become a staple of eleventh-century criticisms of obligatory clerical celibacy, was to loom large in the pages of Protestant polemic.[103] Luther, both in the Wittenberg Disputations and in his *Von den Konziliis und Kirchen* (1539), argued that it was possible in the life of the church that even entire assemblies of bishops might err. Such a drift into heresy could be stemmed, he suggested, by the guidance of the Holy Spirit, inspiring individuals to stand firm to the defence of the truth. Paphnutius, Luther claimed, was one such advocate. His defence of marriage at the Council of Nicaea had prevented the imposition of obligatory continence; 'sometimes one man is able to do more in a council than the whole council besides', Luther wrote, as even 'the papists themselves do witness'.[104] The Catholic church of the sixteenth century, however, refused to let a 'Paphnutius'

---

[100] See pp. 72–4 above.

[101] See, for example, Foxe, *Acts and Monuments* (1563), p. 4; Melanchthon, *Defence*, sig. B3r; Calvin, *Institutes*, p. 1251.

[102] Melanchthon, *Defence*, sig. B4v.

[103] For the development of the legend, see pp. 65–7 above.

[104] Luther, *Commentary on Galatians* (LW 26 and 27) c.2; cf Luther, *Church Postils, 1522*, in J.N. Lenker (ed.), *Sermons of Martin Luther: Church Postils* (2 vols, Baker Book House, 1989), vol. 1 p. 13: 'Hence it is very foolish for the councils to wish to determine and establish what a man must believe, when there is often not a single man present who ever tasted the least of the divine Spirit. So it was in the Council of Nice, when they undertook to enact laws for the spiritual orders that they should not marry, which was all false because it has no foundation in the Word of God. Then a single man arose, by the name of Paphnutius, and overthrew the whole affair'.

speak. The Fathers at Nicaea had been persuaded by the arguments of the bishop, but at the Council of Constance the church had denounced as heretics two Paphnutius figures, and condemned them to death. John Calvin cited the words of Paphnutius to support the assertion that chastity was comprised in lawful cohabitation with a wife, and that clerical marriage should therefore be permitted.[105] Likewise, Philip Melanchthon used the figure of Paphnutius to argue that marriage was a form of chastity, and one that imbued the priesthood with a greater honour than promises of celibacy that the clergy failed to observe.[106] The legend was also discussed in the Wittenberg Articles of 1536, a statement of faith forged as a result of the dialogue between the Lutherans and a delegation from England in 1535. Negotiations floundered in the mire of Henry VIII's marital concerns, but a draft Confession had already been started, probably by Melanchthon. 'Purity before God', it was asserted in the fourteenth article, 'consists in not polluting one's conscience but in obeying God. Therefore celibacy is not purity, but marriage is purity since it is sanctified by the word of God. Thus Paphnutius said that conjugal custom is continency.'[107] Henry VIII was unconvinced, and in a letter to the Germans in August 1538 defended clerical celibacy as the logical application of the 'eunuchs for the sake of the kingdom' principle in Matthew's Gospel, and from a wealth of patristic sources. In an aside directed towards Luther, the king also suggested that the inability of a man to live in celibacy was not in itself an argument in favour of a married priesthood, but rather an argument against the ordination of unsuitable candidates to the ministry.[108] However Paphnutius was again to be marshalled to the defence of clerical marriage by English evangelicals in the 1540s and beyond, who cited his assertion of the sanctity of marriage as an example of the attitude of the primitive church to clergy and celibacy.[109]

---

[105] Calvin, *Institutes*, p. 1252.

[106] Melanchthon, *Defence*, sigs C2r, D2r.

[107] G. Bray, *Documents of the English Reformation 1526–1701* (Cambridge, 2004), pp. 118ff; quotation at p. 151.

[108] G. Burnet, *History of the Reformation of the Church of England* (6 vols, London, 1825), vol. 4, pp. 384–91.

[109] See, for example, Becon, *Matrimony*, sigs IIir, LLl1r; Matthew Parker, *Defence of Priestes Mariages*, sig. G8r–v. For the use and exposition of the Paphnutius story by Catholic writers in the seventeenth century, see the comments of the Dominican Noel Alexandre in his *Dissertationum Ecclesiasticarum Trias. Prima de Divina Episcoporum supra presbyteros eminentia Blondellum. Altera de sacrorum ministrorum coelibatu, sive de historia Paphnutii cum Nicaeno canone concilianda. Tertia de vulgate Scripturae sacrae versione* (Paris, 1678), and the commentary of the Bollandist Jan Stiltinck, 'An Veresimile sit S Paphnutium se in Concilio Nicaeno Opposuisse legi de Continentia Sacerdotum et Diaconorum', in *Acta*

The eleventh-century *Rescript of Ulric* that had served to popularise the legend of Paphnutius was also exploited by evangelicals in England and on the continent in the sixteenth century.[110] The German humanist Johannes Nauclerus printed a copy of the letter of Ulric that was to be used by Robert Barnes, Matthias Flacius, and a number of English polemicists to criticise the reforms of the eleventh century.[111] An English translation of Ulric's denunciation of the Gregorian reforms was printed in 1547 as *An Epistle of Moche Learni[n]g sent … vnto Nicholas, Bysshope of Rome*, and the text of the letter was reproduced in the 1570 edition of John Foxe's *Actes and Monuments*. Foxe was clearly aware of the questions surrounding the authenticity of the letter, and when confronted by accusations from the Catholic apologist Nicholas Harpsfield that the letter was less than authentic and its chronology contradictory, defended its inclusion in his history by presenting the text as the work of Volusianus.[112] Such an assertion was no doubt facilitated by Matthew Parker's publication of two letters purporting to be the work of Volusianus in 1569, *Epistolae Duae D. Volusiani Episcopi Carthaginensis*.[113] However this attribution would appear to have been no more accurate than the traditional association of the letter with Ulric, to whom credit was given by Melanchthon, Aeneas Sylvius, and Matthias Flacius.[114] Flacius and John Bale were both clear in their identification of Ulric as the author of the letter, although Foxe suggested that it was likely that both were mistaken in this, given the clear concordance between the complaint in the letter that married priests were prevented from saying Mass, and the reforms implemented in the pontificate of Nicholas II.[115] The authorship of Ulric was certainly assumed by Thomas Becon, who presented two letters in his *Booke of Matrimonye*, the first identical to that which was included in Foxe's *Acts and Monuments*, and the other, rather shorter, which paraphrased the text which was to be printed as the second of Foxe's letters. Becon's *Booke of Matrimony* was included in his

---

Sanctorum Septembris (Venice, 1761) vol. 3, pp. 784–7, quoted in C. Cochini, *The Apostolic Origins of Priestly Celibacy* (San Francisco, 1990), pp. 23ff.

[110] See pp. 114–15 above.

[111] *MGH LdL*, vol. 1, pp. 254–60; R. Barnes, *Supplication unto the most Gracious prince Henry VIII* (London, 1534), sig. T3r; J. Ponet, *An Apology Fully Aunswering by Scriptures and Aunceaunt Doctors … D.Steph Gardiner* (Strasbourg, 1555).

[112] N. Harpsfield, *Dialogi Sex* (Antwerp, 1566), sig. K1r; Foxe, *Actes and Monuments (1570)*, p. 1320.

[113] Parker's copy of the letter is in CCCC MS 101 fols 201ff.

[114] Parish, *Clerical Marriage*, p. 101; Foxe, *Actes and Monuments (1570)*, p. 1321.

[115] J. Bale, *Scriptorum Illustrium Maioris Brytanniae Quam Nunc Angliam & Scotiam Vocant: Catalogus* (Basle, 1557), p. 65; M. Flacius Illyricus, *Catalogus Testium Veritatis, Qui Ante Nostram Aetatem Reclamarunt Papae* (Basle, 1566), pp. 92, 99ff; M. Judex and J. Wigand, *Ecclesiastica Historia* (Basle, 1560–74), Cent. IX, cols 540–42.

Whole Worckes, printed by John Day, who also acted as Foxe's printer for the 1570 edition of the *Acts and Monuments*. However, the two English translations are not identical, and it may be more likely that it was not Foxe, but Day, or even John Bale, who introduced Becon to the source.[116] Both the account of Paphnutius' intervention at the Council of Nicaea, and the complaints against obligatory clerical celibacy contained in the letter of Ulric, provided vital evidence for those who wished to argue that marriage had not been prohibited to the clergy until at least the second millennium of Christian history. Where the Fathers of the church had wavered in the fourth century, they had been deterred from enacting legislation against clerical marriage by the words of a saintly bishop, and when the bishops of Rome had asserted the requirement to priestly celibacy, they had been criticised and corrected by another holy bishop, Ulric (or Volusianus).

The decrees of the councils of the early church were similarly subject to employment in the service of evangelical polemic. Peter Martyr, in the *Defensio ... in Schola Tigurina*, presented a comprehensive overview of the councils of the early church and their rulings on clerical celibacy and marriage. In defence of clerical marriage he turned to the Councils of Ancyra (314), Neocaesarea, Nicaea, Gangra, Chalcedon and Carthage.[117] The most controversial of these assertions of the legitimacy of clerical marriage was based upon the tenth canon of the Council of Ancyra, which Martyr argued provided evidence that deacons who were not able to live in chastity were permitted to marry. Such a concession was indeed evident in some of the histories of the council, but it had no enduring effect, and if it was regarded as a legitimate concession, soon fell into disuse.[118] The Council of Gangres was exploited by the author of the English *Confutation of Unwritten Verities*, with the intention of undermining the legitimacy of the prohibition of clerical marriage, and indeed the validity of the argument from conciliar tradition altogether. The council had held the penalty of excommunication over the faithful who refused the sacraments of married clergy, yet in the sixteenth century, the writer protested, priests faced excommunication if they continued to live with their wives. The Gangres canon was presented as evidence not only of the continued acceptance of the married priesthood, at least in theory, well into the fourth century, but also of failure of the church to abide by its own conciliar decisions.[119] Apparent contradiction in the canonical tradition was also used by John Foxe to argue against the assertion that the second Council of Carthage

---

[116] Parish, *Clerical Marriage*, p. 103.

[117] Martyr, *Defensio*, vol. 2, sig. G5vff.

[118] For a fuller discussion, see R. Cholij, *Clerical Celibacy in East and West* (Worcester, 1989), pp. 75–8 and chapter 2 above.

[119] E.P., *A Confutatio[n] of Unwritte[n] Verities* (Wesel, 1556), sig. G3vff.

had legislated in favour of clerical celibacy. Foxe had in his sights the prohibition of clerical marriage in the English Six Articles of 1539, and the assertion that such a prohibition could claim its origins in the Carthage canons. Just as some letters had been wrongly attributed to the Fathers, Foxe claimed, so it was entirely possible that the canons of councils had been fabricated by the bishops of Rome. The third canon of the Council of Carthage was presented as one such example, which ran contrary to the assertion at Gangres that the sacraments of the married clergy were valid, in itself testimony to the toleration of clerical marriage in the fourth century.[120] The popularity of the Gangres canon among evangelical polemicists is predictable, given the penalties that it imposed upon those who impugned the sacraments of married clergy. However, the frequency with which the Gangres canon was cited perhaps also reflected the ready availability of a new vernacular history of the council; Luther provided a preface to Kymeus' German edition, *Ein Alt Christlich Concilium fur 1200 jaren zu Gangra jnn Paphlagonia gehalten, wider die hoch genante heiligkeit der München vnd Wiederteuffer . . . verdeutscht und ausgelegt*, of 1537, which was highly critical of Anabaptists, but which also brought the decrees of the Council to a German audience.

It is worth noting that many of the decrees of the councils that were cited as evidence that clerical marriage was permitted in the early church were assemblies of the Eastern church. This is not surprising, given the continued presence of a married ministry in the Greek churches, and the potential value of the exploitation of this precedent to the proponents of clerical marriage in the Latin West. A commentary on the Pauline Epistles by the French humanist Jacques Lefevre d'Etaples included amongst its criticisms of Catholic piety and practice a denunciation of the obligatory celibacy demanded of priests. It was, he proposed, legitimate to argue that celibacy was a superior state to marriage, but there was no justification for extrapolating from this that celibacy was necessary for the priesthood. History showed that priests and deacons had been married men until the pontificate of Gregory VII in the West, and the Greek church, he argued, had remained faithful to the apostolic tradition in retaining the custom of marriage.[121] The argument that the practice of the Greek church reflected the traditions established in the early church, and that it was therefore the Latins who had innovated on the matter of clerical celibacy, was clearly fruitful for those writing in defence of clerical marriage in the sixteenth

---

[120] Foxe, *Actes and Monuments (1583)*, p. 1163.

[121] J. Lefevre d'Etaples, *Commentaires sur les épîtres de Saint Paul* (Paris, 1512). Luther had read this work, which was only condemned by the Sorbonne in 1521, when the issues that it raised became all the more controversial after the publication of Luther's writings on faith and grace.

century.[122] Indeed, the example of the Greek church had been used from the early years of the Reformation to assert the infidelity of the Roman church to the faith of the apostles. Luther, at the Leipzig Disputation of 1519, defended his assertion that the normative authority claimed by the pope in matters of doctrine was without foundation by asserting the example of the Christians of the Greek church, who for the preceding millennium had been outside the authority of the bishop of Rome.[123] There were, he argued, similarities in faith and practice between the Greek church and the nascent evangelical congregations, not least in the utraquism that was practised in the East, and which had been demanded by the Hussites.[124] Links between the Lutheran churches and the Greek church were to become more than a rhetorical device as the linguistic barriers between the two churches were eroded by figures such as Philip Melanchthon, Paul Dolscius, and Martin Crusius. Personal contact came first, it appears, through an elderly priest named Demetrios, who met Melanchthon in Wittenberg in the late 1550s, and returned to Greece with a translation of the Augsburg Confession based upon the 1540 variata, and a personal letter from Melanchthon addressed to the patriarch.[125] No reply was forthcoming from Constantinople, and negotiations between the churches commenced in seriousness only in more auspicious times, and when a more receptive Patriarch occupied the See. In 1573, a new imperial ambassador, the evangelical von Sonnegk, arrived in Constantinople in the company of his Lutheran chaplain and bearing letters from Crusius and Jakob Andreae. This initial contact opened up a theological dialogue between the Lutheran theologians of Tübingen and the Greek church which lasted between 1574 and 1581, and extended into a variety of doctrinal and pastoral concerns, including the question of clerical celibacy and marriage, and monastic vows, which had been criticised in the Augsburg Confession.[126] Despite evident areas of disagreement, not least over the sacraments and the eucharist, the saints, and the theology of justification, there were clear issues upon which

---

[122] See, for example, Melanchthon, *Defence*, sig. A2r.

[123] LW 31, p. 322.

[124] LW 32, p. 58–9; for a more general discussion of the relationship between the Lutherans and the Greek churches, see B.F. Korte, 'Early Lutheran Relations with the Eastern Orthodox', *Lutheran Quarterly*, 9 (1957): 53–9.

[125] E. Benz, 'Die grechische Übersetzung der Confession Augustana aus dem Jahre 1559', in his *Wittenberg und Byzanz* (Munich, 1971), pp. 94ff; Benz identifies Melanchthon himself as the most credible author of the document, which went beyond the Confession in attempting to establish the ecumenicity of Lutheranism.

[126] G. Mastrantonis, *Augsburg and Constantinople: The Correspondence Between Patriarch Jeremiah II and the Tubingen Theologians* (Brookline, MA, 1982); Benz, *Wittenberg und Byzanz*; E. Benz, *Die Ostkirche im Lichte der Protestantischen Geschichtsschreibung* (Freiburg, 1952), pp. 17–20.

there was common ground, most evidently in the rejection of compulsory clerical celibacy. The intention, at least on the part of the Lutherans, was to establish precisely this evidence of shared faith and praxis in order to rebut accusations of novelty and innovation. On the subject of clerical marriage, this was more readily accomplished, but on other fundamental matters of faith, the Greek patriarch was insistent that it was in the tradition of the East that there was the greatest fidelity to the practice and counsels of the patristic church.

The foundations of the clerical marriage discipline in the Greek church had been laid at the Council in Trullo in the late seventh century, and in asserting the controversial right of married priests to continue in the use of their marriages after ordination the Trullan Fathers had attempted to anchor the practice sanction in the so-called Apostolic Canons of the late fourth century.[127] This same source was also utilised in the defence of clerical marriage in the sixteenth century, and particularly in defence of the assertion that the practice of the primitive church had been to admit married men to the priesthood. The sixth canon, which threatened with excommunication any cleric in higher orders who put away his wife under the 'pretext of piety', was particularly useful in this respect, apparently providing evidence of both a married higher clergy in the apostolic church, and of a conscious decision to condemn those who asserted that for a priest to leave his wife was conducive to religious duty.[128] Catholic writers, however, were equally willing to exploit the canons to demonstrate the antiquity of the discipline of celibacy by drawing upon the parts of the collection that prohibited the ordination of digamists, or of those who kept concubines.[129] The canons themselves had been virtually unknown in the west until the sixteenth century, and their authenticity and validity was not accepted by all those who made mention of them. John Calvin, for example, while referring to the threats held over those clerics who might attempt to put away their wives, cautioned that the canons were often contradictory, and that the epithet 'apostolic' was no guarantee of provenance.[130] In the search for evidence of the apostolic origins of the married priesthood, however, such caution was often thrown to the wind of polemical expediency.

---

[127] See pp. 74–6 above.

[128] Becon, *Matrimony*, sig. NNn3r; Martyr, *Defensio*, sig. U6r.

[129] In this respect, Catholic polemicists such as Richard Smith were in agreement with more recent research, including that of Cholij, who suggests that the refusal to ordain digamists on the basis of a defect of chastity implies the origins of a continence discipline in the early church. Cholij, *Clerical Celibacy*, p. 15.

[130] J. Calvin, *The Necessity of Reforming the Church* (tr. J.K.S. Reid), *Library of Christian Classics*, 22 (1954), p. 215.

To assert that clerical marriage was a part of the apostolic tradition was to locate the origins of obligatory priestly celibacy within the later history of the medieval church, as a papal innovation rather than a custom that dated from the time of Christ. Antiquity was not the foundation of doctrinal authority, but by reclaiming that antiquity from the narrative of Catholic history it was possible to position evangelical demands for change within a broader chronology and geography that blunted accusations of novelty and schism. Evangelical polemicists fashioned a history of Christianity in which the nascent reformed churches acquired roots in the events of the past, and the apparent innovations of the sixteenth century their origins in the ancient practices of the early church. However, the history of the medieval church remained a significant part of this polemical scheme, as a rich vein to be plundered for illustrations of doctrinal decay, a proliferation of changes in practice, and the evident need for urgent moral reform. The history of the true church was a history of continuity of faith, rather than institution, it was argued, and by reconstructing the narratives of the medieval past it was possible for evangelicals to assert that it was the institutional Catholic church, and not their own, which had broken apart this chain of belief. The history of clerical celibacy and marriage was a case in point. In presenting evidence of a married priesthood in the first Christian centuries, critics of the discipline of celibacy argued in straightforward terms that it was a law of the church which lacked apostolic origins. By constructing a narrative of the imposition of obligatory celibacy by popes and councils in the post-apostolic era, it was possible to locate the precise moment at which the Catholic church had broken with tradition and drifted into error. Popes and prelates had a significant role to play in this unfolding drama of the Reformation.

Attempts to break apart the traditional histories of the church frequently relied upon the ability to manipulate that same evidence to a different end, and the Protestant narrative of the history of clerical celibacy in the medieval church was constructed upon a broadly familiar base. The deliberations of the early councils and synods were scrutinised in detail and exploited to new ends, and the decrees of the popes were likewise subject to this same process. The authority of the bishop of Rome in the present might be challenged, but the character and custom of the popes of the past remained very much the foreground of the debate. It is no surprise, therefore, that the pontificate of Gregory VII emerged as a defining moment in evangelical narratives of ecclesiastical history, and in the history of clerical marriage. Until this period, it was argued, the Latin church had been served largely by a married clergy, in a millennium of historical continuity that was to be unravelled by the actions of one man. John Bale denounced the eleventh-century reforms as 'profane novelties' which turned honest married priests into 'secret whoredome' and set in train a custom whereby the clergy cultivated a feigned holiness in order to preserve their careers, but led a life which had little in common with the ideal of the celibate priest.[131] John Foxe, drawing upon Bale's work, argued that the Gregorian reforms, particularly in their insistence upon clerical celibacy, ran counter not only to Scripture and the custom of the early church, but also to the laws of nature, in the pope's insistence that the clergy should lead the life of angels.[132] Opposition on the part of the clergy in France and in Germany to the imposition of clerical celibacy was presented as evidence that the papal reforms were perceived as innovation on a grand scale. The violence at the Council of Erfurt was described by several writers, including Robert Barnes, alongside the assertion of the French clergy that they would prefer to leave their altars than their wives.[133] The sources exploited in the construction of this narrative of Gregory's pontificate were varied, and included both 'papal' materials, and the rather more critical letters and chronicles of those who opposed the imposition of mandatory celibacy, and other components of the Hildebrandine reforms. Matthias Flacius Illyricus, for example, reproduced the pope's denunciation of the married clergy in his letter to the clergy of Constance, and John Foxe borrowed heavily from both this and from Bale's *Catalogus* in compiling his own account of the eleventh-century church.[134] Bale, Foxe, Flacius and others also drew substantially upon the newly available letters of Cardinal Benno, whose contemporary condemnations of Gregory VII included a detailed dissection of his pontificate and reforms, alongside the assertion that the pope practised necromancy in order to secure his own ends.[135] The chronicle of Lambert of Hersfield, which had presented a stridently critical picture of the moral conduct of the clergy and the reforms of the pope, was also clearly accessible to Flacius and to Foxe, and provided further valuable evidence of opposition to Gregory's actions. Collections of canon law charted the evolution of doctrine and practice in

---

[131] J. Bale, *The First Two Parts of the Actes, or unchast examples, of the Englysh Votaryes* (London, 1551), Part 2, p. 32vff.

[132] Foxe, *Actes and Monumentes (1570)*, p. 227r.

[133] Becon, *Matrimony*, sig. MMm2v; Ponet, *Defence*, sig. C3r–v; R. Barnes, *Vitae Romanorum Pontificum* (Basle, 1555), pp. 196–216; Barnes, *Supplication*, sig. U1r–v; Foxe, *Actes and Monumentes (1570)*, p. 227; R. Gualther, *Antichrist. That is to say a True Report that Antichriste is come* (tr. J. Old), (Emden, 1556), sig. L6r.

[134] Flacius, *Catalogus*, p. 239. For a fuller discussion of these themes, see Parish, *Monks, Miracles and Magic*, p. 134, and the exceptionally useful detailed analysis of Tom Freeman in 'St Peter did not do thus': http://www.hrionline.ac.uk/johnfoxe/apparatus/freemanStPeterpart1.html

[135] O. Gratius, *Fasciculus rerum expetendarum ac fugiendarum* (Cologne, 1535) was a collection of historical treatises on a variety of subjects, both ecclesiastical and profane, which included a number of anti-papal documents.

the church, but for evangelical polemicists it was the medieval chronicles such as Hersfield's annals, and the bitter condemnations of writers such as Benno, that allowed the denunciation of mandatory clerical celibacy as an invention of the eleventh-century papacy. The reformation debate over the history of clerical celibacy was not only informed, but also shaped, by the controversies of an earlier age. The recourse to the record of the past did not simply provide a basic chronology, but also a context and vocabulary for the defence of clerical marriage in the sixteenth century.

A similar process was evident in the construction of a Protestant history of clerical celibacy in England. The clergy of the English church, it was contested, had been free to marry at least until the advent of Roman influence in the pontificate of Gregory the Great, and even into the tenth century, when the monastic reforms of Dunstan, Oswald and Anselm marked the ascendancy of the 'votaries' over the married secular clerks.[136] A new history of the tenth-century church appeared in the works of Bale, Foxe, and the Magdeburg Centuriators, from which the reforming saints, Dunstan in particular, emerged as the villains of the piece, guilty of subverting secular authority, persecuting the married clergy, and feigning false miracles in support of their newfangled notion of clerical celibacy.[137] The foundation for this narrative lay in the medieval chronicles, hagiographies, and contemporary commentaries. Bale, and Foxe and Flacius after him, drew their account of Dunstan and the reform of the church from his early biographers, including Osbern and William of Malmesbury, and the later chroniclers and historians Fabian, Capgrave, and Johannes Nauclerus. The purpose was to demonstrate both the flawed foundations of clerical celibacy in the English church, and the apparent novelty of the celibacy laws. If the English clergy had not been married throughout the first millennium, it was argued, there would have been no need to take action against them in the tenth century. Thus it was, Bale argued, in the reforms of Dunstan that 'the face first of the Brytonysh and then of the Englysh church sore changed'.[138] The opposition of the clergy of Mainz and Constance to the imposition of obligatory celibacy in the eleventh century had parallels in the protests of the clergy of York and Norwich in the face of Anselm's action against the married clergy.[139] Bale and Foxe gleaned from Matthew Paris a comic vignette in the form of the actions of the papal legate John of Crema in 1125, who had, by contemporary accounts, been apprehended with a prostitute the very night that he had forbidden clergy the company

---

[136] See, for example, Bale, *Votaries*, Part I, pp. 54ff; Foxe, *Actes and Monumentes (1570)*, pp. 207ff.

[137] For a more detailed discussion, see Parish, *Monks, Miracles and Magic*, chapter 5.

[138] Bale, *Votaries*, Part 1, p. 62v.

[139] Bale, *Votaries*, Part 2, p. 60r–v; Foxe, *Actes and Monumentes (1570)*, p. 247.

of their wives.[140] A new meaning for debates in the present was to be found by locating them within an ecclesiastical history that contextualised them within a polemically useful past; Reformation was restoration rather than innovation, and the foundations of Catholic tradition, through a selective approach to the sources, were portrayed as fanciful, if not farcical.

The evangelical assertion of the authority of scripture in determining matters of faith and practice did not render obsolete the narrative of ecclesiastical history. Rather than rejecting outright the precedent of the medieval church, the attack on clerical celibacy in the sixteenth century pressed the historical narrative into the service of the Reformation. This same appropriation of the records and rhetoric of Catholicism was also evident in the evangelical presentation of the relationship between clerical celibacy and the sacrificial function of the priest at Mass. In Catholic devotional and polemical literature, the obligation to celibacy on the part of the priest was a function of his proximity to the sacred in the handling of the consecrated eucharistic elements, and his agency in the transformative miracle of the Mass. In the hands of evangelical polemicists, this link between priestly function and conduct was asserted in equally confident terms, but twisted to a different end. The basic assertion that the nature of the sacrament demanded that its celebrant make a commitment to celibacy was rejected; if Christ were not materially present in the bread and wine, then the character of the priest could not be construed as dishonouring God. More polemically powerful, however, was the notion that the failure of the Catholic clergy to fulfil their obligation to celibacy cast doubt upon not only that obligation, but also the theology of the Mass that underpinned it. This was not a simple assertion of the widely condemned principle that the sacraments of incontinent clergy were in some way inefficacious, but a penetrating proposition that the theology of transubstantiation was erroneous. Thus, it was not the rejection of Catholic sacramental theology that argued in favour of the abolition of obligatory celibacy, but rather the perceived failure of that obligation that justified the redefinition of doctrine. The concubinary priest was not just the embodiment of an argument in favour of clerical marriage on the basis that it was 'better to marry than to burn', but also an argument for more sweeping doctrinal change. John Bale examined the historical foundations of the Catholic Mass, and asserted that a link between clerical incontinence and the doctrine of transubstantiation was evident in the twelfth century. Again, Catholic doctrine was argued to be condemned by its own history. The theology of the Mass, Bale argued, had been tied not only to the principle of clerical celibacy but also to the practice of clerical concubinage

---

[140] See p. 158 above; Bale, *Catalogus*, p. 175; Foxe, *Actes and Monumentes (1570)*, p. 256.

since the seventh century, and this association continued to be evident in the centuries that followed. Peter Lombard, he argued, 'gaue unto [the church] transubstanciacyon', but was himself the child of a nun in breach of her vow of chastity.[141] In one narrative, Strasbourg priests extolled the Mass as 'the chefe upholder of our liberte, wherby our whores a[n] harlots euerychone were mayntayned in ryche felicite'.[142] Such arguments were particularly popular in the perorations of the anti-Mass tracts circulating in English in the late 1540s, particularly in the works of Luke Shepherd and William Turner.[143] However, the general argument was common across the spectrum of evangelical writing. Luther's 1521 treatise *The Misuse of the Mass* included a denunciation of the celibacy that was imposed upon a clergy that was unwilling or unable to fulfil the obligation. 'The devil working through the pope is nowhere so raging and senseless as in the matter of chastity and unchastity', Luther complained, suggesting that the prohibition of marriage in the service of the sacrament was little more than an injunction to 'Go ahead and fornicate'.[144] It was surely better, Luther argued, to allow priests to marry than to live with the consequences of a compulsory celibacy to which many did not adhere. 'So holy is the holiness of this most holy sacrament', he mocked, 'that no man can become a priest if he has married a virgin and his wife is still living... but if one has defiled six thousand harlots, or violated countless matrons and virgins, or has kept many Ganymedes, that would be no impediment to his becoming a bishop or cardinal or pope.'[145]

Luther was not alone in such views. Desiderius Erasmus suggested that there was no good reason to prohibit clerical marriage, 'especially when there is such a horde of priests among whom chastity is rare'. The church would be better served by priests who lived in the chastity of marriage than those who practised the false chastity of celibacy.[146] John Calvin complained bitterly that the Catholic defenders of clerical celibacy argued from the Old Testament example of the Levitical priests that abstinence was required before approaching the sacred, and that it would be 'unseemly' for Christian priests to administer the sacraments if they were married. But the function

---

[141] Bale, *Romyshe Foxe*, sig. C8r; *Mysterye*, sigs 4r–v, 33v, 39v.

[142] William Roy, *Rede me and be nott wrothe*, (np, 1528), sig. A7r.

[143] See Parish, 'Beastly is their Living and their Doctrine. Celibacy and Theological Corruption in Reformation Polemic', in Gordon (ed.), *Protestant History and Identity*, vol. 1, pp. 138–52.

[144] LW 36, p. 206.

[145] Luther, *Babylonian Captivity*, LW 36, p. 114.

[146] A. Hyma, 'Erasmus and the Sacrament of Marriage', in *Archiv fur Reformationsgeschiche*, 48 (1957): 145–64; R. Bainton, *Erasmus of Christendom* (New York, 1969), pp. 49–50; P.S. Allen et al. (eds), *Erasmi Epistolae*, vol. 9, pp. 1197–1214.

of the Levitical priests was not the same as that of the Christian minister, he argued, 'therefore the apostle boldly proclaims without exception, that marriage is honourable among all men'.[147] Yet despite this, marriage came to be seen as inferior to virginity, and the 'too superstitious admiration of celibacy became prevalent'.[148] God might provide an individual with the gift of chastity for specific reasons, but there was no suggestion that celibacy was superior to marriage in any way.[149] Marriage, ordained by God, it was argued, defiled neither the priest nor the sacraments that he celebrated. Even when clerical marriage was tolerated in England, John Jewel protested, there was those who believed that the sacraments were defiled if the priest were 'a good and honest man that hath a wife'.[150] Yet the 'honest' character of a priest, whether defined by promised celibacy or faithful marriage, remained very much in the eye of the beholder. The pre-Reformation faithful who sought out the services of priests whose character was beyond reproach had their counterparts in those who complained against the married clergy of the sixteenth century, and impugned the validity of their sacraments. Visitation articles for the English church in the reign of Edward VI reflect the concern of evangelical bishops on this score, and Thomas More was not the only Englishman to deploy vituperative terms such as 'harlot' in his description of the wives of priests.[151]

In his study of *Lollards and Protestants in the Diocese of York*, A.G. Dickens asserted that clerical marriage and clerical celibacy were not matters that were best discussed 'along doctrinal lines'. Many of the pre-Reformation clergy, he suggests, would have married had the opportunity been presented to them; the Reformation made clerical marriage possible, but it did not create Protestants of those clergy who married.[152] The coincidence of clerical marriage and clerical Protestantism continues to be contested. Marjorie Plummer makes a largely convincing case for clerical

---

[147] Calvin, *Institutes*, p. 1251.

[148] Calvin, *Institutes*, p. 1252.

[149] Calvin, *Sermon on I. Timothy* in *Corp. Ref.*, vol. 53, pp. 254–5.

[150] J. Jewel, 'Defence of the Apology of the Church of England', in J. Ayre (ed.), *The Works of John Jewel* (4 vols, Cambridge, 1849), vol. 4, p. 413.

[151] W.H. Frere, *Visitation Articles and Injunctions for the period of the Reformation* (3 vols, London, 1910), vol. 2, pp. 189, 274, 292–3; M. Prior, '"Reviled and Crucified Marriages". The Position of Tudor Bishops' Wives', in M. Prior (ed.), *Women in English Society 1500–1800* (London, 1985), pp. 118–48; P. Marshall, *The Catholic Priesthood and the English Reformation* (Oxford, 1994), pp. 51–3; A. Barstow, 'The First Generation of Anglican Clergy Wives: "Heroines or Whores?"', *Historical Magazine of the Protestant Episcopal Church*, 52 (1983): 3–16; Dickens, 'Robert Parkyn's Narrative of the Reformation', in Dickens (ed.), *Reformation Studies* (London, 1982), pp. 293–312.

[152] A.G. Dickens, *Lollards and Protestants in the Diocese of York 1509–1558* (London, 1959), pp. 189ff.

marriage as a 'litmus test' for clerical Protestantism in her study of the first generation of married clergy in Lutheran Germany.[153] Those clergy who married, and took to the defence of their marriages in the early 1520s, did so with a solid grounding in the rhetoric of reform, and with an ability to turn to arguments from conscience, scripture and tradition in defence of their actions. In the English context, there is some evidence that the conduct of the married clergy supports Robert Parkyn's observation that those priests who married were the same priests who refused to elevate the elements at the consecration. A priest in the diocese of Chichester, George Fairbank, refused to put away his wife in the face of the Marian restoration of Catholicism, and coupled his defence of clerical marriage with a rejection of the theology of transubstantiation and the teaching of the Catholic church on original sin.[154] However, any attempt to map evangelical sympathies onto the topography of clerical marriage is fraught with danger; the personal beliefs of those clergy who chose to marry are nigh impossible to fathom, and for every priest who married in accordance with evangelical principles, it is possible to adduce evidence of another for whom convenience, or even popular persuasion, was a more compelling motive.[155] While it is possible to argue that many evangelical clergy in England chose to marry, it is rather harder to demonstrate that married clergy as a group were sympathetic to the Reformation.[156]

Yet it is hard to divorce entirely the debate over clerical celibacy and marriage from its theological context. If not actively embracing the Reformation, those clergy who married were surely expressing a willingness to jettison the laws and traditions of Catholicism.[157] And to those who sat in the pews of parish churches, the marriage of priests was a highly visible sign of change. On some issues, it was possible to temporise, or construct a middle ground, but a priest was either married, or he was not. It would push the argument too far to suggest that the married clergy were, by dint of their marriage alone, responsible for the dissemination of the reformation in the parishes, but the presence of a wife in the vicarage

---

[153] Plummer, 'Partner in his Calamities', p. 209; compare with Parish, *Clerical Marriage*, pp. 198–217; A.G. Dickens, 'The Marian reaction in the Diocese of York', in *Reformation Studies* (London, 1982) pp. 93–158, p. 109.

[154] Parykn, *Narrative*, pp. 297, 308; S.Brigden, *London and the Reformation* (Oxford, 1989), pp. 399–400; D. Peet, 'Mid Sixteenth Century Parish Clergy, with particular consideration of the Diocese of York and Norwich', (University of Cambridge unpublished Ph.D., 1980), pp. 272–3; Parish, *Clerical Marriage*, p. 209.

[155] See M. Bowker, *The Secular Clergy in the Diocese of Lincoln 1495–1520* (Cambridge, 1968); C. Haigh, *Reformation and Resistance in Tudor Lancashire* (Cambridge, 1975); Dickens, 'The Marian Reaction in the Diocese of York', pp. 105–6.

[156] Parish, *Clerical Marriage*, p. 217.

[157] Marshall, *Catholic Priesthood*, p. 167.

and married priest in the pulpit may well have contributed in part to the reception process, even if they did not guarantee how positive that reception would be. Clerical marriage was iconoclastic in the multiple meanings of the word. For a priest, or more properly, a religious, to marry in defiance of a vow of chastity was, in the eyes of evangelicals, to destroy an idol that had been erected in the heart. In their rejection of clerical celibacy, and defence of the godliness of clerical marriage, evangelical polemicists were committing an act of doctrinal and historical iconoclasm, breaking apart the traditions of the church and asserting the supremacy of their interpretation of the law of God over and above the disciplines and doctrines of the church. At the pastoral level, clerical marriage shattered the image of the priest set apart from his congregation by sacred function and sole life. Luther's marriage was perhaps the most hotly debated, but the questions that it raised were significant well beyond the Black Cloister, and the intensity of the debate over clerical marriage in the mid-sixteenth century England both reflected and informed the legal position and the presence of married priests in the parishes. Learned Latin and popular polemical writings positioned marriage and celibacy at the heart of religious controversy, and extended the scope of the debate beyond the acts of the individual priest. The reality of clerical marriage in the sixteenth century, for the first time in half a millennium, reopened debates over history and tradition, scripture and canon law, and the fragmentation of East and West. The controversy over clerical celibacy in the sixteenth century leaned heavily upon the lexicon of earlier dialectic, but also opened new avenues of discourse. Clerical marriage in print, if not yet in practice, was a mark of confessional identity, and one that raised questions not only about the discipline of obligatory celibacy, but also issues of discipline, dogma, and direction in the institutional church.

CHAPTER SIX

'Contrary to the state of their order and the laudable customs of the church': Clerical Celibacy in the Catholic Church after the Reformation

To look upon the first generation of evangelicals, Thomas More suggested, and see 'the very father of theyr holy sect ... fallen to flesshe and caryn and lyue in lechery with a nunne under the name of wedlock... and all the chyfe heddys of them, late monkys & freres and now apostatas & lyuynge with harlotes vnder the name of wyues', might lead the observer to the conclusion that the Reformation was 'a sorte of freres folowynge an abotte of misrule in a Christmas game'.[1] The marriage of priests and nuns was tangible evidence of a religious change that was apparent to all, and a visible sign of the rejection of the laws and traditions of the Catholic church. Whether or not clerical marriage and clerical Protestantism went hand in hand in practice, the two were strongly linked in Catholic polemic, and this association, once made, provided a mechanism by which creed and conduct might together be disparaged, and accusations of immorality on the part of the pre-Reformation clergy turned against the nascent reformed churches.[2] By the time that the Council of Trent made its formal pronouncement on the discipline of clerical celibacy, a generation of married priests had left their mark upon the landscape of sixteenth-century religious culture. Forty years of clerical marriage had begun to erode the apparent novelty of the practice, and presented the Catholic church with a problem that was practical and pastoral, as well as disciplinary. However, clerical marriage was no less controversial in the middle decades of the century than it had been at the start; the printed debate was still very much alive, and the position of the married clergy, at least in some parts of

---

[1] T. More, *Confutation of Tyndale's Answer*, L.A. Schuster, R.C. Marius, J.P. Lusardi, R.J. Schoek (eds), *The Yale Edition of The Complete Works of St Thomas More*, 8 (New Haven, Conn., 1973), pp. 41–2.

[2] This issue is discussed in more detail in chapter 5, pp. 146–50 above.

Europe, still precarious and contested. The promulgation of the Tridentine decrees certainly marked a forceful initiative on the part of the church to act against breaches of ecclesiastical discipline and defend the law of obligatory clerical continence, but objections to clerical marriage were repeatedly articulated even before the council convened, and the debate was to continue in the decades that followed.

As David Bagchi has observed, Catholic controversialists who took up their pen against Luther were confronted by a conceptual problem. There was, in the time-honoured tradition of doctrinal debate, deemed to be little purpose in disputing with a heretic. Since heresy was inspired by the devil, Luther and his followers might be assumed to be deaf to any reasoned argument. The papal condemnation of Luther in the Bull *Exurge Domine*, and the judgements on his work published by the universities of Louvain and the Sorbonne, summarised the errors in his writings, but provided no explanation. For some Catholic commentators there was a clear imperative to expand upon such brief propositions, in order that the determinations of the church might appear comprehensible and well founded, but for others, to do so was to imply that it was not enough that the works of Luther were simply condemned, such condemnations required justification. Thus, few Catholic writers could be certain of the support of the curia for their labours in defence of the church, and at least one was wounded by the accusation that to debate with Luther was to fan the flames of heresy.[3] Luther's marriage, and the more general issue of clerical marriage, did, however find a place in the writings of opponents of the Reformation in the 1520s and 1530s. One solution was to dismiss Luther as the successor of heretics already condemned by the medieval church, and to associate his theology with the views of individuals whose reputation had been effectively undermined in the past. The several condemnations of the errors contained in Luther's works by the Sorbonne in the 1520s, including the *Determinations* of its syndic, Beda, repeated the suggestion that his views were those of the fourth century heretic, Vigilantius, against whom Jerome had written with some force.[4] Alternatively, as Cochlaeus and Eck were to discover, there were both sound polemical and theological points to be made in the excoriation of Luther's actions, and the association of heresy and immorality certainly provided Thomas More with countless comic and

---

[3] D. Bagchi, *Luther's Earliest Opponents: Catholic Controversialists, 1518–1525* (Minneapolis, 1991); Bagchi, 'Luther's Catholic Opponents', in A. Pettegree (ed.), *The Reformation World* (Abingdon, 2000), Chapter 6, pp. 99ff.

[4] The identification of Luther with various manifestations of heresy in the medieval church was a more general feature of Beda's work, which accused Luther of treading in the footsteps of the Manichaeans, Waldensians and Cathars.

scatological caricatures with which to paint the Reformation. Other denunciations of clerical marriage were constructed from the scurrilous; Johannes Emser's Epithalamia presented a crude caricature of Luther's own marriage, and the same broad approach was evident in his *Venatione Luteriana Aegocerotis assertio* (1525).

Other responses were rather more erudite in their presentation. The Dominican novice Ambrosius Catharinus composed two Latin works against Luther in 1520, the *Apologia Pro Veritate Catholicae* and the *Excusatio Disputationis*.[5] The two works betrayed a familiarity with Luther's writings, and with Prieras' earlier Catholic attack on Luther and his theology. The *Apologia*, dedicated to the emperor Charles V, ran to five books, of which the final presented an overview and rejection of Luther's entire theology, including the argument that it was permissible for priests to marry and monks to break their vows. Catharinus, in the first book, detailed the eleven 'deceptions' of Luther, and denounced the reformer's efforts to use the morality of the Catholic clergy and the conduct of the popes as a justification for doctrinal reform in the church.[6] Luther's errors and deceits, he argued, identified him as the Antichrist. Luther's reply returned the favour. Clerical celibacy, he argued, was one face of the Antichrist, along with images, fasting, and the Mass.[7] The following year, Emser's *Wider das Unchristliche Buch Martin Luthers an dem Deutschen Adel Vorlegung* presented a point by point dissection of Luther's writings, incorporating a defence of the scriptural and historical origins of clerical celibacy, and the actions that the church had taken against clerical concubinage, against Luther's assertion of the legality and necessity of clerical marriage. Henry VIII's *Assertio Septem Sacramentorum*, published in the same year, similarly took Luther to task for his rejection of clerical celibacy. The king's antipathy toward the married priesthood was justified again in his letter to the Germans in 1538. The celibacy of the clergy, he argued, was founded in Scripture in the Gospel of Matthew (19:12, 'eunuchs for the kingdom of heaven') and in the promise that man would not be tempted beyond that which he could bear (I. Cor. 10:13). The Pauline assertion that it was the

---

[5] Ambrosius Catharinus Politus, *Apologia pro Veritate Catholicae et Apostolicae Fidei ac Doctrinae*, J. Schweizer (ed.) (Münster, 1956); Ambrosius Catharinus Politus, *Excusatio Disputationis contra Martinum* (Florence, 1521); For further detail on Catharinus, see J. Schweizer, *Ambrosius Catharinus Politus (1484–1553), ein Theologe des Reformationszeitalters* (Münster, 1910); F. Lauchert, *Die italienischen literarischen Gegner Luthers* (Freiburg im Breisgau, 1912); and for the most informative English writing on his debate with Luther, P. Preston, 'Catharinus vs Luther 1521', *History*, 88 (2003): 364–78.

[6] Catharinus, *Apologia*, 26ff.

[7] M. Luther, 'Ad librum eximii Magistri Nostri Magistri Ambrosii Catharini, defensoris Silvestri Prieriatis acerrimi, responsio', in *D. Martin Luthers Werke Kritische Gesamtausgabe*, vii (Weimar, 1897), pp. 722ff, especially 735

'doctrine of devils' to prohibit marriage did not apply in this case, Henry argued, because the call to celibacy was heard only by those who were able to abide by the law. Rather than use clerical marriage as a 'remedy' for clerical immorality, he suggested, it would surely be better simply to exclude from the priesthood whose who could not abide by the law of continence.[8]

Just as the evangelical defence of clerical marriage had drawn upon the history of the church, and the writings of Fathers, Catholic polemicists marshalled both history and patristic tradition to the defence of the celibate priesthood. Johannes Faber, vicar of Constance, turned to the example of the apostolic church, including the contested *Apostolic Canon*, to argue that the origins of clerical celibacy lay in the practice of the church in the first Christian centuries. The writings of the fathers and the decrees of the early councils testified to the importance attached to celibacy in the primitive church, and the demands and contentions of Luther, Faber argued, identified him as the successor not of the apostles but of Mohammed.[9] John Fisher presented a defence of clerical celibacy from both scripture and tradition, asserting the authoritative position of extra-scriptural traditions in the determination of faith and practice. The apparent repudiation of these traditions of the church by Luther and his followers was denounced by Fisher in his sermon against Luther in May 1521, and again in his *Assertionis Lutheranae Confutatio*, printed in 1523.[10] The publication in Antwerp of St John Chrysostom's *De Virginitate* perhaps reflected this ongoing debate over the place of virginity, celibacy and marriage in the history of the early church. Johannes Eck's detailed refutation of the views of Luther and Melanchthon, the *Enchiridion Controversarium Seu Locorum Communium* (Ingolstadt, 1525), also included a defence of clerical celibacy, again grounded in scripture and in the traditions of the church, and Jacobus Latomus' condemnation of evangelical theology identified the defence of clerical celibacy as a critical part of the preservation of traditional theology and practice.[11] Catholic opposition to Luther's marriage in particular and clerical marriage more generally continued to be articulated throughout the 1520s and 1530s. The conciliar nuncio Peter van der Vorst included clerical celibacy among his list of contested issues in Germany, although it was presented as a matter

---

[8] G. Burnet, *History of the Reformation of the Church of England*, N. Pocock (ed.), (7 vols, Oxford, 1865), vol. 4, pp. 384-91.

[9] J. Fisher, *Adversus Nova Quaedam et a Christiana Religione Prorsus aliena dogmata mart. Lutheri* (Rome, 1522).

[10] *The English Works of John Fisher*, J.E.B. Mayor (ed.), (EETS extra ser. 27 1876), pp. 311-17; R. Rex, *The Theology of John Fisher* (Cambridge, 1991).

[11] J. Latomus, *De Confessione Secreta* (Antwerp, 1525).

of less immediate and widespread concern than the papal supremacy, the cult of the saints, and purgatory.[12] The evangelical assertion of the necessity and legitimacy of clerical marriage as a remedy for fornication provoked a vigorous response from conservatives at the Diet of Augsburg. The proposition that marriage was a suitable 'remedy for infirmity' was dismissed, and alternative solutions proposed for those clergy who struggled with celibacy, including fasting, vigils, and the avoidance of the temptations that might be apparent in the company of women.[13] In one of the few full-length works devoted to clerical celibacy in this period, Sadoleto set out the case in favour of the apostolic origins of the law in his *Sententia de Coelibatu Clericorum Post Consilium Anni 1538*. The priest, he asserted, was by necessity devoted to the service of God, and such commitment required him to remain unmarried. Although some of the apostles had been married at the time of their calling, he argued, those who were unmarried had not taken wives, sacrificing themselves to the preaching of the Gospel. Established by the apostles, the principle of clerical celibacy was underpinned by the ascetic practices of the first Christians, and, he argued, even supported by the law of the Greek church, which prohibited marriage after ordination.

Sadoleto's work was composed against the backdrop of a commitment to investigate and report on the necessity of reform on the part of Pope Paul III (1534–49). To this end, the pope had sought the opinions of the cardinals, along with Pole, Caraffa and Contarini, and their verdict, the *Concilium de emendanda ecclesia* (1537), both detailed the abuses in the life of the church and proposed a programme of reform that commanded the attention of both Catholic and Protestant.[14] Several recommendations related to the priesthood and to clerical discipline. Dispensations, its authors complained, were all too readily offered to enable the sons of priests to possess the benefices of their fathers, despite the re-enactment of 'ancient law' by Pope Clement VIII. Priests were also, it was suggested, too readily dispensed from holy orders in order that they might marry, when such a dispensation should be reserved only for 'the preservation of a people or a nation'. It was all the more important that this particular issue be addressed, 'in these times when the Lutherans lay such great stress

---

[12] Bagchi 'Catholic theologians of the period before Trent', in Bagchi and D. Steinmetz (eds), *Cambridge Companion to Reformation Theology* (Cambridge, 2006), p. 223.

[13] Confutation Art. XXIII, in *Corp. Ref.*, vol. 27, cols 136ff.

[14] J. le Plat, *Monumenta ad historiam Concilii Tridentini* (7 vols, Louvain, 1781–87), vol. 2, pp. 596–7; J.C. Olin, *The Catholic Reformation: Savonarola to Ignatius Loyola* (New York, London, 1969), pp. 186–97; T.F. Mayer, *Cardinal Pole in European context: a via media in the reformation* (Aldershot, 2000).

on this matter'.[15] The remedy proposed was in no real sense an assertion of the merits of clerical marriage, but the *Concilium de emendenda ecclesia* surely served to establish clerical discipline, and especially clerical continence, as an issue worthy of the attention of the church. The suggestion that some consideration of the celibacy of the clergy was all the more urgent in light of the criticisms of the Lutherans was not without a grounding in reality. Clerical incontinence had been presented in evangelical polemic as more than just a pastoral or moral problem, but as an issue which impinged upon authority, doctrine, and history. By the middle of the century it appeared to have become, if not a prime motivation for conversion to the Reformation, at least a bargaining point for some clergy who sought to withstand the force of ecclesiastical and secular discipline. In 1542, the representative of Albrecht, Archbishop of Brandenburg, protested that many of the diocesan priests lived with concubines, but that attempts to enforce separation had been met with the threat that any further action on the part of the bishop would prompt the priests to align themselves with the Lutherans. 'Many other men who are aware of the current state of affairs in Germany ... believe that chaste marriage would be preferable to sullied celibacy', it was suggested, and 'the most able and knowledgeable men in the populace would rather have wives without ecclesiastical benefices than benefices without wives'.[16] Toleration of clerical marriage was regarded by some as an effective path to conciliation with the reformers, and the emperor Ferdinand, the duke of Cleves and Duke Albert of Bavaria were to make just such a proposition to the pope at the Council of Trent.[17] No promise of a relaxation of the law was likely to be forthcoming, particularly before the celibacy of the clergy was discussed at the council, but a small concession was made to the papal nuncios in Germany that sanctioned the recognition of the marriages of priests on the understanding that those individuals who were appropriately dispensed would refrain from the exercise of their priestly ministry, or any other sacred function.[18]

---

[15] K. Bartlett, M. McGlynn (eds), *Humanism and the Northern Renaissance* (Canadian Scholars' Press, 2000), 175ff.

[16] U. Ranke-Heinemann, *Eunuchs for the Kingdom of God: Women, Sexuality, and the Catholic Church* (tr. P. Heinegg (New York, 1990, German edn 1988), p. 113; J. Brundage, *Law, Sex and Christian Society in Medieval Europe* (Chicago, 1987), p. 568; LePlat, *Concil. Trid.* vol. 8, p. 624.

[17] Le Plat, *Concil Trid.*, vol. 8, pp. 468, 484, 485; 202; 919–26.

[18] Pope Paul III to bishops Petrus of Fano, Aloysius of Verona, and Sebastianus of Ferentino, quoted in J. Lynch, 'Critique of the Law of Celibacy in the Catholic Church from the Period of the Reform Councils', in W. Bassett and P. Huizing (eds), *Celibacy in the Church* (New York, 1972), pp. 57–75.

The availability of a dispensation to individual priests who had entered into marriage would not provide a practicable solution to the more general question of the legalisation of clerical marriage, nor would it answer the criticisms of the reformers who argued that the law of celibacy was fundamentally flawed. When Pope Paul III convened the Council of Trent in 1545, it was at least in part a response to the significance of the issues that had been hotly contested in the three decades since Luther's first protest.[19] Complaints about clerical continence, non-residency, or simony before general councils were nothing new, but the criticisms of Catholic theology and practice contained in the works of evangelicals across Europe posed a more fundamental challenge, particularly in the realms of authority, scripture and tradition, the sacraments, and soteriology. In some respects, as Michael Mullett has argued, the council had its precedents in the conciliar reforms of the fifteenth century and indeed 'may be seen as the fulfillment of those late medieval councils'.[20] However, by the time that the council was summoned, Cardinal Caraffa, at least, was of the opinion that the doctrinal debates were no longer a dispute within Catholicism, but an exchange between the church and those who had positioned themselves outside its walls.[21] The issues to be discussed by the members of the council were proposed by the cardinal legates, and drawn up by a chosen commission, the *congregatio theologorum minorum*. Dogmatic and legal questions were settled in separate preparatory sessions by the *congregatio proelatorum theologorum* and *congregatio proelatorum canonistarum*. The matter was then presented for general debate, and the final form of the decrees determined. The decrees of the council were confirmed on 26 January 1564 in the papal Bull of Pius IV, *Benedictus Deus*, and carried the subscriptions of 215 Fathers. The proceedings of the council amounted to a discussion and rejection of almost every substantive point levelled against the church by its critics.[22]

---

[19] The best modern study of the Council is still H. Jedin, *Geschichte des Konzils von Trient* (6 vols, Freiburg, 1949–1975); some translated into English as *History of the Council of Trent* (tr. E. Graf) (2 vols, London 1957–61); Le Plat, *Concil. Trid.*; J. von Dollinger, *Ungedruckte Berichte und Tagebücher zur Geschichte des Concilii von Trient* (2 parts, Nördlingen, 1876). On the issue of clerical celibacy at Trent see also, E. Ferasin, *Matrimonio e celibate a concilio di Trento* (Rome, 1970); A. Franzen, *Zolibat und Priesterehe in der Auseinandersetzung der Reformationszeit und der katholischen Reform des 16. Jahrhunderts* (Munster, 1969); P. Delehaye, 'Breves remarques historiques sur la legislation du celibat ecclesiastique', *Studia Moralia*, 3 (1965): 389–94; E. Schillebeeckx, *Clerical Celibacy Under Fire. A Critical Appraisal* (London and Sydney, 1968), p. 52.

[20] M. Mullett, *The Catholic Reformation* (New York, 1999), p. 3.

[21] D.C. Steinmetz, 'The Council of Trent', in *Cambridge Companion to Reformation Theology*, p. 234.

[22] S. Ozment, *The Age of Reform 1250–1550* (New Haven, CT, 1980), p. 407.

The council did not debate the issue of clerical celibacy and marriage until 4 March 1563.[23] In accordance with the processes determined in the opening sessions, the subject had been referred to a group of seventeen *theologi minores* who were charged with responding to two separate but related propositions taken from the views of the Protestants.[24] First, 'that marriage should not be relegated to second rank; it is superior to chastity, and God gives married couples a greater grace than the unmarried', and second, 'that western priests can marry, notwithstanding ecclesiastical vows or law, and that to affirm the contrary is to condemn marriage. All those who are not aware of having received the gift of chastity can enter into marriage'.[25] The discussion occupied thirteen sessions, the major part of the time being spent upon the second proposition, in light of the reality of clerical marriage in the reformed churches. In considering the first question, how marriage was to be considered in relation to virginity, there was little dissent from the anticipated line of argument that virginity was deemed superior both in scripture, particularly the Pauline epistles, and in patristic writings. Unsurprisingly, much of the debate turned upon the question of the scriptural and apostolic origins of the law of celibacy, again perhaps reflecting the criticisms levelled against clerical celibacy by the evangelical reformers. None of those who spoke on the issue were German representatives, however, although it was in the German lands that the practical challenge to clerical celibacy was most immediate and intense. The theologians concluded that the nature of the priesthood required a total dedication to God, in the administration of the sacraments, in preaching, and in a life of perpetual prayer. Marriage was prohibited to the clergy on this basis, because it distracted man from this life of total service. The obligation to celibacy was not, therefore, anything that was demanded of the priest above and beyond that to which he was already committed by entry into holy orders. Investigation of the practice of the apostles yielded evidence that while some had been married

---

[23] *Histoire des Conciles d'Apres les Documents Originaux*, C.H. Hefele and J. Leclerq (eds), (19 vols, Paris, 1907–52), vol. 10, p. 507.

[24] Cochini identifies the 17 as: five diocesan priests (Jean Peletier, Antonio Solisius, Richard du Pre, Lazare Brochot, Ferdinand Tricus), three Franciscans (Miguel of Medina, Jean Lubera, Francis Orantes), five Dominicans (Francis Ferror, Jean Gallo, Jean de Ludenna, Basil of Pisis, Sanctus Cithius), two Augustinian hermits (Simon Florentinus, Anthony of Modulpho), one Carmelite (Desire de St Martin), and one regular canon of St Augustine (Claude de Saintes, who was later B. Evreux). Other delegates were invited to take the floor on occasion, including Lucius Anguisciola and Didacus of Pavia: C. Cochini, *The Apostolic Origins of Priestly Celibacy* (San Francisco, 1990), pp. 19–20.

[25] *Concilium Tridentium Diariorum, Actorum, Epistolarum, Tractatuum Nova Collectio*, Societas Goerresiana (ed.), (Freiburg im Breisgau: Herder, 1901–), vol. 9 pt. 6, pp. 380–82 and 425–70, upon which Cochini bases his narrative.

at the time of their calling, they had lived in continence after this point, giving up everything, including their wives, to follow Christ. The fact that married men had been accepted into holy orders in the early church was not disputed, and the fact that ordination carried with it for these men an obligation to perfect and perpetual continence was accepted. However, the roots of this obligation were the subject of some controversy, spawning an argument as to whether continence was demanded of priests *de jure divino*, or by the laws of the church. More significantly, there was a clear and firm distinction made between the ordination of married men, from whom continence was demanded, and the marriage of men who had been single at the time of their ordination, but had then attempted marriage while in orders. In this context, reference was made to the practice of the Greek church, but such comment was brief. Unmarried men, once ordained, the *Theologi minors* asserted, were not, and never had been, permitted to marry. On this basis, there was no grounding in scripture, apostolic tradition, or the law of the church, for the marriage of priests after ordination, and those who were married prior to ordination were bound by a law of perpetual continence.

On July 20, the theologians placed before the Fathers of the Council two canons, the first asserting the binding nature of clerical celibacy, and the second asserting the superiority of virginity over marriage. Canon 7 read 'if anyone says that Western clerics who have received sacred orders or religious who have solemnly professed chastity can validly contract matrimony, ecclesiastical law or vow nothwithstanding, and that to maintain the opposite is only to condemn matrimony; and that all can contract marriage who do not feel themselves to have the gift of chastity, although they have vowed it: let him be anathema', and Canon 9 'If anyone says that matrimony must be placed before virginity or celibacy, and that it is not better and more blessed to remain in virginity or celibacy, than to be joined in matrimony, let him be anathema'. This latter statement was reinforced in the Catechism, in the instruction that 'it should be remembered that the Apostle admonishes: They that have wives, let them be as though they had them not, and that St. Jerome says: The love which a wise man cherishes towards his wife is the result of judgment, not the impulse of passion; he governs the impetuosity of desire, and is not hurried into indulgence. There is nothing more shameful than that a husband should love his wife as an adulteress', although the Catechism did present marriage as a 'remedy' in accordance with I. Cor. 7.[26] The two decrees were approved, on the fifth presentation, in the twentyfourth session of the council.[27] The impact of

---

[26] T.A. Buckley, *The Catechism of the Council of Trent* (London, 1852), pp. 332–50.

[27] *Concil. Trid.*, Vol. 9, p. 968. The earlier objections related in part to the representation of the precedent of the Greek church, and to the addition of a comment on chastity given as

the Tridentine ruling on clerical celibacy was felt in two forms. At the level of doctrinal definition and jurisdictional authority, the Fathers at Trent had asserted the authenticity and apostolicity of clerical celibacy, and had debated and rebutted the arguments that had been made against it in recent years, but also across the centuries. After some debate, the theologians and Fathers stopped short of the assertion that the law of celibacy was simply a law of the church, which could therefore be altered at will. In this respect, the outcome of the deliberations over celibacy did indeed carry an air of finality. H.C. Lea summarised his narrative of the council in the statement that it was here, for the first time, that 'the simple rule of discipline was elevated to the dignity of a point of belief'.[28] Clerical celibacy, it has been argued, became 'the standard-bearer of the Catholic Counter-Reformation, the proof that Catholicism was not going to yield an inch to Protestants'.[29] There were, of course, many other issues upon which the verdict of the council upon the assertions of the Protestants was 'anathema sit', but the determination of the council on obligatory clerical celibacy was a decision that would be highly visible outside the conciliar chambers. Just as clerical marriage was a tangible sign of doctrinal challenge, so the continued insistence upon clerical celibacy was evidence of the determination of the Catholic church to possess the precedent of the apostles, reclaim the narrative of history, and assert an interpretative authority over Scripture. Clerical celibacy came to mean, after Trent, not only perpetual continence, but also a rigid insistence upon the prohibition of marriage to priests after ordination.

The conviction with which clerical celibacy was asserted did not stifle demands for a more accommodating approach, particularly within the Empire. August Baumgartner had already warned in 1562 that the enforcement of clerical celibacy would drive the Catholic clergy into the hands of the Protestants.[30] The Emperor Ferdinand continued to argue for the two concessions that he deemed essential if Protestants within the empire were to be brought back to the Catholic fold, communion in both kinds, and an acceptance of clerical marriage. After the close of the council, Ferdinand and Albert, Duke of Bavaria, appealed once more to the pope for concession on these grounds, and secured permission to grant the chalice to the laity. On clerical celibacy, however, the pope was immoveable, leading Ferdinand to the sarcastic retort that there was little benefit in allowing communion in both kinds if there were no unmarried clergy available to

---

a gift from God, and the assurance that man would not be tempted beyond what he could bear. See Lynch, 'Critique of the Law of Celibacy', 61.

[28] H.C. Lea, *History of Sacerdotal Celibacy* (2 vols, London, 1907), vol. 2, p. 205.

[29] P. de Rosa, *Vicars of Christ* (New York, 1988), p. 421.

[30] *Concil. Trid.*, vol. 5, p. 340.

serve in the parishes. It was a necessity, he argued, for the church to tolerate those clergy who had already married, if the faithful were to have priests at all. Ferdinand's son, Maximilian, also took up the fight, and appeared to have persuaded Pius IV that such a concession was indeed appropriate in order to safeguard the future of the church in Germany. However, there were fears that to allow clerical marriage in one part of the church would be to set a poor example to the others. Philip II of Spain protested that if the pope were to make a concession in the German case, it would being about the destruction of Christendom. With the election of Pius V in 1566, all such talk of toleration ceased.[31] The model of the post-Tridentine priest, educated, committed, and celibate, therefore needed all the more urgently to be realised and sustained in the generations to come, primarily through the seminary training system upon which the provision of suitable candidates to the priesthood depended. Indeed Stickler asserts that it was in the eighteenth canon of the twentythird session, which obliged all dioceses to establish seminaries for the training of priests, that the greatest impact of the deliberations over clerical celibacy was to be felt.[32]

The commitment of the council to the foundation of seminaries held out the promise of an improvement in the quality of the next generation of Catholic clergy, but efforts were also made to eradicate the most contentious clerical conduct among priests already in parishes. To this end, the problem of clerical concubinage was discussed at Trent, and the resulting canon was explicit in its condemnation of the 'shameful and unworthy' clerics who 'dedicated themselves to the service of God and live in the filth of impurity and unclean cohabitation'. Priests were instructed to put away their women, 'wherefore that the ministers of the church may be brought back to that continency and purity of life which is proper to them, and that for this reason the people may learn to reverence them the more, the more

---

[31] G. Constant, *Concession a l'Allemagne de la communion sous les deux especes* (2 vols, Paris, 1923); Lynch, 'Critique of the Law of Celibacy', 62; Dollinger, *Geschichte des Concilii*, vol. I, pp. 588–93.

[32] J.A. O'Donohoe, Tridentine Seminary Legislation: Its sources and its formation (Louvain, 1957); A.M. Cardinal Stickler, *The Case for Clerical Celibacy. Its Historical Development & Theological Foundations* (tr. Fr Brian Ferme) (San Francisco, 1995), p. 53; K.M. Comerford, 'Italian Tridentine diocesan seminaries: A historiographical study', *Sixteenth Century Journal*, 29 (1998): 999–1022; idem., *Reforming priests and parishes, Tuscan dioceses in the first century of seminary education* (Leiden, Boston, 2006); idem, *Ordaining the Catholic Reformation: priests and Seminary Pedagogy in Fiesole (1575–1675)* (Florence, 2001); A. Barnes, 'The Social Transformation of the French Parish Clergy 1500–1800', in B. Diefendorf and C. Hesse (eds), *Culture and Identity in Early Modern Europe 1500–1800* (Ann Arbor, 1993); M. Forster, *The Counter-Reformation in the Villages: Religion and Reform in the Bishopric of Speyer, 1560–1720* (Ithaca, NY, 1992); J.M. Headley and J.A. Tomaro (eds), *San Carlo Borromeo: Catholic Reform and Ecclesiastical Politics in the Second Half of the Sixteenth Century* (Washington DC, 1988).

honourable they see them in their conduct, the holy council forbids all clerics whatsoever to presume to keep concubines or other women concerning whom suspicion can be had in their house or elsewhere, or to presume to have any association with them; otherwise they shall be punished with the penalties imposed by the sacred canons or the statutes of the churches'.[33] The twentyfifth session of the council also reasserted many of the penalties that had traditionally been imposed upon priests who failed to fulfil their obligation to celibacy, and reiterated the long-standing exclusion of the sons of priests from their father's benefices. Clergy who were found to have maintained a concubine were to be admonished by their superiors, and those who refused to amend their ways faced a loss of income, the forfeit of first fruits and tenths, and eventually deprivation from all offices and functions. Efforts to suppress clerical concubinage continued after the council. In 1566, Pope Pius V instructed the bishops of the church to enforce with rigour the Tridentine decrees against clerical concubinage, and conduct visitations of their dioceses, with the intention of depriving recalcitrant clergy and expelling their concubines.[34] The celibacy canons were repeated at series of local synods and councils in the second half of the sixteenth century, including Milan (1565), Ravenna (1568), Florence (1573), Naples (1576), and Avignon (1594).

Understandably, however, the council could not produce an immediate transformation in clerical conduct. As the repeated efforts of local councils and bishops to eliminate clerical concubinage make clear, the reassertion of the law of celibacy at Trent could not create instantly a parish clergy who were as committed to the principle. Political interference impeded the implementation of the Tridentine decrees in parts of Europe, but elsewhere the reformers were simply confronted by the age-old problem of 'mulieres subintrodoctae' and their position in the life of the church. The papal nuncio repeated the complaint of the duke of Cleves that there were barely five priests in his territory who did not live in concubinage in 1561, and the bishop of Munster resigned in 1566 rather than act against concubinary priests in his diocese, and in other parts of the empire clergy had entered into clandestine marriages, or even open unions.[35] Seventeenth century secular courts in Burgundy asserted jurisdiction over incontinent clergy who were not properly disciplined by the church, and in some cases

---

[33] Session 25 c.14; H.J. Schroeder, *Canons and Decrees of the Council of Trent* (Rockford, Ill: 1978), pp. 246–8.

[34] Pius V, *Cum Primum* s.12, in *Bullarium Romanum* (10 vols, Luxembourg 1727–30), vol. 4, chap. 2, pp. 284–6.

[35] Franzen, *Zolibat*, pp. 66, 166–7; S. Lacqua, 'Concubinage and the Church in Early Modern Munster', in R. Harris and L. Roper (eds), *The Art of Survival. Gender and History in Europe 1450–2000* (Past and Present Supplements, vol. 1, 2006), pp. 72–100.

imposed the death sentence upon both priest and concubine.[36] In 1631, there was a complaint at the Synod of Osnabruck that priests in the diocese kept women that they dignified with the title of wife, and twenty years later the bishop of Munster complained that the concubinary priests of his diocese still presented a threat to the authority of the church. The bishop of Autun protested in 1652 that clerical concubinage was sufficiently common in his diocese that priests openly maintained women, fathered children, and provided them with dowries, and that this was accepted by the faithful as the norm.[37] Simone Lacqua's study of church and clergy in early modern Munster suggests that the imposition of clerical celibacy and the abolition of clerical concubinage was an uphill struggle. Some pastors were prepared to maintain their women in the face of repeated censure and the threat of ever more serious penalties, and local archdeacons preferred to fine the guilty clergy rather than bring down the full weight of the canons upon them. A handful of priests even argued that they were not bound by the discipline of celibacy at all, while others found powerful patrons who were prepared to defend their actions and protect their marriages. Even the cathedral chapter could not be remodelled upon the Tridentine ideals.[38] Overall, however, the picture was not entirely bleak. A series of reforming bishops in the diocese of Wurzburg had managed to reduce clerical concubinage by 95% in the century after Trent, but across much of the empire, the fear of the bishops that the conduct of their parish clergy worked to the detriment of religion was no doubt very real. Clerical concubinage and illicit marriages continued to be a source of contention and concern in the church. The Council of Trent, by its rejection of clerical marriage, and articulated intention to reform clerical conduct, had established clerical celibacy as a visible symbol of the distinctiveness of the Catholic priesthood and its function, and therefore the eradication of clerical concubinage as a tangible sign of the effectiveness of Catholic reform. Writing in 1599, the bishop of Ruremond complained that clerical concubinage had eroded the respect that the faithful had for the church, had led the laity to view the clergy with contempt, and had encouraged the spread of heresy that had eventually led to revolt and war.[39] Both Cuyck and the orator at Osnabruck in 1631 who had suggested that the conduct of the clergy placed the authority of the church under threat were no doubt

---

[36] M.E. Wiesner-Hanks, *Christianity and Sexuality in the Early Modern World. Regulating Desire, Reforming Practice* (London, 2000), p. 118.

[37] J.F. Schannat and J. Harzheim (eds), *Concilia Germaniae* (11 vols, Cologne, 1759–90), vol. 9, pp. 431, 787; Barnes, 'French Parish Clergy', 142.

[38] Lacqua, 'Concubinage'.

[39] Heinrich van Cuyck, *Speculum concubinariorum sacerdotum, monachorum ac clericorum* (Coloniae, 1599).

exploiting a rhetorical tool in order to make the point more compelling, but the basic argument made perfect sense. The Fathers at Trent had asserted the authenticity of the law of celibacy and rejected all calls for the toleration of clerical marriage. If the church failed on this most visible and contentious of assertions, the door was pushed wide open for its critics.

On two occasions in the early modern period, and once in the early nineteenth century, the Catholic church did provide general faculties for priests who had married, and thereby defected from the clerical estate, to obtain a virtually unconditional reduction to the lay state. Thomas Aquinas had identified 'apostasia a sacro ordine' among various other forms of apostasy, but the situation of 'lapsed' priests in canon law had its origins in the early church.[40] Penalties of excommunication and deprivation were imposed in the fourth century upon priests who left the church in order to return to secular life, to marry, or to enter military service. By the seventh century, it was expected that such priests would be apprehended and returned to clerical life. Those clergy who married 'in sacris', were deemed to be guilty of apostasy, and faced an automatic penalty of excommunication, and deprivation from all benefices. There was no relaxation of the law at Trent, nor indeed in the centuries between the Tridentine canons and the publication of the Code. Indeed, as Abo notes, ecclesiastical discipline became all the more severe as a result of Pius IX's *Apostolicae Sedis* of October 1869, which imposed the same ipso facto penalty faced by clergy who had attempted to enter into marriage upon their 'pseudo-wives'.[41] The return of apostate clerics to their livings was not only possible, it was required of them as a duty, after a suitable period of penance and evidence of a continent life.[42] This discipline was relaxed on three occasions; in 1801 to address the problem of married French priests after the Revolution, and twice in response to the toleration of clerical marriage in territories that embraced the Reformation. The first such instance followed the petition of the Charles V to the pope regarding the secular clergy in the empire who had attempted marriage. In August 1548 the papal bull *Ad diligentem patrem familias pertinent* provided the papal nuncio in Germany with the faculty to validate the marriages of these priests, although those who took advantage were to be prohibited from

---

[40] Aquinas, *Summa Theologica*, II–II q.12 art. 1 (tr., Fathers of the English Dominican Province) (second edition, London, 1923). The most helpful discussion is in J.A. Abo, 'The Problem of Lapsed Priests', *The Jurist*, 23 (1963): 153–79; see also Franzen, *Zolibat*, pp. 64–88.

[41] Abo, 'Lapsed Priests', 156.

[42] *Decretals of Gregory IX*, CIC c.4 X.III.3; Abo, 'Lapsed Priests', 156.

the exercise of sacred function as a result.[43] A parallel process, described in a letter from Bishop Lipomano to Cardinal Farnese in December of the same year was put in train for the readmission of lapsed priests to sacred function upon separation from their 'wives'.[44]

The second faculty was granted to Cardinal Pole in 1554, to address the situation of clergy in England who had entered into marriages after the legalisation of clerical marriage by Edward VI's parliament in 1549.[45] Again, the clergy were excluded from the celebration of Mass, and from entry into ecclesiastical benefices. They were absolved from the penalty of excommunication, and dispensed in order that they might enter into a valid marriage, but, the faculty made clear, only on this occasion. No subsequent marriage was permitted, and disciplinary action against this first generation of English married priests was a priority for Mary and Pole. Several senior clergy were removed from their posts, including bishops Bird, Bush, Coverdale, Barlow, Ferrer, Scroy, Holgate and Ponet, the majority of whom were married men. The first Parliament of the reign repealed the Edwardian religious legislation, including the 1549 act which permitted clerical marriage, and the 1552 act which had declared the children of such unions legitimate. A disciplinary process was established against married clergy in the first Act of Repeal, and outlined in the royal injunctions issued in March 1553/4. Bishops and ecclesiastical judges, on the instructions of Bishop Bonner of London, were to 'act with all celerity and speed' to deprive of their benefices any clergy 'who contrary to the state of their orders and the laudable custom of the church, have married and used women as their wives'.[46] Those married priests whose wives had died were to be treated more leniently, as were those who promised, in the presence of the bishop, to abstain. Pole's Legatine Constitutions of 1555 repeated the demand that the married clergy be disciplined in accordance

---

[43] 'Bulla Super Connubio Clericorum Germaniae', in W. Friedensburg (ed.), *Nuntiatur des Bischofs Pietro Bertano von Fano, 1548–1549* (Berlin, 1910), pp. 461–3.

[44] Friedensburg, *Nuntiatur*, pp. 197–8.

[45] Julius III's constitution *Dudum cum charissima in Christo Filia Nostra Maria*, March 8, 1554; D. Wilkins, *Concilia Magnae Britanniae et Hiberniae* (4 vols, London, 1737), vol. 4, pp. 91–3.

[46] E. Cardwell, *Documentary Annals of the Reformed Church in England* (2 vols, Oxford, 1839), vol. I. 109–13; I Mary c.2; for a fuller discussion of these events, see H.L. Parish, *Clerical Marriage and the English Reformation* (Aldershot, 2000), pp. 187ff; E.J. Carlson, 'Clerical Marriage and the English Reformation', *Journal of British Studies*, 31 (1992): 1–31; M. Prior, 'Reviled and Crucified Marriages. The Position of Tudor Bishops' Wives', in Prior (ed.), *Women in English Society 1500–1800* (London, 1985) pp. 118–48; R. Spielman, 'The Beginning of clerical marriage in the English Reformation', *Anglican and Episcopal History*, 56 (1987): 251–63.

with the 'ancient canons'.[47] The simplicity of the statement concealed the complexity of the process. Proceedings against the individual clergy could take several weeks to complete, and if a priest sought to continue in ecclesiastical service, a promise of separation was required, along with a public penance. Even if, as Baskerville has argued, the majority of the clergy sought and secured reappointment to a new benefice, the degree of disruption and dislocation caused by the disciplinary action against married clergy was substantial. In Sandwich in Kent it was reported that the deprivation of the married clergy had left the church with no priests to celebrate the sacraments, and although few areas were as badly affected, the sight of priests performing penance, confessing to living under the 'pretence' of matrimony, in violation of the laws of the church, would have done little to raise the esteem in which the priesthood was held. Catholic polemicists denounced the married clergy and their wives with the same enthusiasm and vocabulary with which their evangelical counterparts had described concubinary priests. Thomas Martin's *Treatise declarying and plainly proving that the pretensed marriage of priestes ... is no marriage*, dedicated to the queen in 1554, warned that the position of the entire priesthood was threatened by the actions of the 'unworthy' who had entered into such 'pretensed' marriages. The views of the 'old fathers and founders of oure religion' were contrasted with the licentiousness of the 'new proceders', and Martin derided those married clergy who presumed to celebrate Mass in defiance of the laws of the church and the sanctity of the sacrament. The marriage of priests, he argued, was no marriage at all, and the actions of those clergy who had presumed to take wives no better than concubinage and fornication.[48] Martin's stance was no doubt legitimate within the terms of canon law. Unless validated, the marriage of priests was indeed 'no marriage', and this denunciation of the women involved as harlots and concubines translated readily into the popular imagination. Others certainly shared his view; Robert Parkyn noted with some pleasure that the married clergy found no joy in the accession of Mary, and that their wives were pointed at in the street.[49] The battle between 'old' and 'new' religion was played out in the parishes, in the personal life of those priests who had married in violation of the law of the church, but in accordance with the law of the land.

The practical obstacles to the imposition of obligatory clerical celibacy in England, and indeed to the implementation of the Tridentine decrees

---

[47] Cardwell, *Documentary Annals*, I.153.

[48] T. Martin, *Treatise declarying and plainly proving that the pretensed marriage of priestes ... is no marriage* (London, 1554), sigs A2r–v.

[49] A.G. Dickens, 'Robert Parkyn's Narrative of the Reformation', in Dickens, *Reformation Studies* (London, 1982), p. 308.

were substantial, not least because clerical celibacy was an issue that was both public and personal, practical and polemical, and tied to both past and present. Such problems would not, and could not, melt away overnight. Likewise, the debate over clerical celibacy and marriage was not brought to an end by the simple anathema pronounced by the Fathers at Trent. Indeed the formal reiteration of the position of the Catholic church at the council prompted a further flurry of writing in the 1560s, from both sides of the debate, which addressed the issue of clerical celibacy and monastic vows in the present, reopened the controversy over the historical roots of the discipline, or took up the question in the context of a broader defence (or derogation) of Catholic theology and practice. In 1564, the Polish churchman and diplomat Martin Cromerus published a full length discussion of clerical celibacy and marriage, *Orichovius, sive de Coniugio et Coelibatu Sacerdotum Commentarius* (Cologne, 1564), and in the same year Johannes Cochlaeus' polemic against Luther, which had mocked the marriage of the reformer, was printed as *Septiceps Luthereus Ubique Sibi Suisque Scriptis Contrarius* (Paris, 1564). Cardinal Clement Monilianus presented a broad defence of Catholic theology and practice, clerical celibacy included, in his *Catholicarum Institutionem ad Christianam Theologiam Compendium* (Rome, 1565), which argued from the evidence of the Fathers and councils that the law of celibacy had its origins in the apostolic church. In the same year, the Italian lawyer de Susani presented a detailed case for desirability of clerical celibacy, *Tractatus Caeloibatu Sacerdotum non Abrogando* (Venice, 1565).

From a more critical standpoint came the Lutheran Martin Chemnitz's history of the Council of Trent, the *Examen Concilii Tridentini* (1565–73). Volume 3 presented an assessment of the debates over purgatory, the cult of the saints, and the celibacy of the clergy, set against the backdrop of the history of the church, and the scriptural foundation and apostolic origins of each key assertion of orthodoxy at the council.[50] The significance attached to the history of the church in mid-century Lutheranism was exemplified in the *Magdeburg Centuries*, which asserted a late origin and chequered history for obligatory clerical celibacy. Such attempts to reconstruct and re-present the history of medieval Catholicism did not go unchallenged, and several of the Catholic writers who picked up their pens to reply to Flacius and the Magdeburg group included a historical defence of clerical celibacy within their more general assertion that the evangelical enterprise was flawed and inaccurate. Conrad Brunus' *Admonitio Catholica Adversus Novam Historiam Eccles. Quam Matthaeus Illyricus* (Dillingae

---

[50] A.C. Piepkorn, 'Martin Chemnitz' Views on Trent: The Genesis and the Genius of the Examen Concilii Tridentini', *Concordia Theological Monthly*, 37 (January 1966): 5–37; R. Mumm, *Die Polemik des Martin Chemnitz gegen das Konzil von Trent* (Leipzig, 1905).

1565) was a detailed refutation of the historical narrative contained in the *Centuries*, and both this work, and Eysengrein's *Catalogus Testium Veritatis Locupletissimus* (1565) also painted a more favourable picture of the origins and history of clerical celibacy as part of their challenge to Protestant history writing. Cardinal Bellarmine devoted several chapters of his *Disputationes* to the question of clerical celibacy, including a detailed refutation of Luther's views, and a deconstruction of the narrative presented in the *Magdeburg Centuries*, alongside an examination of the debate over the question of whether the obligation to celibacy was a law of divine or human origin.[51]

In 1556, the Jesuit Turrianus took to the defence of monastic vows, including the vow of chastity, in a Latin work which was greatly informed by his reading of the history of the church, including the Greek church. He had been present at the Council of Trent at the request of the pope, and had worked with both Hosius and Baronius on the revisions to the Vulgate. Baronius had entered into the debate over the history of clerical celibacy in his *Annales*, including the vexed question of the role of Paphnutius at Nicaea, and Hosius was also to take up the defence of the apostolic origins of clerical celibacy. Turrianus' interest in the practice of the early church was evinced in his consideration of the authenticity of the *Apostolic Canons*, and in his translations of Greek patristic texts, which informed his defence of chastity and clerical celibacy.[52] There was nothing overtly contentious about Turrianus' interest in the Greek Fathers, but the precedent of the Greek church in the debate over clerical marriage continued to demand the attention of the popes of the sixteenth century. No serious attempt was made at Trent to assert that the ordination of married men in the East presented a case for the adoption of a similar practice in the West, but the married priesthood of the Greek church was frequently deployed in evangelical defences of clerical marriage, ensuring that the example of the East remained at the forefront of debate. There were also some practical considerations in the second half of the sixteenth century, particularly in the context of the discussions between Rome and the Ukrainian churches, and in the more general issue of the position of married clergy, particularly from Albania, seeking union with the Catholic church after emigrating to escape oppression at the hands of the Turks. The assertion of the validity of Greek practice was dependent upon the assumption that the Trullan canon 13 was of ecumenical standing; this had been part of the defence

---

[51] R. Bellarmine, *Disputationes de Controversiis Christianae fidei adversus hujus temporis Haereticos* (3 vols, Ingolstadt, 1586–93); Bellarmine, *Opera Omnia* (12 vols, Paris 1870) vol. 2, *Quinta Controversia Generalis. De Membris Ecclesiae lib 1. De Clericis.* Cap XVIII, Cap XIX, Cap XXII, Cap XXIV.

[52] F. Turrianus, *De Votis Monasticis Liber* (Rome, 1566).

used by Nicetas in the controversy with Rome in the eleventh century.⁵³ Its ecumenicity was not, however, accepted in the Latin church, although this did not translate into an assertion that the married clergy of the East, and their continued use of marriage after ordination, constituted a bar to the union of the two churches.⁵⁴

A general consideration of the married clergy of the Oriental churches was presented in the *Perbrevis Instructio Super Aliquibus Ritibus Graecorum* of August 1563, and Pope Gregory XIII convened the 'Congregatio de Rebus Graecorum' in 1573 in order to consider the particular position of the Albanian clergy. The conclusion of the Congregation was that married priests were to abstain from their wives prior to the celebration of Mass, although the period of abstinence recommended was set at somewhere between three days and one week. As Cholij notes, there was nothing in the canonical discipline of the Eastern churches that would support this demand.⁵⁵ The union of the Ukrainian church with the Roman church in the pontificate of Clement VIII (1592–1605) was accomplished with assurances from the pope that the married clergy of the former would not be condemned as a result, although it was made clear that this did not amount to papal approval of clerical marriage, and that the imposition of the Latin law of celibacy remained a priority.⁵⁶ The example of the Greek church, and indeed the papal toleration of the use of marriages in other churches, remained lively topics of debate, and featured in the correspondence between the bishop of Meaux, Bossuet, and Leibniz at the end of the seventeenth century. The focus of the exchange was the possibility of reunion between the Lutheran and Roman Catholic churches, and one of the potential obstacles identified by Leibniz was the position of the married Lutheran clergy, who would, he suggested, be alarmed by any threat to their position. Bossuet responded that the pope had never sought to undermine the practice of the Greek church, and noted that the Maronites had been received into communion with the church of Rome without rejection of local custom.⁵⁷ Married clergy did not present an obstacle to union. In the mid-eighteenth century, Benedict XIV (1740–1758) asserted that the primary motivation in the actions of his predecessors in relation to the tradition of the Greek church with regard

---

⁵³ PL 143 982a.

⁵⁴ See R. Cholij, *Clerical Celibacy in East and West* (Leominster, 1988), p. 181; Council of Florence 1439.

⁵⁵ Cholij, *Clerical Celibacy*, p. 168.

⁵⁶ See Cholij, *Clerical Celibacy*, p. 183, who suggests that toleration was proposed out of prudence rather than any sense of recognition.

⁵⁷ See F. Gaquière, *Le Dialogue Irenique Bossuet-Leibniz: La Reunion des Eglises en echec (1691–1702)*, (Paris, 1966).

to clerical marriage was to avoid any deepening of divisions between East and West. The use of marriage was identified as a particular custom of the Eastern church, and not one that the pope sought to overturn, but neither was it fully recognised in the West.

Debate over clerical celibacy and marriage continued well into the seventeenth and eighteenth centuries, with the publication of substantial volumes that charted the history of the discipline, and contested the principles that underpinned it. The most significant contribution in the seventeenth century came from the Lutheran George Calixtus, in his *De Conjugio Clericorum Liber*. First printed in 1631, Calixtus' work was a survey of clerical celibacy and marriage through the laws of the church and the decrees of the popes, which included a detailed examination of the eleventh-century reforms of Hildebrand, and a refutation of Catholic defences of clerical celibacy. Its prime targets were the works of Baronius and Bellarmine, both of whom had asserted the apostolic origins of clerical celibacy. Such views, he argued, were untenable, since scripture, tradition and ecclesiastical history all pointed to the married priesthood as the practice of the apostolic church, and a state that was in accordance with the will of God as voiced in scripture. Calixtus ventured in some detail into the works of the church Fathers, both Latin and Greek, and attempted to argue from the flawed foundations of clerical celibacy that it was evident that the pope had erred in matters of faith and doctrine.[58] The publication of such substantial compendia of materials relating to the history of clerical celibacy no doubt equipped its opponents with the ammunition that they needed to keep the issue alive. John Lynch has noted the frequency with which the Sorbonne censured propositions taken from works of theology and history that argued against clerical celibacy, including the personal assertion that a professed religious may marry if he believed he had received a dispensation from God, and the more general claim that until the pontificate of Leo IX, priests and bishops in the Latin church had been married men.[59]

In the early eighteenth century, the Oratorian Louis Thomassin examined both the practice of the Greek church and the custom of the Latins, in a detailed history of the origins of clerical celibacy. He argued stridently for the apostolic foundation of the discipline of the church,

---

[58] G. Calixtus, *De Conjugio Clericorum Liber*. (Helmstadt, 1631; 2nd edn, Frankfurt, 1651).

[59] Lynch, 'Critique of the Law of Celibacy', 63; see also A. de Roskovany, *Coelibatus et Breviarium: duo gravissima clericorum official, e monumentis omnium seculorum demonstrate. Accessit completa literature*. 11 vols, (Pest-Neustra 1861–88), and *Supplementa ad collections monumentorum et literature III. De Coelibatu et Breviario* (Neutra, 1888), especially volume 6.

and asserted the birth of Christ to a virgin mother as evidence of the superiority of virginity over marriage. The first followers of Christ had been either virgins, he argued, or men who committed to continence at their calling, and this had been the custom of the church ever since.[60] The breadth and depth of the eighteenth-century polemical debate is evident in the substantial work of Francesco Antonio Zaccaria in the 1770s. Zaccaria, an Italian Jesuit, took to the defence of the apostolic origins of clerical celibacy in his *Storia Polemica* printed in 1774, and a decade later in the *Nuova Giustificazione del celibate*. Both were written in response to contemporary criticisms, and in the latter, Zaccaria identified some of the critics who had not been silenced by his first volume by name, including the now married Oratorian, Gaudin.[61] A whole section of the *Storia Polemica* was devoted to the practice of the Greek church, and a further section to the defence of the tradition of the West. The general observation of clerical celibacy had been demanded in the Apostolic church, he claimed, and it was clerical marriage which was, in fact, the innovation. Occasional dispensations granted had encouraged the Latin clergy in the erroneous belief that marriage was permitted, and gave the false impression that a married clergy had been the practice of the early church. Instead, Zaccaria argued, the tradition of clerical celibacy and continence was far older, and the practice of the Catholic church in the eighteenth century more authentically faithful to the traditions of the early church than that of the Protestant married ministry. In the case of those apostles who had been married, he argued, there was no evidence that they had continued in the use of their marriage, and indeed plenty to suggest that they had left their wives to follow their calling. Celibacy was a higher state than marriage, as the praise of virginity throughout the New Testament evinced. It also carried practical advantages for the priest and the church, freeing men from the cares of marriage and the necessity to care for wife and family. A celibate priest was in a better position to commit his life to prayer, and the advantages of this were evident to the Catholic faithful, who respected and valued the unmarried priesthood.[62]

---

[60] L. Thomassin, 'Du Celibat des Beneficiers dans l'Eglise Orientale pendant les cinq premiers siecles', and 'Du Celibat des Beneficiers dans l'Eglise Latine pendant le cinq premiers siecles', in *Ancienne et Nouvelle Discipline de l'Eglise touchant les Benefices et les Beneficiers* (3 vols, Paris 1678–1679, revised 1725), vol. 2, c.52.

[61] Gaudin had written in defence of clerical marriage in his *Les Inconveniens du Celibat des Pretres, prouves par des recherché historiques* (Geneva, 1781). For further discussion of the late eighteenth-century French context, see the following chapter pp. 209–12.

[62] F.A. Zaccaria, *Storia Polemica del celibato sacro da contraporsi ad alcune detestabili opera uscite a questi tempi (Rome, 1774); Nuova giustificazione del celibate scaro dagli inconvenienti oppostogli anche ultimamente in alcuni infamissimi libri dissertazioni Quattro* (Fuligno, 1785); the discussion of the issue of dispensations is in *Storia Polemica*, p. 65.

The final section of the *Storia Polemica* was a refutation of the views of Pierre Desforges and other eighteenth-century protagonists in the debate who had argued in favour of clerical marriage. For the first time since the early sixteenth century, substantive criticisms of clerical celibacy had come from the pens of Catholic authors, particularly among the French writers of the Enlightenment. Voltaire, Bayle and Diderot were entirely unsympathetic to the principle of clerical celibacy, and a highly critical entry on the subject was written for the *Encylopedia*.[63] Among the multitude of works on the topic printed in the 1700s, Desforges' was one of the most substantial, although the presentation of the case rested more upon the weight of material rather than the clarity of thought. The argument in *On the Advantages of Marriage* ranged from the creation narrative contained in Genesis to natural law and human rights, with an excursus into the priesthood of all believers and a more general attack on the authority of the institutional church. The marriage of priests, he argued, would mirror the marriage of Christ and his church. There was no sacramental impediment to marriage in orders; if, Desforges argued, it was possible to marry after baptism and confirmation, there was no justification for the assertion that marriage was not permitted to those who had received the sacrament of orders.[64] The book was highly controversial, and was quickly suppressed and its author imprisoned. However, German and Italian translations secured a wider audience, particularly the Italian edition which appeared timed to coincide with the unpopular pontificate of Pope Clement XIII. The sudden involuntary exodus of Jesuits from their houses gave the question of clerical celibacy an immediate practical as well as philosophical application and opened up a wider debate over the binding nature of vows of chastity within Catholicism, as well as between Catholic and Protestant.

Desforges' work acquired thus a prominent place in Zaccaria's defence of celibacy, which was commissioned by Pope Clement XIV in response to the controversy that the publication of Desforges' work had opened. A French response, less encyclopedic than that of Zaccaria, and dependent upon the presentation of passages in favour of celibacy culled from patristic writings, came from the pen of the Abbé de Villiers, in the *Apologie du Celibat Chretien*. Neither work silenced critics of the

---

[63] For example, P. Bayle's *Dictionnaire historique et critique* (8 vols, Rotterdam, 1692) considered homosexuality to be the result of clerical celibacy. For a more general discussion, see P. Picard, *Zolibatsdiskussion im katholischen Deutschland der Aufkalrungzeit* (Dusseldorf, 1975); B. Plongeron, *Théologie et politique au siècle des Lumières (1770–1820)* (Genève, 1973), pp. 192–8.

[64] Roskovany, *Coelibatus et Breviarium*, vol. 4 nos 1065–1796, lists the volumes published.

'apostolic origins' thesis, however, and a further assertion of the practice of clerical marriage in the early church was published in 1781, Jacques Gaudin's *Les Inconvenients du Celibats des Prêtres*. Gaudin argued that the apostles and the priests of the early church had been free to marry, and that it was perfectly clear from both Old and New Testaments that there was no scriptural prohibition of clerical marriage. Marriage itself was a worthy institution, and the raising of children encouraged a more noble demeanour than the false continence of priests. Celibacy was futile, and mere decadence, and a self-centred way of life that undermined the economy and society of the nation, concentrated land and income in the hands of the church and contributed to the underpopulation of contemporary France. 'Une observation qui m'a toujours frappé en lisant', he wrote, 'l'histoire, c'est que le célibat s'accrédite chez toutes les nations à mesure que les mœurs s'y détériorent'.[65] A refutation, and a defence of clerical celibacy, was composed by Gabriel-Nicolas Maultrot, and printed as *La discipline de l'Église sur le mariage des prêtres* late in 1790. Alongside the assertion of the legitimacy of clerical marriage from scripture and tradition came rather more lurid descriptions of the failure of obligatory celibacy, focusing upon solicitation in the confessional and other such abuses.[66] Some were polemical, others, such as *Venus dans le Cloitre ou la religieuse en chemise*, more vivid, but no doubt serving to keep the issue alive in the public imagination.[67]

The conduct of the Catholic clergy remained, in 1764 as in 1564, a highly public illustration of the effectiveness of the efforts of the church and papacy to put its house in order. Clerical marriage had been established as a popular and polemical battle-line in the early years of the Reformation, in accusations of widespread clerical incontinence that turned priestly conduct into a call for reform and an indictment of traditional theology, and in the public marriages of the first generation of evangelicals that flouted the laws of the church and provided visible testimony to doctrinal change. Contributions to the debate, both Catholic and Protestant, rapidly ranged well beyond accusations of sexual misconduct, deeper into biblical precedent and exegesis, an argument from apostolic tradition, and the reconstruction of the history of celibacy as part of the history of the

---

[65] Gaudin, *Les Inconveniens*, p. 9; the work was also published also with the new title (but identical pagination) *Recherches philosophiques et historiques sur le célibat*; a similar argument based on population was articulated in L'Abbé de Saint-Pierre, *Ouvrages de Politique* (Paris, 1658–1749).

[66] S. Haliczer, *Sexuality in the Confessional* (New York: Oxford, 1996).

[67] Composed by the Abbé du Prat, *Venus* was translated into English and published in London in 1724 by Edmund Curll. See also Gaudin, *Les Inconveniens*, pp. 316–20 and 355–8. Further fictional representations of clerical celibacy in the honour and the breech include Matthew Lewis, *The Monk* (1796) and Harriet Beecher Stowe, *Agnes of Sorrento* (1862).

church. Clerical marriage was not simply a matter between man and wife, it was also an issue of authority, broadly interpreted. A priest who married stood in flagrant breach of the discipline of the church, but to argue that scriptural support for a married priesthood undermined centuries of ecclesiastical law and tradition was to make a broader statement about the nature of authority in doctrine and praxis. At the Council of Trent, Gaudin argued, Pius IV had refused to concede to demands for clerical marriage, because to do so would undermine the authority of the church, and particularly the pope, 'les détacheroit en même tems de la dépendance où ils étoient du Saint-Siège et que, leur permettre de se marier, se seroit autant que détruire la hiérarchie et réduire le pape à n'être qu'évêque de Rome'.[68] The link between the position of the pope and the marriage of priests was perhaps overstated for polemical gain, but the assumption was testimony to the deep roots that the debate over clerical celibacy had planted in wider debate and controversy.

---

[68] Gaudin, *Les Inconveniens*, p. 373.

CONCLUSION

'One of the chief ornaments of the Catholic clergy'?: Celibacy in the Modern Church

Early modern polemicists had attached a theological, moral, historical, and confessional meaning to the question of clerical celibacy, and as the debates continued into the eighteenth century, these familiar battle-fields continued to be contested. The Council of Trent had established a ruling on clerical celibacy that was to provide the foundation for the stance of the modern church, and which constructed an image of Catholic priesthood that was visibly different to that of the reformed churches. However, the church still needed to respond to practical challenges to the celibate priesthood posed by factors that were not always entirely within its control. One such challenge arose in the aftermath of the French Revolution, which marked a watershed not only for the church in France, but also for Catholicism in Europe. The Revolution shattered the link between faith and state, in a country in which Catholic reform had made more progress than any other.[1] With regard to clerical celibacy, the critical moment came in 1789–90. In October 1789, the Assembly voted to suspend the taking of monastic vows, and in February of the following year formally abolished such vows, and required monks and nuns who refused to leave the cloister, or to accept relocation to one of a small number of surviving houses. The *Civil Constitution of the Clergy*, approved in August 1790, enacted the principle that no occupation could be used to debar an individual from marriage, and that no public notary could refuse to ratify a marriage on the grounds

---

[1] N. Atkin and F. Tallett, *Priests, Prelates and People. A History of European Catholicism Since 1750* (London and New York, 2003), chapter 2. For more detail on the French church in the late eighteenth and early nineteenth centuries, see J. McManners, *Church and Society in Eighteenth Century France* (2 vols, OUP, 1998); G. Cholvy and Y-M. Hilaire, *Histoire Religieuse de la France Contemporaine* (Toulouse, 1985–8); J. Le Goff and R. Remond, *Histoire de la France Religieuse* (Paris, 1988–92); J. McManners, *The French Revolution and the Church* (London, 1969); N. Aston, *Religion and Revolution in France 1780–1804* (Basingstoke, 2000) and *Christianity in Revolutionary Europe, c1760–1830* (Cambridge, 2002); R. Gibson, *A social history of French Catholicism* (London, 1989); T. Tackett, 'The Social History of the Diocesan Clergy in Eighteenth Century France', in R.M. Golden (ed.), *Church, State and Society under the Bourbon Kings of France* (Lawrence, KS, 1982).

of profession. Mirabeau had made no specific mention of the marriage of priests, but his speech to the Assembly amounted to a summary of the traditional arguments advanced in favour of clerical marriage, and the intention was clear. The consequence for the Catholic priesthood was that clerical celibacy was now inferred as an implicit protest against the new regime, and marriage as a symbol of political loyalty to the Revolution. In the aftermath of the *Civil Constitution,* many priests in orders entered into open marriages, while others chose civil marriage, perhaps for political reasons; any priest who had presented banns of marriage was immune from imprisonment under the terms of a decree of 1793. Abbé Gaudin of the Oratory took advantage of the apparent relaxation of the law of celibacy, as did several other high-profile clerics, including the bishops of Bourges and Beauvais. There remained, however, a strong commitment to clerical celibacy both on the part of some priests, and on the part of the faithful, who were less than tolerant of those clergy who had entered into marriage after 1791. The Archbishop of Rouen composed a stinging condemnation of clerical marriage in July 1792, and the fact that the stipends of married priests were formally secured in August of the same year suggests that there were some parts of the country in which those priests who had taken wives either encountered local opposition, or had been driven from their cures. Indeed, the majority of the constitutional bishops remained opposed to the marriage of priests, although Thomas Lindet did choose to marry, and Gobel appointed at least one married priest to a Paris church. In July 1793 the Convention adopted a law which held the threat of deprivation and exile over any bishop who sought to prevent the marriage of priests in his diocese, and Jean-Baptiste-Guillaume Graziani of Rouen was excluded from the Episcopal palace on the basis of his denunciation of clerical marriage. The process of 'dechristianisation' included, for many clergy, a perceived requirement to enter into marriage as a visible sign of their renunciation of priestly office and dignity. As Atkin and Tallett suggest, such an attitude on the part of the Convention and its representatives was a 'back-handed compliment to the success of the Counter-Reformation church'; to position marriage as the ultimate proof of the rejection of clerical status was to give tacit recognition to the assumption that celibacy was indeed a defining characteristic of the priesthood.[2]

After the Terror, the restoration of clerical celibacy emerged as one of the priorities for ecclesiastical reform. In March 1795 an encyclical letter was issued from Paris by a group of *assermentés* bishops that denounced clerical marriage in the strongest terms.[3] It was not acceptable, the bishops

---

[2] Atkin and Tallett, *Priests, Prelates and People*, p. 57.

[3] H. Grégoire, *Histoire du mariage des prêtres en France: particulièrement depuis 1789* (Brussels, 1826), p. 109.

argued, for married clergy to claim that they had entered into such unions on the basis of political circumstance, and these priests were deemed to be unworthy of office, and guilty of a sin from which there was no absolution. The national council of 1797 reduced clerical marriages to the status of civil unions, but the final blow was to come in the 1801 Concordat which restored Latin discipline in the French church. The Concordat failed to confront the issue of clerical marriage directly, but its implications were clear in the actions of over 3200 priests who petitioned either for the regularisation of their marriages, or for reinstatement in the church. Well over half of these, around 2000, chose marriage over the ministry.[4] A collective faculty for dispensation, issued to the legate Cardinal Caprara, was the third such example of papal intervention to resolve the particular problem of priests who had entered into marriages authorised by civil law.[5] Primarily as a result of the interventions of Cardinal Consalvi, who argued that matters of individual conscience were not subject to diplomatic agreement, the Concordat had made no provision for the position of the married clergy. However, the papal bull that equipped Caprara with faculties to deal with married French priests indicated that the pope's actions were a response to 'the request made by the government in their favour', and were modelled upon the precedent provided by Julius III.[6] Not all accepted that this was a valid precedent. The bishop of Dijon, for example, argued that Caprara's actions were contrary to the canons of Trent, but the legate simply moved with celerity to address the local situation when necessary.[7] While prepared to offer dispensation to married lower clergy, and reduction to the lay estate, Pius VII refused to extend this principle to former religious, or to bishops who requested the validation of their marriages. The bishop of Autun, Talleyrand, was perhaps the most infamous among the latter group of petitioners. Already unpopular with the church by virtue of his participation in the secularisation of ecclesiastical property, he had also consecrated the Constitutional bishops, and had attempted to secure the position of married clerics during the negotiations that led to the signing of the Concordat in 1801. Talleyrand was denied

---

[4] J. Lynch, 'Critique of the Law of Celibacy in the Catholic Church from the Period of the Reform Councils', in W. Bassett and Peter Huizing (eds), *Celibacy in the Church* (New York, 1972), p. 66, quoting S. Delacroix, *La réorganisation de l'Église de France apres la Révolution, 1801–1809* (Paris, 1962), chapter 20, 'La reconciliation des Prêtres et religieux maries', pp. 443–56.

[5] J. Abo, 'The Problem of Lapsed Priests', *The Jurist*, 23 (1963): 153–79, especially 159. For the two early modern examples see chapter 6 above.

[6] *Bullarii Romani Continuatio* (19 vols, Rome, 1835), vol. 7, part 1, pp. 187, 188; see also G. Cardinal Caprara, *Concordat et Recueil des Bulles et Brefs de NSP le Pape Pie VII* (Paris, 1802), pp. 14–53, quoted in Abo, 'Lapsed Priests', 159.

[7] G. Constant, *L'Eglise de France sous le Consulat et l'Empire* (Paris, 1928), p. 211.

permission to marry, in a decision communicated by Cardinal Consalvi in June 1802. The argument against permission was historical; there was, it was claimed, no evidence in eighteen centuries of history that a bishop had been offered a dispensation to marry, but there were plenty of other cases in which such requests had been denied.[8] Condemnation of clerical marriage in civil law came in 1807, with an assertion by the emperor that there was to be no toleration of marriage for those individuals who had exercised priestly function after 1802. The general faculty facilitated the restoration of union between France and Rome, but it did little to improve standards of the clergy, or the esteem in which they were held by their congregations. As had been the case in England in 1554, the laity in France were, in the early nineteenth century, confronted by a clerical estate in turmoil. Those priests who had married and petitioned for readmission were hardly a model of steadfastness and sacerdotal continence, but one fifth of French parish churches were still without a priest a decade after the Concordat. The instability of previous years had done little to improve recruitment levels, and the church could not count upon the services of the ageing pre-revolutionary clergy indefinitely. Caprara's handling of the married clergy might have been sympathetic, but the broader issues raised by the position of married priests in the French church in 1802 would be harder to resolve.

The Concordat, and the faculties issued by the pope, offered a solution to the specific problem of those priests who had married in revolutionary France. The Church did not, however, address the more general calls for toleration of clerical marriage which extended beyond the French church. The relaxation of the obligation to celibacy was debated in Austria under Joseph II, although such discussions came to an abrupt end at the instruction of the emperor in 1783. Clerical marriage, Caprara observed, was a step beyond the limits of radicalism that Joseph was prepared to entertain from Eybel and others.[9] There was further debate over celibacy in the German-speaking lands in the early nineteenth century. In 1828 the lay professors of Freiburg petitioned in favour of clerical marriage, supported by seminarians and many ordained clergy, and an association in the diocese of Rottenburg was formed to facilitate the abrogation of the celibacy law. Over a hundred clergy in Baden appended their names to a petition in favour of clerical marriage in 1828, and similar demands

---

[8] F. Mathieu, *Le Concordat de 1801* (Paris, 1904), p. 348; H.C. Lea, *History of Sacerdotal Celibacy* (2 vols, London, 1907), vol. 2, pp. 317–18, quoting Bernard de Lacombe. 'Le Mariage de Talleyrand', *Le Correspondant*, Paris, 25 Aout et 10 Septembre 1905.

[9] Lynch 'Critique of the Law of Celibacy', 67; S.K. Padover, *The Revolutionary Emperor: Joseph II of Austria* (2nd edition, London, 1967), pp. 164–5; P.G.M. Dickson, 'Joseph II's Reshaping of the Austrian Church', *Historical Journal*, 36 (1993): 89–114, n. 97.

were articulated by Catholic clergy in Silesia in 1831.[10] In Baden, the liberal Karl von Rotteck argued that clerical celibacy was a matter that was both civic and religious, not confined to the church but impinging upon the welfare of the state. An explicit attempt to 'secularise' the question of clerical celibacy was made in the appeal to the precedent of the Reformation. If, it was argued, the German princes had risen in support of their married priests in the sixteenth century, it was reasonable to expect the prince to do the same in the nineteenth century. Other petitioners argued that the apparent failure of the clergy to abide by the law of celibacy was reason enough for its abrogation. To demand celibacy of the clergy, it was suggested, was to limit their freedom beyond that which was possible or permissible, in the service of a law which dated not to the time of the apostles, but to the era of Gregory VII.[11] History and precedent were again contested, and the rejection of the apostolic origins of the law of celibacy provided the underlying theme of the massive work of two brothers, Johann and Augustine Theiner. The publication of *Die Einfuhrung der erzwungenen Ehelosigkeit bei den christlichen Geistlichen und ihre Folgen. Ein Beitrag zur Kirchengeschichte* (Altenburg, 1828) led to the condemnation of Johann, then an ordained priest and professor of canon law at Breslau, although Augustine was later to enter the Oratory and rise to the position of Prefect of the Vatican Archives. Running to more than 1500 pages, the three-volume work was essentially a compilation of examples and illustrations of the decline of religion since the time of the apostles. Mandatory clerical celibacy was presented as one such example of the corruption of the faith at the hands of the institutional church, a corruption that had created numerous problems for the church, its pastors, and people, throughout its history.[12]

Such polemical and political criticisms did not go unanswered. Joseph Mohler vigorously debated the issue through the mouthpiece of the *Theologische Quarterlschrift* in the 1820s, arguing against clerical marriage from both a theological and practical standpoint. There were, he believed, far too many priests, where there should and could only be a few. This was particularly true where celibacy, a rare gift, was concerned. However, Mohler argued, there was no merit in the proposal that the

---

[10] Lynch 'Critique of the Law of Celibacy', 67–8; Lea, *Sacerdotal Celibacy*, vol. 2, p. 325.

[11] For a fuller discussion of the literature and context, see D. Herzog, *Intimacy and Exclusion: Religious Politics in Pre-Revolutionary Baden* (Princeton, 1997), chapter 1.

[12] O. Chadwick, *Catholicism and History: The Opening of the Vatican Archives* (Cambridge, 1978), pp. 32–71 provides a summary of the career of Augustine; see also C. Cochini, *The Apostolic Origins of Priestly Celibacy* (San Francisco, 1990), pp. 29–30; E. Peters, 'History, Historians, and Clerical Celibacy', in M. Frassetto (ed.) *Medieval Purity and Piety. Essays on Medieval Clerical Celibacy and Religious Reform* (New York and London, 1998), pp. 3–21.

solution to clerical incontinence came through the legalisation of clerical marriage. The precedent of the Greek church might permit the ordination of married men to the priesthood, but it did not support the claim that marriage was legitimate after ordination, a claim which ran contrary to the tradition, dating back to the apostles, that a total commitment was required of those who entered into the priesthood.[13] To attack clerical celibacy, Mohler argued, was to attack the very essence of the church and its authority, by calling into doubt the infallibility of the church in matters of doctrine and practice. The defence of clerical marriage, he suggested, in a tone that would not have been out of place in the works of Thomas More two centuries earlier, was the preoccupation of 'fleshly minded' individuals.[14] A direct response to the work of the Theiner brothers came from Theodore Klitsche in 1830, in his *Geschichte des Colibats der katholischen Geistlichen von der Zeiten der Apostel bis zum Tode Gregors XIII*. Klitsche's historical scope was as broad as that of his opponents, but his defence of clerical celibacy on the basis of apostolic precedent and ecclesiastical tradition relied heavily upon the earlier work of Zaccaria.[15] Forceful papal condemnation of the German calls for the legalisation of clerical marriage came in August 1832, in Gregory XVI's Bull *Mirari Vos*.[16] Clerical celibacy, the pope complained, was under threat from a conspiracy, a 'foedessima conjuratio', which included both laymen and priests, and was motivated by the wishes of the 'lascivious', who sought to enlist the support of the secular powers for their actions. The bishops were instructed to 'strive with all your might to justify and to defend the law of clerical celibacy as prescribed by the sacred canons'. A similar sentiment was evident a decade later in the Bull *Qui Pluribus* of Pius IX, in which the pope complained that 'the sacred celibacy of clerics has also been the victim of conspiracy. Indeed, some churchmen have wretchedly forgotten their own rank and let themselves be converted by the charms and snares of pleasure'.[17] The defence of clerical marriage was presented as an error

---

[13] Lynch, 'Critique of the Law of Celibacy', 67; H. Savon, *Johann Adam Mohler. The Father of Modern Theology* (tr. C. McGrath) (Glen Rock, 1966).

[14] Mohler's works were edited after his death by Dellinger, *Gesammelte Schriften und Aufsatze* (2 vols, Ratisbon, 1839–40). On celibacy, see his 'Beleuchtung der Denkschrift fur die Aufhebung des den katholischen Geistlichen vorgeschriebenen Celibates', *Katholik*, 8 (1828): 1–32, 257–97.

[15] For a response, see Friedrich Wilhelm Carové, *Über das Cölibatsgesetz des römisch-katholischen Klerus* (Frankfurt, 1833), and his earlier *Vollständige Sammlung der Cölibatgesetze* (Frankfurt, 1823).

[16] *Mirari Vos*, 15 August 1832, in *Acta Gregorii XVI*; Consistorial Allocution, 16 December 1920 (*AAS*, 12, 1920), p. 587.

[17] *Qui Pluribus*, 9 November 1846. [http://www.papalencyclicals.net/Pius09/p9quiplu.htm]; Pius also condemned such views in his *Syllabus of Errors*, quoted in Lynch,

motivated by moral degeneracy, and a conspiracy to undermine the canons of the church which had remained in place since Trent. There was to be no room for further debate.

Given the continuing vocal opposition to mandatory celibacy, however, it was no surprise that there was substantial discussion of the issue at the first Vatican Council. The council, the first since Trent, enacted no further decrees on clerical celibacy, but consideration of the discipline took place in connection with discussions of concubinage, the relationship with the Lutheran churches, and the position of the Oriental churches. There were requests from bishops that the mandatory celibacy articulated at Trent be imposed more effectively, and a short constitution, *De Vita et Honesta Clericorum*, was presented to the council, and debated in General Congregation.[18] The only specific reference to clerical celibacy came in the statement on the treatment of those who violated the discipline; for example, any cleric who maintained a concubine or cohabited with a suspect woman was to face the penalties that had been laid down at Trent. An Armenian representative painted a positive picture of clerical celibacy, and suggested that married priests were a drain on the resources of the church, too preoccupied with family concerns, and with an alarming tendency to devote their time, and the possessions of the church, to their children. At least one participant suggested that the council should make a powerful statement in favour of clerical celibacy in light of the recently published criticisms of the practice, but there was no formal vote.[19] The position of the Roman church in relation to the law of celibacy and marriage in the Oriental churches was debated in the fourth Congress of the commission *Super Missionibus et Ecclesiis Ritus Orientalis*, in January 1868. The Latin patriarch of Jerusalem asserted that the majority of the bishops of the Eastern churches favoured clerical celibacy, and Augustine Theiner, acting as one of the Consultors, commended the foundation of cathedral chapters composed of celibates as a mechanism by which celibacy might be introduced in the East.[20] However the 37th Congress of May 1870 concluded that the Oriental churches were too 'immature' to accept the universal imposition of clerical celibacy, and instead simply commended those bishops who sought to introduce obligatory celibacy, without making a more general mandate. The discussion of clerical celibacy

---

'Critique of the Law of Celibacy', 69. The pope was also swift to reject the criticisms of clerical celibacy contained in the more wide-ranging treatise *Defensa de la Autoridad de los Gobiernos* (Lima, 1848).

[18] J. Mansi, *Sacrum Conciliorum Nova et Amplissa Collectio* (53 vols in 60, Paris/Leipzig, 1901–27), vol. 50, pp. 517–700; esp. 683d–4d.

[19] Lynch, 'Critique of the Law of Celibacy', 71.

[20] Mansi, *Sacrum Conciliorum*, vol. 50, p. 1003.

in the East did not reach the general sessions of the council, which ended abruptly with the spread of hostilities in the Franco-Prussian war.

The dogmatic definition of papal infallibility at the council created dissent, primarily among those German, Swiss and Austrian priests and congregations in which lie the roots of the 'Old Catholics'.[21] Whilst papal infallibility was the prime cause of separation, the Old Catholic churches also departed from the Roman Catholic position on the language of liturgy and on the issue of the celibacy of priests. The obligation to celibacy began to be relaxed in Old Catholic churches in the years that followed separation from Rome, although it was only in 1922 that the Dutch church lifted the requirement from its priests. Old Catholics in Switzerland abolished compulsory clerical celibacy in 1875, German priests were permitted to marry (with the approval of the bishop or, if necessary, the synod) in 1877, and in 1880 the first Austrian Synod lifted the prohibition on clerical marriage.[22] Among the participants at the Munich assembly of 1871 was Ignaz von Döllinger, who had been excommunicated after addressing a letter to the Archbishop of Munich in which he described papal infallibility as contrary to apostolic tradition, the decrees of the general councils, and the precedent of history.[23] However, the abrogation of the law of celibacy by the Old Catholics did not find favour with Döllinger, who regarded celibacy as the duty of any priest committed to the service of his people. In a letter to an Anglican friend, Döllinger wrote

> You in England cannot understand how completely engrained it is into our people that a priest is a man who sacrifices himself for the sake of his parishioners. He has no children of his own, in order that all the children in the parish may be his children. His people know that his small wants are supplied, and that he can devote all his time and thought to them. They know that it is quite otherwise with the married pastors of the Protestants. The pastor's income may be enough for himself, but it is not enough for his wife and children also. In order to maintain them he must take other work, literary or scholastic, only a portion of his time can be given to his people; and they know that when the interests of his family and those of his flock collide, his family must come first and his flock second. In short, he has a profession or trade, a *Gewerbe*,

---

[21] B. Hasler, *Wie der Papst Unfehlbar Wurde: Macht und Ohnmacht eines Dogmas* (Munich, 1979); J. O'Connor (ed. and tr.) *The Gift of Infallibility: The Official Relatio on Infallibility of Bishop Vincent Gasser at Vatican Council I* (San Francisco, 2008); C.B. Moss, *The Old Catholic Movement* (London, 1964).

[22] Lynch notes the rather more complex stance of the German Old Catholics: marriage was not permitted within the first six years after ordination, or within three years of entry into the diocese for priests ordained elsewhere.

[23] G. Denzler and E.L. Grasmück (eds), *Geschichtlichkeit und Glaube. Zum 100. Todestag Johann Joseph Ignaz von Döllingers (1799–1890)* (Munich, 1990).

rather than a vocation; he has to earn a livelihood. In almost all Catholic congregations, a priest who married would be ruined; all his influence would be gone. The people are not at all ready for so fundamental a change, and the circumstances of the clergy do not admit of it. It is a fatal resolution.[24]

Döllinger's argument against papal infallibility was couched in terms of continuity of law and tradition, but the argument against clerical marriage was rather more practical, in the suggestion that it distracted the priest from the care of his congregation, and turned his mind to other things.[25] However, it was the history of the church, and particularly the possession of the heritage of the apostolic church, that was to dominate written exchanges on the subject of clerical celibacy in the aftermath of the Vatican Council.

The application of historical theology to the origins of obligatory clerical celibacy generated a heated debate between the Orientalist and son of a Protestant churchman, Gustav Bickell, and the early-church historian Franz Funk in the decade that followed the Vatican Council. Bickell, ordained as a Catholic priest and educated in Syriac and Hebrew, brought the weight of his scholarship to bear on the question of the apostolic origins of clerical celibacy. The first printed salvo appeared in *Zeitschrift fur Katholische Theologie* (1878) with the title 'Der Colibat eine apostolische Anordnung'. Bickell argued that the origins of clerical celibacy and continence in the West lay in the apostolic era, and not, as its opponents would suggest, in the fourth century letters of Siricius, and asserted that the same was true in the East, although there the tradition had been greatly neglected. Bickell's essay prompted a swift response from Funk, 'Der Colibat keine apostolische Anordnung' published in *Tübinger Theologische Quartalschrift* (1880). Funk had been promoted to the chair of history and theology at Tübingen as the successor to Hefele, and was a recognised authority on the patristic period. His primary contention was that there was no evidence that celibacy had been demanded of priests in the apostolic era. While there was some support for the hypothesis that clerical continence was practised, he argued, it was a voluntary action and not a discipline of the church. The Latin church had innovated by turning this voluntary commitment into an obligation, Funk argued, and it was the Greek church that had remained faithful to the apostolic tradition. Bickell rearticulated his original thesis, in 'Der Colibat dennoch eine Apostolische Anordnung' published in *Zeitschrift fur Katholische*

---

[24] A. Plummer in *The Expositor*, December, 1890, p. 470.

[25] See also his comment that 'When a priest can no longer point to personal sacrifice which he makes for the good of his people, then it is all over with him and the cause which he represents. He sinks to the level of men who make a trade of their work': *Er rangiert dann mit den Gewerbetreibenden*, in M. Michael (ed.), *Ignaz von Döllinger* (Munich, 1894), p. 249.

Theologie (1879), and Funk retaliated with a swift reassertion of his own views, 'Der Colibat noch lange keine Apostolische Anordnung' in *Theologische Quartalschift* (1880), and a further, more moderate rejection of Bickell's 'apostolic origins' argument in 1897, 'Colibat und Priesterehe im christlichen Altertum', in *Kirchengeschichliche Abhandlungen und Untersuchungen*. Funk's particular contribution was to establish the idea that it was at the Synod of Elvira that the discipline of clerical celibacy was first asserted in the Latin church, an assertion which enabled him to turn the documentary evidence that Bickell had cited in defence of clerical celibacy against him. The controversy hinged upon the interpretation of contested episodes and documents from the history of the early church. Funk, for example, continued to use the example of the intervention of Paphnutius at the Council of Nicaea to argue that clerical celibacy was a later innovation, although Bickell, as many before him, had questioned strongly the accuracy of the legend.[26]

It was Funk's thesis that was, in the medium term at least, to prove the most enduring, primarily because it secured the backing of two distinguished scholars of the early twentieth century, Vacandard and Leclerq.[27] Writing in 1905, Vacandard acknowledged his debt to Funk, drawing heavily upon his work to support the assertion that celibacy was voluntary rather than compulsory in the early church, and the contention that obligatory celibacy was a later development in the West.[28] Henri Leclerq, who translated into French Hefele's study of the early church councils, *Conciliengeschichte* (1855–74), also entered into the debate over the apostolic origins of celibacy. Following Funk, he argued that clerical celibacy had been voluntary in the early church, although the esteem in which virginity and celibacy were held was to become more apparent by the fourth century. However, the law of sacerdotal celibacy in the contemporary Catholic church, he contended, could not be traced back to this period. There was nothing in scripture, or in the writings of the Fathers, that proved conclusively that the apostles were unmarried

---

[26] See Cochini, *Apostolic Origins*, p. 35; Peters, 'History, Historians and Clerical Celibacy', p. 11; A.M. Cardinal Stickler, *The Case for Clerical Celibacy. Its Historical Development & Theological Foundations* (tr. Fr Brian Ferme) (San Francisco, 1995), pp. 16–17; A.L. Barstow, *Married Priests and the Reforming Papacy. The Eleventh Century Debates* (Lewiston NY, 1982), pp. 199–200.

[27] E. Vacandard, 'Les origines du Celibat Ecclesiastique', *Etudes de Critique d'histoire religieuse* 1st ser. (Paris 1905; 5th edition, Paris 1913), pp. 71–120; 'Celibat', in *Dictionnaire de theologie catholique* (Paris, 1905), vol. 2, 2068–88; H. Leclerq, 'La legislation conciliare relative au celibate ecclesiastique', in the extended French edition of Josef v Hefele, *Conciliengeschichte* (Paris, 1908), vol. 2 part 2, appendix 6, pp. 1321–48; 'Celibat', in *Dictionnaire d'Archeologie chretienne et de liturgie* (Paris, 1908) 2.2802–32.

[28] Vacandard, 'Les origines du celibate ecclesiastique'.

(or, indeed married). St Paul had urged monogamy rather than celibacy upon candidates for the ministry, but the influence of ascetic groups, Leclerq suggested, including the heterodox Manichaeans, had encouraged Christians to regard celibacy as a superior state. Leclerq followed Funk in identifying the Synod of Elvira as a watershed in the history of clerical celibacy, and argued for the continued toleration of married priests in the fourth century church on the basis of the defence of such unions by Paphnutius.[29] The debate over clerical celibacy turned, in the twentieth century as it had in the sixteenth and the eleventh, upon the examination and re-examination of contested incidents in the history of the church in the search for an accurate narrative of the past that might be pressed into service in the debates of the present.

The opportunity for debate in the present was forcefully curtailed by the early twentieth-century papacy. Perhaps the most definite assertion that the matter was closed came from Pope Benedict XV in 1920, in response to the arguments against clerical celibacy voiced primarily by the Union of the Catholic Czechoslovak Clergy (Jednota). The Union had been founded in 1890 to support demands for the celebration of Mass in the vernacular, and for the relaxation of the law of celibacy, and precipitated the formal establishment of an independent Czechoslovak Hussite Church in 1920. The obligation to celibacy had been recently repeated in the Canon Law Code of 1917, which reasserted forcefully that 'clerics in major orders may not marry and they are bound by the obligation of chastity to the extent that sinning against it constitutes a sacrilege'.[30] Pope Benedict had overseen the completion of this project, which had its origins in the pontificate of Pius X, and was deeply committed to the principles of universality that it contained.[31] He responded in strident terms to the Czech protests both in a letter of January 1920, and in his Consistorial Allocution of 16 December 1920. 'Being one of the chief ornaments of the Catholic clergy and a source of the highest virtues', he wrote, 'the law of celibacy must be retained inviolate in its purity; and the holy see will never abolish or mitigate it.'[32] The church, he proclaimed, considered celibacy to be of such importance that dissidents should not entertain any expectation that the law would be abrogated. The vitality of the Latin church, the pope argued, had its roots in the celibacy of its priests, and the protests of those who

---

[29] Leclerq, 'La Legislation conciliaire relative au celibate ecclesiastique', pp. 1321–48.

[30] The 1917 Code is available in English translation with commentary: E.N. Peters, *1917 Pio-Benedictine Code of Canon Law: in English translation, with extensive scholarly apparatus* (San Francisco, 2001), Canon 132.

[31] Recent biographies of Benedict XV include H.E.G. Rope, *Benedict XV The Pope of Peace* (London, 1941) and J.F. Pollard, *The Unknown Pope. Benedict XV* (London, 1999).

[32] Letter, 3 Jan 1920 (AAS 12 (1920), p. 32).

argued from 'democracy' in the defining of ecclesiastical discipline were both fruitless and erroneous.[33] The celibacy of the clergy was a critical part of the confessional identity of the church, a guarantee of its character, and an enduring standard that would be preserved by its pontiffs.

Benedict's successors were equally insistent in their defence of the discipline. Pius XI (1922–39), in his encyclical *On the Catholic Priesthood* presented a positive endorsement of clerical celibacy for reasons that were pastoral, historical, and scriptural. 'Since God is spirit, it is only fitting that he who consecrates to God's service ought to be in some ways free himself from his body …', the pope wrote, 'ought he not to be obliged to live as far as possible like a pure spirit?' The priest, who ought to be entirely 'about the Lord's business', should be entirely detached from earthly affairs, so that his life was lived in heaven.[34] Clerical celibacy was a part, even the pinnacle, of this perpetual act of priestly renunciation and detachment. It was also a requirement of the sacerdotal function of the priest. The origins of clerical celibacy and the nature of the priesthood, the pope wrote, lay in the precedent of the Levitical priests, in the Gospel of Luke, and in the Pauline letters. The priests of the Old Testament, he asserted, had abstained from their wives prior to their service in the temple, and their example placed a similar obligation to continence upon the priests of the new law, the Christian priests who dispensed the mysteries of God.[35] Celibacy was esteemed in both West and East, where the ordination of married men was permitted, but those in higher office were obliged to live unmarried. Indeed the Fathers of the East were as fulsome in their praise of celibacy as those in the Latin West, the pope argued, citing Chrysostom, and the testimony of Epiphanius on the practice of the fourth-century church. Although the origins of the law of celibacy lay in the decrees of the Council of Elvira, this was not the origin of the expectation that priestly office carried with it a commitment to continence. Rather, the Fathers at Elvira, Pius wrote, made 'obligatory what might in any case almost be termed a moral exigency that springs from the Gospel and the Apostolic preaching'.

This ringing endorsement of clerical celibacy had echoes in the Exhortation *Menti Nostrae* (1950) and more particularly in the Encyclical *De Virginitatis* (1954) written by Pius XI's successor, Pius XII (1939–58). 'By this law of celibacy the priest not only does not abdicate his paternity, but increases it immensely', the pope asserted, 'for he begets not for an earthly and transitory life but for the heavenly and eternal one.'[36] The

---

[33] Benedict XV, *Allocutio*, 16 Dec 1920 (AAS 12 (1920), pp. 85–80).

[34] Pius XI, Encyclical *Ad Catholicii Sacerdotii* (20 December 1935). The pontificate of Pius XI is still best approached through P. Hughes, *Pope Pius XI* (London, 1937).

[35] 'Sic nos existimet homo ut ministros Christi et dispensatores mysteriorum Dei'.

[36] *Menti Nostrae* (AAS 42 (1950), p. 663).

Encyclical opened with the statement 'Holy virginity and that perfect chastity which is consecrated to the service of God is without doubt among the most precious treasures which the Founder of the Church has left in heritage to the society which He established', and argued from the example of the apostolic church and the writings of the church Fathers that consecrated virginity had been prized throughout the long history of the church. The Encyclical presented patristic testimony on the value of virginity and celibacy from a wide range of sources, both Latin and Greek, including Jerome, Cyprian, Augustine, Ambrose, Ignatius and Athanasius, alongside the views of Aquinas, Bonaventure, and Peter Damian. From the latter, Pius took the assertion that 'if Our Redeemer so loved the flower of unimpaired modesty that not only was He born from a virginal womb, but was also cared for by a virgin nurse even when He was still an infant crying in the cradle, by whom, I ask, does He wish His body to be handled now that He reigns, limitless, in heaven?' The exploitation of Damian's powerful rhetoric on the subject no doubt underpins William Phipps' assertion that the pope believed that a priest 'sullied the sacrament' if he touched the elements with the same hands with which he had touched a woman, although there is nothing in the encyclical to suggest such a drift into Donatism.[37] Instead, the obligation to celibacy was presented as a precedent of the Old Testament priesthood, grounded in the Levitical laws, and exemplified in the long tradition of vowed chastity and sacerdotal celibacy in the Catholic church, and also in the voluntary chastity of the faithful who abstained from marriage and sexual pleasure in order to serve God more fully. To abstain from marriage, as Matthew the evangelist indicated, 'for the sake of the kingdom', was, for priest and people, to enjoy a spiritual freedom and liberty that was not possible for those encumbered with the cares of the world. Paul's letter to the Corinthians was cited on numerous occasions to support the assertion that virginity was favoured over marriage in the early church.

However, for the priest, the pope argued, there was an added obligation. The temporary continence of the Levitical priesthood was exceeded in the perpetual continence of the Catholic clergy, which was demanded by their Eucharistic function. 'Consider again that sacred ministers do not renounce marriage solely on account of their apostolic ministry, but also by reason of their service at the altar', Pius wrote. 'For, if even the priests of the Old Testament had to abstain from the use of marriage during the period of their service in the Temple, for fear of being declared impure by the Law just as other men, is it not much more fitting that the ministers of Jesus Christ, who offer every day the Eucharistic Sacrifice, possess perfect chastity?' Christian ministry was perpetual, and the obligation

---

[37] AAS 46 (1954), pp. 165ff ; Damian, *De coelibatu sacerdotum*, c.3 [PL 145: 384].

to celibacy likewise. Both Scripture and the teaching of the church had extolled virginity over marriage, as an angelic virtue and as proof of the mastery of the body by the Spirit, and this had been 'defined as a dogma of divine faith' at the Council of Trent. This, the pope conceded, was not the practice of the Greek church, but there was no evidence that celibacy was not equally prized in the East, as Pius XI had argued. There was nothing to suggest that the discipline might be modified in response to contemporary pressures, or that it was anything but firmly grounded in scripture and the traditions of the church.

Expectation that such a modification of the law of celibacy might be imminent was sharpened in the pontificate of John XXIII, and particularly after the summoning of the Second Vatican Council.[38] The pope was reported to be of the view that obligatory clerical celibacy was written not in stone, but in Latin, and could therefore be amended or even abolished.[39] However, the death of John XXIII in 1965 prevented the full discussion of clerical celibacy at the council; his successor Paul VI indicated that he regarded it as 'inopportune' to debate the topic, and the council reinforced the established law of celibacy.[40] The decree *On the Ministry and Life of Priests (Presbyterorum Ordinis)* was adopted by the council and promulgated on 7 December 1965. Citing Matt. 19:12, it announced that 'perfect and perpetual continence on behalf of the kingdom of heaven' was demanded of priests. Such an obligation, as Aquinas had argued, did not spring from the nature of the priesthood, but 'accords with the priesthood on many scores'. This assertion laid to rest the question of the 'implicit vow' of celibacy made by priests at ordination, an assumption that had been part of the defence of clerical celibacy in the twelfth century, and had continued to be exploited by more recent apologists.[41] Continence had been commended by Christ, and endorsed by the church throughout

---

[38] On the Council, see A. Hastings (ed.), *Modern Catholicism. Vatican II and After* (London, 1991); Hastings (ed.), *A Concise Guide to the Documents of the Second Vatican Council* (2 vols, London, 1968–69); R. Latourelle, *Vatican II. Assessments and Perspectives* (3 vols, New York, 1988); G. Alberigo (ed.), *The Reception of Vatican II* (Washington, 1987), and Alberigo and J.A. Komanchak (eds), *History of Vatican II* (Leuven, 1995–); A. Flannery (ed.), *Vatican Council II. The Conciliar and Post-Conciliar Documents* (New York, 1975) and *Vatican Council II. More post-conciliar documents* (New York, 1983).

[39] W. Phipps, *Clerical Celibacy. The Heritage* (London and New York, 2004), p. 172, quoting *National Catholic Reporter*, 12 May 1995, p. 21; John XXIII certainly removed some of the bureaucracy that was necessary for those priests who wished to leave the priesthood in order to marry.

[40] P. Hebblethwaite, *Paul VI* (New York, Paulist Press, 1993), p. 441.

[41] See, for example, T.L. Bouscaren, *Canon Law: A Text and Commentary* (Milwaukee, 1946), and the works of the Jesuit A. Vermeersch, including, for example, his *Epitome iuris canonici: cum commentariis ad scholas et ad usum privatum* (3 vols, Mechliniæ, 1937–46).

history, first 'recommended to priests' who were engaged in the mission of the church, and then imposed upon all who were called to sacred orders. For those who asked of God such a gift, it would be granted. Due heed was paid in the decree to the custom of the Greek church. The assertion that celibacy was not part of the nature of the priesthood was predicated in part upon the presence of married priests in the East, and the council stated that it had no intention of imposing Latin custom upon the Greek church. Those priests who had been ordained after marriage were simply exhorted to 'spend their lives fully and generously for the flock committed to them'. There was no specific mention of an expectation of purity founded upon the example of the Levitical priesthood, but the moral obligations of priests were not unrelated to their office. 'Priests act especially in the person of Christ as ministers of holy things, particularly in the Sacrifice of the Mass, the sacrifice of Christ who gave himself for the sanctification of men', the decree announced. 'Hence, they are asked to take example from that with which they deal, and inasmuch as they celebrate the mystery of the Lord's death they should keep their bodies free of wantonness and lusts.' However, the discussion of clerical celibacy took place within the more general context of the character expected of priests, and the assumption that 'as leaders of the community they cultivate an asceticism becoming to a shepherd of souls'. An unmarried priest was better able to devote himself to the service of his flock, and to 'adhere to [Christ] more easily with an undivided heart'. The celibate priesthood was a living sign of the kingdom of God that was yet to come, in which 'the children of the resurrection neither marry nor take wives'.[42]

Two years later, Pope Paul VI returned once again to the issue of clerical celibacy in his encyclical *Sacerdotalis Caelibatus* of June 1967.[43] The celibacy of the clergy, he argued, had been a constant throughout history, and continued to be so even in the modern world. 'Priestly celibacy has been guarded by the Church for centuries as a brilliant jewel', he wrote, 'and retains its value undiminished even in our time when the outlook of men and the state of the world have undergone such profound changes.' The pope had provided assurances to the delegates at Vatican II that he would give 'new lustre and strength' to the discipline, and in the face of concern from priests and from the faithful, the encyclical would fulfil this promise.[44] Paul VI detailed the objections that had been raised against clerical celibacy, including the assertion that it lacked a biblical

---

[42] W.M. Abbot and J. Gallagher (eds), *The Documents of Vatican II* (London, 1966), pp. 565–6; *Decree on the Ministry and Life of Priests*, 16, 13.

[43] AAS 59 (1967), pp. 657–97.

[44] See letter of 10 Oct. 1965, to Cardinal Tisserant, read in the general session of the next day.

or apostolic precedent, that the Fathers of the church had recommended abstinence rather than celibacy, and that there was a shortage of vocations in the modern church, which could be resolved if priests were permitted to marry. Others had argued that celibacy was psychologically detrimental, and that those priests who made a commitment to celibacy in their youth were insufficiently mature to understand the problems that they might encounter in abiding by this promise. To these objections, the pope presented a full and wide-ranging response, over 13,000 words in length. As the Second Vatican Council had asserted, virginity was not demanded of the priesthood by its nature. It was, however, particularly suited to the ministry, and as such had been considered on many occasions in the past.[45] The celibacy of priests was modelled upon the celibacy of Christ, 'The minister of Christ and dispenser of the mysteries of God, therefore, looks up to Him directly as his model and supreme ideal', and it was in this sharing in the life of Christ that the priest was best able to share in His dignity and mission.[46] The first followers of Christ had been called to leave their families and their homes, and a commitment to celibacy was part of the response to the divine call to sacrifice for the kingdom of heaven.[47] Such a commitment was, as the church recognised, 'a symbol of and stimulus to, chastity' and a life dedicated to the service of others.[48] The unmarried priesthood possessed, the pope stated, an ecclesiological significance, manifesting the love of Christ for the church, and exemplified the perfection of the kingdom of God after the second coming of Christ, and the promise that 'in the resurrection they neither marry nor are given in marriage, but are like angels in heaven'.[49]

Paul VI's encyclical presented a history of clerical celibacy in the life of the church, from the voluntary practice of continence in the first Christian centuries, through the formalisation of the law in the fourth century, to the reinforcement of its principles at Trent and in the Code of Canon Law.[50] The pope recognised the independent discipline of the Greek church established at the Council in Trullo (692), but also the positive

---

[45] *Sacerdotalis Caelibatus*, c.17, 18.

[46] Ibid., c.19, 31.

[47] Ibid., c.22.

[48] Ibid., c.24, referring to *Dogmatic Constitution on the Church*, no. 42: AAS 57 (1965), p. 48; see also c.32.

[49] *Sacerdotalis Caelibatus*, c.26, 34; Matt. 22:30; see also Second Vatican Council, *Decree on the Adaptation and Renewal of the Religious Life*, no. 12 (AAS 58 (1966), p. 107.)

[50] C.35ff with reference to, among others, Tertullian, *De exhort. castitatis*, 13 [PL 2.930]; St. Epiphanius, *Adv. Haer.* II, 48.9 and 59.4: [PG 41. 869, 1025]; St. Ambrose, *De officiis ministr.*, 1.50 [PL 16.97ff]; St. Augustine, *De moribus Eccl. cath.*, 1.32 [PL 32.1339]; St. Jerome, *Adversus Vigilantium*, 2 [PL 23.340–41]; Council of Elvira, can. 33, *Code*, can. 132, §1.

commendations of virginity in the writings of the Greek Fathers, which testified to a common ground between the two churches.[51] Despite the practice in the East, however, the pope asserted that 'the Church of the West cannot weaken her faithful observance of her own tradition. Nor can she be regarded as having followed for centuries a path which instead of favouring the spiritual richness of individual souls and of the People of God, has in some way compromised it, or of having stifled, with arbitrary juridical prescriptions, the free expansion of the most profound realities of nature and of grace'. The married clergy of the East did not constitute a valid argument against the tradition of the West. Rather than debate the issue further, or make a case for the relaxation of the discipline of celibacy, he argued, it would be more fruitful to 'promote serious studies in defence of the spiritual meaning and moral value of virginity and celibacy'. To this end, the faithful were enjoined to pray for new vocations to the priesthood, so that the mission of the church might increase, in the same way as the prayers of the first Christians had replenished the church with ministers after the apostles. It was in celibacy that human values found their highest expression, in a life filled with the richness of God.[52] The particular failings of individual priests did not invalidate or undermine the law of celibacy for the church as a whole. While it was apparent that some priests had abandoned their obligation to celibacy, the fault lay not with the discipline itself, but with the assessment of the suitability of the candidate for priestly office. The church offered dispensations to those who were clearly unsuited, but for others, the pope suggested, it would be more appropriate for the individual to reflect upon the seriousness of their obligations, and the scandal that was caused by their actions, seeking support from their bishop, and from the whole church, to whom the 'treasure' of celibacy belonged.[53] Sacerdotal celibacy, it seemed, was a central part of the life of both priest and people, in the past and in the present. It was a defining mark of the Catholic priesthood, a reflection of the priesthood of Christ, and, even if not part of the nature of the priesthood, at least a critical aspect of the pastoral function of the priest.

The pope's suggestion that it would be more productive to engage in 'serious study' of the meaning and the value of virginity and celibacy certainly bore fruit in the vast literature on clerical celibacy that was published in the aftermath of the Encyclical. Not all contributions were as positive as Paul might have wished, but the extent of the debate was impressive. The 1969 edition of the *Bibliographie Internationale sur le Sacerdoce et le Ministre* listed nearly 7000 items in the four years between the end of the Vatican

---

[51] *Sacerdotalis Caelibatus*, c.38–40.
[52] *Sacerdotalis Caelibatus*, c.57–9.
[53] *Sacerdotalis Caelibatus*, c.83, 93–6.

Council and the publication of *Sacerdotalis Caelibatus*.[54] This diversity of opinion was not limited to the printed word, and although the Synod of Bishops insisted in 1971 that the 'law of priestly celibacy ... is to be kept in its entirety', such unanimity of voice was in some respects specious.[55] North American priests had petitioned vigorously for the toleration of marriage after ordination, and the Dutch Pastoral Council of the previous year had recommended that celibacy should not be demanded as a condition of admission to the priesthood, and that married priests should be permitted to continue to exercise their ministry.[56] Pope Paul responded with a vigorous assertion of the importance of celibacy to the priesthood, although conceded that in areas in which there was a significant shortage of priests there might be reasons to consider the ordination of mature married men.[57] A commission of theologians presented a paper on the nature of priestly ministry later in the same year, which again raised the possibility of the ordination of married men, although not of the continued ministry of priests who had attempted marriage after ordination.[58] The view of the pope was clear, however, and before the 1971 Synod convened copies of Joseph Coppens' collection of essays on the history of clerical celibacy, *Sacerdoce et Celibat*, were sent to all the delegates. The book included articles written by individuals already active in the debate, and rehearsed historical and theological arguments.[59] When the Synod came to consider the question of clerical celibacy, there was little dissent from the established position of the church. Only one voice was raised in defence of a principle of 'optional' clerical celibacy, and the synod did not consider the possibility of tolerating the marriage of men already admitted to the priesthood. There was rather more debate over the potential benefits of ordaining mature married men to combat a shortage of vocations, but again this proposal was rejected amid the expression of concern that the law of celibacy would be undermined in its entirety by such piecemeal erosion. Nearly half the delegates were prepared to accept such ordinations if the pope deemed it necessary, but the majority still opposed the proposal when the matter was put to a vote on the penultimate day of the synod. Papal confirmation of that decision came in the closing speech delivered by Paul VI, and in his rescript, which asserted in a familiar tone that 'in the

---

[54] *Bibliographie Internationale sur le Sacerdoce et le Ministre* (Montreal, 1971).

[55] AAS 63 (1972), pp. 897ff.

[56] J.A. Coriden, 'Celibacy, Canon Law and Synod 1971', in W. Bassett and Peter Huizing (eds), *Celibacy in the Church* (New York, 1972), pp. 109–24, especially pp. 111–12.

[57] AAS 62 (1970), pp. 98ff, quoted in Coriden, 'Celibacy, Canon Law and Synod', p. 111.

[58] See also *De Sacerdotalis Ministeriali* (Vatican, 1971).

[59] J. Coppens (ed.), *Sacerdoce et Celibat* (Gembloux–Louvain, 1971).

Latin church there shall be continued to be observed in its entirety with God's help, the present discipline of clerical celibacy'.[60]

The demand that the discipline of celibacy be observed in its entirety has not been without its critics and challenges. The obligation to celibacy has, for example, been cited as a primary cause of a decline in the number of candidates presenting themselves for ordination, and a key factor in the decision of ordained priests to leave the ministry.[61] The centrality of the Mass in Catholic religious life, reinforced at the Second Vatican Council, makes a shortage of priests all the more acute. Despite the apparent success of the Council of Trent in establishing celibacy as a defining feature of the priesthood, and the reassertion of this principle in the twentieth century, the results of various public opinion polls have suggested that many of the faithful would be supportive of a decision to make celibacy optional.[62] The unmarried priesthood, however, still has a symbolic value for the laity; as James Dittes has suggested, the celibate priest is fundamental to the 'spiritual ecology' of many of the faithful. The meanings attached to clerical celibacy might be inconsistent and occasionally contradictory, Dittes argues, but 'if priestly celibacy did not exist, laymen would have to provide themselves with the equivalent' in an attempt to distance or dehumanise the clergy.[63] The symbolic value of celibacy, however, does not always override the practical needs of parishioners who lack access to the sacraments. North American Catholic priests who have entered into marriages make themselves available, with the support of organisations such as CITI (Celibacy Is The Issue), for the celebration of the sacraments where the services of a priest are not guaranteed. CITI summarises its position as an 'organization that locates, recruits, certifies and promotes married Roman Catholic priests to fill the spiritual needs of the faithful', and suggests that it would be acceptable for human intervention to overturn the obligation to celibacy, in itself a 'mere ecclesiastical law'.[64] The theme of clerical marriage as a solution to 'pastoral emergency' has been explored in more detail by Adrian Hastings, in an examination of the situation of

---

[60] AAS 63 (1971) 897, quoted in J. Coriden, 'Celibacy, Canon Law and Synod', pp. 113–14.

[61] See for example R. Schoenherr and L. Young, *Full Pews and Empty Altars* (Madison, 1993); E. Abbott, *History of Celibacy* (Boston, 2001); Phipps, *Clerical Celibacy*, pp. 190ff; J. Fichtner SJ, *America's Forgotten Priests* (New York, 1968); D.R. Hige, *The Future of Catholic Leadership. Responses to the Priest Shortage* (Kansas City, 1987); Schoenherr 'Holy Power? Holy Authority? And Holy Celibacy?', in Bassett and Huizing (eds), *Celibacy in the Church*, pp. 126–7; Schoenherr and A.M. Greeley, *American Priests* (Chicago, 1972).

[62] Several such polls are discussed in Phipps, *Celibacy*, pp. 196ff;

[63] J.E. Dittes, 'The Symbolic Value of Celibacy for the Catholic Faithful', in Bassett and Huizing (eds), *Celibacy in the Church*, pp. 84–94.

[64] http://www.rentapriest.com accessed 10 March 2009.

the African church, and particularly by Karl Rahner, for whom practical considerations must override theoretical objections in such circumstances. Writing in 1974, Rahner argued that if there were not enough priests who were prepared to be bound by celibacy, 'it is obvious and requires no further theological discussion that the obligation of celibacy must not be imposed'.[65] Aside from the broad issue of vocations to the priesthood, the law of celibacy has also been held responsible for the conduct of those priests implicated in sexual abuse scandals in the Boston diocese, and elsewhere in North America and beyond. Early in 2002, the *Boston Globe* printed a series of stories exposing the extent to which guilty priests had been concealed by the church, and the articles precipitated a crisis in the local church which rapidly reached as far as Rome, threatening lawsuits totalling more than $100 million, and culminating in the resignation of the cardinal, Bernard Law. The primary issue for the *Globe* was the presence of what it described as 'predator priests' in Boston parishes, known to, and tolerated by, the hierarchy. However, for those who commented upon the scandal in letters and on the dedicated website, events in Boston were also a catalyst for calls for a wider consideration of the merits of obligatory clerical celibacy in light of events in the diocese and the church as a whole.[66]

The fires of debate were fanned further by the admission of married clergy into the Catholic priesthood in the 1990s after the decision taken by the Anglican Communion to ordain women. The acceptance of married priests from other traditions was not new; critics of the law of celibacy pointed to the long-standing toleration of Ukrainian practice, and as early as 1967 Pope Paul VI had raised the possibility that 'married sacred ministers' of other denominations might be admitted to 'full priestly functions' while continuing to cohabit with their families, although future marriages would not be permitted.[67] The celibacy imposed upon candidates for the diaconate was lifted at the Second Vatican Council, opening up this office to married men.[68] However, the welcome afforded to married Anglican clergy after 1994 generated a good deal of antipathy, particularly from Catholic priests who had been unable to marry and

---

[65] K. Rahner, *The Shape of the Church to Come* (New York, 1974); A. Hastings, *A History of African Christianity, 1950–1975* (Cambridge, 1979) and *The Church in Africa, 1450–1950* (Oxford, 1994).

[66] The dedicated website, with message boards and comments, is still accessible at http://www.boston.com/globe/spotlight/abuse/extras/celibacy.htm

[67] Phipps, *Celibacy*, p. 252, quoting the 1967 encyclical; see also Y-M. Congar, *L'Episcopat et l'Eglise Universelle* (Paris, 1962) p. 263, for a discussion of the exercise of priestly functions by a Danish convert to Catholicism, accepted by John XXIII.

[68] *Dogmatic Constitution on the Church*, c.29.

continue in their ministry in the Catholic church. In July 1995, the *Advent* organisation, representing married Catholic priests in England, strongly criticised the actions of Cardinal Basil Hume in commending the ministry of married former Anglican clergy to the Catholic faithful in his pastoral letter which had been read out in churches on the previous Sunday. *Advent* leaders complained that their members felt betrayed by the Cardinal, and resentful of the 'vindictive legal process' that had left them as 'second-class citizens'. The Catholic church, it was argued, faced a problem of its own making, which had its roots in the 'man-made law of compulsory celibacy'. Less than honourable conduct by supposedly celibate priests, and attempts to conceal such conduct, witnessed to the weakness of the law, and should, *Advent* claimed, encourage a more compassionate attitude towards Catholic priests who had married.[69] The debate remained active over a decade later. In an interview with the British newspaper the *Daily Telegraph,* the Rt Rev. Malcolm McMahon, Bishop of Nottingham, suggested that the positive reception given to converts from Anglicanism had reopened the question of the position of Catholic priests who expressed a desire to marry. Marriage, the bishop argued, 'should not bar them from their vocation but they must be married before they are ordained. The justice issue also applies to communities which could be deprived of the Eucharist because there aren't enough priests'. Married Anglican clergy had contributed much to parish ministry, he suggested, although if the Catholic church were to permit married men to be ordained on a wider scale, there would be clear financial and practical issues to address.[70]

The necessity of clerical celibacy continues to be debated from both a practical and theological point of view, and within the more general context of discussions over the nature of the Catholic priesthood.[71] The ordination of married men, dwindling vocations, and an apparent lack of support for mandatory clerical celibacy among the younger generation of Catholic priests has led one commentator to conclude that 'a married clergy in the Latin Rite is inevitable', at least from a sociological standpoint.[72] However, a time of crisis in the church is not, for all, in itself a justification for the relaxation of the law of celibacy. Indeed as A.M. Cardinal Stickler observed in his recent study of the historical foundations of clerical celibacy, the Council of Trent laid down the foundations of the modern law in just such

---

[69] See, for example, the discussion in the *Independent*, 7 July 2005.

[70] The *Daily Telegraph*, 8 November 2008.

[71] J. Ratzinger (Benedict XVI), *Zur Gemeinschaft Gerufen, die Kirche heute verstehen* (Freiburg, 1991) 98–123; F.J. Laumann, *Call and Response. Ordaining Married Men as Catholic Priests* (Berryville VA, 2002); S.L. Jaki, *Theology of Priestly Celibacy* (Front Royal, VA: Christendom, 1997); T. McGovern, *Priestly Celibacy Today* (Chicago, 1998).

[72] Schoenherr, 'Holy Power?', p. 140.

a time of unrest and difficulty for the church.[73] Shifting the focus from the practical problems of clerical celibacy to the figure of the priest as *alter Christus*, Stickler argues, restores the debate to its proper place. Since the Second Vatican Council, the Church has emphasised the position of the priest who acts as the representative of the divine, *in eius persona*, and shares in that 'ontological bond' which joins the priesthood to Christ.[74] Such a bond could not be subject to the exigencies of the age. Pope John Paul II was to write in his Apostolic Exhortation *Pastores Dabo Vobis* (March 1992) of the determination with which the Catholic church had maintained the law of celibacy, 'despite all the difficulties and objections raised down the centuries'. Church and clergy were reminded that 'celibacy is a priceless gift of God for the Church and has a prophetic value for the world today'. It was vital, the pope argued, that celibacy be presented in its 'biblical, theological and spiritual richness', as a sign of the kingdom of God beyond the material world, of the love of God for the world, and the love of the priest for his people. The law of celibacy articulated the will of the church, but the pope commended to the clergy not only celibacy as a discipline, but also its 'theological motivation'; the priest was to love the church, the bride of Christ, as Christ had done, and priestly celibacy was the gift of self in and with Christ to the church. Celibacy was a witness to the 'eschatological kingdom', but also an incentive to pastoral charity, and a step in the footsteps of the apostles, who had left all to follow Christ. Perfect continence for the love of the kingdom had been, from the time of Christ, prized and praised by the church, and in this context, a commitment to celibacy was a necessary part of the priesthood.[75]

Academic and polemical controversy over celibacy has continued alongside (but also informed by) the practical challenges posed by Catholic priests leaving the church to marry, and the apparently dwindling vocations of young men to serve the church. A lively debate was conducted in the pages of *New Blackfriars*, prompted by a defence of clerical marriage penned by Adrian Hastings, printed in the journal in 1978. Hastings, whose early clerical career had been spent in Uganda, was an active participant in the Anglican-Roman Catholic International Commission, and later a university teacher. In 1978, convinced that there was no legitimate obstacle to the marriage of priests, Hastings married Anne Spence, without the permission of the church and, it appeared, without incurring any formal ecclesiastical penalty. A full-length rationalisation of his decision was published as *In Filial Disobedience*, although the basic principles of his argument were laid down in the shorter *New Blackfriars*

---

[73] Stickler, *Celibacy*, p. 85.
[74] AAS 62 (1970), p. 44; AAS 71 (1979), p. 406, quoted in Stickler, *Celibacy*, p. 88.
[75] Pope John Paul II, *Pastores Dabo Vobis*, 25 March 1992.

essay, and in *A Final Word*, published in the same journal in response to his critics. Hastings argued for the necessity of clerical marriage on the basis of pastoral need, falling back upon his missionary experience to provide evidence of congregations who lacked the services of a priest because no candidates were available who would commit to celibacy. In contrast, priests in western Europe who had left the ministry to marry stood as 'prêtres en foyer', willing to continue to serve the church, but prevented from so doing.[76] However, Hastings was convinced that clerical celibacy could not be defended or criticised on purely pragmatic or pastoral terms. The obligation to celibacy had a 'semi-doctrinal' character, and was rooted in the understanding (or misunderstanding) of holiness. Despite the barrage of criticism, and the practical problems that the Catholic church faced, Hastings noted that 'on no point has the position of Rome been more consistent'. Married priests had been laicised, but on no occasion had Rome permitted Catholic priests who attempted marriage to continue in their marriage and ministry. Such a prohibition, he contested, lacked a solid foundation. Paul had recommended that the bishop should be the husband of one wife, and although Hastings argued it would be erroneous to extrapolate universal practice from a single scriptural text, this principle had been, the evidence revealed, the practice of the apostolic church. The restoration of the married priesthood would be the restoration of evangelical practice. The legislation of the fourth century that began to regulate the sexual conduct of the clergy had evolved, he believed, from a sense that there was something incompatible between sex and holiness or proximity to the sacred, a sense that had its origins not in Scripture but in ascetic heresies.[77] Hastings was clear that this was not a recommendation that clerical marriage be compulsory, or that only married men should be accepted into the priesthood, but rather a restoration of the both/and (rather than either/or) principle that that had guided the early church.

The debate has continued in the current pontificate of Benedict XVI. The views of the pope had already been made clear, prior to his elevation, in *Salt of the Earth*, in which the then Cardinal Ratzinger suggested that

---

[76] 'Prêtres en foyer' has become the established name of the French Catholic priests who are members of the pan-European *La Fédération Européenne de Prêtres Catholiques Mariés*, which gathers together the married priests of Europe, along with their spouses in arguing for the supremacy of the person over the law, and protests against apparent discrimination against married priests on the basis of the ecclesiastical discipline of clerical celibacy. See, for example, http://www.marriedpriests.eu/

[77] Hastings, 'On celibacy', *New Blackfriars*, 59 (issue 694, March 1978): 104–11; 'Celibacy. A Final Word', *New Blackfriars*, 59 (issue 700, September 1978): 402–8; *In Filial Disobedience* (Great Wakering, 1978); see also Marcel Boivin's reply to Hastings in 'On Priestly Marriage: A Response To Father Hastings On Celibacy', *New Blackfriars*, 60 (Issue 707, April 1979): 182–4.

although the Church had, and would continually, consider the issue throughout its history, there was much more to be lost than to be gained from a relaxation of the rule of celibacy. Priests were bound to celibacy by the commendation by Christ of those who became 'eunuchs for the sake of the kingdom', by the precedent of the apostolic church, by the example of the Levites whose inheritance was God alone, and by the Christological and apostolic meaning of the discipline. Clerical celibacy, Ratzinger argued, was not a dogma, but 'an accustomed way of life that evolved very early in the Church on good biblical grounds'. It was all the more important in a time of crisis that the commitment to celibacy was reaffirmed; a poverty of faith created problems for both marriage and for celibacy, not celibacy alone, and clerical marriage was not the answer to the difficulties faced by the church. To argue for clerical marriage from the example of the Greek church, or the Reformed churches, was to miss the point. Celibacy was coupled to the Catholic priesthood, but outside the church there was a different understanding of priesthood itself, Ratzinger argued, and therefore a different rule on celibacy and marriage. Married priests, particularly those converts from Anglicanism, were the exception to the rule.[78] A concrete challenge to these principles came in early November 2006, when a group of Catholic clergy under the banner *The Married Priests Now! Prelature* addressed an open letter to the pope, commending marriage as a means by which the dedication of the priest to Christ might be enhanced, and calling for the ordination of married men in the church. At the forefront was the African Archbishop Emmanuel Milingo, who argued that the decline in ordinations required more dramatic action than Rome would countenance, and presented an argument in favour of a married priesthood based upon apostolic precedent, and the need for the healing of wounds within the church.[79] The archbishop was excommunicated after his unsanctioned ordination of four North American married men as bishops. The issue of clerical celibacy, once again thrown into the spotlight, was discussed by Pope Benedict XVI in November 2006, and reaffirmed in confident terms in a statement issued on 16 November. This reassertion of the law of celibacy echoed the earlier statement made at the Synod of Bishops on the Eucharist in November 2005, which affirmed the importance of the 'inestimable gift of ecclesiastical celibacy in the practice of the Latin Church', and urged that

---

[78] *Salt of the Earth: The Church at the End of the Millennium: An Interview With Peter Seewald* (San Francisco, 1997), pp. 194–200.

[79] Pope Paul VI consecrated Milingo as the Bishop of the archdioceses of Lusaka in 1969; Milingo married in 2001, separated from his wife, and then returned to cohabitation. Details of Married Priests Now! are to be found on the bishop's website, http://www.archbishopmilingo.org.

the 'reasons for the relationship between celibacy and priestly ordination be illustrated adequately to the faithful, in full respect for the traditions of the Eastern churches'. Confronted by concerns surrounding the decline in ordinations to the priesthood, the Fathers concluded that the cause of this decline lay not in obligatory celibacy, but rather in the more general trend towards the secularisation of society.[80] A married priesthood was not to be regarded as a panacea for the ills of the church.

The resolve of the bishops in 2005 has parallels in the forceful assertion of Benedict XVI that it is simply not sufficient to understand priestly celibacy in purely functional terms; clerical celibacy is not merely a practical issue with practical solutions. Addressing the Bishops of Brazil in May 2007, the pope expressed his sadness that even within the church there were those who would question the value of the priestly commitment to celibacy. Apostolic celibacy, he suggested, was a 'total entrustment to God', and a 'total openness to the service of souls'. Where ideological, secular, or factional concerns overrode this belief, 'the structure of total consecration to God begins to lose its deepest meaning'.[81] Clerical celibacy, then, is firmly tied to the meaning and function of priesthood, and not something that could, or should, be eroded by contingent temporal concerns. The pope's comments exemplify the complexity of the celibacy debate in past and present. The roots and the meaning of clerical celibacy in the Catholic tradition stretch far beyond the conduct and concerns of the modern clergy, and into the history, traditions, and mysteries of the church and priesthood, and the breadth of the issue has been reflected in the scope of the debate over clerical celibacy and marriage in the modern church and in centuries past. The answer to the basic question of whether married men should be ordained to the ministry, and whether priests in orders should be permitted to marry, encompasses more extensive debates over the interpretation of biblical texts, the understanding of patristic precedent and its place in the determination of doctrine and practice, the relationship between scripture and tradition, the theology of the sacraments, and the role of the priest in the life of the church. The controversy over the origins and the value of priestly celibacy has been conducted against a backdrop provided by these broader questions, but has also provided a powerful and immediate focus for the examination of such issues.

---

[80] Synod of Bishops, November 2005, Proposition 11.

[81] Benedict XVI, *Meeting and Celebration of Vespers with the Bishops of Brazil, 11 May 2007*: http://www.vatican.va/holy_father/benedict_xvi/speeches/2007/may/documents/hf_ben-xvi_spe_20070511_bishops-brazil_en.html; see also Benedict XVI, *Sacramentum Caritatis: Post-Synodal Apostolic Exhortation 22nd February 2007*: http://www.vatican.va/holy_father/benedict_xvi/apost_exhortations/documents/hf_ben-xvi_exh_20070222_sacramentum-caritatis_en.html

The life of the priest, lived within the parish community, is a highly visible manifestation of the pastoral and pedagogical priorities of the church. The commitment to celibacy, most simply understood, leaves the priest unencumbered by the cares of marriage and household, but it also embodies a distinctive view of sex, the sacraments, and service. The eradication of the married priesthood in the eleventh century was tangible testimony to the priorities of the papacy in the reform of the church. Clergy who took wives in the sixteenth century presented a perceptible sign of changes in doctrine and discipline. The reassertion of the commitment to clerical celibacy at the Council of Trent positioned the eradication of concubinage as a barometer of the success of Catholic reform, and the unmarried priesthood as a defining characteristic of post-Reformation Catholicism. Modern critics of the law of celibacy have failed to dent this resolve; indeed the modern Church and papacy has repeatedly reasserted the link between celibacy and priesthood, as a link modelled on apostolic tradition and maintained throughout the history of the church. For this reason, clerical celibacy remains an issue which is simultaneously personal and polemical, individual and institutional, human and historical. At the close of the fourth century, Pope Siricius commended to the church the principle that there be one faith, one tradition, and one discipline; the debate over clerical celibacy in subsequent centuries has embodied these issues of faith, tradition, and discipline, but the unity for which the pope hoped has remained, on the subject of clerical celibacy, elusive.

Bibliography

Councils and Canon Law

Acta Concilii Constanciensis, H. Finke (ed.), (4 vols, Munster: Regensburg, 1896–1928).
Canon Law: A Text and Commentary, T.L. Bouscaren (ed.), (Milwaukee: Bruce, 1946).
Les Canons des Conciles Oecumeniques, P.P. Joannou (ed.), (Rome: Pontifica Commissione per la radazione del conduce di diretto canonico orientale, 1962).
Canons and Decrees of the Council of Trent, H.J. Schroeder (ed.) (Rockford, Ill: Herder, 1978).
Code of Canon Law, 1983 (http://www.vatican.va/archive/ENG1104/_INDEX.HTM).
(Pio-Benedictine) Code of Canon Law: in English translation, with extensive scholarly apparatus, E.N. Peters (ed.), (San Francisco: Ignatius Press, 2001).
Concilia Galliae a.314–a.506, C. Munier (ed.), (Turnhout: Brepols, 1963).
Concilios Visigoticos, J. Vives et al. (eds), (Barcelona: Instituto Enrique Flórez).
Conciliengeschichte, C-J. von Hefele (ed.), (Freiburg im Breisgau: Herdersche Verlags-Handlung, 1873).
Concilia Germaniae, J.F. Schannat and J. Harzheim (eds) (11 vols, Cologne: A. Agrippa, 1759–90).
Conciliorum Oecumenicorum Decreta, J. Alberigo, J. Dossetti, P. Joannou, C. Leonardi (eds), (Freiburg im Breisgau: Herder, 1962).
Corpus iuris canonici in tres partes distinctum: glossis diuersorum illustratum; Gregorij Papæ XIII. iussu editum, complectens Decretum Gratiani, decretales Gregorij IX. Sextum decretalium Bonifacij VIII. Clementinas, Extravagantes Ioannis XXII. Extravagantes communes, &c. Accesserunt Constitutiones nouæ Summorum Pontificum hactenus desideratæ, quæ VII. decretalium loco esse possint, necnon annotationes Antonij Naldi additionibus novis elucidatæ, A. Naldi (ed.), (3 vols, Lyons: Huguetan and Barbier, 1671).
Corpus Juris Civilis: Codex Justiniani Repetitae Praelectionis a 534; Digesta a.533; Institutiones Junstiniani a.533, P. Kreuger, T. Mommsen, R. Schoell, G. Kroll (eds), (3 vols, Berlin: Berolini: Weidman, 1877).
Corpus Reformatortum, Karl Gottlieb Bretschneider et al. (eds) (101 vols, Brunswick, Berlin: Halle, 1834–).

Concilium Tridentium Diariorum, Actorum, Epistolarum, Tractatuum Nova Collectio, Societas Goerresiana (eds), (Freiburg im Breisgau: Herder, 1901–).

Decrees of the Ecumenical Councils, Norman P. Tanner (ed.) (London: Sheed and Ward, 1990).

Disciplinary Decrees of the General Councils: Text, Translation and Commentary, H.J. Schroeder (ed.), (St. Louis: B. Herder, 1937).

Discipline générale antique. t.I, ptie. 1. Les canons des conciles oecuméniques (IIe–IXe s.)–t.1, ptie. 2. Les canons des synodes particuliers (IVe–IXe s.)–t.II. Les canons des pères grecs, P. Joannou (ed.), (Grottaferrata: Tipografia Italo-Orientale S. Nilo, 1962–64).

The Documents of Vatican II, W.M. Abbot and J. Gallagher, (eds) (London: G. Chapman, 1966).

Epitome iuris canonici: cum commentariis ad scholas et ad usum privatum, A. Vermeersch (ed.), (3 vols, Mechliniæ: H. Dessain, 1937–46).

Geschichte des Konzils von Trient, H. Jedin (ed.) (6 vols, Freiburg: Herder 1949–75); some translated into English as *History of the Council of Trent* (tr. E. Graf), (2 vols, London, 1957–61).

Histoire des Conciles d'Apres les Documents Originaux, C.H. Hefele and J. Leclerq (eds), (19 vols, Paris: Letouzey et Ane, 1907–52).

Monumenta ad historiam Concilii Tridentini, J. Le Plat (ed.) (7 vols, Louvain: Typographie académique, 1781–87).

Patrologia Cursus Completus: Series Graeca, J.-P. Migne (ed.), (161 vols, Paris 1857–66).

Patrologia Cursus Completus: Series Latina, J.-P. Migne (ed.), (Paris, 1844–55).

Regesta pontificum Romanorum ab condita ecclesia ad annum post Christum natum MCXCVIII, P. Jaffe (ed.), (2 vols, Leipzig: Wattenbach, 1885–88).

'Responsum a Pio IV datum consiliariis electorum et principum imperii, qui sacerdotum conjugia petebant', in J. Leplat (ed.), *Monumentorum ad Historiam Concilii Tridentini Amplissima Collectio VI* (Louvain: Typographie académique, 1876).

Sacrorum Conciliorum Nova et Amplissa Collectio, J.D. Mansi (ed.), continued and reprinted by L. Petit and J.P. Martin (53 vols in 60, Paris/Leipzig: Weller, 1901–27).

The Seven Ecumenical Councils of the Undivided Church (tr. H.R. Percival), in *Nicene and Post-Nicene Fathers*, 2nd Series, P. Schaff and H. Wace (eds), (repr. Grand Rapids MI: Wm. B. Eerdmans, 1955).

Synodorum generalium et provincialium statuta et canones cum notis et historicis dissertationibus, C. Lupus (ed.) (Louvain: viduae Bernard. Masii, 1665–73).

Vatican Council II. The Conciliar and Post-Conciliar Documents, J. Flannery (ed.), (New York: Liturgical Press, 1975).
Vatican Council II. More post-conciliar documents, J. Flannery (ed.), (New York: Liturgical Press, 1983).

Papal Documents

Acta apostolicae sedis, 12 (Vatican City: Libreria editrice vaticana, 1909–).
Benedict XVI, *Meeting and Celebration of Vespers with the Bishops of Brazil, 11th May 2007*: http://www.vatican.va/holy_father/benedict_xvi/speeches/2007/may/documents/hf_ben-xvi_spe_20070511_bishops-brazil_en.html.
——, *Sacramentum Caritatis: Post-Synodal Apostolic Exhortation 22nd February 2007*: http://www.vatican.va/holy_father/benedict_xvi/apost_exhortations/documents/hf_ben-xvi_exh_20070222_sacramentum-caritatis_en.html.
Bullarium Romanum (10 vols, Luxembourg: Gosse & Soc. 1727–30).
Bullarii Romani continuatio summorum pontificum Clementis XIII. Clementis XIV. Pii VI. Pii VII. Leonis XII. Pii VIII. et Gregorii XVI. Constitutiones, literas in forma brevis epistolas ad principes viros, et alios atque allocutiones complectens (19 vols, Rome: Ex Typographia Reverendæ Cameræ Apostolicæ, 1835).
Bulla Super Connubio Clericorum Germaniae, in W. Friedensburg (ed.), *Nuntiatur des Bischofs Pietro Bertano von Fano, 1548–1549* (Berlin: Deutsches Historisches Inst., 1910).
Decretals of Gregory IX, E.L. Richter and E. Friedberg (eds), *Corpus Iuris Canonici, Pars Secunda: Decretalium Collectiones* (Leipzig: Tauchniz, 1881).
Epistolae Romanorum pontificum, et quae ad eos scriptae sunt, a S. Clemente I. usque ad Innocentium III, P. Coustant (ed.) (Brunsbergae: E. Peter, 1721).
Epistolae Vagantes of Pope Gregory VII, H.E.J. Cowdrey (ed.) (Oxford: OUP, 1972).
Gregorii I papae Registrum epistolarum. Libri I–VII, Paul Ewald and L.M. Hartmann (eds) (Hanover: *Monumenta Germaniae Historica: Epistolae*, 1887–91).
Gregorii I papae Registrum epistolarum. Libri VIII–XIV, P. Ewald and L.M. Hartmann (eds) (Hanover: *Monumenta Germaniae Historica: Epistolae*, 1887–91).
Gregory XVI, *Mirari Vos*, Aug 15th 1832, in *Acta Gregorii XVI. Corpus actorum RR. pontificum* (Graz: Akadem. Druck- und Verlagsanst., 1971).

Innocent I, *Epistola 6*, in *Patrologia Cursus Completus: Series Latina*, J.-P. Migne (ed.) (Paris, 1844–55), vol. 20.

——, *Epistola 2, Ad Victricium Episcopum Rothomoagensem*, in *Patrologia Cursus Completus: Series Latina*, J.-P. Migne (ed.) (Paris, 1844–55), vol. 20.

——, *Epistola Ad Exuperium Episcopum Tolosoanum*, in *Patrologia Cursus Completus: Series Latina*, J.-P. Migne (ed.) (Paris, 1844–55), vol. 20.

——, *Epistola Ad Maximum et Severum Episcopos per Brittios*, in *Patrologia Cursus Completus: Series Latina*, J.-P. Migne (ed.) (Paris, 1844–55), vol. 20.

John Paul II, *Letter to Priests (9 April 1979)*; *Pastores Da Vobis (25 March 1992)*.

Julius III, 'Bulla Papae Julii Potestatem Concedens Cardinali Polo Anglicam Ecclesiae Romanae Reuniendi', in Wilkins, D., *Concilia Magnae Britanniae et Hiberniae ab anno 1546–1717* (London: Gosling and Woodward, 1737), pp. 91–3.

Leo the Great, *Epistola 14*, in *Patrologia Cursus Completus: Series Latina*, J.-P. Migne (ed.) (Paris, 1844–55), vol. 54.

——, *Epistola 167*, in *Patrologia Cursus Completus: Series Latina*, J.-P. Migne (ed.) (Paris, 1844–55), vol. 54.

Constitutiones et acta publica imperatorum et regum, L. Weiland (ed.), (Hanover: Monumenta Germaniae Historica, Legum Section IV, 1893).

Nicholas, *Responsa Nicolai ad Consulta Bulgarorum*, in *Patrologia Cursus Completus: Series Latina*, J.-P. Migne (ed.), (Paris, 1844–55), vol. 119.

Paul VI, *Decree on the Ministry and Life of Priests* (7 December 1965) [http://www.vatican.va/archive/hist_councils/ii_vatican_council/documents/vat-ii_decree_19651207_presbyterorum-ordinis_en.html].

Priestly Celibacy (24 June 1967) [http://www.vatican.va/holy_father/paul_vi/encyclicals/documents/hf_p-vi_enc_24061967_sacerdotalis_en.html].

Pius XI, *Qui Pluribus*, 9 November 1846 [http://www.papalencyclicals.net/Pius09/p9quiplu.htm].

——, *Syllabus of Errors*, 8 December 1864 (Vatican: Holy Office, 1864).

Pius XIII, *Holy Virginity* (25 March 1954) [http://www.vatican.va/holy_father/pius_xii/encyclicals/documents/hf_p-xii_enc_25031954_sacra-virginitas_en.html].

Siricius, *Epistola Ad Himerium*, in *Patrologia Cursus Completus: Series Latina*, J.-P. Migne (ed.), (Paris, 1844–55), vol. 13.

——, *Epistola Ad Gallos Episcopos*, in *Patrologia Cursus Completus: Series Latina*, J.-P. Migne (ed.), (Paris, 1844–55), vol. 13.

Patristic Period

Ambrose of Milan, *Epistola 22*, in *Patrologia Cursus Completus: Series Latina*, J.-P. Migne (ed.) (Paris, 1844–55), vol. 16.
——, *De Viduis*, in *Patrologia Cursus Completus: Series Latina*, J.-P. Migne (ed.) (Paris, 1844–55), vol. 16.
——, *De Virginitate*, in *Patrologia Cursus Completus: Series Latina*, J.-P. Migne (ed.) (Paris, 1844–55), vol. 16.
——, *De Virginibus*, in *Patrologia Cursus Completus: Series Latina*, J.-P. Migne (ed.) (Paris, 1844–55), vol. 16.
Augustine, *City of God* (De Civitate Dei), *Patrologia Cursus Completus: Series Latina*, J.-P. Migne (ed.) (Paris, 1844–55), vol. 41.
——, *Confessionum*, in *Patrologia Cursus Completus: Series Latina*, J.-P. Migne (ed.) (Paris, 1844–55), vol. 32.
——, *De Continentia*, in *Patrologia Cursus Completus: Series Latina*, J.-P. Migne (ed.) (Paris, 1844–55), vol. 40.
——, *De Bono Coniugali*, in *Patrologia Cursus Completus: Series Latina*, J.-P. Migne (ed.) (Paris, 1844–55), vol. 40.
——, *De Sancta Virginitate*, in *Patrologia Cursus Completus: Series Latina*, J.-P. Migne (ed.) (Paris, 1844–55), vol. 40.
——, *De Bono Viduitatis*, in *Patrologia Cursus Completus: Series Latina*, J.-P. Migne (ed.) (Paris, 1844–55), vol. 40.
——, *De Coniugiis Adulterinis*, in *Patrologia Cursus Completus: Series Latina*, J.-P. Migne (ed.) (Paris, 1844–55), vol. 40.
——, *De Nuptiis et Concupiscientia*, in *Patrologia Cursus Completus: Series Latina*, J.-P. Migne (ed.) (Paris, 1844–55), vol. 44.
——, *De Haeresibus*, in *Patrologia Cursus Completus: Series Latina*, J.-P. Migne (ed.) (Paris, 1844–55), vol. 42.
——, *De Peccatorum Meritis*, in *Patrologia Cursus Completus: Series Latina*, J.-P. Migne (ed.) (Paris, 1844–55), vol. 44.
Basil, *De Renunciatione Saeculi*, in L. Schopp (ed.), *The Fathers of the Church. Volume 9: St Basil Ascetical Works* (Washington DC: Catholic University of America Press, 1962).
Chrysostom, *Commentary on the First Epistle to Timothy*, in *Patrologia Cursus Completus: Series Graeca*, J.-P. Migne (ed.) (161 vols, Paris 1857–66), vol. 62.
Clement of Alexandria, *Stromata*, in *Patrologia Cursus Completus: Series Graeca*, J.-P. Migne (ed.) (161 vols, Paris 1857–66), vol. 8.
Epiphanius, *Panarion (Adversus Haereses)*, in *Patrologia Cursus Completus: Series Graeca*, J.-P. Migne (ed.) (161 vols, Paris 1857–66), vol. 8.
——, *Expositio Fidei*, in *Patrologia Cursus Completus: Series Graeca*, J.-P. Migne (ed.) (161 vols, Paris 1857–66), vol. 42.

Eusebius, *Historica Ecclesiastica*, in A. Roberts and J. Donaldson (eds), *Select Library of Nicene and Post-Nicene Fathers*, series 2, vols 1 and 2 (Grand Rapids, Mich.: Eerdmans, 1951–).

——. *Demonstratio Evangelica*, in *Patrologia Cursus Completus: Series Graeca*, J.-P. Migne (ed.) (161 vols, Paris 1857–66), vol. 22.

Gelasius of Kyzikos, *Historia Concilii Nicaeni XXXII*, in *Patrologia Cursus Completus: Series Graeca*, J.-P. Migne (ed.) (161 vols, Paris 1857–66), vol. 85.

Gregory Nazianzen, *Epistola 197*, in *Patrologia Cursus Completus: Series Graeca*, J.-P. Migne (ed.) (161 vols, Paris 1857–66), vol. 37.

Ignatius, *Letter to Polycarp*, in *Patrologia Cursus Completus: Series Graeca*, ed. J.-P. Migne (161 vols, Paris 1857–66), vol. 5.

Irenaeus, *Adversus Haereses*, in *Patrologia Cursus Completus: Series Graeca*, J.-P. Migne (ed.) (161 vols, Paris 1857–66), vol. 7.

——, *Against the Heresies, Book One*, D.J. Unger and J.J. Dillon (eds) (New York: Paulist Press, 1992].

Jerome, *Adversus Jovinianum*, in *Patrologia Cursus Completus: Series Latina*, J.-P. Migne (ed.) (Paris, 1844–55), vol. 23.

——, *Contra Vigilantium*, in *Patrologia Cursus Completus: Series Latina*, J.-P. Migne (ed.) (Paris, 1844–55), vol. 23.

——, *Epistola 22 to Eustochium*, in *St. Jerome: Letters and Select Works* (tr. W.H. Fremantle), *Select Library of Nicene and Post-Nicene Fathers*, Ser. 2, vol. VI (Grand Rapids, Mich.: Eerdmans, 1951–).

——, *Epistola 48*, in *Corpus Scriptorum Ecclesiasticorum Latinorum*, vol. 54 (Vienna: C. Gerodi et al., 1866–).

——, *Commentarius In Titum*, in *Patrologia Cursus Completus: Series Latina*, J.-P. Migne (ed.) (Paris, 1844–55), vol. 26.

——, *De Perpetua Virginitate B. Mariae Adversis Helvidium*, in *Patrologia Cursus Completus: Series Latina*, J.-P. Migne (ed.) (Paris, 1844–55), vol. 23.

Justin Martyr, *Apology*, in *Patrologia Cursus Completus: Series Graeca*, J.-P. Migne (ed.) (161 vols, Paris 1857–66), vol. 6.

Origen, *Commentary on the Gospel of Matthew*, in *Patrologia Cursus Completus: Series Graeca*, J.-P. Migne (ed.) (161 vols, Paris 1857–66), vol. 13.

——, *Homilies on Numbers*, in *Patrologia Cursus Completus: Series Graeca*, J.-P. Migne (ed.) (161 vols, Paris 1857–66), vol. 12.

——, *Homilies on Leviticus*, in *Patrologia Cursus Completus: Series Graeca*, J.-P. Migne (ed.) (161 vols, Paris 1857–66), vol. 12.

Polycarp, *Letter to the Philippians* in *The Ante-Nicene Fathers*, volume one, A. Roberts, J. Donaldson, and A. Cleveland Coxe (eds) (Buffalo, NY: Christian Literature Publishing Co., 1885).

Socrates, *Historia Ecclesiastica*, in *Patrologia Cursus Completus: Series Graeca*, J.-P. Migne (ed.) (161 vols, Paris 1857–66), vol. 67.
Sozomen, *Historia Ecclesiastica*, in *Patrologia Cursus Completus: Series Graeca*, J.-P. Migne (ed.) (161 vols, Paris 1857–66), vol. 67.
Tatian, *On Perfection According to the Saviour*, in *The Ante-Nicene Fathers*, volume two, A. Roberts and J. Donaldson (eds) (Grand Rapids, Mich.: Eerdmans, 1989–90).
Tertullian, *De Exhortatione Castitatis*, in *Patrologia Cursus Completus: Series Latina*, J.-P. Migne (ed.) (Paris, 1844–55), vol. 2.
——, *De Monogamia*, in *Patrologia Cursus Completus: Series Latina*, J.-P. Migne (ed.) (Paris, 1844–55), vol. 2.
——, *Ad Uxorem*, in *Patrologia Cursus Completus: Series Latina*, J.-P. Migne (ed.) (Paris, 1844–55), vol. 1.
——, *Adversus Marcionem* (tr. and ed. E. Evans) (Oxford: Clarendon Press, 1972).

Printed Primary Sources

Abbatis Panormitani Commentaria in Tertium Decretalium Librum (7 vols, Venice: Iuntas, 1588).
Adam von Bremen, *Gesta Hammaburgensis ecclesiae pontificum in Scriptores Rerum Germanicarum in Usum Scholarum Separatim Editi*, B. Schmeidler (ed.) (Hanover: Monumenta Germaniae Historica, 1917).
Aguirre, J.S. de, *Collectio Maxima Conciliorum Omnium Hispaniae, et Novi Orbis* (6 vols, Rome: Catalini, 1753–5).
Alexandre, N., *s Dissertationum Ecclesiasticarum Trias. Prima de Divina Episcoporum supra presbyteros eminentia Blondellum. Altera de sacrorum ministrorum coelibatu, sive de historia Paphnutii cum Nicaeno canone concilianda. Tertia de vulgate Scripturae sacrae versione* (Paris, 1678).
The Anglo Saxon Chronicle, D. Whitelock, D.C. Douglas, S. Tucker (eds) (London: Eyre and Spottiswoode, 1961).
Anon, *Vita S. Altmanni*, in *Patrologia Cursus Completus: Series Latina*, J.-P. Migne (ed.) (Paris, 1844–55), vol. 148.
Anselm, *History of the Dedication of the Church of St Remigius*, in *Patrologia Cursus Completus: Series Latina*, J.-P. Migne (ed.) (Paris, 1844–55), vol. 142.
Antonius, J., *Aurea at Singularis Lectura Super IV Decretalium in Ca. De Clere. Coniugatis* (Pavia, 1497).
Apel, J., *Defensio Johannis Apelli ad Episcopum Herbipolensem pro suo Coniugio* (Wittenberg, 1523).

Aquinas, *Summa Theologica* (tr. Fathers of the English Dominican Province) (2nd edn, London, 1923).
Arnulf of Milan, *Liber Gestorum Recentium in Scriptores Germanicarum in usum scholarum separatim 67*, C. Zey (ed.) (4 vols, Hanover: Monumenta Germaniae Historica, 1994).
Augustus de Ancona, *Summa de potestate ecclesiastica* (Venice, 1487).
Bacon, F., *Of Marriage and Single Life* (1597), J. Pitcher (ed.), *The Essays of Francis Bacon* (Penguin Classics, 1985).
Bale, J., *A Mysterye of Iniquyte Contayned within the Heretycally Genealogye of Ponce Pantolabus* (Antwerp, 1545).
——, *The Apology of John Bale Agaynste a Ranke Papyst* (London, 1550).
——, *Yet a Course at the Romyshe Foxe* (Antwerp, 1543).
——, *Scriptorum Illustrium Maioris Brytanniae Quam Nunc Angliam & Scotiam Vocant: Catalogus* (Basle, 1557).
——, *The First Two Parts of the Actes, or unchast examples, of the Englysh Votaryes* (London, 1551).
Bayle, P., *Dictionnaire historique et critique* (8 vols, Rotterdam, 1692).
Barnes, R., *That By Gods Law it is Lawfull for Priestes that hath not the gift of chastite to marry wiues*, in *The Whole Workes of W.Tyndall, Iohn Frith and Doct. Barnes, three worthy martyrs and principall teachers of this churche of Englande*, J. Foxe (ed.) (London, 1573).
——, *Vitae Romanorum Pontificum* (Basle, 1555).
——, *A Supplication unto the most Gracious prince Henry VIII* (London, 1534).
Baronius, C., *Annales Ecclesiastici Ann.390 c.47* (Venice, 1740).
——, *Annales Ecclesiastici*, G.D. Mansi (ed.) (30 vols, Lucca, 1738–59).
Becon, T., *Book of matrimony*, in *The Worckes of Thomas Becon whiche he hath hitherto made and published with diuerse other newe books added* (2 vols, 1564).
Beecher Stowe, H., *Agnes of Sorrento* (Boston, 1862).
Bellarmine, R., *Disputationes de Controversiis Christianae fidei adversus hujus temporis Haereticos* (3 vols, Ingolstadt, 1586–93).
——, *Opera Omnia*, J. Fevre (ed.) (12 vols, Paris, 1870).
Bernold of Constance, *Chronicon*, in *Annales et chronica aevi Salici. Scriptores V*, Georg Waitz (ed.) (Hanover, Monumenta Germaniae Historia, 1844).
Bossardus, G., *De Continentia Sacerdotum sub hac Quaestione: utrum papae possit com sacerdote dispensare, ut nubat?* (Paris, 1505).
Bray, G., *Documents of the English Reformation 1526–1701* (Cambridge: CUP, 2004).
Brunus, C., *Admonitio Catholica Adversus Novam Historiam Eccles. Quam Matthaeus Illyricus* (Dillingae, 1565).

Bucer, M., *De Coelibatu Sacerdotum* (Basle, 1548).
——, *The Gratulation of the Most Famous Martin Bucer* (tr. T. Hoby) (London, 1549).
Bullinger, H., *The Golden Boke of Christen Matrimonye* (tr. M. Coverdale) (London, 1543).
Burchard, *Decretum (Brocardus)*, in *Patrologia Cursus Completus: Series Latina*, J.-P. Migne (ed.) (Paris, 1844–55), vol. 140.
Burnet, G., *History of the Reformation of the Church of England*, N. Pocock (ed.), (7 vols, Oxford, 1865).
——, *History of the Reformation of the Church of England* (6 vols, London, 1825).
Caesarius of Heisterbach, *The Dialogue on Miracles* (tr. H. von E. Scott and C.C. Swinton Bland), with an introduction by G.G. Coulton (London: Routledge, 1929).
Calixtus, G., *De conjugio clericorum tractatus quo ostenditur pontificiam legem, qua sacris ministris conjugium universim et simpliciter interdicitur, sacrae scripturae, rectae rationi justarumque legum naturae, et ecclesiasticae primaevae antiquitati prorsus adversari ... .* (Helmstadt, 1631).
Calvin, J., *Institutes of the Christian Religion*, J.T. McNeill (ed.) (2 vols, London, 1961).
——, *The Necessity of Reforming the Church* (tr. J.K.S. Reid), Library of Christian Classics, 22 (1954).
——, *Jean Calvin Opera* (Brunswick, 1871).
Capitularia regum Francorum, Alfred Boretius (ed.) (Hanover: Monumenta Germaniae Historica, 1883).
Caprara, G. Cardinal, *Concordat et Recueil des Bulles et Brefs de NSP le Pape Pie VII* (Paris, 1802).
Cardwell, E., *Documentary Annals of the Reformed Church in England* (2 vols, Oxford: Oxford University Press, 1839).
Carlstadt, A., *Axiomata Super Coelibatu, Monachatu et Viduitate* (Wittenberg, 1521).
——, *The Essential Carlstadt. Fifteen Tracts by Andreas Bodenstein (Carlstadt) from Karlstadt*, E.J. Furcha (ed.) (Scottdale Penn, Waterloo Ontario: Herald Press, 1995).
Carové, F.W., *Über das Cölibatsgesetz des römisch-katholischen Klerus* (Frankfurt, 1833).
——, *Vollständige Sammlung der Cölibatgesetze* (Frankfurt, 1823).
Casinensis, P., *Historia gentis Langobardorum*, in *Scriptores rerum Langobardicarumet Italicarum saec. VI–IX*, Georg Waitz (ed.) (Hanover: Monumenta Germaniae Historica, 1878), pp. 45–187.
Catharinus, *Ambrosius, Apologia pro Veritate Catholicae et Apostolicae Fidei ac Doctrinae*, J. Schweizer (ed.) (Münster: Aschendorff, 1956).

——, *Excusatio Disputationis contra Martinum* (Florence, 1521).
Catholic Encyclopedia (15 vols, New York: Appleton, 1907–12).
Celtis, C., *Quatuor libri amorum secundum quatuor latera Germanie* (Nuremberg, 1502).
Chaucer, G., *The Canterbury Tales*, in G. Benson, C. Cannon (eds) The Riverside Chaucer (3rd edn, Oxford: OUP, 1988).
Chemnitz, M., *Examen Concilii Tridentini* (1565–73).
Cochlaeus, J., *Commentarii de Actis et Scriptis Martini Lutheri Saconis* (1549).
——, *Septiceps Luthereus Ubique Sibi Suisque Scriptis* Contrarius (Paris 1564).
Constitutiones et acta publica imperatorum et regum inde ab a. DCCCCXI usque ad a. MCXCVII (911–1197), L. Weiland (ed.) (Hanover: Monumenta Germaniae Historica, 1893).
Coupe, W., *German Political Satires from the Reformation to the Second World War* (3 vols, White Plains, NY: Kraus, 1993).
Cromerus, M., *Orichovius, sive de Coniugio et Coelibatu Sacerdotum Commentarius* (Cologne, 1564).
Crowley, R., *A Confutation of xiii articles wherunto Nicholas Shaxton ... subscribed* (London, 1548).
Cuyck, H. van, *Speculum concubinariorum sacerdotum, monachorum ac clericorum* (Coloniae, 1599).
Dante, *The Divine Comedy*, G.L. Bickersteff (ed.) (Oxford: Blackwell, 1972).
De Castitate et Munditia Sacerdotum et Ceterorum Alteris Ministrorum (Paris, c.1492).
Desforges, P., *Avantages du mariage, et combien il est nécessaire & salutaire aux prêtres et aux évêques de ce tems-ci d'épouser une fille chrétienne* (2 vols, Brussels, 1760).
Dickens, A.G., 'Robert Parkyn's Narrative of the Reformation', in Dickens (ed.), *Reformation Studies* (London, 1982), pp. 293–312.
Die Entstehung des papstlichen Investiturverbots fur den Deutschen Konig, R. Schieffer (ed.), (Stuttgart: Monumenta Germaniae Historica, 1981).
Doctrinal of Sapience, J. Gallagher (ed.), *Middle English Texts* 26 (Heidelberg, 1993).
Dionysius the Carthusian, *The Lyfe of Prestes* (London, 1533).
Dungersheim, J., *Schriften Gegen Luther Theorismata Duodecim Contra Lutherum, Articuli Sive Libelli Triginta*, Theobald Freudenberger (ed.) (Munster: Aschendorff, 1987).
Durandus, W., *Tractatus de modo generalis concilii celebrandi* (Paris: Clousier, 1671).
Emser, J., *Epithalamia Martini Lutheri Wittenbergensis et Johannes Hessi Vratislavtensis ed Id Genus Nuptiarum* (1525).

——, *Venatione Luteriana Aegocerotis assertio* (1525).
E.P., *A Confutatio[n] of Unwritte[n] Verities* (Wesel, 1556).
Epistolae Selecta: Die Briefe des heiligen Bonifatius und Lullus, M. Tangl (ed.) (Hanover: Monumenta Germaniae Historia, 1916).
Erasmus, D., *A Right Fruitfull Epistle... In Laud and Praise of Matrimony* (tr. Richard Taverner) (London, 1532/6).
——, *Opus epistolarum Des. Erasmi Roterodami*, P.S. Allen, H.W. Garrod (eds) (12 vols, Oxford: Clarendon Press, 1906–58).
Faber, J., *Defensio Adversus Johannem Fabrum ... pro conjugio sacerdotali defensio* (Wittenberg, 1523).
——, *Faber's Opus adversus nova quaedam et a Christiana religione prorsus aliena dogmata Martini Lutheri* (Rome, 1523).
Fasciculi Zizaniorum, W.W. Shirley (ed.) (London: Rolls Series, 1858).
Fisher, J., *Adversus Nova Quaedam et a Christiana Religione Prorsus aliena dogmata mart. Lutheri* (Rome, 1522).
——, *The English Works of John Fisher*, J.E.B. Mayor (ed.), *Early English Texts Society*, extra ser. 27 (1876).
Flacius Illyricus, M., *Catalogus Testium Veritatis, Qui Ante Nostram Aetatem Reclamarunt Papae* (Basle, 1566).
Foxe, J., *The Actes and Monuments of these latter and perillous days* (London, 1563).
——, *The Actes and Monuments of these latter and perillous days* (London, 1570).
——, *The Actes and Monuments of these latter and perillous days* (London, 1583).
Frere, W.H., *Visitation Articles and Injunctions for the period of the Reformation* (3 vols, London: Alcuin Club, 1910).
Frith, J., *Pistle to the Christen Reader. The Reuelacion of Antichrist* (Antwerp, 1529).
Gaudin, Abbe, *Les inconvéniens du célibat des prêtres, prouvés par des recherché historiques* (Geneva, 1781).
Gerson, J., *Dialogus de Celibatu Ecclesiasticorum* (1423), in Grévy-Pons, N., *Célibat et nature, une controverse médiévale: A propos d'un traité de début de XVe siècle* (Paris: Centre national de la recherche scientifique, 1975), pp. 162–95.
Gerung, C., *Der Actus und Des Geschicht* (Augsburg, 1523).
Gonzalez, F. de P., *Defensa de la autoridad de los gobiernos y de los obispos contra las pretensiones de la curia romana* (Lima: Juan Sanchez, 1848–56).
Gotti, V.L., *Colloquia Theologico-Polemica in tres classes distribute* (Bologna, 1727).
Gower, J., *Vox Clamantis*, in *The Complete Works of John Gower: vol. 4, The Latin Works*, G.C. Macauley (ed.) (Oxford: OUP, 1902).

Gratian, Decretum (*Concordia discordantium canonum*), in *Corpus iuris canonici in tres partes distinctum; glossis diuersorum illustratum; Gregorij Papæ XIII. iussu editum, complectens Decretum Gratiani, decretales Gregorij IX. Sextum decretalium Bonifacij VIII. Clementinas, Extravagantes Ioannis XXII. Extravagantes communes, &c. Accesserunt Constitutiones nouæ Summorum Pontificum hactenus desideratæ, quæ VII. decretalium loco esse possint, necnon annotationes Antonij Naldi additionibus novis elucidatæ*, A. Naldi (ed.) (3 vols, Lyons: Huguetan and Barbier, 1671).

Gratius, O., *Fasciculus rerum expetendarum ac fugiendarum* (Cologne, 1535).

Grévy-Pons, N., *Célibat et nature, une controverse médiévale: A propos d'un traité de début de XVe siècle* (Paris: Centre national de la recherche scientifique, 1975).

Gualther, R., *Antichrist. That is to say a True Report that Antichriste is come* (tr. J. Old) (Emden, 1556).

Gunzberg, E. von, *Syben Frumm Aber Trostloss Pfaffen Klagen Ihre Not* (Basle, 1521).

Harpsfield, N., *Dialogi Sex* (Antwerp, 1566).

Henry VIII, *A copy of the Letters Wherin … King Henry VIII… made answer unto … Martyn Luther* (London, 1528).

——, *Assertio Septem Sacramentorum* (Corpus Catholicorum vol. 43, Munster, 1992).

Henry of Huntingdon, *Historia Anglorum*, T. Arnold (ed.) (London: Rolls Series 74, 1879).

Hooper, J., 'A Brief and Clear Confession of the Christian Faith', in C. Nevinson (ed.), *The Later Writings of Bishop Hooper* (Cambridge: Parker Society, 1852).

Huggarde, M., *The Displaying of the Protestantes and Sondry their Practises* (London, 1556).

Hulton, W.A. (ed.), *The Coucher Book of Whalley Abbey* (2 vols, Manchester: Chetham Society, 1847–9).

Humbert, Cardinal Silva, *Adversus Nicetam*, in *Patrologia Cursus Completus: Series Latina*, J.-P. Migne (ed.) (Paris, 1844–55), vol. 141.

Humbert, *Responsio sive contradiction adversus Nicetae Pectorati libellum*, in *Patrologia Cursus Completus: Series Latina*, J.-P. Migne (ed.) (Paris, 1844–55), vol. 143.

Innocent III, *Die Register Innocenz' III. 6: 6. Pontifikatsjahr, 1203/1204, Texte und Indices*, O. Hageneder, J.C. Moore, and A. Sommerlechner (eds) with Christoph Egger and H. Weigl (Graz: H. Böhlaus Nachf, 1964).

James, T., *A Manvduction or Introdvction unto Divinitie* (Oxford, 1625).

Jewel, J., 'Defence of the Apology of the Church of England', in J. Ayre (ed.), *The Works of John Jewel*, vol. 4 (Cambridge: Parker Society, 1849).

Joye, G., *The Defence of the Mariage of Priestes Agenst Steuen Gardiner* (Antwerp, 1541).

——, *The Letters which Joh Ashwell… sente secretlye to the byschope of Lincolne* (Antwerp, 1531).

Judex, M. and Wigand, J., *Ecclesiastica Historia* (Basle, 1560–74).

Klingebeil, S., *Von Priester Ehe* (Wittenberg, 1528).

Lambert of Hersfeld, *Annales*, in *Annales et chronica aevi Salici. Scriptores V*, G. Pertz (ed.) (Hanover: Monumenta Germaniae Historica, 1844).

Latomus, J., *De Confessione Secreta* (Antwerp, 1525).

Lefevre d'Etaples, J., *Commentaires sur les épîtres de Saint Paul* (Paris, 1512).

Le Maistre, *Questiones morales magistri Martini Magistri perspicacissimi theologie professoris, de fortitudine feliciter incipiunt* (2 parts, Paris, 1510).

Leopardi, Count M., *Vita di Niccolò Bonafede vescovo di Chiusi* (Pesaro, 1832).

Les Registres d'Innocent IV, E. Berger (ed.) (4 vols, Paris: BEFAR, 1884–1920).

Lewis, M., *The Monk*, edited with an introduction by H. Anderson (London: OUP, 1973).

Libelli de lite imperatorum et pontificum saeculis XI. et XII. Conscripti I, Ernst Dümmler, Friedrich Thaner, Lotkar von Heinemann (eds) (Hanover: Monumenta Germaniae Historica, 1891).

Libelli de lite imperatorum et pontificum saeculis XI. et XII. Conscripti II, Ernst Dümmler, Friedrich Thaner, Ernst Sackur (eds) (Hanover: Monumenta Germaniae Historica, 1892).

Libelli de lite imperatorum et pontificum saeculis XI. et XII. Conscripti III, Ernst Dümmler, Ernst Sackur (eds) (Hanover: Monumenta Germaniae Historica, 1897).

Liber Landavensis: The text of the Book of Llan Dav, J.G. Evans (ed.) (Oxford: J. Bellows, 1893).

Luther, M., *Luther's Works*, J. Pelikan, H.C. Oswald, H. Grimm, T. Lehmann et al. (eds) (56 vols, St Louis: Concordia Publishing, 1955–86).

——, *Martin Luthers Werke. Briefweschel*, J.F.K. Knaake, G. Kawerau, et al. (eds) (15 vols, Weimar: Herman Bohlaus Nachfolger, 1930–48).

——, *Luther's Correspondence and Other Contemporary Letters*, P. Smith (ed.) (2 vols, Philadelphia: Lutheran Publication Society, 1918).

——, *Ursach und Antwort, das jungfrauen kloster gottlich verlassen mogen* (Wittenberg, 1523).

——, 'Ad librum eximii Magistri Nostri Magistri Ambrosii Catharini, defensoris Silvestri Prieriatis acerrimi, responsio', in *D. Martin Luthers Werke Kritische Gesamtausgabe*, vii (Weimar: Herman Bohlaus Nachfolger, 1897).

——, *The Interpretation of the Two horrible figures: The papal Ass in Rome and the Monk Calf found in Freiburg in Meissen 1523*, in *Weimarer Ausgabe: Martin Luther Werke* (90 vols, Weimar: Herman Bohlaus Nachfolger, 1883–) vol. 11, pp. 369–85.

——, *Sermons of Martin Luther: Church Postils*, J.N. Lenker (ed.) (2 vols, Grand Rapids, MI: Baker Book House, 1989).

Maior, J., *Quartus Sententiarum* (Paris, 1509).

Marianus Scotus, *Chronicon*, in *Annales et chronica aevi Salici. Scriptores V*, G. Pertz (ed.) (Hanover: Monumenta Germaniae Historica, 1844).

Martin, T., *A traictise declaryng and plainly prouyng, that the pretensed marriage of priestes, and professed persones, is no mariage, but altogether vnlawful* (London, 1554).

Maultrot, G-N., *La discipline de l'Église sur le mariage des prêtres* (Paris: Lejay Fils, 1790).

Martyr, P., *Defensio Doctrinae Veteris et Apostolicae de Sacrosanto Eucharistiae Sacramento* (Zurich, 1559).

——, *Defensio de Petri Martyris Vermilii* ... Basle? 1559).

——, *The Commonplaces of the Most Famous and Renowned Diuine Doctor Peter Martyr* (tr. A. Marten) (London, 1583).

Melanchthon, P., (tr. George Joye), *A very godly defense full of lerning defending the mariage of preistes* (Antwerp, 1541).

——, *De Votis Monasticis et an Coniugum sit Concedendum Puellae Qui in Monasterio Aliquamdiu Vixerat* (Wittenberg, 1521).

——, *De Ecclesia et de Auctoritate Verbi Dei*, in C.L. Hill (ed.), *Melanchthon, Selected Writings* (Minneapolis: Augsburg, 1963).

Metochites, T., *Miscellanea Philosophia et Historica*, C. Muller and T. Kiessling (eds) (Leipzig: C.J. Vogel, 1821).

Monilianus, C., *Catholicarum Institutionem ad Christianam Theologiam Compendium* (Rome, 1565).

More, T., *Responsio ad Lutherum*, J.M. Headley (ed.), in *The Yale Edition of The Complete Works of St Thomas More*, 5 (New Haven, Conn.: Yale UP, 1969).

——, *A Dialogue Concerning Heresies*, T.M.C. Lawler, G. Marc'hadour, R.C. Marius (eds), in *The Yale Edition of The Complete Works of St. Thomas More*, 6 (New Haven, Conn.: Yale UP, 1981).

——, *Letter to Bugenhagen, Supplication of Souls, Letter against Frith*, F. Manley, G. Marc'hadour, R. Marius, C.H. Miller (eds), in *The Yale Edition of The Complete Works of St Thomas More*, 7 (New Haven, Conn.: Yale UP, 1990).

——, 'The Confutation of Tyndale's Answer', L.A. Schuster, R.C. Marius, J.P. Lusardi, R.J. Schoek (eds), *The Yale Edition of The Complete Works of St. Thomas More*, 8 (New Haven, Conn.: Yale UP, 1973).

Myers, A.R., *English Historical Documents 1327–1485* (London: Routledge, 1995).

Odo of Cluny, *Collationes*, in *Patrologia Cursus Completus: Series Latina*, J.-P. Migne (ed.) (Paris, 1844–55), vol. 133.

Orderic Vitalis, *Historia Ecclesiasticae*, A. Le Prevost (ed.) (5 vols, Paris: Société de l'histoire de France, 1838–55).

Panormitanus (Nicolaus de Tudeschis), *Abbatis Panormitani Commentaria in Tertium Decretalium Librum* (Venice, 1588).

Parker, H., *Dives and Pauper* (London, 1536).

Parker, M., *A Defence of Priestes Mariages* (London, 1567).

Pellens, K. (ed.), *Die Texte des Normannischen Anonymus* (Wiesbaden: Steiner, 1966).

Peter Damian, *Contra Intemperantes*, in *Patrologia Cursus Completus: Series Latina*, J.-P. Migne (ed.) (Paris, 1844–55), vol. 145.

——, *De Caelibatu Sacerdotum*, in *Patrologia Cursus Completus: Series Latina*, J.-P. Migne (ed.) (Paris, 1844–55), vol. 145.

——, *Opuscula*, in *Patrologia Cursus Completus: Series Latina*, J.-P. Migne (ed.) (Paris, 1844–55), vol. 145.

——, *Liber Gomorrhianus*, in *Patrologia Cursus Completus: Series Latina*, J.-P. Migne (ed.) (Paris, 1844–55), vol. 145.

——, *Die Briefe des Petrus Damiani in Epistolae: 2, Die Briefe der deutschen Kaiserzeit*, K. Reindel (ed.) (4 vols, Munich: Monumenta Germaniae Historica, 1983–89).

Peter Lombard, *Libri Quatuor Sententiarum*, in *Patrologia Cursus Completus: Series Latina*, J.-P. Migne (ed.) (Paris, 1844–55), vol. 192.

Platina, *Vitæ Pontificum Platinæ historici liber de vita Christi ac omnium pontificum qui hactenus ducenti fuere et XX* (Venice, 1479).

Ponet, J., *A Defence for the Mariage of Priestes* (London, 1549).

——, *An Apology Fully Aunswering by Scriptures and Aunceaunt Doctors ... D.Steph Gardiner* (Strasbourg, 1555).

Pseudo-Udalrici Epistola de Continentia Clericorum, in *Libelli de Lite I*, Lothar von Heinemann (ed.) (Hanover: Monumenta Germaniae Historica), pp. 244–60.

Raemond, F. De, *L'Histoire de la Naissance, Progrez et Decadence de l'heresie* (Rouen, 1647).

Raine, J.A., *The Priory of Hexham: its chroniclers, endowments, and annals* (Durham: Surtees Society, 1864–65).

Ratramnus, *Contra Graecorum Opposita*, in *Patrologia Cursus Completus: Series Latina*, J.-P. Migne (ed.) (Paris, 1844–55), vol. 121.

Ratherius, *De Contemptu Canonum*, in *Patrologia Cursus Completus: Series Latina*, J.-P. Migne (ed.) (Paris, 1844–55), vol. 136.

——, *De Nuptio Illicitu*, in *Patrologia Cursus Completus: Series Latina*, J.-P. Migne (ed.) (Paris, 1844–55), vol. 136.

Reformatio Sigismundi in Staatsschriften des späteren Mittelalters 6: Reformation Kaiser Siegmunds, H. Koller (ed.) (Stuttgart: Monumenta Germaniae Historica, 1964).

Das Register Gregors VII. (Gregorii VII Registrum), in Epistolae Selecta V, E. Caspar (ed.) (2 vols, Hanover: Monumenta Germaniae Historica, 1920, 1923).

The Register of Pope Gregory VII, 1073–1085: An English Translation, H.E.J. Cowdrey (ed.) (Oxford: Oxford University Press, 2002).

Robert of Brunne, *Handlyng Synne*, J. Furnivall (ed.), *Early English Texts Society*, Old Series, 119 and 123 (1901 and 1903).

Robinson, J.H., *Readings in European History* (Boston: Ginn & Co., 1904).

Roskovány, A., *Coelibatus, et Breviarium: duo gravissima clericorum officia, e monumentis omnium seculorum demonstrate* (5 vols, Pest, 1861).

Roy, W., *Rede me and be nott wrothe* (n.p., 1528).

De Sacerdotalis Ministeriali (Sacra Congregatio Pro Doctrina Fidei: Vatican, 1971).

Saignet, G., *Lamentationem ob coelibatum sacerdotum, seu dialogum Nicenaenae Constitutionis et Naturae ea de re Conquerentis (1417/8)*, in Grévy-Pons, N., *Célibat et nature, une controverse médiévale: A propos d'un traité de début de XVe siècle* (Paris: Centre national de la recherche scientifique, 1975), pp. 135–61.

Schmid, N., *Teufeln oder Lastern, damit die bosen, unartigen Weiber Besessen Sind* (n.p. (Leipzig), 1557).

Scriptores rerum Langobardicarumet Italicarum saec. VI–IX, Georg Waitz (ed.) (Hanover: Monumenta Germaniae Historica, 1878).

Smith, R., *Defensio Sacri Episcoporu[m] & sacerdotum coelibatus contra impias & indoctas Petri Martyris* (Paris, 1550).

Somerville, R., *The Councils of Urban II* (Amsterdam: Hakkert, 1972).

Stambaugh, R. (ed.), *Teufelbucher in Auswahl* (4 vols, Berlin: De Gruyter, 1970).

Stephen of Tournay, *Summa Stephani Tarnacensis*, V. Schulte (ed.) (Giessen, 1891).

Study on Priestly Life and Ministry (Washington DC: National Conference of Catholic Bishops, 1971).

Thomassin, L., 'Du Celibat des Beneficiers dans l'Eglise Oreintale pendant les cinq premiers siecles' and 'Du Celibat des Beneficiers dans l'Eglise Latine pendant le cinq premiers siecles', in *Ancienne et Nouvelle*

Discipline de l'Eglise touchant les Benefices et les Beneficiers (3 vols, Paris: Louis Roulland, 1678–79, revised 1725).

Thorpe, B., *Ancient Laws and Institutes of England* (2 vols, London: Eyre and Spottiswoode,1840).

——, (ed. and tr.), *The Homilies of the Anglo-Saxon Church. The First Part, Containing The Sermones Catholici, or Homilies of Ælfric. In the Original Anglo-Saxon, with an English Version* (2 vols, London: Richard and John E. Taylor, 1844, 1846).

Turner, W., *The Rescuyng of the Romishe Fox other vvyse called the Examination of the Hunter* (Bonn, 1545).

——, *Huntynge and Fyndynge Out of the Romyshe Foxe which more than seuen years hath bene hyd among the bisshopes of England* (Basle, 1543).

Turrianus, F., *Apostolicarum Constitutionum et Catholicae Doctrinae Clementis Romani Libri VIII* (Antwerp, 1578).

——, *De Votis Monasticis Liber* (Rome, 1566).

Tyndale, W., *An Answer unto Sir Thomas More's Dialogue*, in *The Whole Workes of W. Tyndall, Iohn Frith and Doct. Barnes, three worthy martyrs and principall teachers of this churche of Englande*, J. Foxe (ed.) (London, 1573).

——, *The Obedience of a Christian Man*, in *William Tyndale: Doctrinal Treatises*, H. Walter (ed.) (Cambridge: Parker Society, 1848).

Villiers, M.A. (Abbe) de, *Apologie du Celibat Chretien* (Paris: Damonneville & Musier, 1761).

Vita Altmanni Episcopi Pataviensis, in *Historiae aevi Salici. Scriptores XII*, W. Wattenbach (ed.) (Hanover: Monumenta Germaniae Historica, 1856).

Walter Map, *Apocalypse of Goliae*, in T. Wright (ed.), *The Latin Poems Commonly Attributed to Walter Mapes* (2 vols, London: Camden Society, 1841).

Wenrici scolastici Treverensis Epistola sub Theoderici episcope Virdunensis Nomine Composita, in *Libelli de lite imperatorum et pontificum saeculis XI. et XII. Conscripti I*, Ernst Dümmler, Friedrich Thaner, Lotkar von Heinemann (eds) (Hanover: Monumenta Germaniae Historica, 1891).

Whitford, R., *Pype or Tonne of the Lyfe of Perfection* (London, 1532).

Wilkins, D. (ed.), *Concilia Magnae Britanniae et Hiberniae, a synodo Verolamiensi, AD 446 ad Londinensem, AD 1717* (2 vols, London: Gosling and Woodward, 1737).

Will, C., *Acta et Scripta quae de controversiis ecclesiae Grecae at Latinae saeculo composite extant* (Paris: Lipsiae et Marpurgi, 1861).

Working paper on the Ministerial Priesthood in Preparation for Synod 1971 (Ottowa: Canadian Catholic Conference, 1971).

Wycliffe, J., *Tracts and Treatises of John de Wycliffe, D.D. with Selections and Translations from his Manuscripts, and Latin Works*, Robert Vaughan (ed.) (London: Blackburn and Pardon, 1845).

——, *Hou Sathanas & his prestos and his feyned religious casten by pre cursed heresies to distroie all good lyuynge and meytenen alle manere of synne*, in W.W. Shirley (ed.), *A Catalogue of the Original Works of John Wyclif* (Oxford: Clarendon Press, 1855).

Zabarella, F., *Capita Agendorum in Concilio Const. De Reformatione, Magnum Oecumenicum Constantiense Concilium*, H. van der Hardt (ed.) (Frankfurt: Zetzneri, 1700).

Zaccaria, F.A., *Storia polemica del celibato sacro da contrapporsi ad alcune detestabili opere uscite a questi tempi* (Rome, 1774).

——, *Nuova giustificazione del celibate scaro dagli inconvenienti oppostogli anche ultimamente in alcuni infamissimi libri dissertazioni Quattro* (Fuligno, 1785).

Zwingli, U., *Supplicatio quorumdam apud Helvetios Evangelistarum*, in M. Schuler and J. Schulthess (eds), *Zwingli Opera*, (8 vols, Zurich, 1828–42).

Secondary Sources

Abbott, E., *A History of Celibacy* (Boston: da Capo, 2001).
Abo, J.A., 'The Problem of Lapsed Priests', *The Jurist*, 23 (1963): 153–79.
Acquaviva P., and Petric, J. (eds), *Dante and the Church: Literary and Historical Essays* (Dublin: Four Courts Press. 2007).
Adam, A., 'Das Fortwirken des Manichäismus bei Augustin', *Zeitschrift fur Kirchengeschichte*, 69 (1958): 1–25.
Alberigo, J. (ed.), *The Reception of Vatican II* (Washington DC: Catholic University, 1987).
Alberigo, J., and Komanchak, J.A. (eds), *History of Vatican II* (Leuven: Peters, 1995–).
Aston, M., *Lollards and Reformers. Images and Literacy in Late Medieval Religion* (London: Hambledon, 1984).
Aston, N., *Religion and Revolution in France 1780–1804* (Basingstoke: Macmillan, 2000).
——, *Christianity in Revolutionary Europe, c.1760–1830* (Cambridge: Cambridge University Press, 2002).
Atkin, N., and Tallett, F., *Priests, Prelates and People. A History of European Catholicism Since 1750* (London and New York: IB Tauris, 2003).
Aubert, R. (ed.), *Sacralisation and Secularisation* (Concilium 47, New York, 1969).

Audet, J-P., *Mariage et celibat dans le service pastoral de l'Eglise, Histoire et Orientation* (1st edn, Paris, 1929; 2nd edn, Quebec: Editions des Sources, 1999).
——, *Structures of Christian Priesthood. Home, Marriage and Celibacy in the Pastoral Service of the Church* (tr. R. Sheed) (London and Melbourne: Sheed and Ward, 1967).
Bagchi, D., *Luther's Earliest Opponents. Catholic Controversialists 1518–1521* (Minneapolis: Fortress, 1991).
——, 'Luther's Catholic Opponents', in A. Pettegree (ed.), *The Reformation World* (Abingdon: Routledge, 2000), chapter 6.
Bailey, D.S., *Sexual Relations in Christian Thought* (New York: Harper 1959).
Bainton, R., *Erasmus of Rotterdam* (New York: Scribner, 1969).
Baldwin, J., 'A campaign to reduce clerical celibacy at the turn of the twelfth and thirteenth centuries', in *Etudes d'histoire du droit canonique dediees a Gabriel Le Bas* (2 vols, Paris: Sirey, 1965).
——, *The Language of Sex. Five Voices from Northern France Around 1200* (Chicago and London: University of Chicago Press, 1994).
Barlow, C.W., *Martini Episcopi Bracarensis Opera Omnia* (New Haven, Conn.: Yale UP, 1950).
Barnard, L.W., 'The Origins and Emergence of the Church in Edessa during the First Two Centuries AD', *Vigiliae Christianae*, 22.3 (Sept. 1968): 161–75.
Barnes, A., 'The Social Transformation of the French Parish Clergy 1500–1800', in B. Diefendorf and C. Hesse (eds), *Culture and Identity in Early Modern Europe 1500–1800* (Ann Arbor: Univ. Michigan Press, 1993).
Barstow, A.L., *Married Priests and the Reforming Papacy, The Eleventh Century Debates* (Lewiston, NY: Edward Mellen Press, 1982).
——, 'The First Generation of Anglican Clergy Wives: "Heroines or Whores?"', *Historical Magazine of the Protestant Episcopal Church*, 52 (1983): 3–16.
Bartlett, K., McGlynn, M. (eds), *Humanism and the Northern Renaissance* (Ontario: Canadian Scholars' Press, 2000).
Beaudette, P., 'In the World but not of it: Clerical Celibacy as a Symbol of the Medieval Church', in M. Frassetto (ed.), *Medieval Purity and Piety. Essays on Medieval Clerical Celibacy and Religious Reform* (New York and London: Taylor and Francis, 1998), pp. 23–47.
Baumert, N., *Ehelosigkeit und Ehe im Herrn: Eine Neuinterpretations von I Kkor 7* (Wurzburg: Echter, 1984).
Beatrice, F., 'Continenza e matrimonio nel Christianesimo primitivo', in R. Cantalamassa (ed.), *Etica sessuale e Matrimonio nel Cristianesimo delle Origini* (Milan: Vita e Pensiero, 1976).

Benz, E., 'Die grechische Übersetzung der Confession Augustana aus dem Jahre 1559', in his *Wittenberg und Byzanz* (Munich: Wilhelm Fink, 1949).

——, *Die Ostkirche im Lichte der Protestantischen Geschichtsschreibung* (Freiburg: K. Alber, 1952).

Berman, C.H., *Medieval Religion. New Approaches* (London and New York: Routledge, 2005).

Bernstein, P., *The Power of Gold. The History of an Obsession* (New York: John Wiley and Sons, 2000).

Bickell, G., 'Der Colibat eine apostolische Anordnung', *Zeitschrift fur Katholische Theologie*, 2 (1878): 20–64.

——, 'Der Colibat dennoch eine apostolische Anordnung', *Zeitschrift fur Katholische Theologie*, 3 (1879): 792–9.

Bickell, J.W., 'Apostolischen Kirchenordnung', in *Geschichte des Kirchenrechts* (Giessen, 1843).

Bjorklund, N.B., '"A Godly Wife is an Helper": Matthew Parker and the Defence of Clerical Marriage', *Sixteenth Century Journal*, 34.2 (2003): 347–65.

Blenkinsopp, J., *Celibacy, Ministry, Church* (New York, London: Burns and Oates, 1968).

Blinzer, J., '"Zur Ehe unfahig ..." Auslegung von Mt. 19,12', in *Gesammelte Ausfatze*, 1 (1969): 30–40.

Blumenthal, U.-R., 'Pope Gregory VII and the Prohibition of Nicolaitism', in Frassetto, M. (ed.), *Medieval Purity and Piety: Essays on Medieval Clerical Celibacy and Religious Reform* (New York and London: Taylor and Francis, 1998), pp. 239–67.

——, *The Investiture Controversy: Church and Monarchy from the Ninth to the Twelfth Century* (Philadelphia: University of Pennsylvania Press, 1988).

Bocquet, L., *Étude sur le célibat ecclésiastique jusqu'au concilie de Trente* (Paris: Giard & Brière, 1894).

Boelens, M., *Die Klerikerehe in der Gesetzgebung der Kirche unter besonderer Berücksichtigung der Strafe* (Paderborn: Schöningh., 1968).

——, 'Die Klerikereche in der kirchlichen Gesetzgebung zwischen den Konzilien von Basel und Trent', *Archiv fur katholisches Kirchenrecht*, 138 (1969): 62–81.

Boivin, M., 'On Priestly Marriage: A Response To Father Hastings On Celibacy', *New Blackfriars*, 60 (Issue 707, April 1979): 182–4.

Booty, J., *John Jewel as Apologist of the Church of England* (London: SPCK, 1963).

Borst, A., *Die Katharer* (Stuttgart: Hiersemann, 1953).

Bowker, M., *Secular Clergy in the Diocese of Lincoln, 1485–1520* (Cambridge: CUP, 1968).

Brady, T., '"You hate us priests": Anticlericalism. Communalism, and the Control of Women at Strasbourg in the Age of the Reformation', in P. Dykema and H. Oberman (eds), *Anticlericalism in Late Medieval and Early Modern Europe* (Leiden: Brill, 1993), pp. 167–207.

Brecht, M., *Martin Luther. Volume II. Shaping the Defining the Reformation 1521–1532* (tr. J.L. Schaff) (Minneapolis: Fortress Press, 1985–93).

Brennan, B., 'Episcopae: Bishops' Wives Viewed in Sixth Century Gaul', *Church History*, 54 (1985): 313–23.

Brigden, S., *London and the Reformation* (Oxford: Clarendon Press, 1989).

Brooke, C.N.L., 'Gregorian Reform in Action: Clerical Marriage in England 1050–1200', *Cambridge Historical Journal*, 12.1 (1956): 1–21.

Brooke, C.N.L., 'Married Men among the English Higher Clergy 1066–1100', *Cambridge Historical Journal*, 12.2 (1956): 187–8.

Brown, P., *The Body and Society. Men, Women and Sexual Renunciation in Early Christian Society* (New York: Columbia UP, 1988).

——, *Augustine of Hippo* (Berkeley: University of California Press, 1967).

Brown, R.E., *An Introduction to the New Testament* (New Haven, Conn.: Yale UP, 1997).

Brundage, J., 'Sexuality, Marriage and the reform of Christian Society in the thought of Gregory VII', *Studia Gregoriani*, 14 (1991): 69–73.

——, 'Concubinage and Marriage in Medieval Canon Law', in *Sexual Practices and the Medieval Church*, V.L. Bullough and J.A. Brundage (eds) (Buffalo, NY: Prometheus, 1982), pp. 118–28.

——, *Law, Sex and Christian Society in Medieval Europe* (Chicago and London: University of Chicago Press, 1987).

Buckley, T., *The Catechism of the Council of Trent* (London: Routledge, 1852).

Bullough, V.L., 'Introduction: The Christian Inheritance', in V.L. Bullough and J. Brundage (eds), *Sexual Practices and the Medieval Church* (Buffalo: Prometheus, 1982).

Bullough, V.L., and J. Brundage (eds), *Sexual Practices and the Medieval Church* (Buffalo: Prometheus, 1982).

Bunnik, R.J., 'The Question of Married Priests', in *Cross Currents*, XV.4 (Fall, 1965): 407–14.

Callam, D., 'Clerical Continence in the Fourth Century: Three Papal Decretals', *Theological Studies*, 41 (1980): 3–50.

——, 'The Origins of Clerical Celibacy' (University of Oxford, unpublished D.Phil., 1977).

Camenhausen, H. von, *Ecclesiastical Authority and Spiritual Power in the Church of the First Three Centuries* (Peabody, Mass.: Hendrickson, 1997).

Cameron, E., 'Medieval Heretics as Protestant Martyrs', in D. Wood (ed.), *Studies in Church History*, 30 (Oxford: Blackwell, 1993), pp. 185–207.

Caner, D.F., 'The Practice and Prohibition of Self Castration in Early Christianity', *Vigilae Christiani*, 51 (1997): 396–415.

Cantor, N.F., *Church, Kingship and Lay Investiture in England 1089–1135* (Princeton: Princeton UP, 1958).

Carlson, E., 'Clerical Marriage and the English Reformation', *Journal of British Studies*, 31 (1992): 1–31.

——, *Marriage and the English Reformation* (Oxford: Blackwell, 1994).

Carry, E., *Le célibat ecclésiastique devant l'histoire et devant la conscience* (Geneva: Garin, 1905).

Chadwick, H., *The Early Church* (London, New York: Penguin 1968).

Chadwick, O., 'The Early Reformation on the Continent', in H. and O. Chadwick (eds), *The Oxford History of the Christian Church* (OUP: Oxford 2001).

——, *Catholicism and History: The Opening of the Vatican Archives* (Cambridge: CUP, 1978).

Chasteigner, J. De, 'Le célibat sacerdotale dans les écrits de Saint Pierre Damien, in *Doctor Communis*, 24 (1971): 169–83 and 261–77.

Cholij, R., *Clerical Celibacy in East and West* (Worcester: Fowler Wright, 1988).

——, 'The lex continentiae and the impediment of orders', *Studia canonical*, 21 (1987): 391–418.

Cholvy, G., and Hilaire, Y.-M., *Histoire Religieuse de la France Contemporaine* (Toulouse: Privat, 1985–88).

Clark, E., *Reading Renunciation. Asceticism and Scripture in Early Christianity* (Princeton NJ: Princeton UP, 1999).

Classen, A., 'Anticlericalism in Late Medieval German Verse', in P. Dykema and H. Oberman (eds), *Anticlericalism in Late Medieval and Early Modern Europe* (Leiden and New York: Brill, 1993), pp. 91–114.

Clerq, V. De., *Ossius of Cordova* (Washington DC: Catholic University of America Press, 1954).

Cochini, C., *The Apostolic Origins of Priestly Celibacy* (San Francisco: Ignatius Press, 1995).

Cohn, H.J., 'Anticlericalism in the German Peasants' War 1525', *Past and Present*, 83 (1979): 3–31.

Coleman, E., 'Representative Assemblies in Communal Italy', in P.S. Barnwell and Marco Mostert (eds), *Political Assemblies in the Early Middle Ages* (Turnhout: Brepols, 2003), pp. 193–210.

Collins, P., *Mixed Blessings. John Paul II and the Church of the Eighties. The Crisis in World Catholicism and the Australian Church* (Ringwood: Penguin, 1986).
Colson, J., *Les Fonctions ecclesiales aux deux premiers siecles* (Paris: Desclee de Brouwer, 1954).
Comerford, K., 'Italian Tridentine diocesan seminaries: A historiographical study', *Sixteenth Century Journal*, 29 (1998): 999–1022.
——, *Reforming priests and parishes, Tuscan dioceses in the first century of seminary education* (Leiden, Boston: Brill, 2006).
——, *Ordaining the Catholic Reformation: priests and Seminary Pedagogy in Fiesole (1575–1675)* (Florence: Biblioteca della Rivista di storia e letteratura religiosa, 2001).
Congar, Y-M., *Tradition and Traditions. An Historical and a Theological Essay* (London: Burns and Oates, 1966).
——, *L'Episcopat et l'Eglise Universelle* (Paris: Les Éditions du Cerf, 1962).
Constant, G., *Concession a l'Allemagne de la communion sous les deux especes* (2 vols, Paris: Boccard, 1923).
——, *L'Eglise de France sous le Consulat et l'Empire* (Paris: J. Gabalda et fils, 1928).
Constantelos, D., 'Marriage and Celibacy of Clergy in the Orthodox Church', in W. Bassett and Peter Huizing (eds), *Celibacy in the Church* (New York: Herder, 1972), pp. 30–38.
Coolen, G., 'Les origines du célibat ecclésiastique', *Bulletin trimestriel de la Société Académique des Antiquaires de la Morinie*, 20 (1967): 545–58.
Coppens, J., 'Le Sacerdoce Veterotestamentaire', in Coppens (ed.), *Sacerdoce et célibat: études historiques et théologiques* (Gembloux: Bibliotheca Epemeridum theologicarum Lovaniensium, 1971), pp. 3–21.
Coriden, J.A., 'Celibacy, Canon Law and Synod 1971', in W. Bassett and Peter Huizing (eds), *Celibacy in the Church* (New York: Herder, 1972), pp. 109–24.
Cousar, C.G., *The Letters of Paul. Interpreting Biblical Texts* (Nashville: Abingdon Press, 1996).
Cowdrey, H.E.J., *The Cluniacs and the Gregorian Reform* (Oxford: OUP, 1970).
——, 'Pope Gregory VII and the Chastity of the Clergy', in M. Frassetto (ed.), *Medieval Purity and Piety. Essays on Medieval Clerical Celibacy and Religious Reform* (New York and London: Taylor and Francis, 1998), pp. 269–302.
——, 'The Papacy, the Patarenes and the Church of Milan', in *Transactions of the Royal Historical Society*, 5th series, 18 (1968): 25–48.

——, *Pope Gregory VII, 1073–1085* (Oxford: Oxford University Press, 1988).
Coyle, J.K., 'Recent views on the origins of clerical celibacy: a review of the literature from 1980–1991', *Logos: a journal of eastern Christian studies*, 34 (1993): 480–531.
Cronin, H.J., 'The Twelve Conclusion of the Lollards', *English Historical Review*, 22 (1907): 292–304.
Cross, F.L., 'History and Fiction in the African Canons', *Journal of Theological Studies*, 12 (1961): 227–47.
Crouzel, H., 'Le célibat et la continence ecclésiastique dans l'église primitive, leurs motivations', in J. Coppens (ed.), *Sacerdoce et célibat: études historiques et théologiques* (Gembloux: Bibliotheca Epemeridum theologicarum Lovaniensium, 1971), pp. 333–71.
——, 'Les Origines du célibat ecclésiastique: A propos d'un livre recent', *Nouvelle Revue Theologique*, 6 (1970): 649–53.
Cullum, P., 'Clergy, Masculinity and Transgression in Late Medieval England', in Hadley (ed.), *Masculinity in Medieval Europe* (London: Longman, 1999), pp. 178–96.
Cushing K., *Papacy and Law in the Gregorian Revolution, Oxford Historical Monographs* (New York: Oxford University Press, 1998).
Dale, A.W., *The Synod of Elvira and Christian Life in the Fourth Century* (London: Routledge, 1882).
Darlington, R.R., 'Ecclesiastical Reform in the Late Old English Period', *English Historical Review*, 51 (1936): 385–428.
Dauvillier, J., and de Clerq, C., *Le Mariage en Droit Canonique Oriental* (Paris: Sirey, 1936).
Davis, L.D., *The First Seven Ecumenical Councils (325–787)* (Collegeville, Minn.: Liturgical Press, 1983).
Deansley, M., *The Pre-conquest Church in England* (London: A & C Black, 1963).
Deen, H., *Le Celibat des pretres dans les premiers siecles de l'Eglise* (Paris: Du Cedre, 1969).
Delacroix, S., *La réorganisation de l'Église de France apres la Révolution, 1801–1809* (Paris: Éditions du Vitrail, 1962).
Delehaye, P., 'Breves remarques historiques sur la legislation du célibat ecclésiastique', *Studia moralia*, 3 (1965): 362–96.
——, 'Le Dossier Antimatrimonial de l'Adversus Jovinianum et son influence sur quelques ecrits latins du XII siecle', *Medieval Studies*, 13 (1951): 65–86.
Deming, W., *Paul on Marriage and Celibacy: The Hellenistic Background of I Corinthians 7* (Cambridge/New York/Oakleigh: Cambridge University Press, 1995).

Denifle, H., *Luther und Luthertum: in der ersten Entwickelung, quellenmäßig dargestellt* (2 vols, Mainz: Kirchheim, 1905–06).

Denzler, G., *Das Papsttum und der Amstzolibat. Erster Teil: Die Zeit bis zue Reformation; Zweiter Teil: Von der Reformation bis in die Gegenwart* (Papste und Papsttum, Band 5 I, II: Stuttgart, 1973, 1976).

Denzler, G., 'Zur Geschichte des Priesterzölibats', in K. Pennington (ed.), *Proceedings of the Tenth International Congress of Medieval Canon Law* (Monumenta iuris canonici; Ser. C: Subsidia 11), pp. 311–30.

Denzler, G., and Grasmück, E.L. (eds), *Geschichtlichkeit und Glaube. Zum 100. Todestag Johann Joseph Ignaz von Döllingers (1799–1890)* (Munich: Erich Wewel, 1990).

Deveruex, E.J., *Renaissance English Translations of Erasmus: A Bibliography to 1700* (Toronto: University of Toronto Press, 1983).

Dickens, A.G., 'The Shape of Anticlericalism and the English Reformation', in E. Kouri and T. Scott (eds), *Politics and Society in Reformation Europe* (Basingstoke: Macmillan, 1987).

——, *The English Reformation* (2nd edn, London: Penguin, 1989).

——, *Lollards and Protestants in the Diocese of York 1509–1558* (London: OUP, 1959).

——, 'The Marian reaction in the Diocese of York', in his *Reformation Studies* (London: Hambledon, 1982), pp. 93–158.

Dickson, P.G.M., 'Joseph II's Reshaping of the Austrian Church', *Historical Journal*, 36 (1993): 89–114.

Dipple, G., *Antifraternalism and Anticlericalism in the German Reformation: Johann Eberlin von Gunzburg and the Campaign Against the Friars* (Aldershot: Ashgate, 1996).

Dittes, J.E., 'The Symbolic Value of Celibacy for the Catholic Faithful', in W. Bassett and Peter Huizing (eds), *Celibacy in the Church* (New York: Herder and Herder, 1972).

Döllinger, I. von, *Ungedruckte Berichte und Tagebücher zur Geschichte des Concilii von Trient* (2 parts, Nördlingen, 1876).

——, *Er rangiert dann mit den Gewerbetreibenden*, in M. Michael (ed.), *Ignaz von Döllinger* (Munich:, 1894),

Dondaine, A., 'L'origine de le'heresie medievale', *Rivista di Storia della Chiesa in Italia*, 6 (1952): 47–78.

Dortel-Claudot, M., 'Le prêtre et le marriage: évolution de la législation canonique des origines au XIIe siècle', *L'année canonique: recueil d'études et d'information*, 17 (1973): 319–44.

Douglas, J.D., *Women, Freedom and Calvin* (Philadelphia: Westminster Press, 1985).

Douglas, M., *Purity and Danger. An Analysis of Concept of Pollution and Taboo* (London: Routledge, 2002).

Dresdner, A., *Kultur-und Sittengeschichte der Italienischen Geistlichkeit im 10 un 11 Jahrhundert* (Breslau: Verlag, 1890).

Duchesne, L., 'Le concile d'Elvira et les flamines chrétiennes', *Mélanges Renier* (Paris: F. Vieweg, 1887).

Duffy, E., *Saints & Sinners: A History of the Popes* (New Haven: Yale University Press, 1997).

Dummler, E., 'Eine Streitschrift fur Priesterehe', in *Sitzungberichte der koniglich-preussichen Akademie der Wissenschaften*, 21 (1902): 418–41.

Durkheim, E., *The Elementary Forms of the Religious Life* (tr. J.W. Swain) (London: Allen and Unwin, 1915).

Dykema, P., and Oberman, H. (eds), *Anticlericalism in Late Medieval and Early Modern Europe* (Leiden and New York: Brill, 1993).

Elliott, D., 'The Priest's Wife. Female Erasure and the Gregorian Reform', in C.H. Berman (ed.), *Medieval Religion. New Approaches* (London and New York: Routledge, 2005), pp. 123–56.

Engen, J. Van, 'Anticlericalism among the Lollards', in Dykema, P., and Oberman, H. (eds), *Anticlericalism in Late Medieval and Early Modern Europe* (Leiden and New York: Brill, 1993), pp. 53–63.

Erickson, J.H., 'The Council in Trullo: issues relating to the marriage of clergy', *The Greek Orthodox Theological Review*, 40 (1995): 183–99.

Evans, G., *Problems of Authority in Reformation Debates* (Cambridge: CUP, 1992).

Fairbank, C., *Hiding Behind the Collar* (Frederick, MD: Publishamerica, 2002).

Fairfield, L.P., *John Bale. Mythmaker for the English Reformation* (West Lafayette, Indiana: Purdue University Press, 1976).

Farner, O., 'Anna Reinhart, die Gatten Ulrich Zwingli', *Zwingliana*, 8 (1916): 230–45.

Ferasin, E., *Matrimonio e celibate a concilio di Trento* (Rome: Facultas Theologica Pontificiae Universitatis Lateranensis, 1970).

Fichtner, J., *America's Forgotten Priests* (New York: Harper and Row, 1968).

Fliche, A., *La Reforme Gregorienne* (Paris and Louvain: Universite Catholique de Louvain, 1924–37).

Fluchter, A., *Der Zolibat Zwischen Devianz und Norm. Kirchenpolitil und Gemeidealltag in der Herzogtumern Julich und Berg im 16 und 17 Jahrhundert* (Cologne: Bohlau, 2006).

Forster, A., *The Counter-Reformation in the Villages: Religion and Reform in the Bishopric of Speyer, 1560–1720* (Ithaca, NY: Cornell UP, 1992).

Fraade, S.D., 'Ascetical Aspects of Ancient Judaism', in A. Green (ed.), *World Spirituality*, vol. 13: *Jewish Spirituality from the Bible to the Middle Ages* (New York: Crossroads, 1986), pp. 253–88.

Franzen, A., *Zölibat und Priesterehe in der Auseinandersetzung der Reformationszeit und der katholischen Reform des 16. Jahrhunderts* (Munster: Aschendorff, 1969).

Frassetto, M., *Medieval Purity and Piety: Essays on Medieval Clerical Celibacy and Religious Reform* (New York and London: Taylor and Francis, 1998).

Freudenberger, T., *Hieronymus Dungersheim von Ochsenfurt an Main, 1465–1540, Theologieprofessor in Leipzig: Leben und Schriften* (Munster: Aschendorff, 1988).

Frazee, C.A., 'The origins of clerical celibacy in the western church', *Church History*, 57 (1988) Suppl.: 108–26.

Freedman, P.H., *Images of the Medieval Peasant* (Stanford: Stanford UP, 1999).

Fudge, T.A., 'Incest and Lust in Luther's Marriage: Theology and Morality in Reformation Polemics', *Sixteenth Century Journal*, 34.2 (2003): 319–45.

Funk, F.X., 'Der Colibat keine apostolische Anordnung', *Tübinger theologische Quartalschrift*, 61 (1880): 202–21.

——, 'Colibat und Priesterehe im Christlichen Alterum', in *Kirchengeschichtliche Abhandlungen und Unterschungen*, I (1897): 121–55.

——, *Didascalia et Constitutiones Apostolorum* (2 vols, Paderborn: Schoeningh., 1905).

Gabler, U., *Huldrych Zwingli. His Life and Work* (tr. Ruth Gritsch) (Edinburgh: T&T Clark, 1986).

Gaposchkin, M.C., 'Boniface VIII, Philip the Fair, and the sanctity of Louis IX', *Journal of Medieval History*, 29.1 (2003): 1–26.

Gaquière, F., *Le Dialogue Irenique Bossuet-Leibniz: La Reunion des Eglises en echec (1691–1702)* (Paris: Beauchesne, 1966).

Garrity, R.M., 'Spiritual and canonical values in mandatory priestly celibacy', *Studia canonical*, 27 (1993): 217–60.

Gaudemet, J., 'Le célibat ecclésiastique. Le droit et la practique du XIe au XIIIe siècles', *Zeitschrift der Savigny Stiftung für Rechtsgeschichte, Kanonistiches Abteilung*, 68 (1982): 1–31.

Gerrish, B., 'Priesthood and Ministry in the Theology of Luther', *Church History*, 34 (1965): 402–22.

Gibbon, E., *The History of the Decline and Fall of the Roman Empire*, J.B. Bury (ed.) (8 vols, London: Methuen, 1909).

Gibson, R., *A social history of French Catholicism* (London: Routledge, 1989).

Gilchrist, J., 'The reception of pope Gregory VII into the Canon Law 1071–1141', in *Zeitschrift der Savigny Stiftung fur Rechtsgeschichte, Kanonistische Abteilung*, 56 (1973): 35–82.

Goertz, H-J., '"What a tangled and tenuous mess the clergy is": Clerical Anticlericalism in the Reformation Period', in Dykema, P., and Oberman, H. (eds), *Anticlericalism in Late Medieval and Early Modern Europe* (Leiden and New York: Brill, 1993), pp. 499–519.

Golb, N., *Who Wrote the Dead Sea Scrolls? The Search for the Secret of Qumran* (New York: Scribner, 1985).

Gordon, B., *The Swiss Reformation* (Manchester: MUP, 2002).

——, 'The Changing Face of Protestant History and Identity in the Sixteenth Century', in his *Protestant History and Identity in Sixteenth Century Europe, vol. I The Medieval Inheritance* (Aldershot: Ashgate, 1996), pp. 1–22.

Grane, L., *The Augsburg Confession* (tr. J.H. Ramussen) (Augsburg: Fortress Press, 1987).

Greenslade, S., 'The authority of the Tradition of the Early Church in Early Anglican Thought', *Oecumenica* (1971–2): 9–33.

Greenspan, K., 'Lessons for the Priest, Lessons for the People: Robert Mannyng of Brunne's Audiences for Handlyng Synne', *Essays in Medieval Studies*, 21 (2004): 109–21.

Gregg, J.Y. (ed.), *Devils, Women and Jews. Reflections of the Other in Medieval Sermon Stories* (New York: SUNY Press, 1997).

Grégoire, H., *Histoire du mariage des prêtres en France: particulièrement depuis 1789* (Brussels: Baudouin, 1826).

Grévy-Pons, N., *Célibat et nature: Une controverse médiévale. A propos d'un traité du début du XVe siècle* (Paris: Centre Nationale de la recherché Scientifique, 1975).

Griffe, É., 'Le concile d'Elvire et les origines du célibat ecclésiastique', *Bulletin de littérature ecclésiastique*, 77 (1976): 123–7.

——, 'A propos du canon 33 du concile d'Elvire', *Bulletin de littérature ecclésiastique*, 74 (1973): 142–5.

Gryson, R., *Les origins du celibate ecclesiastique* (Gembloux: Ducolot, 1970).

——, 'Dix ans de recherches sur les origines du célibat ecclésiastique', *Revue théologique de Louvain*, 11 (1980): 157–85.

Guthrie, D., *New Testament Introduction* (Nottingham: Intervarsity Press, 1990).

Haigh, C., 'Anticlericalism and the English Reformation', *History*, 68 (1983): 391–407.

——, *Reformation and Resistance in Tudor Lancashire* (Cambridge: CUP, 1975).

Haliczer, S., *Sexuality in the Confessional. A Sacrament Profaned* (Oxford: OUP, 1995).

Hargreaves, H., 'Sir John Oldcastle and Wycliffite Views on Clerical Marriage', *Medium Aevum*, 42 (1973): 141–5.

Hardin, R.F., 'Caricature in More's Confutation', *Moreana*, 24 (1987): 41–52.
Harper-Bill, C., 'A Late medieval visitation: The diocese of Norwich in 1499', in *Proceedings of the Suffolk Institute of Archaeology and History*, 34 (1977).
Harrington, J.F., *Reordering Marriage and Society in Reformation Germany* (Cambridge: CUP, 1995).
Hasler, B., *Wie der Papst Unfehlbar Wurde: Macht und Ohnmacht eines Dogmas* (Munich: R. Piper & Co. Verlag, 1979).
Hastings, A. (ed.), *Modern Catholicism. Vatican II and After* (London: SPCK, 1991).
——, *A Concise Guide to the Documents of the Second Vatican Council* (2 vols, London: Darton, Longman & Todd, 1968–69).
——, *A History of African Christianity, 1950–1975* (Cambridge: Cambridge University Press, 1979).
——, *The Church in Africa, 1450–1950* (Oxford: Clarendon Press, 1994).
——, 'On celibacy', *New Blackfriars*, 59 (issue 694, March 1978): 104–11.
——, 'Celibacy. A Final Word', *New Blackfriars*, 59 (issue 700, September 1978): 402–08.
——, *In Filial Disobedience* (Great Wakering: Mayhew-McCrimmon, 1978).
Hayne, T., *The Life and Death of Martin Luther* (London: Jo. Stafford, 1643).
Headley, J.M., 'The Reformation as a Crisis in the Understanding of Tradition', *Archiv Fur Reformationsgeschichte*, 78 (1987): 5–22.
Headley, J.M., and Tomaro, J.A. (eds), *San Carlo Borromeo: Catholic Reform and Ecclesiastical Politics in the Second Half of the Sixteenth Century* (Washington DC: Folger Shakespeare Library, 1988).
Heal, F., *The Reformation in Britain and Ireland* (Oxford: OUP, 2003).
Heath, P., *The English Parish Clergy on the Eve of the Reformation* (London: Routledge, 1969).
Hebblethwaite, P., *Paul VI* (New York: Paulist Press, 1993).
Hefele, C.J., 'Die Entwicklung des Cölibats und die kircheliche Gesetzgebung über denselben sowohl bei den Griechen als Lateinern', *Beiträge zur Kirchengeschichte, Archäologie und Liturgik*, 1 (1864): 122–39.
Heid, S., *Clerical Celibacy in the Early Church. The Beginnings of Obligatory Continence for Clerics in East and West* (tr. Michael J. Muller) (San Francisco: Ignatius Press, 2001).
——, 'Grundlagen des Zolibats in der fruhen Kirche', in K.M. Becker and J. Eberle (eds), *Der Zolibat des priesters*, Sinnund Sendung 9 (St Ottilien, 1995).

Hendrix, S., 'Luther on Marriage', *Lutheran Quarterly*, 14.3 (2000): 335–50.
Herzog, S., *Intimacy and Exclusion: Religious Politics in Pre-Revolutionary Baden* (Princeton: Princeton UP, 1997).
Hige, D.R., *The Future of Catholic Leadership.Responses to the Priest Shortage* (Kansas City: Sheed, 1987).
Hodl, L., 'Die lex Continentia: Eine Problemgeschichtliche Studie uber den Zolibat', *Zeitschrift fur Kirchengeschichte*, 83 (1961): 325–44.
Hogan, W., *A Synopsis of Popery as It was and Is* (Hartford: Andrus, 1847).
——, *Auricular Confession and Popish Nunneries* (2 vols, Hartford: Andrus, 1847).
Honigmann, E., 'The Original Lists of the Members of the Councils of Nicaea, the Robber-Synod, and the Council of Chalcedon', *Byzantion*, 16 (1942/3): 20–28.
Houlbrooke, R.A., *Church Courts and the People During the English Reformation* (Oxford: OUP, 1979).
Hudson, A., *The Premature Reformation. Wycliffite Texts and Lollard History* (Oxford: Clarendon Press, 1988).
Hughes, P., *Pope Pius XI* (London: Sheed and Ward, 1937).
Hunter, D.G., 'Rereading the Jovinianist Controversy: Asceticism and Clerical Authority in Late Ancient Christianity', *Journal of Medieval and Early Modern Studies*, 33.3 (2003): 453–70.
——, 'Clerical Celibacy and Veiling of Virgins: new Boundaries in Late Ancient Christianity', in W.E. Klingshirn and M. Vessey (eds), *The Limits of Ancient Christianity: Essays on Late Antique Thought and Culture in Honour of R.A. Markus* (Ann Arbor: University of Michigan Press, 1999), pp. 139–52.
——, 'Resistance to the Virginal Ideal in Late Fourth-Century Rome: The Case of Jovinian', *Theological Studies*, 48 (1987): 45–64.
Hyma, A., 'Erasmus and the Sacrament of Marriage', in *Archiv fur Reformationsgeschiche*, 48 (1957): 145–64.
Jaki, S.L., *Theology of Priestly Celibacy* (Front Royal, VA: Christendom Press, 1997).
James, C., 'Ban Wedy I Dynny: Medieval Welsh Law and Early Protestant Propaganda', *Cambrian Medieval Celtic Studies*, 27 (1994): 61–81.
Jenkins, P., *Paedophiles and Priests* (Oxford: OUP, 2001).
Jestice, P.G., 'Why Celibacy? Odo of Cluny and the Development of a New Sexual Morality', in M. Frassetto (ed.), *Medieval Purity and Piety. Essays on Medieval Clerical Celibacy and Religious Reform* (New York and London: Taylor and Francis, 1998), pp. 81–116.
John, E., 'St Oswald and the Tenth Century Reformation', *Journal of Ecclesiastical History*, 9 (1958): 159–72.

——, *Orbis Britanniae and other Studies* (Leicester: Leicester University Press, 1966).

Johnson, F.L., and Weideman, A.J., 'The Crisis of Celibacy at the Council of Trent', in *The Law on Celibacy: Soundings from its History* (St Meinrad, Indiana: Resonance, 1966).

Johnson, S., 'Luther's Reformation and (un)holy Matrimony', *Journal of Family History*, 17.3 (1992): 271–88.

Jong, M. De, 'Imitatio Morum. The Cloister and Clerical Purity in the Carolingian World', in M. Frassetto (ed.), *Medieval Purity and Piety Essays on Medieval Clerical Celibacy and Religious Reform* (New York and London: Taylor and Francis, 1998), pp. 49–80.

Kalb, H., *Studien zur Summa Stephans von Tournai. Ein Beitrag zur kanonistischen Wissenschaftsgeschichte des späten 12. Jahrhunderts* (Innsbruck: Universitatsverlag Wagner, 1983).

Kaufmann, T., 'Pfarrfrau und Publizistin – Das Reformation Amt der Katharine Zell', *Archiv für Reformationsgeschichte*, 88 (1997): 169–218.

Kawerau, W., 'Die Reformation und die Ehe', *Reformationsgeschichte*, 8 (Halle: Verein fur Reformationsgeschichte): 1–104.

Kelleher, M.A., '"Like man and wife": Clerics Concubines in the Diocese of Barcelona', *Journal of Medieval History*, 28 (2002): 349–60.

Kelly, J.N.D., *Jerome, His Life, Writings and Controversies* (New York: Harper and Row, 1975).

Kemp, B., 'Hereditary benefices in the medieval English church: a Herefordshire example', *Bulletin of the Institute of Historical Research*, 43 (May 1970): 1–15.

Klauck, H-J., *Hausgemeinde und Hauskirche im fruhen Christentum* (Stuttgart: Verlag Katholisches Bibelwerk, 1981).

Kleist, A., 'Matthew Parker, Old English, and the Defence of Priestly Marriage', in *Anglo-Saxon Books and their Readers: Papers in Honour of Helmut Gneuss*, T. Hall and D. Scragg (eds) (Kalamazoo: Medieval Institute Publications, 2003).

Klinger, E., *Luther und der Deutsche Volksaberglaube* (Berlin: Mayer & Muller, 1912).

Klitsche, T.F., *Geschichte des Cölibats der katholischen Geistlichen von den Zeiten der Apostel bis zum Tode Gregors VII* (Augsburg: Kollmann und Himmer, 1930).

Knetes, C., 'Ordination and matrimony in the eastern orthodox church', *The Journal of Theological Studies*, 11 (1910): 348–400; 481–513.

Knowles, D., *Monastic Order in England: a history of its development from the times of St. Dunstan to the Fourth Lateran Council, 940–1216* (Cambridge: CUP, 1949).

Kochutara, G.S., *The Concept of Sexual Pleasure in the Catholic Moral Tradition* (Rome: Editrice Pontificia Universita Gregoriana, 2007).

Korte, B.F., 'Early Lutheran Relations with the Eastern Orthodox', *Lutheran Quarterly*, 9 (1957): 53–9.

Kottin, B., *Der Zolibat in der Alten Kirche* (Munster: Aschendorff, 1970).

Krause, H-G., *Das Papstwahldekret von 1059 und seine Rolle in Investitursreit* (Rome: Studi Gregoriani, 1960).

Krodel, G., 'Luther: An Antinomian?', *Luther Jahrbuch*, 63 (1996): 69–101.

Kuttner, S., 'Pope Lucius III and the Bigamous Archbishop of Palermo', in J.A. Watt, J.B. Morrall, F.X. Martin (eds), *Medieval Studies Presented to Aubrey Gwynn SJ* (Dublin: Colm O Lochlainn, 1961), pp. 409–45.

Pope John Paul II, *The Theology of Marriage and Celibacy* (Boston: Pauline Books and Media, 1986).

Laeuchli, S., *Power and Sexuality: the Emergence of canon law at the synod of Elvira* (Philadelphia: Temple University Press, 1972).

Lacqua, S., 'Concubinage and the Church in Early Modern Munster', in R. Harris and L. Roper (eds), *The Art of Survival. Gender and History in Europe 1450–2000* (Past and Present Supplements, vol. 1, 2006), pp. 72–100.

Lauchert, F., *Die italienischen literarischen Gegner Luthers* (Freiburg im Breisgau: Herder, 1912).

Lambert, M., *Medieval Heresy: Popular Movements from the Gregorian reform to the Reformation* (Oxford: Blackwell, 1992).

Latourelle, R., *Vatican II. Assessments and Perspectives* (3 vols, New York: Paulist Press, 1988).

Laumann, F.J., *Call and Response. Ordaining Married Men as Catholic Priests* (Berryville VA: Dialogue Press, 2002).

Laurent, V., 'L'Oeuvre Canonique du Concile in Trullo 691–2', *Revue des Etudes Byzantine*, 23 (1965): 7–41.

Lea, H.C., *History of Sacerdotal Celibacy in the Christian Church* (3rd edn, 2 vols, London: Williams and Norgate, 1907).

Leclerq, H., 'La legislation conciliaire relative au celibate ecclesiastique', in C.J. von Hefele (ed.), *Conciliengeschichte* (Freiburg: Herdersche Verlags-Handlung, 1908).

——, 'Celibat', in *Dictionnaire d'Archeologie chretienne et de liturgie* (Paris, 1908).

——, 'S. Pierre Damian et les femmes', in *Studia Monastica*, 15 (1973): 43–55.

Le Goff, J., and Remond, R., *Histoire de la France Religieuse* (Paris: Éditions du Seuil, 1988–92).

Legrand, L., 'St Paul and Celibacy', in J. Coppens (ed.), *Priesthood and Celibacy* (Milan, Rome: Ancora, 1972), pp. 427–50.

Le Saint, W.P., *Tertullian, Treatises on Marriage and Remarriage* (Westminster, Md., 1951).

Levy, J.C., 'Was John Wyclif's Theology of the Eucharist Donatistic?', *Scottish Journal of Theology*, 53 (2000): 137–53.
Leyser, C., 'Peter Damian's "Book of Gomorrah"', *Romantic Review*, 86 (1995): 191–211.
L'Huillier, P., 'Mandatory celibacy as a requirement for episcopacy', *The Greek orthodox theological review*, 40 (1995): 213–19.
Liotta, F., La *Continenza dei chierici nel penserio canonistico classico da Graziano a Gregorio IX* (Milan: Giuffre, 1971).
Loades, D., 'Anticlericalism in the Church of England before 1558: an "eating canker"?', in N. Aston and M. Cragoe (eds), *Anticlericalism in Britain c.1500–1914* (Stroud: Sutton, 2000), pp. 1–17.
Lohkamp, B., 'Cultic Purity and the Law of Celibacy', *Review for Religious*, 30 (1971): 119–217.
Lupton, J., *Life of John Colet* (2nd edn, London: G. Bell & Sons, 1909).
Lynch, J.E., 'Marriage and Celibacy of the Clergy: The Discipline of the Western Church: An Historico-Canonical Synopsis', *The Jurist*, 32.1 and 2 (1972): 14–38 and 189–212.
Lynch, J., 'Critique of the Law of Celibacy in the Catholic Church from the Period of the Reform Councils', in W. Bassett and Peter Huizing (eds), *Celibacy in the Church* (New York: Herder and Herder, 1972), pp. 57–75.
MacDonald, W.W., 'Anticlericalism, Protestantism and the English Reformation', *Journal of Church & State*, 15 (1973): 21–32.
MacGovern, T., 'Der priesterliche Zölibat in historischer Perspektive', *Forum Katholische Theologie*, 14 (1998): 18–40.
McCutcheon, R., 'The Responsio ad Lutherum: Thomas More's Inchoate Dialogue with Heresy', *Sixteenth Century Journal*, 22 (1991): 77–90.
McGovern, T., *Priestly Celibacy Today* (Chicago, Midwest Theological Forum, 1998).
McGrath, A., *Reformation Thought, An Introduction* (Oxford: Blackwells, 1988).
McKee, E.A., *Katharina Schutz Zell* (2 vols, Leiden, Boston, Cologne: Brill, 1999).
McManners, J., *Church and Society in Eighteenth Century France* (2 vols, Oxford: OUP, 1998).
——, *The French Revolution and the Church* (London: SPCK, 1969).
McNamara, J., 'The herrenfrage: The Restructuring of the Gender System, 1050–1150', in C. Lees (ed.), *Medieval Masculinities Regarding Men in the Middle Ages* (Minneapolis: University of Minnesota Press, 1994), pp. 3–29.
——, 'Chaste Marriage and Clerical Celibacy', in Bullough, V.L., and Brundage, J. (eds), *Sexual Practices and the Medieval Church* (Buffalo: Prometheus, 1982), pp. 22–33.

Maimbourg, L., *Histoire du Lutheranisme* (2 vols, Paris: Elsevier, 1681).
Marshall, P., 'Anticlericalism Revested? Expressions of Discontent in Early Tudor England', in C. Burgess and E. Duffy (eds), *The Parish in Late Medieval England: Proceedings of the 2002 Harlaxton Symposium* (Donington: Shaun Tyas, 2006).
——, *The Catholic Priesthood and the English Reformation* (Oxford: Clarendon Press, 1994).
——, 'The Debate over Unwritten Verities in Early Reformation England', in B. Gordon (ed.), *Protestant History and Identity in Sixteenth Century Europe. vol. I The Medieval Inheritance* (Aldershot: Ashgate, 1996), pp. 60–77.
Martene, E., *Thesaurus Novus Anecdotorum* (Paris: Delaulne, 1717).
Marx, A., 'Les Racines du celibat essenien', *Revue de Qumran*, 7 (1970): 323–42.
Mastrantonis, G., *Augsburg and Constantinople: The Correspondence Between Patriarch Jeremiah II and the Tubingen Theologians* (Brookline, MA: Holy Cross Press, 1982).
Mathieu, F., *Le Concordat de 1801: ses origines-son histoire* (Paris: Perrin, 1903).
Mathisen, R., *Ecclesiastical Factionalism and Religious Controversry in Fifth Century Gaul* (Washington DC: Catholic University of America Press, 1989).
Matthews, G., *Augustine* (Oxford: Blackwell, 2005).
Mayer, J., *De Catharina Lutheri Conjugye, Dissertatio* (Leipzig, 1698).
Mayer, T.F., *Cardinal Pole in European context: a via media in the Reformation* (Aldershot: Ashgate, 2000).
Migne, M., 'Concile ou collection d'Elvire', *Revue d'Histoire Ecclesiastique*, 70 (1975): 361–87.
Miller, M.C., 'Masculinity, Reform, and Clerical Culture: Narratives of Episcopal Holiness in the Gregorian Era', *Church History*, 72 (2003), pp. 25–52.
Mohler, J.A., 'Beleuchtung der Denkschrift fur die Aufhebung des den katholischen Geistlichen vorgeschriebenen Celibates', *Katholik*, 8 (1828): 1–32, 257–97.
Moore, R.I., *The Origins of European Dissent* (Oxford: Blackwell, 1985).
Morris, C., *The Papal Monarchy: The Western Church from 1050 to 1250* (Oxford History of the Christian Church, New York: Oxford University Press, 1991).
Moss, C.B., *The Old Catholic Movement* (London: SPCK, 1964).
Muller, K., *Aus der Akademischen Arbeit: Vortage und Aufsatze* (Tubingen, 1930).

Muller, M., *Die Lehre des hl. Augustinus von der Paradiesesehe und ihre Auswirkung in der Sexualethik des 12. und 13. Jahrhunderts bis Thomas von Aquin* (Regensburg: Friedrich Pustet, 1954).
Mullett, M., *Martin Luther* (London: Routledge, 2004).
——, *The Catholic Reformation* (New York: Routledge, 1999).
Mumm, R., *Die Polemik des Martin Chemnitz gegen das Konzil von Trent* (Leipzig: Lippert, 1905).
Murphy-O'Connor, J., *Paul the Letter-Writer: His World, His Options, His Skills* (Collegeville, MN: Liturgical, 1995).
Nelson, J.L., 'Kingship, Law and Liturgy in the Political Thought of Hincmar of Rheims', *English Historical Review*, 92 (1977): 241–79.
Niederwimmer, K., *Askese und Mysterium. Ubere Ehe, Ehescheidung und Eheverzicht in den Anfangen des christlichen Glaubens* (Gottingen: Vandenhoeck und Ruprecht, 1975).
Oberman, H., *Luther. Man Between God and the Devil* (tr. Eileen Walliser-Schwarzbart) (London and New Haven: Yale UP, 1989).
——, *Dawn of the Reformation. Essays in Late Medieval and Early Reformation Thought* (Edinburgh: T&T Clark, 1992).
O'Brien, J.M., 'Henry Charles Lea: The Historian as Reformer', *American Quarterly*, 19 (1967): 104–13.
O'Connor, J. (ed and tr.), *The Gift of Infallibility: The Official Relatio on Infallibility of Bishop Vincent Gasser at Vatican Council I* (San Francisco: Ignatius Press, 2008).
O'Donnell, J., *Augustine: A new biography* (New York: ECCO, 2005).
——, *The Canons of the First Council of Arles, 314 AD* (Washington: Catholic University of America Press, 1961).
O'Donohoe, J., *Tridentine Seminary Legislation: Its sources and its formation* (Louvain: University of Louvain, 1957).
Olin, J.C., *The Catholic Reformation: Savonarola to Ignatius Loyola* (New York, London: Harper and Row, 1969).
Olsen, C., *Celibacy and Religious Traditions* (Oxford: OUP, 2007).
Owst, G., *Literature and Pulpit. a neglected chapter in the history of English letters & of the English people* (Oxford: Blackwell, 1961).
Ozment, S., *When Fathers Ruled, Family Life in Reformation Europe* (Cambridge, Mass., and London: Harvard UP, 1983).
——, *The Age of Reform 1250–1550* (New Haven, CT: Yale UP, 1980).
Padover, S., *The Revolutionary Emperor: Joseph II of Austria* (2nd edn, London: Eyre & Spottiswoode, 1967).
Palazzini, P., 'S. Pier Damiani e la polemica anticelibataria', *Divinitas*, 14 (1970): 127–33.
Pampaloni, P., 'Continenza e celibate del clero: Leggi e motive nelle fonti canonistiche dei sec IV et V', *Studia Patavina*, 17 (1970): 18–19.

Parish, H.L., *Clerical Marriage and the English Reformation* (Aldershot: Ashgate, 2000).
——, *Monks, Miracles and Magic Reformation Representations of the Medieval Church* (London: Routledge, 2005).
——, 'Beastly is their Living and their Doctrine. Celibacy and Theological Corruption in Reformation Polemic', in B. Gordon (ed.), vol. I *The Medieval Inheritance* (Aldershot: Ashgate, 1996), pp. 138–52.
Parsons, E.W.C., *Religious chastity: an ethnological study* (New York: AMS Press, 1975).
Partner, N., 'Henry of Huntingdon: Clerical Celibacy and the Writing of History', *Church History*, 42 (1973): 467–75.
Peet, D., 'Mid Sixteenth Century Parish Clergy, with particular consideration of the Diocese of York and Norwich' (University of Cambridge unpublished Ph.D., 1980).
Peters, C., 'Gender Sacrament and Ritual. The Making and Meaning of Marriage in Late Medieval and Early Modern England', *Past and Present*, 169.1 (2000): 63–96.
Peters, E., 'Henry Charles Lea 1825–1909', in Helen Damico and Joseph Zavadil (eds), *Medieval Scholarship: Biographical Studies in the Formation of a Discipline. Vol. One: History* (New York: Routledge, 1995), pp. 89–100.
——, 'History, Historians, and Clerical Celibacy', in M. Frassetto (ed.), *Medieval Purity and Piety. Essays on Medieval Clerical Celibacy and Religious Reform* (New York and London: Taylor and Francis, 1998), pp. 3–21.
Pettegree, A.D.M., *Reformation and the Culture of Persuasion* (Cambridge: CUP, 2005).
Phipps, W., *Clerical Celibacy. The Heritage* (London and New York: Continuum, 2004).
——, 'Did Ancient Indian Celibacy Influence Christianity?', *Studies in Religion*, 4 (1974): 49–50.
Picard, P., *Zolibatsdiskussion im katholischen Deutschland der Aufkalrungzeit* (Dusseldorf: Patmos, 1975).
Piepkorn, A.C., 'Martin Chemnitz' Views on Trent: The Genesis and the Genius of the Examen Concilii Tridentini', *Concordia Theological Monthly*, 37 (January 1966): 5–37.
Pitsakis, C.G., 'Clergé marié et célibat dans la législation du concile in Trullo', in George Nedungatt (ed.), *The council in Trullo revisited* (Rome: Kanonika: 1995), pp. 262–306.
Plongeron, B., *Théologie et politique au siècle des Lumières (1770–1820)*, (Genève: Droz, 1973).

Plummer, M.E., 'Clerical Marriage and Territorial Reformation in Ernestine Saxony and the Diocese of Merseburg in 1522–1524', *Archiv für Reformationsgeschichte*, 98 (2007): 45–70.

——, '"Partner in his Calamities": Pastors Wives, Married Nuns and the Experience of Clerical Marriage in the Early German Reformation', *Gender and History*, 20.2 (2008): 207–27.

Po-Chia Hsia, R., 'Anticlericalism in German Reformation Pamphlets', in Dykema, P., and Oberman, H. (eds), *Anticlericalism in Late Medieval and Early Modern Europe* (Leiden and New York: Brill, 1993), pp. 491–8.

Pollard, J.F., *The Unknown Pope. Benedict XV* (London: G. Chapman, 1999).

Porter, M., *Sex, Marriage and the Church. Patterns of Change* (Victoria, Aus.: Harper Collins, 1996).

Powell, D., 'Tertullianists and Cataphrygians', *Vigiliae Christianae*, 29 (1975): 33–54.

Preston, P., 'Catharinus vs Luther 1521', *History*, 88 (2003): 364–78.

Prior, M., '"Reviled and Crucified Marriages". The Position of Tudor Bishops' Wives', in M. Prior (ed.), *Women in English Society 1500–1800* (London: Methuen, 1985), pp. 118–48.

Quesnell, Q., 'Make themselves Eunuchs for the Kingdom of Heaven (Mt. 19:12)', in *Catholic Biblical Quarterly*, 30 (July, 1968): 335–8.

Puff, H., 'Localising Sodomy: The "Priest and Sodomite" in Pre-Reformation Germany and Switzerland', *Journal of the History of Sexuality*, 8 (1997): 165–95.

Rackam, R.B., 'The Texts of the Canons of Ancyra', in *Studia Biblica et Ecclesiastica*, 3 (1891): 139–216.

Rahner, K., *The Shape of the Church to Come* (New York, Seabury Press, 1974).

Ranke-Heinemann, U., *Eunuchs for the Kingdom of God: Women, Sexuality, and the Catholic Church* (tr. P. Heinegg) (New York: Doubleday, 1990, German edn 1988).

Rankin, D., *Tertullian and the Church* (Cambridge: Cambridge University Press, 1995).

Ratzinger, Cardinal J. (Pope Benedict XVI), *Zur Gemeinschaft Gerufen, die Kirche heute verstehen* (Freiburg: Herder, 1991).

——, *Salt of the Earth: The Church at the End of the Millennium: An Interview with Peter Seewald* (San Francisco: Ignatius Press, 1997).

Reinburg, V., 'Liturgy and Laity in Late Medieval and Reformation France', *Sixteenth Century Journal*, 23 (1992): 526–46.

Rex, R., *The Theology of John Fisher* (Cambridge: CUP, 1991).

Richardson, P., 'The Parish Clergy of the Thirteenth and Fourteenth Centuries', *Transactions of the Royal Historical Society*, 3rd series, 6 (1912): 89–128.

Robinson, A., *St Oswald and the Church of Worcester* (London: British Academy, 1919).

Robinson, I.S., *The Papal Reform of the Eleventh Century: Lives of Pope Leo IX and Pope Gregory VII* (Manchester: Manchester University Press, 2004).

——, *The Papacy, 1073–1198: Continuity and Innovation* (New York: Cambridge University Press, 1990).

Rope, H.E.G., *Benedict XV The Pope of Peace* (London: J. Gifford, 1941).

Roper, L., 'Luther, Sex, Marriage and Motherhood', *History Today*, 33 (1983): 33–8.

——, *Oedipus and the Devil. Witchcraft, Sexuality and Religion in Early Modern Europe* (London and NY: Routledge, 1994).

Rosa, P. De, *Vicars of Christ* (New York: Crown, 1988).

Roskovány, A., *Coelibatus et breviarium, duo gravissima clericorum officia, e monumentis onmium seculorum demonstrata, accessit completa literature* (11 vols, Pestini: Beimel et Kozma, 1860–81).

Rublack, H-V., 'Anticlericalism in German Reformation Pamphlets', in Dykema, P., and Oberman, H. (eds), *Anticlericalism in Late Medieval and Early Modern Europe* (Leiden and New York: Brill, 1993), pp. 461–89.

Rublack, U., 'Zur Reception von Luthers De Votis Monasticis Iudicium', in R. Postel and F. Kopitzch (eds), *Reformation und Revolution. Beiträge zum politischen Wandel und den sozialen Kräften am Beginn der Neuzeit: Festschift für Rainer Wohlfeil zum 60 Geburtstag* (Stuttgart: Steiner, 1989), pp. 224–37.

Ryan, J.J., *St Peter Damiani and His Canonical Sources* (Toronto: Univ. Toronto Press, 1956).

Savon, H., *Johann Adam Mohler. The Father of Modern Theology* (tr. C. McGrath) (Glen Rock, NJ: Paulist Press, 1966).

Schaff, P., *History of the Christian Church* (New York, 1914).

Shagan, E., *Popular Politics and the English Reformation* (Cambridge: CUP, 2003).

Scheeben, M.J., *Die Mysterien des Christentums. Wesen, Bedeutung und Zusammenhang derselben nach der in ihrem übernatürlichen Charakter gegebenen Perspektive* (Mainz: Matthias-Grünewald-Verl., 1931).

Schillebeeckx, E., *Clerical Celibacy Under Fire. A Critical Appraisal* (London and Sydney: Sheed and Ward, 1968).

——, *Marriage: Human Reality and Saving Mystery* (New York, 1965).

Schimmelpfennig, B., 'Zolibat und Lage der "Priestersohne" vom 11 bis 14 Jahrhundert', *Historische Zeitschrift*, 27 (1978): 2–44.

Schoenherr, R., *Goodbye Father: The Celibate Male Priesthood and the Future of the Catholic Church* (Oxford and New York: OUP, 1997).

——, 'Holy Power? Holy Authority? And Holy Celibacy?', in W. Bassett and P. Huizing (eds), *Celibacy in the Church* (New York: Herder, 1972), pp. 126–7.

Schoenherr, R., and Young, L., *Full Pews and Empty Altars* (Madison: Univ. Wisconsin Press, 1993).

Schoenherr, R., and Greeley, A.M., *American Priests* (Chicago: National Opinion Research Center of the University of Chicago, 1972).

Schofield, J., *Philip Melanchthon and the English Reformation* (Aldershot: Ashgate, 2006).

Scholz, R., *Die Publizistik zur Zeit Philipps des Schonen und Bonifaz VIII* (Stuttgart, 1903; repr. Amsterdam: P. Schippers, 1962).

Schweizer, J., *Ambrosius Catharinus Politus (1484–1553), ein Theologe des Reformationszeitalters* (Münster: Aschendorff, 1910).

Sculley Bradley, E., *Henry Charles Lea. A Biography* (Philadelphia: University of Pennsylvania Press, 1931).

Selderhuis, H.J., *Marriage and Divorce in the Thought of Martin Bucer* (tr. J. Vriend and L.D. Bierma) (Kirksville, MO: Thomas Jefferson Univ. Press, 1999).

Siegel, A., 'Italian Society and the Origins of Eleventh-Century Western Heresy', in Michael Frassetto (ed.), *Heresy and the Persecuting Society in the Middle Ages: Essays on the Work of R.I. Moore* (Leiden: Brill, 2006), pp. 43–72.

Sipe, A.W.R., *Celibacy in Crisis. A Secret World Revisited* (New York and Hove: Brunner-Routledge, 2003).

Slattery, J.T., *Dante's attitude toward the church and the clergy of his times* (Philadelphia: J.J. McVey, 1921).

Sloyan, G., 'Biblical and patristic motives for the Celibacy of Church Ministers', in W. Bassett and Peter Huizing (eds), *Celibacy in the Church* (New York: Concilium, vol. 78, 1972), pp. 13–29.

Smith, J.C., 'Katharina von Bora Through Five Centuries: A Historiogaphy', *Sixteenth Century Journal*, 30.3 (1999): 745–74.

Sommerville, R., 'The Council of Pisa 1135: A Re-examination of the Evidence of the Canons', *Speculum*, 45 (1970): 98–114.

——, *Pope Urban II. The Collectio Britannica and the Council of Melfi* (Oxford: OUP, 1996).

Spielman, R., 'The Beginning of clerical marriage in the English Reformation', *Anglican and Episcopal History*, 56 (1987): 251–63.

Stafford, W.S., *Domesticating the Clergy. the inception of the Reformation in Strasbourg, 1522–1524* (Missoula, Mont.: Scholars Press, 1976).

Stancliffe, C., *St Martin and his Hagiogapher: History and Miracle in Sulpitius Severus* (Oxford: Clarendon Press, 1983).

Staniforth, M. (ed.), *Early Christian Writings: The Apostolic Fathers* (Middlesex: Penguin books, 1968).

Stein, A., 'Martin Luthers Bedeutung dur die Anfange des Evangelischen Eherechts', *Osterreichisches Archiv fur Kirchenrecht*, 34.1 and 2 (1983–84): 29–95.

Steinmetz, D., 'The Council of Trent', in David Bagchi and David C. Steinmetz (eds), *The Cambridge Companion to Reformation Theology* (Cambridge: CUP, 2004).

Stickler, Cardinal A.M., *The Case for Clerical Celibacy. Its Historical Development & Theological Foundations* (tr. Brian Ferme) (San Francisco: Ignatius Press, 1995).

——, 'A New History of Papal Legislation on Celibacy', *Catholic Historical Review*, 65 (1979): 76–84.

Strauss, G., *Manifestations of Discontent in Germany on the Eve of the Reformation* (Bloomington: Indiana University Press, 1971).

——, 'Ideas of Reformatio and Renovatio from the late middle ages to the Reformation', in J.D. Tracy and H. Oberman (eds), *Handbook of European History* (Leiden: Brill, 1994).

Swanson, R., 'Problems of the Priesthood in Pre-Reformation England', *English Historical Review*, 105 (1990): 845–69.

——, 'Angels Incarnate: Clergy and Masculinity from Gregorian Reform to Reformation', in D. Hadley (ed.), *Masculinity in Medieval Europe* (London: Longman, 1999), pp. 160–77.

Tackett, T., 'The Social History of the Diocesan Clergy in Eighteenth Century France', in R.M. Golden (ed.), *Church State and Society under the Bourbon Kings of France* (Lawrence KS: Coronado Press, 1982).

Tanner, N., *The Councils of the Church: A Short History* (New York, 2001).

——, *Heresy Trials in the Diocese of Norwich 1428–1431*, Camden Society, 4th series, 20 (London, 1977).

Tavard, G.H., *Holy Writ or Holy Church. The Crisis of the Protestant Reformation* (London: Burns and Oates, 1959).

Tellenbach, G., *Libertas. Kirche und Weltordnung im Zeitalter des Investiturstreites* (Stuttgart: Kohlhammer, 1936).

Theiner, J.A., and Theiner, A., *Die Einfuhrung der erzwungenen Ehelosigkeit bei den christlichen Geistlichen und ihre Folgen. Ein Beitrag zur Kirchengeschichte* (3 vols, Altenburg, 1828).

Thibodeaux, J.D.,'Man of the church or man of the village? Gender and Parish Clergy in Medieval Normandy', *Gender and History*, 18.2 (2006): 380–99.

Thomson, J., *Early Tudor Church and Society 1485–1529* (London: Longmans, 1993).
Thouzellier, C., *Heresie et heretiques: Vaudois, Cathares, Patarines, Albigeois* (Rome: Edizioni di Storia e letteratura, 1969).
Tibiletti, C., 'Verginità e matrimonio in antichi scrittori cristiani', *Annali della Facoltŕ di Lettere e Filosofia dell'Universita di Macerata*, 2 (1969): 9–217.
Tierney, B., *Crisis of Church and State* (New Jersey: Prentice-Hall, 1964).
Tinsley, B.S., *History and Polemics in the French Reformation: Florimund de Raemond: Defender of the Church* (London: Associated University Presses, 1992).
Ullmann, W., *The Inquisition of the Middle Ages* (New York: Harper Torchbook, 1969).
Vancandard, E.F., 'Les origines du Celibat Ecclesiastique', *Etudes de Critique d'histoire religieuse*, 1st ser. (Paris 1905; 5th edn, Paris 1913): 71–120.
——, 'Celibat', in *Dictionnaire de theologie catholique*, 2 (Paris, 1905): 2068–88.
Vasella, O., *Reform und Reformation in der Schweiz: Zur Würdigung der Anfänge der Glaubenskrise* (Munster: Aschendorff, 1965).
Vasiliev, A., *History of the Byzantine Empire* (Madison Wisconsin: Univ. Wisconsin Press, 1952).
Verkamp, B., 'Cultic Purity and the Law of Celibacy', *Review for Religious*, 30 (1971): 199–217.
Vermes, G., *The Dead Sea Scrolls in English* (Harmondsworth, 1968).
Vleeschouwers-van Melkebeek, M., 'Mandatory celibacy and the Priestly Ministry in the Diocese of Tournai at the end of the Middle Ages', in *Peasants and Townsmen in Medieval Europe: Studia in Honorem Adriaan Verhulst*, J-M Duvosquel and Erik Thoen (eds) (Ghent: Snoeck-Ducaju & Zoon, 1995), pp. 681–92.
Vogels, H-J., *Priester Durfen Heiraten: Biblische geschichtliche und rechtliche Grundegegen den Pflichtzolibat* (Bonn: Kollen, 1992).
Voobus, A., *Celibacy. A Requirement for Admission to Baptism in the Early Syriac Church* (Stockholm, 1951),
Weiskotten, H.T., *The Life of Saint Augustine: A Translation of the Sancti Augustini Vita by Possidius, Bishop of Calama* (Merchantville, NJ: Evolution Publishing, 2008).
Wemple, S.F., *Women in Frankish Society: Marriage and the Cloister, 500 to 900* (Philadelphia: University of Pennsylvania Press, 1985).
Wertheimer, L., 'Children of Disorder: Clerical Parentage, Illegitimacy, and Reform in the Middle Ages', *Journal of the History of Sexuality*, 15:3 (2006): 382–407.

Wiesner-Hanks, M.E., *Christianity and Sexuality in the Early Modern World. Regulating Desire, Reforming Practice* (London: Routledge, 2000).

Wilks, M., *The Problem of Sovereignty in the Later Middle Ages. The Papal Monarchy with Augustinus Triumphus and the Publicists* (Cambridge: CUP 1963).

Williams, G., The Welsh Church from Conquest to Reformation (Fayetteville: University of Arkansas Press, 1993).

Williams, G.H., *The Norman Anonymous of 1100 AD* (Cambridge Mass.: Harvard Theological Studies, 1951).

Winkelmann, F., 'Paphnutios, der Bekenner und Bischof', *Probleme der Koptischen Literatur*, 1 (1968): 145–53.

Winning, T., 'Church Councils in Sixteenth-Century Scotland', in D. McRoberts (ed.), *Essays on the Scottish Reformation* (Glasgow: Burns, 1962).

Witte, J., Jr, *From Sacrament to Contract: Marriage, Religion and Law in the Western Tradition* (Louisville: John Knox Press, 1997).

Wood, C.T., *Philip the Fair and Boniface VIII: State vs Papacy* (Huntingdon, NY: Krieger, 1976).

Wright, A.D., *The Counter Reformation. Catholic Europe and the Non-Christian World* (London: Weidenfeld and Nicolson, 1982).

Yost, J.K., 'The Reformation Defence of Clerical Marriage in the Reigns of Henry VIII and Edward VI', *Church History*, 50 (1981): 152–65.

Index

Adrian I, pope 75
Agapetus, pope 52
Alexander II, pope 98–9
Alexander III, pope 107
Alexandria 27–8, 60, 62
Ambrose 27, 33, 40–41, 221
Ambrosiaster 33–4
Ambrosius, Catharinus Politus 187
Ancyra, Council of 45–6, 63–4, 66, 69, 74, 76–7, 105, 112, 172
Anglican-Roman Catholic International Commission 230
Anglo-Norman church 106
Anonymous, Norman 118
Anselm 97, 106–7, 111, 119, 178
Antichrist 4, 12, 132, 146, 165, 177, 187
Anticlericalism 123, 129, 151
Antinomianism 146
Antwerp 81, 149, 155, 162–3, 165, 171, 188
Apel, Johannes 151
Apostles 8–9, 11, 13, 15, 24, 27–9, 31, 36, 48, 53, 55, 61, 78, 81, 83, 132–3, 163, 165–7, 174, 181, 188–9, 192, 194, 205, 207, 213–14, 218, 225, 230
Apostolic Canons 77–80, 82–3, 115, 175, 202
Apostolic church 18, 49, 55, 81, 84, 86–7, 131, 136, 139–41, 166–7, 175, 188, 201, 204–5, 217, 221, 231–2
Apostolic origins of clerical celibacy, debate 3–4, 11, 26, 16, 18, 28–9, 31–4, 40, 42–50, 52–3, 55–6, 61–4, 66, 71–2, 75, 78–82, 115–16, 131, 139, 166, 175–6, 189, 192, 201, 204–5, 207, 213, 217–88
Apostolic tradition 9, 13, 74, 79, 173, 176, 193, 207, 216–17, 234
Aquinas, Thomas 113, 198, 221–2
Arles, Council of 44–6

Athanasius 221
Augsburg Confession 158, 160, 174
Augustine, Saint 34–5, 38–41, 213, 221
Authority 10, 12–13, 41, 70–71, 75, 82–4, 90–91, 98, 109, 116–17, 122, 151, 154, 169, 174, 176, 190–91, 197, 206, 208, 214, 217
  papal 13, 117, 130–31

Bacon, Francis 22
Bale, John 149, 156, 162, 171, 177–80
Barnes, Robert 155, 171, 177, 195
Baronius, Cesare 70, 84, 120, 168, 202, 204
Basle, Council of 127, 135, 137–8
Becon, Thomas 164, 166, 170, 172, 175, 177
Bede 75
Bellarmine, Robert, Cardinal 70, 202, 204
Benedict VIII, pope 95
Benedict XIV, pope 203
Benedict XV, pope 219–20
Benedict XVI, pope 229, 232–3
Benefices, hereditary 91–2, 95, 107
Benno, cardinal 178
Bernold of Constance 69–70, 72–3, 97, 114, 116–17
Bernold of St Blasien 116
Bickell, Gustav 4, 26, 31, 55, 60, 81, 217–18
Bishops 1, 7–8, 25–6, 31–3, 38, 41–3, 45–50, 52–4, 59, 62–4, 67–8, 72, 76–7, 79, 81–4, 87, 90, 95–7, 99, 101, 103, 105–7, 109, 111–12, 114–15, 121, 124, 126–7, 134, 151–3, 157, 166, 168–70, 180, 196–7, 199, 203–4, 210–12, 214–16, 225–6, 231–3
  constitutional 210–11
  married 32, 61–2, 77, 107
Boniface VIII, pope 130–31
Bora, Katherine von 146–8, 157

Bremen, Arnold of 96–7
Bromyard, John 126
Bucer, Martin 152, 164, 168
Byzantine church 64, 85

Caesarius of Heisterbach 120
Calixtus, Pope 204
Calvin, Jean 22, 166, 168–70, 175, 181
Cambrai, clergy of 102, 105
Campeggio, cardinal 152
Canon law 3, 6–7, 10–11, 42, 71, 95, 100, 139, 143, 150, 160, 177, 183, 198, 200, 213, 219, 222, 224
Canonists 67, 74, 84, 98, 112–14
Cantors 73–4, 77, 89, 118
Caprara, Cardinal 211
Carafa, Cardinal 191
Carlstadt, Andreas 134, 152, 155
Carové, Friedrich Wilhelm 214
Carthage 31
Carthage, Council of 38, 47–8, 53, 78, 80, 84, 172–3
Casinensis, Paul 75
Catharinus, Ambrosius 187
Celtis, Conrad 139
Chalcedon, Council of 64, 73–4, 172
Chastity 9, 22, 32, 35–6, 38, 47–8, 61–2, 64–5, 68, 85, 92, 98, 102, 106, 108, 113, 115, 131, 133, 137–40, 148, 152–6, 159, 163, 168, 170, 172, 175, 180, 192–3, 206, 219, 224
  conjugal 33, 138
Chaucer, Geoffrey 120–21
Chemnitz, Martin 201
Chobham, Thomas of 113
Christ 2, 6, 13, 19, 22–3, 26, 29–30, 36, 39, 108–10, 112, 120, 122, 132–3, 136, 140, 146, 154, 166, 176, 179, 193–4, 206, 222–4, 230, 232
  first followers of 21, 27–8, 48, 166, 205, 224
  priesthood of 88, 225
Christian liberty 147, 153
Christian priesthood 9, 13, 16, 22, 24, 61–2, 85, 137, 162, 180, 220
Church history, use of 12, 87, 90, 136

CITI 227
Clement VI, pope 131
Clement VIII, pope 189, 203, 206
Clement of Alexandria 27–8, 60
Clergy wives 110, 119, 121, 150
Cochlaeus, Johannes 146
Code of Canon Law 3, 6, 219, 224
Colet, John 129
Coppens, Joseph 226
Concubinage, priests 6, 92, 97, 104, 113, 121, 124, 126–8, 136, 139, 141, 149–50, 157, 179, 196–7, 200
Concubines 4, 38, 66, 76, 82, 87, 95–8, 105, 109, 112, 120–21, 125, 140, 150, 162, 175, 190, 196–7, 200, 215
Constance, council of 135–6, 170, 177–8,
Constantinople 73, 174
Continence 3, 5, 13, 16–17, 19, 21, 24, 26, 28–32, 37–9, 41–2, 44, 47–51, 53, 55–6, 59, 61–3, 65, 68–9, 73–4, 76, 79–81, 85–7, 90, 92, 105, 110, 112–13, 115, 122, 133, 135–7, 139, 193, 205, 217, 220, 222, 224
Continence, of clergy 2–5, 25, 30–31, 37, 39, 41, 45, 48, 50, 52–3, 55–6, 61–2, 64, 69, 74, 85, 87, 92–3, 96, 102, 108, 137, 186, 190–91, 217
  complete 18–19, 90
Corinthians, letter to 23–4, 27, 118, 140, 162–3, 166, 221
Crema, John of 119–20, 178
Cunibert of Turin 111

Damasus, pope 48, 50
Damian, Peter 7, 84, 97–8, 108–10, 221
Dante 132
Deacons 25–6, 29, 42–3, 45–6, 48–50, 52–3, 60, 63–4, 66, 68, 76–8, 82–3, 92, 95–6, 98, 101–3, 105, 108, 172–3
Dead Sea Scrolls 18–19
Decree on the Ministry and Life of Priests 223
Desforges, Pierre 206
Devil 34, 110, 121, 143, 145, 149, 153, 165, 180, 186, 188, 191, 195

Döllinger, I. 216–17
Dolscius, Paul 174
Donatism 6, 45, 93, 98, 109, 129, 221
Drenss, Augustin 151
Dungersheim, Jerome 146
Dunstan, Saint 178
Durandus, William 135–6

Eastern churches, clerical marriage in 3–4, 11, 46, 59–63, 69, 71, 73–5, 77, 79–86, 115, 136, 174–5, 183, 202–4, 215–17, 220, 222–3, 225, 233
Eck, Johannes 186
Elvira, synod of 10, 41–2, 56, 66, 69, 76, 87, 218–20
Emser, Johannes 187
England, church in 89, 91, 107, 119, 123, 126, 167, 170, 178, 181, 188
Epiphanius 29, 220
Epiphanius of Constantia 61, 109
Epiphanius of Salamis 50
Erasmus, Desiderius 126, 146, 180
Erfurt, Council of 177
Essenes 18–19
Ethelred 94–5
Eunuchs 2, 20–21, 60, 170, 187, 190, 232
Eusebius 21, 45, 52, 61, 70
Eustochium 26, 36

Faber, Johannes 188
Faculties, general 198–9, 211–12
Fairbank, George 182
Fisher, John 188
Flacius, Matthias Illyricus 171, 201
Fliche, Augustin 10
Florentinus, Simon 192
Fornication 24, 102, 108, 111, 119, 127, 132–3, 138, 155, 158–9, 162, 164, 189, 200
Foxe, John 155–6, 169, 171–3, 177–9
Frith, John 165

Gaul, church in 37–8, 77, 169
Gangres, council of 32, 71, 73, 172
Gardiner, Stephen bishop of Winchester 171

Gaudin, Jacques 205, 207–8
Gelasius, pope 82
Gerson, Jean 12, 137
Gospels 19–21, 22–3, 28–9, 98, 132, 137, 149, 187, 189, 220
Gratian 28, 72, 75, 112–3
Greek church 11, 59, 71, 73, 82–4, 116, 131, 138, 140, 173–5, 189, 193, 202–5, 214, 217, 222–3, 232
Gregorian Reform 11, 48, 73, 87–9, 91, 93, 95, 97, 99, 101, 103, 105, 107, 109, 111, 113–5, 117, 119, 121, 134, 140, 159, 171, 177
Gregory of Nyssa 52
Gregory VII, pope 10, 69, 72, 87, 89, 99–103, 105–6, 109, 111–18, 122, 139, 151, 173, 176–7, 213
Gregory IX, pope 121
Gregory XIII, pope 203
Gregory XVI, pope 214
Gregory the Great, pope 115
Gualther, Rudolph 177

Harpsfield, Nicholas 171
Hasenberg, Johann 146
Heaven 1, 13, 21, 36, 61–2, 105, 118, 187, 220–22, 224
Hedio, Caspar 151
Henry I 107
Henry V 117
Henry VIII 144, 147, 163, 170, 187
Himerius, bishop of Tarragona 48–9
Hippo, Council of 53
Huggarde, Miles 147–8, 150
Hugo, bishop of Constance 126, 157
Humbert, Cardinal 71, 75, 83, 108–9, 111
Hume, cardinal Basil 229
Huntingdon, Henry of 107
Hus, Jan 136, 141
Hussites 174

Ignatius 20, 32, 60, 221
    letter of 26, 32, 167
Incontinence 66, 93, 96, 130–31, 134
    of clergy 73, 112, 116, 121, 126, 128, 132, 135, 137, 179, 190, 196, 207, 214

Innocent III, pope 121
Institutes of the Christian Religion, The 166, 168–70, 181

Jerome 28–9, 34–40, 52, 55, 60, 62–3, 168, 186
Jewel, John 167, 181
John the Baptist 19
John, disciple of Jesus 29
John XII, pope 75
John XXIII, pope 222, 228
John Paul II, pope 13, 20, 230
Joseph II, emperor 212
Jovinian 28–9, 33, 35–7, 40, 51, 168
Juhel, bishop of Dol 106

Klingebeil, Steffan 167

Lambert, Francis 158
Lanfranc 106
Lateran Council 1123 103–4, 112
Latomus, Jacobus 188
Lea, H.C. 7–9, 13, 35, 45, 64–5, 67, 84, 89, 91, 122, 124–5, 194, 212–13
Leipzig Disputation 174
Leo I, pope 101
Leo IX, pope 97–8, 109, 204
Levitical priesthood 5, 18, 48, 133, 161, 180–81, 220–21, 223
Lindet, Thomas 210
Lollards 132–4, 181
Lombard, Peter 16, 180
London, council of 106, 119
Lorsch, monks of 117
Louis IX 130
Lucius III, pope, 113–14
Luther, Martin 27, 69, 124, 141, 143–9, 151, 153–6, 158, 160, 162–3, 165–70, 173–4, 180, 186–8, 191, 201–2
  marriage, 143–9, 183, 186, 188

Maior, John 138
Manichaean 34, 39 186
Map, Walter 120
Martin, Thomas 27, 147
Marriage, second 25–6, 31–2, 76, 82

after ordination 46, 56, 63–5, 81, 199
  valid 151, 199
Martyr, Peter 150, 167, 172
Mary 33, 150, 199–200
Melanchthon, Philip 158, 162–6, 168–71, 174, 188
Melfi, synod of 103
Milan 38, 111
Milingo, Archbishop Emmanuel 232
Mohler, Joseph 213–14
Monasticism 67–8, 77, 85, 93, 154
Monastic vows 152–6, 158–60, 168, 174, 187, 201–2, 209
Monks, marriage of 49, 143, 148–9, 154–5
More, Thomas 147, 150, 155, 181, 185–6, 214
Munster, bishop of 196–7
Muntzer, Thomas 152
Murphy-O'Connor, Cardinal Cormac 23

Neocaesarea, council of 64–6, 76–7, 172
Nicaea, first council of 48, 65, 68–71, 96, 98, 100, 105, 112, 115, 116, 169–70, 172, 202, 218
  second Council of 67, 75
Nicetas 71, 83, 85, 203
Nicholas I, pope 73
Nicholas II, pope 98–9, 110–11, 171
Nicolaitism 83, 96, 101–2, 108
Novatian 70
Nuns 49, 145–8, 154, 185, 209

Odo of Cluny 92–3
Odo Rigaldus 125
Old Catholics 216
Old Testament 11, 16, 41, 49, 52, 115, 140, 161–2, 180, 220–21
Origen 21, 60–61
Osnabruch, synod of 197
Ossius, bishop of Cordoba 44
Otto, bishop of Constance 101

Palermo 113–14
Paphnutius 47, 65, 67–71, 80, 115–16, 169–72, 202, 219
Paris, Council of 127, 131

INDEX

Parker, Matthew 163–4, 170–71
Parkyn, Robert 181–2, 200
Patarenes 99, 111
Paul 23–7, 30, 50, 98, 159, 162, 165–7, 231
Paul III, pope 189–91
Paul VI, pope 20, 22, 223, 227–88, 232
Pavia, synod of 47, 96
Peter 28–30
Philip 29, 130
Philip II 195
Philip IV 131
Philo 18–19
Pius II, pope 138, 159
Pius IV, pope 191, 195, 208
Pius V, pope 195–6
Pius XI, pope 220
Pius XII, pope 23, 222
Pole, Cardinal Reginald 189, 199
Polycarp 20, 30, 32
Ponet, John 165, 171, 177, 199
Prayer 24, 37, 50, 52–3, 61, 78–9, 86, 102, 113, 118, 163, 205, 225
Prêtres en foyer 207, 210–11
Priests, lapsed 198–9, 211
Pseudo-Udalrici 99, 114–15

Raemond, Florimund de 148
Rahner, Karl 228
Ratherius of Verona 90
Reinhard, Anna 156
Roman Synod 51, 97–9, 105, 117
Roskovány, Augustin, bishop of Neutra 8–9, 124
Roy, William 180
Rusticus of Narbonne 53

Sacraments 6, 12, 34, 37, 42, 51, 53, 72–3, 86, 89, 93, 95, 97–8, 102, 104–5, 109, 111–12, 117–18, 129–30, 134, 136, 173–4, 179–81, 191–2, 200, 227, 233–4
 of incontinent clergy 73, 179
Saignet, Guillaume 12, 136–7
Schurf, Jerome 148
Seminaries 195
Shepherd, Luke 180

Siegfried of Mainz, archbishop 100
Simony 96, 100–102, 112, 132, 191
Siricius, pope 34, 49–53, 55, 82, 169
Socrates 63, 68, 70–71
Sola scriptura 41, 160–61, 166
Sons of priests 86, 103, 105–6, 113, 118–19, 125–6, 189, 196
Sozomen 68, 70–71, 116
Stiltinck, Jan, 170
Subdeacons 50, 53, 64, 66, 77–8, 95–6, 98, 101–3

Talleyrand, bishop of Autun 211–12
Tertullian 28, 31–2, 34
Thaner, Friedrich 72
Theiner, Augustin 41, 213–5
Timothy, Letter to 25, 50, 60, 62, 153, 165–6, 181
Toledo, council of 124
Trent, Council of 2, 10, 12, 40, 166, 185–6, 189–91, 193–8, 200–202, 208–9, 211, 215, 222, 224, 227, 230, 234
Trullo, council in 26, 46, 63, 67, 71, 74–80, 82–6, 112, 175, 202, 225
Tübingen 30, 84, 174, 217
Tudeschi, Nicholas 138
Turrianus, Francisco 81, 202
Tyndale, William 156, 161–2

Ukraine, churches 202–3
Ulric of Augsburg 114–15, 171–2
Urban II, pope 98

Vatican Council I 216–17, 226
Vatican Council II 5, 20, 222, 224, 227–8, 230
Vatican II 222–3
Vigilantius 29, 35, 37–8, 40, 62, 168, 186
Virginity 17, 20, 29, 32–3, 35–7, 39–41, 54–5, 60, 62, 133, 162, 168, 181, 188, 192–3, 205, 218, 221, 224–5
Vitricius of Rouen 51–2
Volusianus 171–2
Vows 89, 105, 154–9, 187, 206, 209

Walden, Thomas 133

Waldensians 186
Wales, church in 122, 125
Wittenberg 145, 151, 153, 164
Wycliffe, John 132–4, 141

Zabarella, Francesco 136

Zaccaria, Francesco Antonio 40, 205–6, 214
Zachary, pope 92
Zell, Katharina Schutz 158
Zurich 46, 156–7
Zwingli 156–7